Model Immigrants and Undesirable Aliens

Model Immigrants and Undesirable Aliens

The Cost of Immigration Reform in the 1990s

Christina Gerken

University of Minnesota Press
Minneapolis
London

Portions of chapter 1 were previously published as "U.S. Immigration Policies: 1986–2008," in *Immigrants in American History: Arrival, Adaptation, and Integration*, ed. Elliott Barkan. Copyright 2012 by Elliott Barkan and ABC-CLIO. Reproduced with permission of ABC-CLIO, Santa Barbara, California.

Published by the University of Minnesota Press
111 Third Avenue South, Suite 290
Minneapolis, MN 55401-2520
http://www.upress.umn.edu

Library of Congress Cataloging-in-Publication Data

Gerken, Christina.
 Model immigrants and undesirable aliens : the cost of immigration reform in the 1990s / Christina Gerken.
  Includes bibliographical references and index.
  ISBN 978-0-8166-7472-5 (hc)
  ISBN 978-0-8166-7473-2 (pb)
   1. United States—Emigration and immigration—Government policy. 2. United States—Emigration and immigration—Political asepcts—History—20th century. 3. Immigrants—Government policy—United States—History—20th century. 4. Emigration and immigration law—United States—History—20th century. 5. Immigration enforcement—United States—History—20th century. 6. United States—Politics and government—1993–2001. I. Title.
 JV6483.G47 2013
   325.7309'049—dc23   2013030778

Printed in the United States of America on acid-free paper

The University of Minnesota is an equal-opportunity educator and employer.

20 19 18 17 16 15 14 13   10 9 8 7 6 5 4 3 2 1

Contents

Introduction: Building a Neoliberal Consensus   1

1. Exclusionary Acts: A Brief History of U.S. Immigration Laws   19

2. Family Values and Moral Obligations:
   The Logic of Congressional Rhetoric   73

3. Dehumanizing the Undocumented:
   The Legislative Language of Illegality   111

4. Manufacturing the Crisis: Encoded Racism in the Daily Press   151

5. Entrepreneurial Spirits and Individual Failures:
   The Neoliberal Human-Interest Story   195

Conclusion: Legacies of Failed Reform   235

Acknowledgments   251

Notes   253

Bibliography   287

Index   309

Building a Neoliberal Consensus

Congressional debates from the mid-1990s suggest that the U.S. immigration system had reached a point of crisis. According to the dominant political rhetoric, immigration laws failed to protect U.S. citizens from an overwhelming influx of undesirable immigrants who, unlike previous generations of newcomers, were reluctant to blend in with the majority culture and contribute to the economy. Politicians frequently referred to this seemingly unprecedented crisis in their calls for immediate and drastic immigration reform measures. For example, when Senator Richard Shelby (R-AL) spoke in favor of the Immigration Control and Financial Responsibility Act of 1996 (S. 1664), he argued that immigrants "put a crippling strain on the American education system" and placed a burden on taxpayers by committing crimes, displacing U.S. workers, and using public welfare services, including emergency medical care (United States Congress, Senate, April 25, 1996). In a carefully worded remark (interspersed with proclamations that he was neither anti-immigrant nor racist), Senator Shelby also contended that current immigrants were less desirable because they were culturally and ethnically different from "our domestic population" and were thus slower to assimilate, especially in a society where "multiculturalism is favored over the 'melting pot' concept" (United States Congress, Senate, April 25, 1996).

Over time, many have pushed to reduce overall admissions and reform admission criteria because of the changing cultural and ethnic heritage of immigrants; this idea is far from original. In the late nineteenth century, the *New York Times* expressed a similar concern over the increasing number of Eastern and Southeastern European immigrants. In an article from 1892, the *New York Times* argued that past generations of Northwestern European immigrants "were readily assimilated and made good citizens." However, with a new wave of immigrants, "new and unclean fountains burst in the east and southeast, the swelling streams pouring in a people wholly different in race, character, traditions, purpose and social life" ("Immigration Problems," *The New York Times*, November 26, 1892). In the 1920s, in an effort to justify the passage of a national quota law, politicians warned of the potentially disastrous effects of turning America into a "conglomeration of racial groups each advocating a different set of ideas and ideals according to their bringing up" (James Davis, "One Hundred Years of Immigration," *The New York Times*, February 17, 1924). But despite obvious similarities, Senator Shelby's comments are also fundamentally different from his predecessors' concerns. Not only is Shelby careful to refrain from using openly racist language by focusing on the damaging effects of multiculturalism instead of race/ethnicity itself, but he expresses his views on the racial/ethnic makeup of the immigrant population as part of a much larger concern about the economic and social consequences of large-scale immigration.

This book argues that the immigration reform discourse of the mid-1990s represents a new way of thinking and talking about immigration. In particular, later chapters discuss the productive tension between Congress's pronounced effort to discuss immigration reform as an economic issue and the underlying anxieties about immigrants' race, class, gender, and sexuality. As part of a larger neoliberal reform process in the mid-1990s, politicians linked proposals to develop a nationwide system to identify "legal" and "illegal" immigrants with welfare legislation, measures that were supposed to prevent/fight terrorism, encourage economic security, and provisions concerning marriage/family structure.[1] Within this larger reform discourse, immigrants were repeatedly cited as one of the principal causes of the nation's high poverty rate, the increasing costs of social welfare, a decline in traditional values, and the need to pass ever more invasive and restrictive immigration and welfare reform measures.

The legal discourse—congressional debates, committee reports, and speeches by politicians—contained little specific information about who these immigrants were. In an attempt to appear nondiscriminatory, politicians developed an elaborate, abstract way of talking about immigrants without directly addressing the dynamics of race and gender. Instead of directly addressing these issues, the discourse contained a variety of code words, metaphors, and images alluding to racial characteristics. For example, similar to Senator Shelby's aforementioned remarks, countless politicians juxtaposed past immigrants' eagerness to assimilate quickly with the unwillingness of contemporary immigrants to give up their own customs, religious beliefs, and languages. Instead of joining the melting pot—an outdated, problematic metaphor often used in congressional debates—recent immigrants were portrayed as reluctant to assimilate. This kind of rhetoric downplays the fact that most immigrants do not *refuse* to assimilate; deep-seated prejudices, structural discrimination, and racism effectively prevent immigrants, especially immigrants of color, from "blending in" with the majority. Even more important, this seemingly race-neutral language about multiculturalism, assimilation, and the melting pot was used to keep up the pretense that concerns about immigration were not about race or racist anxieties but about immigrants' willingness and ability to behave a certain way and adhere to the expectations of the general population.

In contrast to this general reluctance to talk openly about race, congressional debates and media representations of immigrants and immigration reform were heavily influenced by a larger discourse about "family values." The concept of family values is inherently flexible and dependent on a society's economic, political, cultural, and religious systems and beliefs. In a U.S. context, the phrase *family values* has been used to justify a wide variety of perspectives—everything from conservative Christian values (e.g., promarriage and traditional heteropatriarchal gender roles and opposition to cohabitation, premarital sex, and abortion) to calls for parent-friendly employment laws, affordable child care, access to birth control and abortion, and support of alternative family and kinship structures. By the mid-1990s, *family values* became largely synonymous with a conservative ideology that promoted the traditional nuclear family as the only living arrangement worthy of governmental support and protection. The Defense of Marriage Act (DOMA) became law in 1996, and family-values issues also became prevalent in a number of other public policy debates. Most prominently, the U.S. government decided to use the Illegal Immigration Reform and Immigrant Responsibility Act of 1996 (IIRIRA) and the Personal Responsibility and Work Opportunity Reconciliation Act of 1996 (PRWORA) as a way to force immigrants (and poor citizens, in the case of the Personal Responsibility Act) to conform to heteronormative notions of the family. The acts effectively imposed restrictions and limitations on people who were unable to adhere to the neoliberal norm of living in self-supportive family units with minimal needs for public assistance.[2]

One important part of the immigration debate focused on reforming the family reunification category, which allows U.S. citizens and legal permanent residents to sponsor relatives for immigration to the United States. Predictably, most politicians agreed that the ability to reunite with immediate family members was an important cornerstone of the American immigration system. In accordance with the customary family-values rhetoric, politicians claimed it would be un-American to separate married couples from their young children. The legal status of other family members—such as the adult children of U.S. citizens and legal permanent residents, as well as their brothers and sisters—was open to question, and several representatives wanted to discontinue the practice of allowing U.S. citizens and legal permanent residents to sponsor family members other than their parents and minor children.

While the discourse about immigration reform was closely connected to family-values rhetoric, later chapters in this book will demonstrate that the driving force behind the 1995–96 immigration reform discourse was a concern about immigrants' economic impact. The debates and policy suggestions focused on maximizing immigration-related profits while dismantling the welfare state and minimizing public expenditures for immigrants. For example, the explicit commitment to family values and family reunification not only helped portray the state as a benevolent and humanitarian force but also opened up an avenue for recruiting much-needed low-wage migrant workers while effectively eliminating any financial risk. The state mandated that the petitioning family must assume financial responsibility and absorb the potential costs if their relative became unable to support himself. Accordingly, the state was no longer forced to explicitly exclude anyone and was now able to transfer the risk to the petitioning family and let them decide how they wanted to act and whether they would be able to meet the minimum requirements for sponsoring a relative.

Academic findings on the economic impact of immigration vary widely. On one end of the spectrum, a number of researchers argue that the current generation of immigrants poses a drain on the U.S. economy. Estimates in the 1990s varied from a net loss of $29.14 billion (Simcox 1994) to $42.5 billion per year (Huddle 1993). On the other end of the spectrum, Michael E. Fix and Jeffrey S. Passel of the Urban Institute developed models that suggest contemporary immigrants are in fact net contributors who pay more in taxes than they receive in benefits. Based on their estimates,

Fix and Passel conclude that immigrants created a surplus of $28.7 billion in 1992 (Fix and Passel 1994). Despite these variations in numbers, economists agree that the costs for newly arrived immigrants are unevenly distributed (Fix and Passel 1994; Light 2010). Since most of immigrants' taxes are paid to the federal government, states like California and Texas complain about unfunded mandates (i.e., they do not receive enough state and local taxes from immigrants to cover all their expenses).

In addition to this general cost–benefit assessment, economists also emphasize that an individual's potential to develop into a so-called net contributor was largely dependent on his or her level of education and marketable job skills. The discourse thus made a sharp distinction between skilled and unskilled immigrants. On one hand, the discourse recognized that certain skilled workers—such as computer specialists, doctors, and nurses—were needed to fill an increasing number of job openings. These educated immigrants could become net contributors and lead middle-class lives. This class status caused anxiety, and some people felt threatened by immigrants' undeniable success. As a result, there was a lengthy discourse about measures to protect American workers from "unfair" competition and the possibility of giving out temporary visas to make sure that immigrants could be forced to leave if they were no longer needed.

Unskilled workers, on the other hand, caused a different kind of anxiety. Oftentimes, politicians implied that unskilled immigrants were also undocumented—a conflation that is not correct. In addition, migrant farm laborers, as well as unskilled workers in restaurants, hotels, and certain factories, were described as an unassimilated, foreign underclass that posed a threat to American society and culture. These individuals were frequently forced to accept extremely low wages and dangerous working conditions, and consequently many of them were unable to have a stable home and live in prototypical nuclear families. Thus they were perceived as a danger to the American value system. The following chapters not only identify the specific nature of these anxieties, but they also show how exactly these anxieties influenced the immigration discourse.

It is also important to note that the immigration reform discourse in the mid-1990s framed immigration as a purely national concern and precluded a more in-depth engagement with the transnational forces that led to the presumed crisis in immigration. As the following chapters will show, immigrants were often portrayed as individual actors in a free market who migrated for better jobs and were rewarded—or punished—on the basis of the decisions that they made. Within this discursive frame-work, immigrants are only able to access rights if they play by the rules, migrate legally, and eventually pursue naturalization. However, as several migration scholars have noted, migration is not a purely personal deci-sion; it is "a direct result of displacement induced by structural adjustment programs and neoliberal policies forced on the Third World" (Das Gupta 2006, 13). Free trade agreements such as NAFTA have left millions bereft of land and livelihood and "have created the conditions for the United States to become a magnet for cheap, exploitable and illegal migrant labor" (Green 2011, 369). Yet while free trade agreements facilitate the movement of goods and capital, they aggressively prevent the free movement of peo-ple and deny them access to legal migration options (Sassen 1996, 1998). Instead, this system produces a docile and easily exploitable illegal labor force that is subject to a plethora of human- and civil-rights abuses.

While the following chapters examine mainstream immigration reform discourse, with all its limitations and exclusions, I encourage readers to keep in mind that many questions are left unexamined by this discourse—questions scholars are just beginning to explore. For example, we should question the delinking of immigration policies from geopolitics and trans-national trade agreements and analyze how exactly they have affected the economies in foreign countries as well as the United States. Going a step further, I would also suggest that we critically examine the United States' much-proclaimed right to aggressively protect its southern border and criminalize certain forms of entry. While the mainstream discourse has seemingly naturalized the distinction between law-abiding legal immi-grants and "illegal aliens," in reality, it has helped to construct and reaffirm those very categories. In light of the aforementioned global trade devel-opments, we need to rethink the role of undocumented immigrants. Are they really just lawless individuals who refuse to play by the rules and fail to live up to the demands of neoliberal citizenship? Or does their existence serve an important economic and ideological function in response to the needs of an increasingly global economy?

Furthermore, as Monisha Das Gupta has suggested, activists and schol-ars need to "imagine possibilities at which most balk: that rights do not have to be contained within borders; that claims can crisscross national borders and draw on different rights regimes; that national membership does not have to be the coveted goal; and that migrant rights are precisely that—rights particular to people who cross borders" (2006, 257). Instead of continuing to battle over who can access certain immigration categories and what rights and privileges go along with each category, we could start to envision a radically different system and construct a "transnational complex of rights" (Das Gupta 2006). Finally, this study questions the commonly held perception that neoliberal free market and free trade policies not only are race and gender neutral but might actually lead to greater equality. Instead, the following analysis will demonstrate how neoliberal discourse disguises the reality that racism and sexism continue to affect social and economic processes.

Discourse Analysis

Critical discourse analysis is concerned with the discursive reproduction of power and social inequality and seeks to uncover the racist, sexist, and heterosexist assumptions that inform political discourse and media representations (Jäger and Maier 2009; Lazar 2005; van Dijk 1999, 2000; Wodak 1999). Building on these critical approaches to discourse, the following chapters will examine the 1995–96 immigration discourse and demonstrate how it represented a new way of interpreting social reality. As in all societal discourses, the immigration reform discourse touched on a great variety of topics and concerns. However, as my analysis will demonstrate, the discourse was dominated by a few key issues, which are commonly referred to as *discourse strands* or *discursive strands*. Concerns and issues beyond or outside these few discourse strands were deemed either too controversial (e.g., for reasons of political correctness) or otherwise too problematic to be reconciled with the dominant discursive framework. For example, while several expert witnesses who testified before Congress made explicit connections between migration, NAFTA, and free trade, politicians were reluctant to further examine this issue and successfully disengaged the debate over immigration reform from the related discourse about NAFTA.[3] My data thus reveals that the connection between free trade and free movement of workers (i.e., migration) became overshadowed by other concerns.

My analysis uses Foucault's work on truth, knowledge, power, and discourse to examine how exactly the 1990s immigration reform discourse produced a consensus that stricter immigration laws, which shifted financial responsibility onto immigrants and their sponsors, were necessary, rational, and economically profitable. In addition, I investigate how politicians and the mainstream media juxtaposed an idealized image of responsible, self-sufficient legal immigrants who eagerly adhered to heteronormative family values with altogether negative depictions of undocumented workers who were commonly perceived as an unassimilable underclass. Based on this discursive distinction, politicians and the media were able to justify invasive new measures that supposedly rewarded desirable behavior and punished those who had forfeited their right to remain in the United States and access widely available services such as welfare benefits and public education. In short, I demonstrate how this explicit focus on "rational" neoliberal reform measures was used to disguise the racist and heterosexist effects of the discourse and the resulting reform measures.

The following chapters will treat the debate surrounding immigration reform as a heterogeneous, contradiction-ridden discursive formation that cannot and should not be analyzed in isolation. As Foucault argued in *The Archaeology of Knowledge and the Discourse on Language*, "a discursive formation is not . . . an ideal, continuous, smooth text that runs beneath the multiplicity of contradictions. . . . It is rather a space of multiple dissensions; a set of different oppositions whose levels and roles must be described" (1972, 155). As such, the discourse draws on a wide variety of issues and connects them in complicated and sometimes contradictory ways. The following chapters will address the important intersections among immigration, antiterrorism, and welfare reform and demonstrate how the rhetorical connection of these issues shaped the popular perception of the "immigration crisis."

The Emerging Neoliberal Consensus

This book situates the immigration discourse in 1995–96 in the larger theoretical framework of neoliberalism. Scholars of neoliberalism have argued that neoliberal governments are characterized by the attempt to restructure the social welfare system in such a way that it becomes more economically profitable. As part of this neoliberal project, governments shift responsibility from the state to individual citizens and their families. Welfare benefits are regarded as investments in promising individuals who are willing and able to follow certain rules and are expected to take calculated risks and invest in their own abilities. They are supposed to act as entrepreneurs of themselves. Building on the already extensive body of work discussing U.S. attempts to reorganize the welfare state in accordance with neoliberal objectives, I argue that neoliberalism is also an extremely useful lens for examining the immigration reform discourse of the mid-1990s (Brown 1999; Bryson and Lister 1994; Cammisa 1998; Fox, Piven, and Cloward 1993; Fraser and Gordon 1992; Gilens 1999; King 1999; Larner 2000; Naples 2003; Orloff 1993; Quadagno 1994).

Following Nikolas Rose's work on neoliberalism (or "advanced liberalism"), I will show how the U.S. government negotiates conflicting interests and rationalizes its proposed immigration reform measures. In *Powers of Freedom*, Nikolas Rose criticizes scholars who "suggest that the contemporary reconstruction of government is an inevitable response to a transformation of the conditions that made social government and the welfare state possible" (1999, 139). Instead, Rose argues that government is an entity intentionally created and fostered by the politics of power, and not merely a byproduct of social, economic, and cultural circumstances. In order to understand the historical significance of the emerging neoliberal consensus, scholars thus need to examine the larger intellectual and political histories that made it possible.

Shortly after World War II, a group of European intellectuals called attention to the dangers inherent in any state-driven social engineering. Friedrich von Hayek, in particular, was critical of the fact that modern states had influence over the tax and welfare system, housing, urban planning, public transportation, and many other important aspects of social life. According to von Hayek, the state had been gradually expanding its power over its citizenry: not only was it able to determine which groups were worthy of support, but it was also able to impose certain values and moral codes on people who sought access to state services. Eventually, he argued, this trend would lead to totalitarianism. Yet instead of promoting a return to classic liberalism, a group of economists and jurists known as the *Ordoliberalen* suggested a new neoliberal framework. They wanted to free the market from subsidies and government regulations, which, in their eyes, had fostered the development of extensive business monopolies while making workers dependent and unmotivated. Within this neoliberal framework, the state would promote a new set of values that would encourage individuals to become actively involved in shaping their own lives. Rather than passively accepting the status quo, citizens were expected to act as self-interested consumers who aggressively sought new opportunities for personal advancement.

In the United States, it took some thirty years for these ideas to enter the public debate over social welfare. As Lyndon B. Johnson's 1960s War on Poverty once again expanded New Deal social welfare programs, neoliberals became increasingly vocal in their critique of big government. In 1980, U.S. voters finally endorsed a presidential candidate who promised to end the era of big government spending. In its stead, President Ronald Reagan proposed a dramatic tax cut, especially for the upper classes, that was supposed to give the economy a boost and reduce unemployment. These results would, in turn, justify abolishing Johnson-era welfare programs. Yet while President Reagan embraced neoliberal ideas about freeing the market, he combined these beliefs with a traditional conservative rhetoric about the importance of family values and Christian beliefs.

The Reagan administration also addressed the growing number of undocumented immigrants present in the United States—an issue that had garnered considerable public attention since the early 1980s. In 1986, President Reagan signed the Immigration Reform and Control Act (IRCA) into law. This act was an interesting compromise between the anxieties of the average American worker and the needs of big business. On one hand, the IRCA made it illegal for employers to hire undocumented immigrants. On the other hand, the law offered legal status to all immigrants who could prove that they had lived in the United States since January 1, 1982. While this amnesty provision was certainly meant as a concession to employers, it also benefited some three million undocumented immigrants who applied for permanent legal residency.[4] Even more important in this context is the fact that by closing the U.S. labor market to additional undocumented workers (at least in theory), this law represented a clear violation of the neoliberal free market doctrine. Despite President Reagan's popularity, he left a problematic legacy for future administrations. While inflation was under control and the economy had started to boom after 1983, these positive achievements were hardly the result of Reagan's domestic politics. President Reagan's neoliberal rhetoric had largely ignored serious social problems and structural weaknesses in the American economy.

The first Bush administration continued this trend. Due to the general improvement of the economy, the cutbacks on the social safety net and the failure to address deeper-seated problems did not show much of an effect at first. As the economy slowed down in the early 1990s, however, the long-term effects of Reaganism began to be felt. The savings-and-loan industry collapsed, America fought a costly war in Kuwait, unemployment rose, and the number of Americans with incomes below the poverty line increased from 31.9 to 34 million in a matter of a few months. Yet apart from tax increases and short-term emergency aid to the most needy, President George H. W. Bush did little to address the problem.

When Bill Clinton was elected in 1992, he faced difficult challenges on the domestic front. The middle class had become increasingly vocal in their critique of the welfare state and the federal tax system. A combination of social issues (e.g., white anxieties over affirmative action; a conservative backlash against abortion, out-of-wedlock births, feminists, and homosexuals; and controversies over the alleged collapse of traditional family values) added to the general dissatisfaction. After the results of the 1994 midterm election, when Republicans won fifty-four seats and gained the majority in the house, President Clinton embarked on a radical reform course that pledged to "end welfare as we know it." In response to Congress's passage of the Personal Responsibility and Work Opportunity Reconciliation Act, President Clinton reassured reporters that he intended to sign the law because "the current welfare system undermines the basic values of work, responsibility, and family, trapping generation after generation in dependency and hurting the very people it was designed to help" (Clinton, July 31, 1996). Even though government spending on social welfare had continually grown since the first half of the twentieth century, government programs had been ineffective in reducing poverty and unemployment. Instead of continuing this trend toward increased government intervention, President Clinton promoted a neoliberal approach that emphasized work, independence, and personal responsibility and reenvisioned the government's role in the distribution of resources. In contrast to Presidents Reagan and Bush, who had merely decreased the funding for certain programs while increasing governmental spending in other areas, President Clinton developed a much more cohesive rhetoric that explained why the welfare state had to be radically restructured. In the 1990s, neoliberalism thus entered its second phase and was elevated "from a market ideology to a mainstream political and social philosophy" (Melamed 2011, 146).

In his analysis of neoliberal reform movements in the United States and much of Western Europe, Nikolas Rose argued that neoliberal governments see the relation of the social and the economic in such a way that "all aspects of social behavior are reconceptualized along economic lines" (1999, 141).[5] Neoliberal governments no longer seek to govern through expansive state apparatuses, "but through the regulated choices of individual citizens" (Rose 1996, 41). Accordingly, citizens are seen as clients who choose to consume certain services and expect to pay a certain price for these choices. Government services represent an investment in a promising individual—one who is likely to develop into a productive citizen.

Even though most critics have focused on welfare reforms to exemplify the logic of emerging neoliberal governments in the United States and in Western Europe, the consequences of this new way of thinking have been much more far-reaching. Neoliberal governments have shifted power and funding from the federal to the state level, limited worker protection laws, put an increasing emphasis on private insurances, restructured the public education and the criminal justice systems, and reorganized immigration laws in accordance with economic objectives. As Eithne Luibhéid has argued, "key concerns for . . . neoliberal governance have been how to produce self-governing individuals, and how to ensure that self-governing relationships are directed toward ends that the state deems appropriate" (2005b, 71). To this end, neoliberal governments employ a combination of different strategies, including financial rewards and penalties, the removal of privileges, and the curtailing of certain fundamental rights (e.g., the right to privacy), in order to control their populations.

This neoliberal approach to governing populations is accompanied by an elaborate discourse explaining how free market policies will maximize societal well-being much more successfully than the redistributive policies of previous governments. Furthermore, neoliberal political rationality depoliticizes notions of race and gender. In contrast to the liberal paradigm, which recognized group-based inequalities as a problem, neoliberal policies are promoted as the avenue to a postracist and postsexist world of opportunity for every rational consumer with an entrepreneurial spirit. Race and gender, among other identity categories, supposedly cease to exist as social divisions and are reframed into economic issues. Through privatization and liberalization of the market, producers and investors will gain access to previously untapped markets and begin to cater to a wider, multicultural group of consumers and their individual tastes. However, evidence suggests that privatization does not automatically lead to greater equality; many race-based exclusions and inequalities continue to flourish in a privatized market. One example is the education system. While public schools were desegregated in the 1950s, recent data shows that many school districts are becoming more and more racially segregated through suburbanization and white parents pulling their children out of public and enrolling them in private schools (Melamed 2011, 221). The discourse driving legislative changes in immigration law is one of the most consequential of these neoliberal discourses. I strongly agree with Mitchell Dean's claim that "discourses on government are an integral part of the workings of government rather than simply a means of its legitimation" (1999, 26). Language is not a second-order phenomenon shaped by a more fundamental logic. Instead, an analysis of the discourse surrounding a particular issue—such as the question of who should be allowed to immigrate—exposes the concerns and values that are at stake.

As my analysis will show, politicians did not argue simply that "economic government is to be desocialized in the name of maximizing the entrepreneurial comportment of the individual," as Nikolas Rose put it (1999, 144). Undoubtedly, a one-sided emphasis on economic objectives would have enabled opponents to launch a powerful critique about the reform plan's lack of empathy and disregard for vulnerable women and children. With this in mind, politicians carefully constructed a complex rhetoric that combined economic interests with a strong focus on fundamental values and virtues worthy of preservation. According to this seemingly compassionate neoliberal discourse, neoliberal reform measures were seen not only as profitable to society but also as beneficial to individuals—an opportunity to improve their chances of becoming contributing members of society and thus increase their feeling of self-worth. In the end, the vigorous debate about values also served the essential ideological function of deflecting attention from the crude economic calculus at the heart of the larger neoliberal project.

The Racial and Sexual Politics of Neoliberalism

While neoliberalism is most commonly defined as a set of economic regulatory policies that disregard race and gender and reward rational decision making and an entrepreneurial spirit, the neoliberal immigration reform discourse of the mid-1990s is not only infused with politically correct notions of race and gender; it also produces new privileged and stigmatized categories of immigrants along racial and gender—and increasingly also religious—lines. This critical analysis of the racial and sexual politics of neoliberal immigration reform discourse has been largely ignored by popular immigration "experts" and scholars alike. An examination of congressional records reveals that expert testimony given by representatives from a variety of (anti-) immigrant organizations—such as the Federation for American Immigration Reform (FAIR), the Heritage Foundation, or Negative Population Growth—has not only foregrounded economic assessments in their arguments to limit immigration levels and immigrants' access to social services but also actively denied any concern about race or gender.

Even conservative critics like CNN anchor Lou Dobbs and reactionary radio talk hosts such as Michael Savage, Roger Hedgecock, and Rush Limbaugh were careful to frame their critique of illegal immigrants in race-neutral terms. For the most part, they were quite reluctant to discuss race and dismissive of guests who brought up the issue. On October 28, 2006, for instance, Dobbs expressed his concern about the "invasion of illegal aliens."[6] In response to this alarmist rhetoric, Rosa Rosales, president of the League of United Latin American Citizens (LULAC), cautiously remarked, "We're not being invaded, you know? What's all this hysteria? Is it because the Latino population is growing in such great numbers that we fear the voting power?" Dobbs, however, did not even acknowledge that most immigrants were indeed Latino. Instead, he reacted quite condescendingly and tried to return to the color-blind discourse he was so comfortable with. He replied, "All right. Rosa, I was so proud of you. Rosa, I was so proud of you, and then you bring up race." When John Trasvina, interim president of the Mexican American Legal Defense and Education Fund (MALDEF) agreed with Rosales's assessment that the anti-immigration discourse was informed by racist anxieties, Dobbs claimed that bringing up race was "the last refuge of people without arguments. It is the last refuge of people without fact."[7]

Scholarly literature on neoliberalism and immigration reform differs widely in the analysis of the relationship between economic/financial concerns and noneconomic factors such as racial anxieties and prejudices. While some scholars argue that economic rather than racial anxieties are at the root of the popular consensus that immigration levels are too high (Bean, Gushing, Haynes, and Van Hook 1997), others call for a multifaceted approach that takes economic as well as racial fears into consideration (Tichenor 2002; Suro 1996). In addition, scholars have examined how immigrants' large families contribute to Americans' opposition to high levels of immigration and generous welfare benefits for immigrants.[8]

Gordon H. Hanson, for example, argues that Americans are primarily concerned about the fiscal effects of immigrants' supposed tendency to have large numbers of children. He writes, "As low wage-earners, these immigrants are likely to pay little in taxes and to make large demands on public expenditures relative to other U.S. residents. Compounding their demands on public services, immigrants also tend to have large families" (Hanson 2005, 27).

Some recent scholarship goes beyond the question of whether economic concerns are the driving force behind immigration reform and instead examines how different anxieties interact with and ultimately shape immigration discourse and policy. In *Targeting Immigrants*, for example, Jonathan Xavier Inda explores how "illegal" immigrants have been constructed as targets of government and problematized as unethical beings (2005). Others specifically challenge the notion of neoliberalism as a gender- and race-blind project. Wendy Brown, for instance, argues that in spite of neoliberalism's attempt to depoliticize notions of race, gender, and class, neoliberal policies actually undermine our commitment to universalism and help create a permanent underclass (2006). Similarly, Martha McCluskey, in her analysis of the neoliberal attack on the welfare state, concludes that "neoliberalism embraces a racialized, genderized, and class-biased vision of social equity and community solidarity that favors the interests of the most privileged members of society" (2003, 785–86).

San Hea Kil and Cecilia Menjivar are more concerned with the effects the dominant discourse has had on the social and political climate in the United States. Kil and Menjivar argue that the current anti-immigrant discourse criminalizes and racializes "illegal aliens" and "contributes to a social and political climate encouraging violence and social polarization between citizen and noncitizen, white and nonwhite" (2006, 165). Hence politicians and the mainstream media not only validate vigilante groups like the "Minutemen Project" but also encourage racist and violent actions against immigrants. While I agree with Kil and Menjivar's assessment that the anti-immigrant discourse has had a number of problematic effects, not least of which is the formation of militia-type organizations, and while I applaud their acknowledgement of the violence involved in immigration control, the discursive focus on economic objectives and the reluctance to talk openly about immigrants' race, ethnicity, and nationality has proved much more damaging than the rare instances of outright racism. In particular, my analysis will demonstrate how the neoliberal framework of immigration reform discourse has systematically downplayed the racist, sexist, and heterosexist implications of contemporary immigration policies and helped cover up the violence produced by their racist and sexist effects. This book thus joins a larger debate about how neoliberal policies subtly draw on a number of anxieties that are deeply embedded in our society and combine them in new and interesting ways that are fundamentally different from earlier immigration reform debates.

Later chapters will examine the discursive strategies that created, shaped, and upheld images of "desirable" and "undesirable" immigrants. I argue that government debates, media discourse, and public perception were part of a larger regime of knowledge/power that continually produced and reinforced the neoliberal ideal of a responsible, self-sufficient subject. This underlying neoliberal logic, with its reductionist insistence on cost–benefit analysis, foreclosed any attempt to engage in a serious moral/ethical debate about the merits and effects of the U.S. immigration system. At the same time, my research demonstrates that despite this limited approach, the mid-1990s discourse on immigration was characterized by a tension between its underlying neoliberal assumptions and other (often contradictory) values and objectives grounded in an earlier liberal discourse on human rights, with its moralistic concerns about civility and its sentimental appeals to humanitarian needs. In particular, I investigate how long-standing and deep-seated anxieties about immigrants' race, class, gender, and sexuality intersected with neoliberal logic in both the public discourse and the legislative process.

Organization of the Book

The following chapters examine congressional debates and mainstream newspapers to illustrate how immigration discourse circulates and how these distinct discursive sites work intertextually within the larger discourse to reinforce, supplement, and even contradict each other. Chapter 2 accomplishes two important objectives: First, it provides a brief overview of major immigration laws and policies from the colonial period until the twenty-first century. This analysis demonstrates how classic liberal notions of citizenship, which combined political, economic, and social criteria, have influenced various historical exclusions in American immigration law. Second, this chapter demonstrates how the immigration, welfare, and antiterrorism measures that were passed in 1996 were fundamentally different from earlier approaches to these concerns. This section determines how these interrelated reform measures can be understood as an integral part of a larger neoliberal framework.

Chapter 3 examines the neoliberal logic behind the restructuring of the family preference category. An analysis of congressional debates and committee reports shows how Congress used an explicit profamily rhetoric to justify measures intended to activate legal immigrants' capacity for self-sufficient citizenship. By focusing on the controversy over the family reunification system, this chapter demonstrates how politicians from both ends of the political spectrum inserted family values and moral obligations into a discourse that was largely dominated by economic considerations.

While chapter 3 is primarily concerned with the congressional discourse about the legal immigration system, chapter 4 examines the discursive construction of "illegal aliens" as "anticitizens." While Congress was eager to portray legal immigrants as responsible, hardworking, community-minded individuals who had the potential to develop into productive members of society, they were reluctant to acknowledge that undocumented immigrants were anything but lawbreakers and low-cost laborers. In contrast to the discourse about legal immigration, which constantly weighed humanistic concerns against economic considerations, Congress was quite comfortable discussing undocumented immigrants' economic impact without much regard to the human side of the issue. Taken together, these two chapters explain how these two discursive depictions of an idealized legal immigrant on the one hand and a threatening illegal alien on the other were mutually constitutive of each other and how these two images worked intertextually.

In chapter 5, I examine three major newspapers—the *New York Times,* the *Houston Chronicle,* and the *San Francisco Chronicle*—to explore the linkages between media and legislative discourse. Even though journalists were critical of overzealous politicians and punitive reform measures, the media's reliance on alarmist language and stereotypical images ultimately reinforced the sense that there was a burgeoning immigration crisis that warranted immediate action. In contrast to linguistic approaches to the immigration discourse, which tend to focus on the role of discriminatory language, my analysis will demonstrate that the neoliberal discourse on immigration of the mid-1990s was radically different from earlier overtly racist discourses (Entman and Rojecki 2000; Jäger and Link 1993; Santa Ana 2002; van Dijk 1997, 1999, 2000). In particular, I examine the different strategies that the mainstream media discourse deployed to disguise its racist effects by mostly refraining from the personalized attacks and overt racism that characterized earlier immigration discourses. Chapter 6 focuses on human-interest stories. This chapter demonstrates how the mainstream media used these stories as an important tool to negotiate widespread anxieties about immigrants' race, class, and sexuality. I contend that human-interest stories represented an integral part of the neoliberal project. In particular, I argue that the dramatic examples of many immigrants' apparent inability to escape poverty and adhere to heteronormative family values were used to validate the discourse's focus on individual deficiencies. My analysis of stories, special reports, and multipart series about documented as well as undocumented immigrants examines how mainstream newspapers juxtaposed negative examples of immigrants who had failed to live up to the neoliberal ideal of an active citizen with stories of successful immigrants whose entrepreneurial spirit had ensured economic stability and happiness for their families.

The conclusion focuses on the aftermath of the immigration, antiterrorism, and welfare reform measures that were passed in 1996. Persistent anti-immigrant anxieties have bolstered the categorical distinction between desirable and undesirable immigrants, and it is no longer up to the federal government to control populations who are deemed a threat. Increasingly, private actors—such as landlords—have been called upon to help enforce immigration laws and police their fellow community members. While some of these invasive new measures have been declared unconstitutional, references to 9/11 and perceived threats to "homeland security" continue to be used to reinforce the anti-immigrant discourse and support ever more intrusive laws. At the same time, a growing coalition of human and immigrant rights organizations has begun to challenge the dominant anti-immigrant rhetoric. The conclusion examines their rhetorical strategies and demonstrates how some of their arguments have confirmed and maybe even strengthened the neoliberal agenda.

1
_____

Exclusionary Acts

A Brief History of U.S. Immigration Laws

Immigration in the United States has had a profound impact on the nation's political, economic, social, and cultural life. Since 1840, some sixty million persons from all over the world have migrated to the United States.[1] The volume of immigration has varied significantly in response to the economic and political situation in both the United States and foreign countries. Most scholars divide the history of U.S. immigration into four periods: During the first wave of immigration (1840–90), almost fifteen million British, Irish, German, and Scandinavian migrants arrived at America's shores. In the second period (1891–1920), an additional eighteen million immigrants settled in the United States, most of them from southeastern Europe (Italy, Austria-Hungary, as well as Russia), with a considerable minority of east Asians.[2] The third period (1920–65) brought another 7.5 million immigrants, including a growing number of Mexicans. The ongoing fourth wave, which began with the passage of the Immigration and Nationality Act (INA) of 1965, has attracted an increasingly diverse group of newcomers from Mexico, Latin America, and various Asian countries (DeSipio 1998; Fix and Passel 1994; LeMay and Barkan 1999). Between 1965 and 2011, approximately thirty million new immigrants entered the United States.

Even though the United States has a long history of actively recruiting foreign workers and encouraging immigrants to settle in the United States, the federal government—as well as individual states—has also made an effort to exclude those persons who were deemed undesirable. Over the course of time, the criteria used to distinguish between desirable and undesirable immigrants have changed considerably. Depending on the domestic situation and the changing characteristics of the immigrant flow, immigration policies have reacted to economic considerations, national security concerns, specific ideas about a unified national identity, immigrants' racial characteristics, and anxieties about immigrants' gender and sexuality. At different points in U.S. history, one or more of these concerns have dominated the debate surrounding immigration legislation, while others were deemed less important.

This chapter will provide a brief overview of major immigration laws and policies. In particular, I am interested in the ever-changing criteria that were used to exclude certain categories of people. Subsequent chapters will argue that the immigration reform debates in 1995–96 were dominated by neoliberal objectives that emphasized both the liberalization of market forces and the importance of personal responsibility. This discourse, which was based on the idea that immigrants were potential risks that needed to be assessed and contained, was accompanied by the elimination of a social safety net for newly arrived immigrants. In the mid-1990s, immigrants became increasingly linked to other risk categories, such as crime, terrorism, and welfare abuse, thus underlining the necessity to manage and control not just the U.S. borders but also the immigrant population that was already present in the United States. As part of this larger neoliberal project, the state shifted more responsibility to immigrants and their sponsors, expecting them to manage economic risks and provide financial support.[3]

This pronounced emphasis on risk-management strategies and economic objectives was linked to cultural, humanistic, and moralistic concerns. The following chapters are particularly interested in the role that race, gender, and family structures play in this context. As critical race scholars have demonstrated, discourses about race and racial difference in the 1990s were embedded in a new multicultural paradigm that masked the centrality of race and racism to social processes (Melamed 2006; Omi and Winant 1994). This ethic of multiculturalism is fundamentally different from earlier liberal notions of race. Gunnar Myrdal's 1944 study *An American Dilemma*, which is one of the foundational texts for liberal discourses about race in the mid-twentieth century, redefined *race* as *culture*. In contrast to earlier notions of race, which emphasized biological differences, Myrdal shifted his focus toward cultural differences and identified black culture and politics as the primary reasons for black poverty and inferiority (Melamed 2006). By disentangling race from biology, Myrdal concluded that racial hierarchies were neither natural nor permanent. Instead, his outlook on race relations in the United States is surprisingly optimistic: he calls for a rational discussion between members of the two races to overcome prejudices and thinks that "a slow but steady cleansing of the American mind is proceeding as the cultural level is raised" (Myrdal 1944, 40). If racism is primarily a psychological problem that could be solved by educating whites and dispelling prejudiced beliefs, no widespread social reforms are needed (Melamed 2011). According to this theory, American society was well on its way to greater racial equality.

Despite the obvious problems inherent in Myrdal's approach—such as his model's inability to account for structural inequalities and his tendency to idealize white Americans' willingness to move toward racial equality—his liberal paradigm acknowledged racial inequality as a problem. By the mid-1990s, neoliberal multiculturalism had successfully "deracialize[d] official antiracism" and no longer recognized race—or other identity categories such as gender or sexuality—as fundamental determinants of a person's status in society (Melamed 2006, 16). Programs to increase "diversity" were mostly rhetorical gestures. These initiatives have displaced racial references and are now linked to concerns about "equal access" and "human rights," thus reinforcing the notion that we live in a postracist/postracial world. This tendency to downplay the importance of race is one of the defining features of the neoliberal immigration discourse. As later chapters will demonstrate, the immigration reform discourse in the mid-1990s not only refrained from discussing race explicitly but was also founded on the belief that the neoliberal reform effort was inherently antiracist. State-sponsored interventions, such as affirmative action policies, were not only framed as violations of the neoliberal free-market agenda; they were also dismissed as ineffective in eliminating racism and sexism. According to this neoliberal logic, admission policies that focus on an immigrant's potential to become a productive member of U.S. society guarantee equal access and are thus race blind.

Similarly, neoliberal reform policies are commonly presented as gender neutral. The following analysis, however, will demonstrate that the immigration reform discourse of the mid-1990s was not only intrinsically gendered but also predicated on a dominant notion of normative heterosexuality. Throughout history, U.S. immigration policies have provided preferential treatment to traditional family structures and gender norms in a variety of ways. For example, at different points in history, unmarried pregnant women were denied entry and women's ability to naturalize was based on their husbands' citizenship. Today, family reunification visas are still limited to members of the traditional nuclear family (spouses, parents, and children) and denied to same-sex partners.

In the late 1980s and early 1990s, however, feminist and LGBTQ advocates of immigration reform won a number of important victories. Immigration lawyers increasingly critiqued the representation of the refugee as a male figure that was fleeing persecution based on his political activism or religious beliefs. Several landmark cases demonstrated that female refugees could be survivors of gender-specific forms of violence—such as female genital mutilation or a culture of rape that was condoned by the police and other public officials—that qualified as persecution based on their membership in a particular social group (Grewal 2005). In 1990, seventeen years after the American Psychiatric Association declared that homosexuality was not a psychiatric disorder, gay and lesbian individuals were no longer issued a class A medical exclusion certificate for a "psychopathic personality" and were granted the right to immigrate (Somerville 2005; Wygonik 2005).

Starting in the early 1990s, the United States began to admit a select few openly gay and lesbian immigrants and asylum seekers. However, evidence suggests that "to gain entrance, immigrants must present themselves as gendered and sexual beings recognizable (and acceptable) to immigration and court officials" (Berger 2009, 659). Immigration judges expected gay and lesbian asylum seekers—as well as women fleeing from gendered violence—to fit into certain stereotypical identity categories and act accordingly. For example, advocates oftentimes advise gay male asylum seekers to appear stereotypically effeminate to convince judges that they did indeed face persecution based on their campy appearance and behavior (Berger 2009; Miller 2005; Morgan 2006). For women making claims on the basis of gender, "numerous negative credibility rulings concern incongruities between the judge's expectations for an appropriate performance of emotionality and what the woman claimant actually performs in court" (McKinnon 2009, 214). In order to meet the gendered expectations of the judge, female survivors of violence are expected to deliver tearful, graphic descriptions of their abuse without appearing hysterical. If a claimant's performance does not match these stereotypical norms, judges are more likely to doubt their credibility and deny their claim. While these recent developments represent hard-won and important victories for immigrants that had been denied entry in earlier decades, they should not be read as a deviation from our dominant sexual regime.

Not only has Congress failed to engage in a more fundamental debate about sex, sexuality, gender, and family reunification in the U.S. immigration system; abolishing the ban on LGBTQ immigrants and admitting a select few gay and lesbian asylum seekers has only reinforced our dominant sexual regime that "normalizes sexuality channeled into childbearing within patriarchal marriage" (Luibhéid 2011, 181). Family reunification, which provides by far the largest number of green cards every year, is still reserved for heterosexual couples. Gay and lesbian immigrants are only admitted for humanitarian reasons (asylum) or through their employers, and they are unable to gain access through sponsorship by their same-sex partners. Women migrants are still much more likely to enter the United States as dependents of their husbands. Although visa categories and eligibility criteria for green cards are formally gender neutral, data show that almost 75 percent of all H-1B visas are issued to men and 75 percent of H-4 dependent visas to women (Lodhia 2010). Recipients of H-4 visas are ineligible for social security numbers and unable to work legally and will find it difficult to open a bank account or rent an apartment without their spouse's consent. A battered immigrant woman residing in the United States on an H-4 visa or whose application for a green card was sponsored by her husband will thus find it extremely difficult to escape a violent relationship (Lodhia 2010).

Furthermore, the neoliberal immigration reform discourse has framed female immigrants' bodies and their reproductive capacity as a threat to the social safety net (Chavez 2007; Segura and Zavella 2007). Latinas, in particular, were oftentimes described as irrational, and their desire to have children was described as a clear violation of the neoliberal emphasis on rational decision making and maximizing earning potential. Female immigrants were particularly vilified if their childbearing happened outside the bounds of patriarchal marriage or if they were unable to financially support themselves and their children. The emphasis on supposedly gender-neutral economic criteria eventually reinforced heteronormative gender identities and a gendered model of economic activity that portrayed men as economic agents and providers and women as caregivers (Griffin 2007).

This neoliberal approach differs significantly from earlier immigration laws and the discourse that surrounded them. In order to understand the significance of this neoliberal shift, it is necessary to provide historical background. The first part of this chapter will highlight some of the major immigration reforms from the colonial period until the late twentieth century and discuss how the United States tried to exclude specific groups at different points in history. In particular, this analysis will demonstrate how classic liberal notions of citizenship, which combined political, economic, and social criteria, have influenced various historical exclusions in American immigration law. In the second part of this chapter, I will provide a detailed analysis of the neoliberal logic behind the immigration reform discourse in 1995–96 and explain how immigration reform became interconnected with a larger discourse about welfare reform and a growing concern about terrorism.

The Exclusionary Logic of Early Immigration Laws

U.S. immigration laws have seen a lot of significant changes over the last three centuries. Until the early twentieth century, immigration laws tended to be fairly eclectic. The United States did not have a federal immigration law until 1875, and most of the early attempts to regulate immigration focused on a few specific groups who were deemed particularly undesirable. Based on a multiplicity of different factors—such as the state of the economy, the social climate, and race and gender relations—Congress determined whether certain groups should be allowed to enter the United States. If Congress came to the conclusion that a particular group did not represent a welcome addition to the national community, this group was excluded.

Furthermore, Congress was quite unapologetic when it came to these explicit exclusions. As a young nation, the United States had a vested interest in preserving national unity and admitting only those individuals who would further its advancement. Since immigration laws were designed to reinforce contemporary norms, values, and social hierarchies, the motivation behind these exclusions was regarded as self-evident and not subject to much discussion. In addition, Congress felt that there was no need to spell out the criteria that should be used to distinguish desirable from undesirable immigrants. Immigration officers were expected to base their decisions on omnipresent social norms and values. When the law called for the exclusion of all "idiots and insane persons," for instance, officers presumably knew what characteristics and types of behaviors they were supposed to look for.

Early immigration laws relied heavily on a person's background to determine exclusion. If a prospective immigrant had committed a crime, violated a social norm, or belonged to a certain racial group, he or she was banned from entering the United States. More recent reform measures, on the other hand, established a complex actuarial system that tried to assess whether immigrants had the *potential* to develop into self-sufficient subjects or whether they were likely to turn into burdens or even threats to society. This new immigration system downplays the importance of race and other inherent characteristics. Instead, it shifts responsibility to each individual immigrant and claims that it is possible for everyone to develop into a desirable candidate, regardless of race, gender, or sexuality. If a person is denied an immigrant visa, it is due to their own lack of ambition or marketable qualifications. The subsequent analysis will demonstrate how U.S. immigration laws have gradually progressed from outright exclusions to a depersonalized system that claims to be color blind and nondiscriminatory.

Due to the American colonies' desire to attract settlers, colonial immigration laws offered special privileges and generous naturalization statutes to all potential European immigrants.[4] Yet, beginning in the eighteenth century, various colonies started to become more selective and enacted statutes that restricted the flow of immigration. On March 12, 1700, for instance, the Massachusetts Bay Colony passed a law that required the master or commander of a ship to provide authorities with a list of passengers. If a passenger appeared to be "impotent, lame, or otherwise infirm, or likely to be a charge to the place," he or she needed someone to provide a bond on his or her behalf. Subsequent provincial laws specified these public charge provisions and gradually increased the bond.[5] In 1756, the Massachusetts Province laws declared that "any sick or otherwise impotent and infirm person" who was unable to post a bond of one hundred pounds should be prevented from entering the United States. Even though the impact of these statutes was fairly limited at the time, scholars have argued that they have served as a model for subsequent national legislation and were thus of major historical importance (LeMay and Barkan 1999).

It was not until March 3, 1875, that the United States enacted its first federal immigration legislation—the Page Law. The passage of this law was preceded by a number of important historical developments, which, taken together, seemed to threaten the dominant white culture. In particular, the end of the Civil War and the passage of the Fourteenth Amendment had led to increased racial tensions and anxieties. At the same time, the racial composition of the immigrant population began to change. By 1875, immigrants from southern, central, and eastern Europe had begun to outnumber those from northwestern Europe, and Asian immigrants had started to enter the West Coast in increasing numbers. In contrast to earlier generations of immigrants, these newcomers were perceived as racially inferior and unassimilable. In an attempt to justify and uphold America's strict racial hierarchy, several eminent scholars—such as Samuel G. Morton, Josiah C. Nott, and Louis Agassiz—developed a comprehensive scientific theory about race as a biological category with meaningful social consequences.[6] According to these theories, new immigrants were not only less intelligent and thus more likely to become public charges but also said to have a stronger tendency to commit crimes, pose a public health risk, and exhibit anti-American behavior. Barring certain racial groups from immigrating was thus "not only socially desirable but also scientifically appropriate" (Hing 2003, 61).

These alarmist arguments effectively ended the prevailing tradition of welcoming almost everyone. Yet instead of developing a comprehensive immigration system that systematically excluded all persons who were deemed inferior, the Page Law narrowly focused on two of the most controversial figures of the time: Asian prostitutes and convicted criminals of all races and nationalities. According to immigration scholar Eithne Luibhéid, the targeting of Asian prostitutes, in particular, "underscores the salience of intersecting racial, gender, class, and sexual categories in constructing alleged 'threats' to white patriarchy" (Luibhéid 2002, 5). In addition, Luibhéid argues that this category—"prostitutes," or as the Page Law phrased it, immigrants who entered the United States "for lewd and immoral purposes"—was neither predetermined nor self-evident, but open to different interpretations. This ambivalent language meant that immigration inspectors had a certain degree of flexibility when it came to determining a prospective immigrant's eligibility to enter. Yet even though these standards were not set in stone, they were not arbitrary either. Immigration officers were expected to base their judgments on social norms and values that had been produced in everyday interactions and popular discourse that continually assaulted female Asian immigrants' character. In an analysis of San Francisco news coverage between 1876 and 1882, George Anthony Peffer found that "the press unanimously informed [readers] that nine of any ten Chinese women stepping off a steamer from

Hong Kong were certain to be prostitutes" (Peffer 1999, 79). Based on these common representations, immigration officers could feel justified to exclude all Asian women. Their race and gender effectively counted as evidence for their likelihood to be a prostitute.

On August 3, 1882, Congress passed a law that further extended the rights and responsibilities of state commissioners of immigration and provided additional grounds for exclusion. In particular, section 2 ruled that "any convict, lunatic, idiot or person unable to take care of himself or herself without becoming a public charge . . . shall not be permitted to land."[7] At first glance, these restrictions focused exclusively on personal characteristics, not on immigrants' group membership, race, class, or nationality. However, it is important to note that these factors certainly impacted the commissioners' attitudes, their willingness to ask specific questions about criminal backgrounds and sexual histories, and most importantly, their interpretation of the information they received. Based on the social norms and the racial attitudes of the time, immigration officers then decided about whether a certain individual seemed desirable or not. Therefore, the impact of these statutes was far from race, class, or gender neutral.

With the passage of the Chinese Exclusion Act in 1882, the United States entered a new phase of racially specific immigration statutes that excluded those persons who were deemed to be a threat to the white patriarchal system. Even though the act's scope was limited specifically to one national group, its symbolic importance should not be underestimated. According to Roger Daniels, "the Chinese Exclusion Act was the hinge on which American immigration policy turned, a hinge on which Emma Lazarus's 'golden door' swung almost completely shut" (Daniels 1990, 271). In marked contrast to the categorical exclusion of the Chinese through both the Page Law and now the Chinese Exclusion Act, Japanese laborers were treated more favorably. Even though they were subject to the same racist anxieties and anti-Asian campaigns as the Chinese, the Japanese were able to benefit from their home country's emergence as a world power. Concerned about the potential political fallout, the U.S. government realized it "could not restrict Japanese immigration in the heavy-handed, self-serving fashion with which it had curtailed Chinese immigration" (Hing 1993, 29). Instead, it negotiated a so-called gentleman's agreement in which the Japanese government agreed to limit the issuance of travel documents, while the United States granted Japanese wives and children the right to be reunited with family members in the United States.

Yet the list of persons who posed a threat to white supremacy continued to grow and the language used to describe these individuals and their perceived defects became gradually more hostile. In 1891, with the passage of the first federal Immigration Control Act, Congress ruled that the following persons were to be excluded: "All idiots, insane persons, paupers or persons likely to become public charges, persons suffering from a loathsome or a dangerous contagious disease, persons who have been convicted of a felony or other infamous crime or misdemeanor involving moral turpitude, polygamists, and also any person whose ticket or passage is paid for with the money of another." As part of the major codification of immigration laws in 1903, Congress made changes to the criteria used to classify excludable immigrants and added scientific language to clarify some of their categories. For example, instead of simply excluding all "insane persons," the law now added that this category consisted of persons "who have been insane within five years previous" and "persons who have had two or more attacks of insanity at any time previously." For the first time, Congress also added anarchists and terrorists to the list of undesirable immigrants. By 1903, potential immigrants could thus be excluded on racial grounds, for economic reasons, because they represented a security or public health threat, because their past behavior had violated the moral code of the United States, or because an immigration officer determined that they were likely to violate U.S. norms and values in the future.

With the passage of the Immigration Act of 1917, the United States further expanded the grounds for exclusion and added a literacy requirement.[8] Every potential immigrant over sixteen years of age had to read a few sentences in their native language—or, even better, English—in front of a state official who then determined whether this person was literate. This new requirement was praised as a major victory by the proponents of more restrictive immigration laws (Smith 1995, 231). Immigration scholars oftentimes quote the literacy requirement as "an important example of the 'who-is-a-real-American' enactments that have pervaded immigration policy throughout the country's history" (Hing 2003, 51; see also Dobkin 2009, 29). Yet, looking at the effects that this law had on immigrant admissions, it is clear that this was little more than a symbolic victory for nativists. From July 1920 to June 1921, less than 14,000 out of over 800,000 potential immigrants were excluded or deported, but merely 1,450 were denied entry on the basis of the literacy test (Daniels 2004, 46).

In addition to passing these new restrictions, Congress also acknowledged that immigration laws not only were supposed to serve economic purposes and select qualified immigrants but also had an obligation to reunite families. Accordingly, the Immigration Act of 1917 exempted the parents, grandparents, spouses, and unmarried or widowed daughters of any U.S. citizen or legal permanent resident from the literacy requirement.[9] Apparently, America's historical commitment to family values outweighed the importance of certain skills, such as the ability to read.

After the categorical exclusion of Chinese immigrants in 1882 and the broadening of this category to all "natives of any country, province, or dependency situated on the Continent of Asia" in 1917, the United States experienced a continuing influx of eastern and southern European immigrants to fill unskilled labor positions. In 1921, the United States thus decided it was no longer sufficient to exclude individual European immigrants who were deemed undesirable. Instead, the United States enacted the first numerical limit for all immigrants from the Eastern Hemisphere, which represented a dramatic shift in immigration policies (Daniels 2004; Tichenor 2002). The First Quota Act of 1921 limited the annual number of immigrants from each country to 3 percent of the number of foreign-born persons of that particular nationality who were present in the United States in 1910. In 1924, Congress adjusted the overall ceiling from 350,000 immigrants per year to a maximum of 150,000 immigrants by 1929. Even more important, the Johnson-Reed Act of 1924 gave preferential treatment to immigrants from northwestern Europe. Instead of basing quotas on the 1910 census, when the proportion of immigrants from southern and eastern Europe was already significant, the Johnson-Reed Act ruled that the allocation of slots should be based on the 1890 census.[10] In addition, the act established the following preference categories: at least 50 percent of the quotas of each nationality should be reserved for the parents of U.S. citizens and, if the quotas were higher than three hundred, to skilled agricultural workers. The remaining slots were open to unmarried dependent children and wives of legal permanent residents.[11]

This newly established preference system represented an explicit attempt to reproduce the dominant white heteropatriarchal structure of American society. The selection criteria imposed a specific version of the nuclear family on potential immigrants and gave preferential treatment to immigrants who adhered to those narrowly defined family structures. In particular, bonds between parents and children and husbands and wives were deemed worthy of protection, while all other forms of relationships were dismissed as less formative and, ultimately, less desirable. Even more important, the Immigration Act of 1924 also contributed to an ongoing racial project. In the past, the concepts of race and nationality had been loosely conflated (Ngai 1999). With the passage of the Johnson-Reed Act, however, the U.S. government made a clear distinction between racial identities that were deemed permanent and unchangeable and nationality-based identities that could be transformed through assimilation (Ngai 1999). This new racial formation (Omi and Winant 1994) affected European and non-European immigrants quite differently. "The new immigration law differentiated Europeans according to nationality and ranked them in a hierarchy of desirability," while nonwhite immigrants were deemed "unalterably foreign and unassimilable to the nation" (Ngai 1999, 69f). Even though nativists deemed southeastern Europeans less desirable than British and German migrants, they never challenged their eligibility to naturalize based on their membership in the white race. In other words, this new system of racial classification further divided European from non-European immigrants. In conjunction with recent Supreme Court decisions (*Ozawa v. United States* and *United States v. Thind*), the Immigration Act of 1924 racialized Asians, in particular, and helped define them as definitely "not white" and thus permanently foreign.

Mexicans, in contrast, were not as easily classified. On the one hand, they were not explicitly precluded from U.S. citizenship, which could be regarded as evidence that they were considered white. On the other hand, the increasing influx of uneducated, lower-class Mexican immigrants had caused widespread anxieties, and Mexicans were commonly discussed in terms of a "race problem" and described as a racial "other" (Ngai 1999, 88). More specifically, the Mexican "race" was portrayed as unclean and likely to represent a public health risk. While medical exams on Ellis Island had recently been eliminated, enforcement efforts moved to the U.S.–Mexico border and Mexican immigrants were subjected to degrading medical procedures (such as delousing the migrants and fumigating their clothing). According to Mae Ngai, "these procedures were particularly humiliating, even gratuitous, in light of the fact that the Immigration Act of 1924 required prospective immigrants to present a medical certificate to the U.S. consul when applying for a visa, that is, before travel to the

United States" (Ngai 2003, 85f). Yet despite these humiliating procedures and the increasing nativism that was directed against Mexican immigrants, Mexican migration—both legal and illegal—to the United States reached unprecedented levels during the 1920s (Gomberg-Muñoz 2009; Massey, et al. 2002).

With the onset of the Great Depression, however, the number of Mexicans in the United States decreased quite dramatically. This was mostly due to widespread deportation efforts and "voluntary" repatriation. Between 1930 and 1940, at least 415,000 Mexican workers were forcibly deported and 85,000 were repatriated (De Genova and Ramos-Zayas 2003, 5). According to Lisa Flores, "the deportation drive and the repatriation campaign of the 1930s served to create rhetorically a border between Mexico and the U.S., between 'Americans' and Mexican/Americans" (Flores 2003, 364). This state-supported deportation drive was buttressed by a media campaign that emphasized two dominant narratives: one expressing the need for docile, easily controllable, short-term laborers and the other defining Mexican immigration as a significant problem (Flores 2003). The former narrative constructed Mexicans as ideal laborers because they were willing to work hard for little money, could be hired on the spot, and could be fired when their work was no longer needed. Unlike other immigrant groups, Mexicans were supposedly unlikely to take up permanent residence in the United States and move into more skilled positions. The competing narrative, however, drew on existing fears of Mexicans as an unassimilable and undesirable group. This narrative was supported by eugenic arguments that described Mexicans as inherently different and inferior and likely to threaten "racial purity and superiority" (Flores 2003, 374). Ultimately, concerns over the economic crisis increased and Mexican immigrants emerged as the scapegoat for anything from poverty and unemployment to crime and drug trafficking. Hence "the Mexican body became a criminal body," and the image of the docile laborer all but disappeared (Flores 2003, 376).

While these two narratives seem contradictory, both of these representations were "deeply embedded within the cultural commonsense" and thus able to coexist quite comfortably (Flores 2003, 381). Even more important, both of these narratives have one concern in common: the concern over which immigrants are deemed desirable and who represents a threat to the nation. During the Great Depression, the collapsing economy overshadowed the need for a pliable workforce. During and after World War II, however, Mexicans were once again praised as the ideal flexible labor force and actively recruited by U.S. farmers. In 1942, the United States and Mexico signed a binational treaty that allowed for temporary labor migration. As part of the Bracero Program, which lasted from 1942 to 1965, nearly five million Mexicans moved northward to find temporary employment in agriculture. These legal workers were joined by large numbers of undocumented immigrants (Massey 1988; Massey et al. 2002). Yet despite the obvious need for low-wage workers from Mexico, the public discourse continued to be dominated by negative images, and Mexicans were routinely subjected to racist attacks and repatriation campaigns such as "Operation Wetback" in 1954. Contrary to the official emphasis on reuniting and protecting families, these campaigns tore apart immigrant families and endangered their economic survival, with little regard for the children that were oftentimes left behind when their parents were deported.

The 1952 INA—commonly referred to as the McCarran-Walter Act—continued to prioritize a narrow version of the white, heteropatriarchal family. This act, which has remained the basic immigration law for more than fifty years, mainly consolidated previous immigration statutes into a single law. As such, the McCarran-Walter Act retained the national quota system; reiterated the long-established exclusion criteria for persons who are likely to become a public charge, pose a public health or national security risk, or violate religious or moral values; and continued to give preferential treatment to northwestern European immigrants. However, the act also contained a number of significant changes. Most notably, the act removed all explicit racial, gender, and nationality barriers to U.S. citizenship and lifted the ban on Asian immigration. While this amendment signified a change in the official attitude toward Asian immigrants, the decision to discontinue this outright exclusion was mainly a symbolic gesture that had little practical impact (Hing 1993). Between 1952 and 1965, the quota of immigrants from the Asia-Pacific Triangle was capped at two thousand. Immigrants from the Western hemisphere, on the other hand, were still allowed to enter the United States without numerical restriction—a feature that "many members of Congress and commentators failed to grasp" (Daniels 2004, 119).

In addition, the McCarran-Walter Act enacted a slight revision of the preference system. Whereas earlier laws had reserved the majority of visas to family members of U.S. citizens and legal permanent residents, the 1952

INA allotted the first 50 percent of the quota to "immigrants whose services are determined by the Attorney General to be needed urgently in the United States because of the high education, technical training, specialized experience, or exceptional ability of such immigrants." The next 30 percent of visas were reserved for parents of U.S. citizens, and the remaining slots were made available to spouses and unmarried children of legal permanent residents.[12] Yet even though economic considerations started to compete with family values, there was no indication that the United States was ready to abandon its historical commitment to the nuclear family.

With more women entering the labor market during World War II, the United States experienced a marked shift in gender relations. When U.S. soldiers came home after the end of the war, they were eager to return to traditional family structures and assert their positions as primary breadwinners. Many women, on the other hand, were reluctant to abandon their careers and resume their lives as mothers and wives. The war also served as a critical divide in the social history of gays and lesbians. While the majority of young men entered a sex-segregated military, young women were offered the opportunity to leave their tight-knit family structures and move to metropolitan areas for wartime employment. This newfound freedom from traditional heteropatriarchal family structures enabled young people to express their sexual identity much more freely. During the war, a vibrant gay subculture developed in cities along both coasts. This new visibility, however, provoked a violent conservative backlash in the early 1950s. Increasingly, Americans linked their anxieties about homosexuals to the widespread panic over Communism.

It is hardly surprising that immigration reform measures reflected these Cold War anxieties. The McCarran-Walter Act contained provisions that facilitated the admission of refugees from Communist nations, because, as Eithne Luibhéid has argued, "the presence of these refugees seemed to validate the United States' claims about the evils of Communism and the desirability of capitalism" (Luibhéid 2002, 19). In addition, Congress stated that the medical exclusion criteria were meant to include gay and lesbian immigrants. Starting with the Immigration Act of 1917, the United States had excluded persons who were found "mentally defective" or who had a "constitutional psychopathic inferiority." Even though these classifications were certainly open to different interpretations, the Immigration and Naturalization Service (INS) made it clear that this classification included self-identified homosexuals. "In 1950, the Senate

Committee on the Judiciary reported that the 'classes of mental defectives should be enlarged to include homosexuals and other sex perverts'" (Green 1987, 141).[13] In reaction to widespread anxiety about the rise of a homosexual subculture, the judiciary committee discussed various options to ensure that homosexual immigrants would be effectively excluded. The Public Health Service observed that instead of creating a separate class for homosexual immigrants, it would be more effective to issue class A medical exclusion certificates—which were reserved for persons who were "afflicted with a psychopathic personality"—to potential immigrants who were judged to be gay or lesbian.[14]

While the language that was used to refer to gay and lesbian immigrants remained intentionally vague in 1952, the 1965 INA added a new class of medical exclusions for "sexual deviants."[15] Gays and lesbians were now explicitly barred from entry. This was not the only measure aimed at imposing traditional heteropatriarchal family values on immigrants. Whereas earlier reform measures had started to shift the focus away from family reunification to a greater emphasis on education and job skills, the 1965 INA reversed this trend. Starting in 1965, 74 percent of all visas were allotted to family members of U.S. citizen and legal permanent residents.[16] Only one-tenth of all immigration visas were reserved for "qualified immigrants who are members of the professions, or who because of their exceptional ability in the sciences or arts will substantially benefit prospectively the national economy, cultural interests, or welfare of the United States." The same number of visas was made available to unskilled workers who were willing and able to fill existing labor shortages. Finally, a mere 6 percent of visas were reserved for refugees.

Concomitantly, the 1965 INA also reflected the dominant values of the Civil Rights era and finally abolished the racially motivated quota system. Instead, the INA ratified a provision that allotted 20,000 immigrant visas to each country and set an overall ceiling of 160,000 immigrants for the Eastern Hemisphere. With regard to the Western Hemisphere, the INA established an annual 120,000 immigrant cap, with no limits for individual nations.[17] While the 1965 INA represented a step toward more racially inclusive immigration politics, its effects were rather limited, and some scholars argue that rather than ending discrimination toward immigrants of color, the law had the exact opposite effect (Daniels 2004; Dobkin 2009). Because non-European immigrants had been effectively barred from the United States for decades, there were few U.S. citizens and legal permanent residents of color who were able to petition for family members after the passage of the 1965 INA. The only groups who really profited from this reform measure were eastern and southern European immigrants. According to immigration scholar David Reimers, this effect was far from accidental. His analysis of congressional documents shows that while the U.S. government felt pressured to strike the most blatantly racist provisions from the law, they were reluctant to initiate a more fundamental reform. Consequently, the legal "changes were intended to be cosmetic rather than substantive."[18]

During the late 1960s and the 1970s, apart from a few minor amendments that were passed with bipartisan consensus, there was little debate about immigration reform. In the early 1980s, however, the political climate began to change and immigration reform became, once again, a hotly debated topic. Congressional debates during the Ninety-Eighth Congress (1983–84) foreshadowed a lot of the issues that continued to dominate the debate in 1995–96. Immigration Subcommittee Chair Alan K. Simpson (R-WY) and ranking members Edward Kennedy (D-MA) and Strom Thurmond (R-SC) developed one of most groundbreaking reform proposals of the early 1980s. They advocated an amnesty program for undocumented immigrants who had resided in the United States for an extended period of time.[19] A few politicians expressed concerns that these legalized immigrants could petition for additional family members and thus cause an already overburdened legal immigration system to collapse. Still others were worried that the amnesty provision might lead to increasing expenditures for social welfare programs and suggested that newly legalized immigrants should be ineligible for public assistance for a minimum of five years. Generally speaking, though, the Immigration and Control Act of 1983 (S. 529) caused surprisingly little controversy and was approved by the Senate by a wide margin (76–18).

By the time the House held general hearings on the Immigration and Control Act (H.R. 1510), the amnesty provision, in particular, had become much more controversial. While most representatives favored an orderly legalization process for some undocumented workers, there was much disagreement about the specific eligibility criteria (Gimpel and Edwards 1999). Representatives were particularly concerned about the lack of reliable statistical data and the possibility that there might be millions of eligible candidates who were all eager to naturalize. Possible solutions to this perceived problem included raising the residency requirement, adding a mandatory English language proficiency exam, or testing immigrants' knowledge of American history and politics.[20] In the end, the conference committee failed to resolve the fundamental differences between the Senate and the House version of the bill.

During the Ninety-Ninth Congress, Alan K. Simpson (R-WY) once again spearheaded the campaign to develop a path to legalization for undocumented immigrants that had resided in the United States for an extended period of time. While the "Immigration Reform and Control Act" (IRCA) of 1986 (Pub. L. No. 99-603) was widely praised as the most significant immigration reform measure since 1965, it was essentially "a schizoid measure reflecting the deep divisions in Congress over immigration policy" (Daniels 2004, 224). On the one hand, the amnesty provision enabled approximately 2.7 million persons to legalize their status and eventually sponsor family members to migrate legally—in some cases without numerical restrictions (e.g., spouses, who are classified as immediate family members and are thus able to migrate without numerical limits).[21] On the other hand, the IRCA also established sanctions for employers who *knowingly* recruited and/or hired undocumented immigrants. While employer sanctions represent an important step toward eliminating one of the major incentives for undocumented immigrants—jobs—it is important to note that Congress emphasized the word *knowingly*, an indication that they had no desire to pass "a statute that would put large numbers of respectable and wealthy citizen into legal jeopardy" (Daniels 2004, 225). It is thus hardly surprising that the enforcement side of this act lacked teeth and that the IRCA expanded rather than restricted immigration (Daniels 2004; McDonald 2010).

Three years later, Congress turned their attention toward reforming the legal immigration system. In the Senate, Senators Edward M. Kennedy (D-MA) and Alan K. Simpson (R-WY) developed a bill that emphasized job skills and shifted visas away from families seeking reunification toward highly qualified immigrants who could make important contributions to the U.S. labor market.[22] The House was divided over two very different reform proposals: On the one hand, Lamar Smith (R-TX) and John Bryant (D-TX) advocated more restrictive policies, especially for unskilled family members. On the other hand, Bruce Morrison (D-CT) and Howard Berman (D-CA) introduced bills to expand immigration and exempt immediate relatives of legal permanent residents from numerical limitations, which would help reunite families and decrease the backlog.

In response to the changing national origins of contemporary immigrants, Charles Schumer (D-NY) introduced a new "Diversity Category" to reserve a number of visas for immigrants from underrepresented nations. Yet, as many scholars suggest, the "diversity" program was not truly about diversity at all. Instead, it represented an affirmative action program for white immigrants from western Europe (Aleinikoff et al. 2007; Dobkin 2009; Gales 2009; Hing 2003; Schuck 2003). In the end, the 1990 INA (Pub. L. No. 101-649) increased the worldwide annual immigration level by 37 percent to 800,000.[23]

The American public perceived this dramatic increase in immigration levels as an affront. Even though the 1990 law did not represent an attempt to liberalize immigration policy (but was actually an effort to align the immigration ceilings with reality and decrease the immigration backlog), the public focus was on numbers. According to the media, the INA of 1990 would encourage even more immigrants to enter the United States and compete for jobs and social services. In reality, however, most people that were able to take advantage of these newly available green cards—especially in the employment category—were already present in the United States and had long attempted to adjust their status to permanent residency (Daniels 2004, 237). In the end, however, the public response to these legal changes was almost exclusively negative. According to Roger Daniels, "public dissatisfaction with immigration . . . reached a post-1924 peak" and set the stage for a divisive immigration reform debate in the mid-1990s (Daniels 2004, 232).

The Neoliberal Reform Discourse in 1995–96

During the 104th Congress, representatives discussed more than a dozen original immigration bills with hundreds of amendments. While the final version of the immigration reform law—which was signed into law by President Bill Clinton on September 30, 1996—primarily focused on border enforcement, undocumented immigrants, and a reform of the sponsorship system, previous debates had contemplated much more far-reaching reform measures. In addition to these immigrant-specific provisions, however, the 104th Congress also passed a comprehensive welfare reform and a new antiterrorism law, both of which affected the rights and responsibilities of immigrants.

The following section will provide a chronological overview of the legislative process in 1995–96 and lay the groundwork for the next two chapters, which will focus on the discursive strategies that linked these three areas of legal reform. Even though my main focus will be on the Illegal Immigration Reform and Immigrant Responsibility Act (IIRIRA), I will briefly discuss two additional acts that were passed in 1996: the Personal Responsibility and Work Opportunity Reconciliation Act (PRWORA) and the Antiterrorism and Effective Death Penalty Act (AEDPA). Taken together, the debates surrounding these three pieces of legislation formed a discursive terrain that created a new interpretation of the role of immigration and immigrants in U.S. society.

As the following analysis will show, these reform measures were primarily motivated by a neoliberal logic that attempted to reorganize the U.S. immigration system as a market-like structure. Under this neoliberal project, potential immigrants were regarded as customers who wished to obtain a desirable commodity—an immigrant visa. In order to obtain this commodity, individuals had to follow certain rules, accept personal responsibility, and provide proof that they were unlikely to become a financial burden or a security threat. In other words, this new neoliberal project subordinated political and social rationales to an economic project. Instead of arguing that family reunification visas were important for social reasons, for instance, politicians claimed that traditional nuclear families represented an important support structure that could help a newly arrived immigrant stay off welfare. In addition, "criminal aliens" and potential terrorists were not only undesirable because they represented a threat to U.S. citizens, but they were also subject to deportation because they had violated the social contract. Therefore, even nonviolent offenses such as tax evasions and fraud were classified as "aggravated felonies" for immigration purposes and could lead to a deportation order.

Yet even though economic considerations drove the legislative process, political, social, and even cultural arguments were strategically used to justify certain provisions. In a way, the market-like structure of the new immigration system was interpreted as an ethic in itself. Not only did this focus on economic principles substitute the traditional emphasis on social norms and moral values, but Congress also implied that the demands of the market should act as a guide for all human action. It thus became potential immigrants' moral duty to take the initiative and reorganize their lives in such a way that they could achieve maximum success in the labor market. This underlying logic was noticeably different from the reasoning behind earlier immigration legislations.

Immigration Reform in the 1990s

The 1990 INA mandated the formation of a bipartisan Commission on Immigration Reform to examine the accomplishments of earlier immigration policies and make recommendations for the future. President Clinton appointed former congresswoman Barbara Jordan (D-TX) to chair this nine-member advisory commission.[24] In September 1994, the U.S. Commission on Immigration Reform (also referred to as the *Jordan Commission*) released its first interim report, which focused solely on illegal immigration. This report, *U.S. Immigration Policy: Restoring Credibility*, found it to be self-evident that undocumented immigrants were undesirable. Since they had no legal right to join the U.S. labor market, it did not even matter whether their hard labor and their willingness to take temporary positions and accept minimal wages had a positive impact on the U.S. market. Undocumented immigrants had disobeyed the rules of the game and should not be rewarded for their behavior.

Therefore, the commission recommended a threefold strategy to reduce the number of undocumented immigrants and decrease public expenditures on this population. First, and most important, the United States needed to prevent as many illegal entries as possible. In order to achieve this, the 1994 report advocated increased resources for border management, additional personnel to patrol the U.S.–Mexico border, the construction of additional barriers (i.e., fences), tighter airport security with more INS officers, improved interagency cooperation (between INS and Customs), and the introduction of a land border crossing fee that could help finance these costly endeavors. Second, the Jordan Commission called for the development and implementation of a fraud-resistant system for verifying work authorizations and a vigorous enforcement of sanctions against employers who knowingly hire undocumented workers. Third, the report proposed that undocumented immigrants should not be eligible for any publicly funded services except emergency care and programs necessary to protect public health and safety. At the same time, however, the commission explicitly stated that they were strongly opposed to "any broad, categorical denial of public benefits to legal immigrants" (U.S. Commission on Immigration Reform 1994, 23).[25]

Soon after the Jordan Commission released its interim report, the Democrats lost their majority in the House and the new Speaker, Newt Gingrich (R-GA), launched a new round of immigration reform debates. Gingrich advocated the formation of several congressional task forces, which were to develop specific policy recommendations. The Congressional Task Force on Immigration Reform,[26] which was chaired by Elton Gallegly (R-CA), a keen supporter of California's Proposition 187 (which denied undocumented immigrants in California access to public schools, health care, and other social services), consisted of fifty-four members and was organized in six topic-oriented working groups.[27] The Jordan Commission and the Congressional Task Force's recommendations—which, apart from some minor differences with regard to numbers, were basically identical—set the tone for the ensuing debate.

On January 24, 1995, Senator Alan K. Simpson (R-WY) introduced the first comprehensive immigration reform bill to warrant significant debate during the 104th Congress: the Immigrant Control and Financial Responsibility Act (S. 269).[28] Simpson's bill contained provisions to increase border patrol; improve the work authorization verification system; reform asylum, exclusion, and deportation procedures; and limit immigrants' welfare usage. It was soon joined by two competing reform proposals. On March 21, 1995, Dianne Feinstein (D-FL) submitted the Illegal Immigration Control and Enforcement Act (S. 580). Six weeks later, Senator Edward M. Kennedy (D-MA) offered yet another comprehensive immigration reform bill (S. 754), which included measures to prevent illegal immigration and reduce employment opportunities of undocumented workers who were already present in the United States. When the Subcommittee on Immigration voted on the combined bill, which was still called S. 269, only Paul Simon (D-IL) and Edward M. Kennedy (D-MA) voiced their opposition.

In June 1995, the U.S. Commission on Immigration Reform sent its second interim report, "Legal Immigration: Setting Priorities," to Congress. According to the commission, the allocation of immigrant visas needed to reflect the demands of the U.S. labor market and make sure that newly arrived immigrants would be self-supporting. This economic rationale was underlined by a number of cultural and social considerations. In the end, the report recommended a significant reduction of legal immigration levels, a reallocation of visas away from unskilled laborers and distant family members to skilled workers and the nuclear family, and an increased emphasis on the "effective Americanization of new immigrants, that is the cultivation of a shared commitment to the American values of liberty, democracy, and equal opportunity" (U.S. Commission on Immigration Reform 1995, xxx). On June 22, 1995, only days after the Jordan Commission's report was released, Representative Lamar Smith (R-TX) took up the report's recommendations on legal immigration reform and sponsored the Immigration in the National Interest Act (H.R. 1915). The first version of this bill cut the number of immigrants to about two hundred thousand a year, eliminated several family reunification categories (e.g., brothers and sisters of U.S. citizens), and introduced an income requirement for U.S. citizens and legal permanent residents who wished to sponsor a family member. Initially, this income requirement was set at 200 percent of the federal poverty line. In addition to these legal immigration reform proposals, Smith's bill also contained an assortment of provisions that would have affected refugees, asylum seekers, and undocumented immigrants. According to Smith, legal and illegal immigration were inextricably linked and could not be looked at separately. Throughout the debate, he strongly advocated reform proposals that tackled both issues in tandem.

Alan K. Simpson (R-WY) championed this comprehensive approach. When he suggested merging the Senate versions of the legal (S. 1394) and illegal immigration reform bills (S. 269) on November 3, 1995, he proclaimed, "Curbing or even stopping illegal immigration is not enough. . . . The American people are increasingly troubled about the impact legal immigration is having on their country. Poll after poll shows us this. The people have made it so very clear they believe the level of immigration is too high" (United States Congress, Senate, November 3, 1995). The new omnibus proposal (S. 1394) represented one of the harshest anti-immigration legislations in decades. Compared to the House version, however, Simpson's bill was slightly more generous. S. 1394 wanted to lower the annual level of nonrefugee admissions from 675,000 to 540,000, reduce employment-based immigration, eliminate several family reunification categories, and establish income requirements for sponsors (at least 125 percent of the poverty line). On November 28, 1995, the Senate Immigration Subcommittee agreed to move S. 1394 out of the subcommittee.[29]

Shortly afterward, various organizations started to question the logic behind these comprehensive reform proposals that combined legal and illegal immigration reform. In particular, representatives of the American

Immigration Lawyers Association (AILA), who served as expert witnesses in multiple committee hearings, voiced their concern: "In this immigration debate there is an overriding myth. That myth is the myth that illegal immigration can be controlled by reforming legal immigration. These are related, but they are distinctly separate" (Daryl R. Buffenstein, AILA, United States Congress, House, June 29, 1995). Representatives from both parties agreed with this assessment and expressed their positive attitudes toward legal immigrants. In addition, high-tech business executives lobbied Congress to remove the provisions concerning skilled workers. According to this business coalition, U.S. companies were dependent on their ability to recruit qualified foreigners if they wanted to survive in a highly competitive international market. In her study of cooperation and competition between economic interest groups and ethnic and human rights advocates, Carolyn Wong (2006) found that, in the 1990s, high-Tech companies such as Microsoft and Intel started to build a coalition with Hispanic and Asian American rights groups. Even though this coalition seems odd at first glance—especially since these disparate groups tend to occupy opposite ends of the political spectrum—their alliance made a lot of sense in this particular historical and political context. This left–right coalition argued that law-abiding legal immigrants who contribute to the nation's economic development should not be punished for the crimes of undocumented immigrants. Yet, while it was hardly surprising that the business lobby focused on the economic aspects of immigration reform, it is remarkable that immigrant rights groups abandoned their traditional concerns about racism, discrimination, and social and cultural rights of minorities and advanced a very similar neoliberal rhetoric. Citing statistics that illustrated legal immigrants' achievements, they underlined the business lobby's demands.

In the end, this unlikely alliance proved successful. On March 14, 1996, Senator Spencer Abraham (R-MI) proposed an amendment to split S. 1394 into two different bills: a legal and an illegal immigration reform bill. Senators Arlen Specter (R-PA), Mike DeWine (R-OH), Russell D. Feingold (D-WI), and Paul Simon (D-IL) immediately endorsed Abraham's proposal. After little debate, the Senate Judiciary Committee decided to split the bill. In the meantime, the House had decided to adopt the Chrysler-Berman-Brownback Amendment, which sought to eliminate the cuts in legal immigration.[30] However, these successes came at a high price. While politicians from both parties had responded positively to the idea that legal immigrants were commendable human beings who contributed to U.S. society in multiple ways, they were far less willing to acknowledge that undocumented workers deserved any kind of protection. Quite to the contrary, the discourse about undocumented immigrants became increasingly more hostile.

Undocumented immigrants were referred to as lawbreakers and criminals who had made a conscious decision to disregard U.S. laws. Politicians insinuated that undocumented immigrants did not stop at violating U.S. immigration laws. They were also allegedly more prone to join gangs, commit violent crimes, and pose a national security threat. This rhetoric about undocumented immigrants as criminals did not emerge in a vacuum, but similar allegations have emerged on a fairly regular basis throughout the twentieth century. In her analysis of media representations of Mexican Americans in the 1920s and 1930s, Lisa Flores found that when jobs became scarce during the Great Depression, not only were Mexican immigrants commonly described as competitors for jobs but the discourse also drew on other latent fears. Mexican immigrants supposedly threatened racial purity, represented public health risks, and perhaps even more important, posed a criminal danger. Newspapers across the nation frequently reported on crimes committed by Mexican immigrants and highlighted their "purported penchant for criminality" (Flores 2003, 374). Yet even though these representations bear an obvious resemblance to the images of "criminal aliens" in the mid-1990s, there is a significant difference: while the media discourse in the 1920s and 1930s was mainly concerned with the fundamental differences between Americans and *Mexican* Americans, more recent debates focus more on the fundamental distinction between legal and illegal immigrants.

In the late twentieth century, legal Mexican immigrants were commonly recognized as an integral part of our nation. In an attempt to draw a sharp distinction between the merits of legal immigration and the problems inherent in illegal immigration, numerous speakers glorified documented immigrants as ambitious, hardworking people who adhered to traditional heteropatriarchal family values and made invaluable contributions to U.S. society and economy. Undocumented immigrants, on the other hand, were oftentimes described as uneducated and unskilled men who had abandoned their families and preferred communal living arrangements.

Much of the debate also focused on undocumented immigrants' use of public services. Elton Gallegly (R-CA), in particular, repeatedly argued that undocumented immigrants "consume precious social benefits that are denied every day to legal residents who are truly entitled to those benefits" (United States Congress, House, September 25, 1996). While most politicians agreed with this statement—and the initial report from the Jordan Commission, which had recommended that all nonemergency public services should be made unavailable to undocumented immigrants—there was much debate over the role that public education should play in this context. When Elton Gallegly originally proposed a Proposition 187–type amendment to allow states to deny undocumented immigrants access to public schools, he was joined by most of his colleagues. Even though the Gallegly Amendment caused an emotional and divisive debate, the amendment was passed (257–163) and integrated into the House version of the bill (H.R. 2202). On March 21, 1996, the House passed H.R. 2202 by a wide margin (333–87).

A few weeks later, the Senate began its debate of two separate bills. On April 10, 1996, Senator Orrin Hatch (R-UT) introduced the Illegal Immigration Act of 1996 (S. 1664) and the Legal Immigration Act of 1996 (S. 1665). Yet several senators were still dissatisfied with the decision to discuss these issues separately. Knowing that it would be much more difficult, if not impossible, to pass an immigration reform bill that solely focused on legal immigrants, Senator Alan K. Simpson (R-WY) made repeated attempts to integrate legal immigration provisions into S. 1664. On April 24, 1996, for example, Simpson presented an amendment to reform the family preference system and decrease the number of visas that were available for family reunification. Instead of exempting immediate family members of U.S. citizens from the quota system, Simpson argued that there should be a firm ceiling of 480,000 family-sponsored immigrants that included everyone. According to Simpson, "chain migration" had caused a deskilling of the immigrant flow and had thus had a negative impact on the U.S. labor market. Senators Abraham (R-MI) and DeWine (R-OH), however, were unwilling to accept this point. Not only did they dismiss Simpson's anecdotal evidence about chain migration as fictional; they also expressed their disapproval of his attempt to reintroduce legal immigration reform into a debate about undocumented immigrants. Not surprisingly, Simpson's amendment was quickly defeated on a decisive 20–80 vote.

After these legal immigration provisions had been deleted from S. 1664, the Senate invoked cloture and passed the bill almost unanimously. Only Senators Russ Feingold (D-WI), Bob Graham (D-FL), and Paul Simon (D-IL) voted nay (Gimpel and Edwards 1999, 268). Interestingly, however, there were a number of other stipulations for legal immigrants that remained in both the Senate and the House bill. Both S. 1664 and H.R. 2202 contained provisions that made the affidavit of support (which required a signature by U.S. citizens and legal permanent residents who wanted to sponsor a family member) legally enforceable. In addition, both versions of the illegal immigration bills established income requirements for potential sponsors and stipulated that a certain percentage of the sponsor's income should be deemed available to the immigrant if he or she applied for public services. Despite the rhetoric about splitting the bills and examining both issues separately, the 104th Congress had come to the realization that the political climate would have made it impossible to pass a comprehensive legal immigration reform to reduce numbers and change priority categories. However, the affidavit of support and the deeming requirements had become entwined into a larger debate about welfare reform, personal responsibility, and self-sufficiency. As prime examples of cost-saving neoliberal reform measures, these provisions had been endorsed by representatives from both parties, as well as minority and immigrant rights organizations. To ensure their ratification, the affidavit of support and the deeming requirements were taken out of the controversial legal immigration reform bill and rejoined with the much more popular illegal immigration bill.

Following the passage of illegal immigration reform bills in the Senate and the House, a conference committee faced the daunting task of combining the two bills and reconciling the differences between them. While previous Congresses had always relied on bipartisan committees, the Republican majority decided to exclude Democrats from the decision-making process in 1996—a decision that would cause a lot of controversy in the end. Yet even the Republican committee members had a difficult time building a consensus among themselves. Although the committee agreed that the neoliberal reform project called for provisions that shifted responsibility to immigrants and their sponsors, members had different ideas about the exact numbers and the list of programs that should be affected. In particular, the Republican conference committee struggled to reconcile three major differences between the House and Senate versions:

First, S. 1664 expected future sponsors to prove that their annual income was at least 125 percent of the federal poverty line, whereas H.R. 2202 set the income requirement at 200 percent. Second, there was much disagreement about which types of public services should be included under the "deeming requirement." Whereas the House version made educational programs and student loans available to all recent immigrants, regardless of their sponsors' incomes, the Senate version applied the deeming requirement to all future applicants for higher education loans and grants. Third, the House version still contained the Gallegly Amendment, which gave states the option to deny undocumented immigrants the right to receive a public education.

In late July, the conference committee finally reached a compromise. After lengthy debates, they had decided to include the Gallegly Amendment in the bill. Knowing that this decision would be highly controversial among their colleagues, they added a provision that exempted all children who were already enrolled in public schools across the nation. This concession satisfied neither their Democratic colleagues, who were already irritated by the Republicans' decision to exclude them from the conference committee, nor President Clinton, who threatened to veto the bill if Congress included any version of the Gallegly Amendment. With the legislative period coming to an end, the Republican conference committee needed to make quick decisions. After all, they did not want to be blamed for jeopardizing a widely popular bill weeks before an important election. As a result, the conference committee eventually removed the Gallegly Amendment and presented their report to the House, which ratified the bill on September 25, 1996.[31]

To the dismay of the conference committee, President Clinton made a few additional requests. In addition to several relatively minor technical amendments, President Clinton disagreed with the idea that employers could only be faced with discrimination charges if the wronged person could provide proof that the employer had intended to discriminate against them. He also insisted that the deeming provisions and sponsor income requirements should be deleted from the bill. Speaker Newt Gingrich (R-GA) was furious. He grudgingly lowered the income requirement to 125 percent of the federal poverty line and deleted the new public charge provision, which would have made immigrants subject to deportation if they received more than twelve months of public benefits during their first five years in the United States. However, "Republican negotiators stood firm against President Clinton's efforts to remove the higher standard of proof for immigration-related discriminatory employment practices lawsuits" (Gimpel and Edwards 1999, 283). Additionally, Congress was unwilling to strike the popular deeming requirements from the bill. President Bill Clinton accepted this as a valid compromise and included the immigration bill, which had passed the House on September 28, 1996, in the Omnibus Consolidated Appropriations Act (Pub. L. No. 104-208).

Compared to the original bills, the final version of the Illegal Immigration Reform and Immigrant Responsibility Act of 1996 (IIRIRA) was slightly more generous. As previously mentioned, the IIRIRA had lowered the income requirements for sponsors to 125 percent of the federal poverty line, protected legal immigrants from deportation as public charges, and restored undocumented immigrants' access to emergency medical care and public schools. However, the IIRIRA still contained a number of provisions that severely restricted the rights and protections of documented as well as undocumented immigrants. In particular, the IIRIRA changed the definition of an "aggravated felony" for immigrant offenders and made even those immigrants who had committed nonviolent crimes and crimes for which no sentence was served subject to deportation. The IIRIRA also limited the opportunities for judicial review; instated three- and ten-year bars of entry for persons who had been unlawfully present in the United States for more than 180 days or one year, respectively; and barred for life persons who misrepresented a material fact on a visa application. With regard to legal immigrants, the IIRIRA limited access to public benefits and turned the affidavit of support between sponsor and immigrants into a legally binding contract. In keeping with the larger neoliberal project, the IIRIRA excluded immigrants who had already violated the social contract (and those potential immigrants who were likely to do so) from the United States.

Restricting Immigrants' Access to Public Benefits: Welfare Reform

Parallel to the lengthy debate about immigration reform, the 104th Congress also deliberated a major welfare reform act, the Personal Responsibility and Work Opportunity Reconciliation Act of 1996 (PRWORA). The PRWORA was signed into law on August 22, 1996 (Pub. L. No. 104-193), a few weeks before President Clinton approved the immigration reform act. Taken together, these two acts represent a two-pronged attempt to limit immigrants' access to certain welfare programs. According to Gimpel and Edwards, the connection between these two acts can be described as follows: "the welfare reform legislation set new, more restrictive standards of eligibility, whereas the immigration bill provided the enforcement mechanisms for those standards" (Gimpel and Edwards 1999, 284).

While this assessment is certainly accurate, I think that Gimpel and Edwards's brief analysis of the PRWORA failed to notice some of the more complex interactions between welfare and immigration reform. Welfare and immigration reform emerged as two of the most hotly debated issues during the 104th Congress. Politicians from both ends of the political spectrum had become increasingly concerned about escalating levels of government spending and the effects of the advanced welfare state on native-born citizens and immigrants. In particular, politicians implied that the current system not only discouraged American welfare recipients from finding work but also served as a magnet for paupers from all over the world. Consequently, politicians were eager to reform the welfare system to meet economic objectives. In accordance with the larger neoliberal project, which I will discuss in more detail in the following chapters, means-tested public services became the prime means for reforming those individuals who had failed to succeed in a highly competitive job market. Welfare checks were described as a reward for applicants who expressed the willingness to fulfill work requirements most often by accepting jobs with limited prospect for advancement. For those individuals who were unable to meet the new work requirements or for single mothers who were unable to live up to heteropatriarchal family values, welfare checks could be reduced or withheld to punish undesirable behavior.

In the end, the 104th Congress enacted a radical reform measure that reorganized the welfare system along economic lines.[32] Even though the act was not primarily focused on the special status of noncitizens, I argue that immigrants' welfare eligibility was much more than a mere afterthought to a reform package that attempted to downsize federal spending. In an attempt to fit immigrants into this larger debate about cost-effectiveness, lucrative investments, and risk-management strategies, politicians raised crucial questions about the meaning of welfare in a neoliberal state. Neoliberal logic assumes that social categories such as race, gender, sexuality, and potentially citizenship status are inconsequential—an approach that is problematic since it explicitly negates the continuing influence of structural inequalities. Instead, it requires that authorities assess an individual's personal characteristics and behaviors to determine whether this person is likely to succeed and thus worthy of support. As long as a person is deemed likely to succeed, citizenship status is inconsequential, and immigrants should continue to have access to the same services as native-born citizens. Since immigrants had made a commitment to stay in the United States permanently, they represented a good potential long-term investment and, with a little public support, might be turned into responsible, self-sufficient members of society. Therefore, it should not matter that they were not (yet) U.S. citizens.

At the same time, many politicians interpreted the neoliberal logic in a slightly different manner and offered other types of solutions. Contrary to America's long history of providing the same services to both legal permanent residents and U.S. citizens, these individuals argued that the United States had no obligation to support and reform immigrants. Instead of establishing an elaborate system of legally binding affidavits, it would be more cost-efficient for the U.S. government to admit only the most promising individuals and deport those who had failed to find a well-paying job. When the Subcommittee on Human Resources held a preliminary meeting to discuss the "Impact of Immigration on Welfare Programs" on November 15, 1993, for instance, Chairman Harold E. Ford (D-TN) argued that the subcommittee needed to determine the exact amount of money that had been spent on immigrants' welfare benefits, verify whether immigrants displaced American workers, evaluate the admission criteria for contemporary immigrants, and most importantly, "determine what would happen if we simply ended welfare for noncitizens" (United States Congress, House, November 15, 1993). From the very beginning of the debate, politicians questioned whether immigrants should be discussed in the context of welfare reform at all, and some representatives preferred a solution that would simply eliminate immigrants' welfare eligibility. The majority, however, supported compromise measures that distinguished between citizens and immigrants, without banning immigrants from all welfare programs. Throughout the 104th Congress, the reform proposals affecting immigrants' welfare eligibility not only grew more complex but also created a careful balance between these conflicting views. Compared to the final version of the bill, early reform proposals appear overly broad and unsympathetic to the effects blanket provisions would have had on an increasingly diverse immigrant population.

On January 4, 1995, Representative Steven C. LaTourette (R-OH)—and 119 Republican cosponsors—introduced the Family Self-Sufficiency Act of 1995 (H.R. 4), the first comprehensive welfare reform act in the 104th Congress. The original version of this act consisted of eight separate titles, one of which was "Restricting Welfare for Aliens."[33] Section 401(a) determined that no future immigrants, with the exception of refugees and, after five years, legal permanent residents who were older than seventy-five years of age, "shall be eligible for any program referred to in subsection (d)." Said subsection lists a total of fifty-two programs, ranging from emergency food and shelter grants, to immunization programs, to a wide variety of higher education benefits. The only federally funded program for which all immigrants remained eligible was emergency medical care.

After various committees held hearings on different sections of the bill, the committees reported the bill back to the House on March 16, 1995 (H.R. Rep. 104-83). A few days later, the House of Representatives started their general debates and discussed numerous amendments, which gradually complicated the blanket ban on immigrants' welfare eligibility. On March 23, 1995, Ileana Ros-Lehtinen (R-FL) introduced the first in a long line of immigrant-specific amendments. Her amendment, which was accepted on the same day, established that legal permanent residents who suffered from "a physical or developmental disability or a mental impairment" could not be denied federal public assistance. Even though this amendment was limited in scope, it set the tone for the later debate. While the majority was reluctant to provide services to newly arrived immigrants who had not made a satisfactory attempt to become self-sufficient, many politicians were sympathetic to those immigrants who had either fallen on hard times through no fault of their own or who needed some specific short-term assistance to finish their education or job training.

In August and September 1995, the Senate held their general debate on the Family Self-Sufficiency Act of 1995. During this debate, the Senate approved special provisions for victims of domestic abuse, restored eligibility for educational programs, and unanimously adopted the Boxer Amendment (No. 2529), which made sure that the immigrant-specific restrictions did not apply to foster-care or adoption-assistance programs. In contrast, all the more radical amendments, which would have either restored eligibility to large parts of the immigrant population or amended the list of programs to cash- and cash-like programs, were rejected by wide margins.[34]

By January 1996, the conference committee had devised seven different versions of the Family Self-Sufficiency Act of 1995, each of which contained significant changes with regard to immigrants' welfare eligibility. Gradually, a straightforward two-section title had grown into a highly complex compromise that distinguished between different classes of immigrants and benefits and introduced additional requirements for immigrants' sponsors.[35] In accordance with the neoliberal reform project, the final version of the act was based on the following two imperatives: "It continues to be the immigration policy of the United States that (A) aliens within the nation's borders not depend on public resources to meet their needs, but rather rely on their own capabilities and the resources of their families, their sponsors, and private organizations, and (B) the availability of public benefits not constitute an incentive for immigration to the United States" (§ 400, H.R. 4, January 3, 1996). Accordingly, H.R. 4 declared all future immigrants—with the exception of veterans and soldiers on active duty—to be subject to sponsor deeming.[36] During the first five years, the income and resources of the person who had signed an affidavit of support should be deemed available to the immigrant and taken into consideration when determining their eligibility for certain means-tested benefits. Significantly, the deeming provision no longer applied to short-term noncash emergency disaster relief, immunization programs, public health assistance for communicable diseases, all benefits under the National School Lunch Act and the Child Nutrition Act, and programs of student assistance under titles IV, V, IX, and X of the Higher Education Act of 1965, as well as local programs such as soup kitchens, crisis counseling and intervention services, and short-term shelters. After a period of five years, immigrants would gain access to the entire list of public benefits, including the four major programs (TANF, SSI, Medicaid, and Food Stamps).

Yet shortly after both the House and the Senate agreed to this conference report, President Bill Clinton vetoed the bill. On June 27, 1996, Representative John R. Kasich (R-OH) introduced a successor to H.R. 4—the Personal Responsibility and Work Opportunity Reconciliation Act of 1996 (PRWORA; H.R. 3734). With regard to immigrants' welfare eligibility, the first version of this act was remarkably similar to its predecessor. After stressing the fact that everyone—including undocumented immigrants—remained eligible for emergency medical services, immunization programs, and public health assistance for testing and treatment of serious communicable diseases, H.R. 3734 established that newly arrived immigrants would be ineligible for most other federal benefits for a minimum of five years. In addition, H.R. 3734 reiterated the sponsor deeming provisions that were already part of the final version of H.R. 4.

The ensuing debate was predominantly concerned with the importance of specific programs and the eligibility of certain groups of immigrants. For instance, politicians questioned the exact meaning of "public health assistance for testing and treatment of serious communicable diseases." While several speakers believed that this term should include the treatment of HIV/AIDS—after all, HIV/AIDS was defined as a communicable disease under immigration law—other politicians were horrified by the idea that the U.S. government would provide publicly funded services to HIV-positive immigrants. Representative Dana Rohrabacher (R-CA) argued that undocumented immigrants who were HIV positive "should be deported from this country to protect our own people instead of spending hundreds of thousands of dollars that should go for the health benefits of our own citizens." His colleague Robert K. Dornan (R-CA) added, "Because we have done this magnificent PR on the only fatal venereal disease in the country, we still go back and forth as though AIDS is a badge of honor. It shows you are a swinger and you are part of the in crowd in this country. Sad" (United States Congress, House, September 25, 1996).

In addition, politicians vacillated when it came to immigrants' eligibility for educational benefits, such as Head Start programs and student loans.[37] Whereas some people argued that these costly services were no different from other public benefits and should thus be unavailable to newly arrived legal immigrants, other politicians maintained that educational benefits represented a particularly important form of support that could not be denied to any human being. Once the majority agreed that educational benefits represented a good long-term investment and were thus an important means to further the neoliberal reform project, the struggle over specific programs started. In particular, some politicians were reluctant to include postsecondary programs in the list of available programs. In the end, Congress decided to exempt all educational support programs from time restrictions and deeming requirements.[38] Other controversial issues included the exact definition of "programs, services, or assistance which are necessary for the protection of life or safety" (also exempt from sponsor deeming), the specific requirements for affidavits of support, as well as the treatment of legal permanent residents who currently received certain forms of public assistance. Yet, despite these significant controversies, the general neoliberal framework remained relatively stable throughout the congressional debates about H.R. 3734.

President Bill Clinton signed the bill, which became Public Law 104-193, into law on August 21, 1996. The immigrant-specific regulations can be found in title IV ("Restricting Welfare and Public Benefits for Aliens"). What had started out as a brief and easily comprehensible two-section title that banned almost all immigrants from all public benefits had grown into a highly complex title that consisted of six separate subtitles with multiple sections each. Most importantly, the final version of the bill declared new immigrants, who had not yet contributed to the system, ineligible for the major federal welfare programs but restored eligibility to preenactment immigrants and made exemptions for some of the aforementioned programs. In addition, the PRWORA also shifted responsibility toward state governments. Within certain limitations, states were now able to decide which groups of immigrants were worthy of public support. At the same time, the PRWORA limited the overall availability of federal funds and earmarked these funds for specific groups and programs. States were only allowed to attribute federal funds to programs that provided TANF and Medicaid to immigrants who had arrived before August 22, 1996. If they wanted to provide the same services to postenactment immigrants, the money would have to come out of the state budget (Zimmerman and Tulmin 1999). As a whole, the PRWORA ended an era of increasingly generous welfare benefits that had made no distinction between U.S. citizens and legal permanent residents.

In accordance with the larger neoliberal project, these welfare reform measures were meant to not only improve the "quality" of new immigrants but also encourage those immigrants who were already present in the United States to make better choices and develop into self-sufficient neoliberal subjects. However, research demonstrates that the PRWORA had a number of unintended consequences. According to a study by Espenshade, "the 1996 reform measures, instead of preserving legal immigration and discouraging illegal immigration, are more likely to reduce the former and expand incentives for the latter" (Espenshade et al. 1997, 770). In addition to increasing levels of undocumented immigration, the PRWORA also pressured legal immigrants to naturalize at a much faster rate to gain access to social services. As a result, the cost savings were lower than anticipated and more legal immigrants were able to both vote and sponsor family members' immigration petitions by the late 1990s. Yet, perhaps most importantly, this neoliberal logic failed to take persistent structural inequalities into consideration. While the welfare reform measures were meant to increase immigrant productivity and self-sufficiency, research shows that immigrants' labor market participation had always been high (Capps, Ku, and Fix 2002; Fix and Passel 2002). Immigrant poverty had not been the result of a lack of ambition or an unwillingness to work hard, but it was primarily a result of the fact that many newly arrived immigrants were concentrated in low-income sectors of the labor market. As a result, denying those immigrants access to much-needed services created poverty, decreased the availability of nourishing foods, and led to more health-related problems, without providing any further incentive to work even harder.[39]

Further Restricting Immigrants' Rights: Antiterrorism Legislation

When Islamic terrorists planted a car bomb in the underground parking garage of the World Trade Center on February 26, 1993, they sent a shock wave through the United States. The bomb, which was meant to destroy the foundation of the north tower and trigger the collapse of both buildings, failed to achieve its proclaimed goal. However, the massive detonation killed six people, injured over a thousand people, destroyed several electrical power lines, and cut off telephone service for much of lower Manhattan. Most importantly, the attack reminded U.S. citizens that terrorism was a reality and that the United States was not immune from terrorist attacks. Almost two years after the bombing, President Clinton introduced a comprehensive antiterrorism legislation—the Omnibus Counterterrorism Act (S. 390).[40] Yet at that point, Congress was no longer convinced that there was an imminent terrorist threat that warranted an immediate response. President Clinton's bill was thus quickly put on the back burner. Two months later, this general apathy came to a sudden end when Timothy McVeigh, a twenty-six-year-old Gulf War veteran, loaded a rented Ryder truck with homemade explosives, drove up to the Alfred P. Murrah Federal Building in Oklahoma City, ignited a timed fuse, and walked away. The explosion killed 167 people.

Immediately after the attack, the media broadcasted interviews with people who had reportedly seen several Middle Eastern–looking suspects. Within a few hours, however, McVeigh was arrested for driving without a license plate and, while in jail, confessed to the attack in Oklahoma City.

McVeigh was soon put on trial, where a jury imposed the death penalty. Up until his death on June 11, 2001, McVeigh maintained that he had acted alone. The American public, however, had a hard time believing that a young, white man with no criminal history could have committed such an atrocious act. Instead, investigators maintained that McVeigh must have had ties to Islamic terrorists. Some people even contended that McVeigh was linked directly to Ramzi Yousef, a member of Abu Sayaf, who had planned the 1993 bombing of the World Trade Center. Despite lengthy investigations, no one ever found sufficient evidence to connect McVeigh to a militant Islamic organization.[41]

Ironically, the acts of this white, native-born U.S. citizen were used to justify the passage of a comprehensive antiterrorism law that would have little effect on terrorists like Timothy McVeigh. Instead, the Antiterrorism and Effective Death Penalty Act (AEDPA) was directed against all foreign-born criminals, not just terrorists. An examination of the genesis of this law led Kevin R. Johnson to conclude that "though the Antiterrorism Act's name obviously suggests concerns with combating 'terrorism,' the law is a political response to deeper uncertainty in the U.S. political order" (Johnson 1997, 838). In the context of the neoliberal debate about immigration and immigrants, the AEDPA could also be interpreted as an attempt to establish a simplified screening system to identify potential lawbreakers and ensure that the U.S. government had the tools to deport those immigrants who had violated the social contract. Since the neoliberal doctrine emphasized the importance of independence, personal responsibility, and self-sufficiency, Congress usually made an effort to protect personal rights and liberties. At the same time, individual actors were supposed to make responsible choices and adhere to the demands of the market. If a person violated these rules, the government became involved and reinstated order. In the case of noncitizen criminals and terrorists, deportation orders represented the most cost-effective way to deal with individuals who were apparently unwilling or unable to submit to these rules.

Knowing that Americans' desire for public safety and security represented a powerful argument, however, politicians were eager to portray the AEDPA as a direct reaction to the Oklahoma City bombing. Only eight days after the attack, on April 27, 1995, Senators Orrin G. Hatch (R-UT) and Bob Dole (R-KS) introduced a bipartisan "bill to prevent and punish acts of terrorism," as the synopsis phrases it.[42] This bill, the AEDPA (S. 735), was passed by the Senate after only four days of debates. In the

House, Representative Henry J. Hyde's (R-IL) version of the antiterrorism bill (H.R. 1710) caused slightly more controversy. On the one-year anniversary of the Oklahoma City bombing, Congress passed the final conference report on both bills. A few days later, on April 24, 1996, President Bill Clinton solemnly proclaimed that the AEDPA "stands as a tribute to the victims of terrorism and to the men and women in law enforcement who dedicate their lives to protecting all of us from the scourge of terrorist activity." At the same time, President Clinton was also acutely aware of the fact that "this bill also makes a number of major, ill-advised changes in our immigration laws having nothing to do with fighting terrorism" (Clinton 1996).

Legal scholar Bruce Robert Marley has argued that, even though many politicians were undoubtedly aware of the problematic consequences this law would have on many noncitizens, it was hardly surprising that the AEDPA met so little resistance. Marley writes, "There was very little political or popular resistance to these measures. After all, disenfranchisement of an unpopular, scapegoat community that does not enjoy suffrage carries no political risk. Who, after all, would speak out in support of immigrant terrorists? Of illegal aliens? Of criminal immigrants? Not surprisingly, few did" (Marley 1998, 858). Congressional records from the 104th Congress prove that representatives from both parties were not shy to express their disdain for terrorists. Melvin L. Watt (D-NC), for example, went on record with the following comment: "I hate terrorists. They are the scum of the earth. There is nothing lower than a terrorist. They are worse even than people who shoot folks in the back" (United States Congress, House, April 18, 1996). Predictably, no one spoke out in opposition to this remark.

However, Representative Watts was also one of the few people who spoke out against the tendency to equate terrorists with other criminal aliens and subject them to the same treatment. Yet despite some protests that "the tragic bombing is not a reason to repeal the sixth amendment," as Maxine Waters (D-CA) phrased it, Congress decided that the Oklahoma City bombing represented a perfect pretext for an invasive law that affected a much larger group than terrorists (United States Congress, House, April 18, 1996).[43] In particular, politicians argued that the bombing should be interpreted as a warning sign to make some fundamental changes. Bill Martini (R-NJ), for example, asserted, "We cannot allow the seeds of destruction to be sewn in our country. We must send the message loud and clear that the United States will act decisively against those who attempt to undermine civility" (United States Congress, House, April 18, 1996). At the end of the day, Congress thus "lumped together lawful permanent residents with illegal aliens, terrorists, and drug traffickers" (Marley 1998, 858). In an effort to ensure maximum national security, President Clinton eventually signed a law that, many legal scholars have argued, sacrificed noncitizens' individual liberties and freedoms all too quickly (Beall 1998; Johnson 1997; Marley 1998; Martin 1999).

This law, the AEDPA (Pub. L. No. 104-132), consists of eight sections: (1) "Habeas Corpus Reform,"[44] (2) "Justice for Victims,"[45] (3) "International Terrorism Prohibitions,"[46] (4) "Terrorist and Criminal Alien Removal and Exclusion," (5) "Nuclear, Biological, and Chemical Weapons,"[47] (6) "Implementation of Plastic Explosives Convention," (7) "Criminal Law Modifications to Counter Terrorism,"[48] and (8) "Assistance to Law Enforcement."[49] While all these sections contain noteworthy reform provisions, I will primarily focus on those stipulations that had a direct effect on all legal permanent residents and future immigrants.

Title IV is of particular interest in this context. The official purpose of this title can be summarized as follows: Title IV amends the mechanism to bar members of terrorist organizations and enables the U.S. government to devise a list of organizations with terrorist intentions, facilitates the removal procedures for alien terrorists who are already present in the United States, modifies the asylum procedures to ensure that terrorists cannot get political asylum, and expands the list of deportable offenses. Taken together, these new procedures established a system that was supposed to protect U.S. citizens from dangerous terrorists and other criminal aliens. As such, these procedures were fairly uncontroversial. Yet these protective measures came at a high price for the entire immigrant community.

If we look at the same title from a defendant's perspective, the law's effect could be more accurately described as follows: Title IV creates special removal procedures that allow the court to introduce "secret" evidence that had been obtained illegally, and it eliminates federal court review of these decisions by denying noncitizens access to habeas corpus examination.[50] Throughout the debate, several politicians were highly critical of these strict limitations. In their opinion, these procedures were not just unethical, but they also stood in clear violation of a defendant's fundamental right to due process. Even after weighing the inherent dangers against the potential benefits, these representatives were unwilling to sacrifice fundamental individual liberties—cornerstones of the American legal system for generations. Jerrold Nadler (D-NY), for example, repeatedly stressed, "We cannot have a procedure for deporting aliens who are allegedly terrorists where they have no opportunity to cross-examine their accusers, no opportunity to see the evidence against them, no opportunity even to know the specific charges" (United States Congress, House, March 13, 1996). His opponents, on the other hand, were convinced that the end justified the means. For them, it was perfectly legitimate to limit a suspected terrorist's constitutional rights in order to protect the American public.

Yet while the majority was willing to support these antiterrorist provisions, many politicians were reluctant to limit judicial review in cases involving other "criminal aliens." In the end, Congress basically agreed that the introduction of secret or classified evidence and evidence that had been obtained illegally should only be admissible if there was some kind of *national* security risk involved. "Alien criminals" who did not pose a national security risk were granted the right to have a counsel and get a public hearing. In addition, their attorneys were granted the right to access all evidence, introduce additional evidence, and cross-examine all witnesses. Importantly, though, the AEDPA also mandated the creation of a special removal court. In all cases involving undocumented immigrants or temporary residents, this court's deportation order would be final, and the defendant would not get a chance to seek judicial review. Legal permanent residents were still able to appeal a deportation order to the Board of Immigration.

In addition, the AEDPA also increased the number of deportable offenses. With the passage of the Anti–Drug Abuse Act of 1988, the United States introduced a new class of crimes: "aggravated felonies." Initially, this category consisted of a small number of crimes that were deemed serious enough to warrant the deportation of a noncitizen after he or she had completed their criminal sentence in a U.S. prison. Outside of immigration law, the term was meaningless. Shortly after the introduction of this new class of deportable offenses, the term "aggravated felony" underwent a rapid expansion and the crimes that were added to the list were "not necessarily aggravated or felonies" (Family 2010). With the enactment of the Immigration Act of 1990, Congress added all violent crimes for which a court had imposed a minimum sentence of five years in prison.[51] In 1996, the AEDPA extended this category even further. Section 435 lowered the "term of imprisonment" threshold from five years to one year in prison. As a result, shoplifting, fraud, bribery, and many other nonviolent crimes were turned into deportable offenses. Even more significantly, the AEDPA also "created an entirely new meaning of the word 'conviction,' which applied only to aliens" (Marley 1998, 867). Under the AEDPA, it was no longer important whether the noncitizen had actually served a prison sentence. Instead, the new language of the law included all cases where the defendant had decided to settle, accept a plea bargain, or went on probation—the important factor was that a judge *could* have imposed a sentence of twelve months or more.

This provision, in and of itself, would have led to the deportation of thousands of relatively minor criminals, who did not pose a threat to society. Yet to make an already overinclusive provision even more broad, Congress decided that this new definition of aggravated felonies should be applied retroactively. Several politicians spoke out against this drastic measure. Senator Edward M. Kennedy (D-MA), in particular, was outraged about the idea that, under this new law, "a refugee from Rwanda could put a bill in the mailbox and realize he forgot to put a stamp on it. When he innocently tries to remove the letter from the mailbox and he is arrested for tampering with the mail—a felony. Due to poor representation, he accepts a plea bargained sentence of one year. To his surprise, he is suddenly subject to expedited deportation with no judicial review" (United States Congress, Senate, June 7, 1995).[52]

Unfortunately, these scenarios soon became reality. Legal scholar Bruce Robert Marley, for example, provides the following description of an actual case that happened shortly after the AEDPA was passed:

Refugio Rubio has been a legal resident of the United States for thirty-four years. He is fifty-seven years old, a field hand and laborer, and the patriarch of a family that includes seven U.S. citizen sons and seven U.S. citizen grandchildren. Recently, Rubio attended an Immigration and Naturalization Service (INS) interview as part of the naturalization process. There he was arrested as an aggravated felon. The reason? Twenty-seven years ago, in 1972, Refugio Rubio was convicted of a possession with intent to distribute marijuana violation. Since then, he has never been in any trouble with the law. He raised a family, built his own home, and has been a model "citizen" in every way. (Marley 1998, 855)[53]

Instead of fulfilling his dream to become a naturalized citizen, the INS detained Refugio Rubio as an "aggravated felon" and subjected him to a brief deportation hearing without any opportunity for discretionary relief. In the past, legal permanent residents were able to petition an immigration judge for a "waiver of deportation" if they had significant ties to the United States (e.g., if they were married to a U.S. citizen or had U.S. citizen children). In other cases that involved extreme hardships to the defendant or his or her family, the immigrant could request a "suspension of deportation," especially if the defendant had been convicted for a less serious offense. The AEDPA, though, mercilessly eliminated all forms of discretionary relief.

By increasing the number of deportable offenses to include even relatively minor misdemeanors and by eradicating measures that allowed judges to prevent injustices and grant discretionary relief to some of the most deserving noncitizens, U.S. Congress made it clear that they were not simply concerned with America's national security. Instead, Marley has argued, the evidence suggests that "an aggravated felony was no longer a protective device to shield American society from the most heinous crimes. Rather, an aggravated felony became a sword, one that hewed indiscriminately through the ranks of the immigrant community" (Marley 1998, 865). Unfortunately, subsequent events have shown that the AEDPA was only the first in a long line of overly invasive laws that, under the pretense of protecting Americans from terrorist attacks, severely limited the fundamental rights of all noncitizens and, increasingly, U.S. citizens as well.

Current Debates

After the rise in anti-immigrant feelings in the mid-1990s, public sentiments slowly started to change at the dawn of the twenty-first century. Low unemployment rates and a positive economic outlook provided an ideal climate for more generous immigration reform measures. In February 2000, the AFL-CIO executive council called for an overhaul of immigration policy to protect workers' rights, help reunite families, enforce worker protection laws, and hold employers accountable who knowingly hire and exploit undocumented immigrant workers. Their resolution from February 16, 2000, also emphasized that "a new amnesty program is needed to provide permanent legal status for undocumented workers and their families, millions of whom have made and continue to make enormous contributions to their communities and workplaces." Congress endorsed the idea to protect immigrant workers and their families, but they were not quite ready for another debate about a potentially large-scale amnesty provision.

In the Senate, Edward Kennedy (D-MA) sponsored the Latino and Immigration Fairness Act (S. 3095), while Representatives Henry Bonilla (R-TX) and Lamar Smith (R-TX) introduced the Legal Immigration Family Equity Act (LIFE Act; H.R. 4942) in the House. Congress ultimately passed the House version of the act. This legislation expands the use of "K" visas, which used to be restricted to fiancées of U.S. citizens and to spouses and minor children who have petitions for legal permanent residency pending. It also creates a new "V" visa category that grants employment authorization and protection from removal to spouses and minor children of legal permanent residents who have been waiting more than three years for an immigrant visa. Perhaps most importantly, the LIFE Act also reinstated Section 245(i) of the INA (enacted in 1994 as an amendment to the original INA or 1952). This section allows undocumented persons who qualify for permanent residency but are ineligible to adjust status in the United States because of an immigration status violation to pay a $1,000 penalty to continue processing in the United States. On October 3, 2000, Congress also passed the American Competitiveness in the Twenty-First Century Act (S. 2045), which added an additional 297,500 H-1B visas over the next three years. Senators eventually rejected the proposed measure to increase the number of H-2A visas for agricultural workers.

During his first presidential campaign, George W. Bush had made a clear commitment to further improve trade relations with Mexico and develop a temporary worker program that would enable much-needed migrant laborers to enter the United States through legal channels. Shortly after he took office, President Bush began talks with newly elected Mexican President Vincente Fox, who had run on a decisive promigration platform and promised to protect the interests of Mexican workers abroad and prevent further deaths of illegal border crossers. This initial meeting in Guanajuato, Mexico, not only was of symbolic importance (since it was Bush's first foreign visit) but also lead to the formation of the high-level Mexico–U.S. Migration Working Group, which was chaired by U.S. Attorney General John Ashcroft, Secretary of State Colin Powell, Mexico's Foreign Minister Jorge Castañeda, and Interior Secretary Santiago Creel.

During their second meeting in September 2001, which took place in Washington, D.C., Fox and Bush instructed the working group "to reach mutually satisfactory results on border safety, a temporary worker program and the status of undocumented Mexicans in the United States." At the time, the working group was in the process of exploring a variety of options, including a temporary "guest worker" program, a legalization program with a path to U.S. citizenship or a possible combination of both. President Bush maintained that he was vehemently opposed to a "blanket amnesty" but open to a limited legalization program—without specifying either one. He also continued to support plans for a new temporary worker program.

The terrorist attacks of September 11, 2001, put an abrupt end to the movement toward more generous immigration laws and instead turned immigration into a homeland security issue. As an immediate response to the attacks, Congress passed three highly restrictive laws that would significantly diminish the legal rights of current and future immigrants. The USA Patriot Act (PL 107-56), which was passed by a wide margin in both houses and signed into law on October 26, 2001, enabled law enforcement agencies to access personal information (including e-mails, phone conversations, and financial records) of terrorism suspects and gave them more leeway in detaining, investigating, and deporting noncitizens suspected of terrorist activity. In addition, the USA Patriot Act broadened the definition of "terrorist" and "terrorist activity." On March 14, 2002, President George W. Bush signed the Enhanced Border Security and Visa Entry Reform Act of 2002 (PL 107-113) into law. This act required the INS, which had been widely criticized for its inability to identify and deport those terrorists who were in the United States illegally, to develop a database that would allow federal law enforcement and intelligence agencies to share data with the INS and the U.S. State Department. On November 22, 2002, the Homeland Security Act (PL 107-296) disbanded the INS and created the U.S. Department of Homeland Security.

Ten months after the USA Patriot Act was passed, former attorney general John Ashcroft and the Department of Justice enacted the National Security Entry and Exit Registration System (NSEERS), which required citizens of twenty-five predominantly Muslim countries to go through a special registration process. Under this special registration, new arrivals who were male, between the ages of sixteen and forty-five, and citizens of one of these twenty-five countries had to register at a specially determined port of entry. Immigrants and visitors who were already present in the United States had to appear at a domestic registration center to be fingerprinted, photographed, interrogated, and in many cases, detained. In a press release from December 3, 2003, the U.S. Department of Homeland Security reported that as of September 30, 2003, they had collected information on 93,741 individuals at the ports of entry and 83,519 individuals at the former INS offices. A total of 13,799 of these individuals were placed in deportation proceedings due to a variety of immigration violations. Not a single one of these 177,260 boys and men were charged with terrorist activities.

While the government eventually suspended the special registration measure in December 2003, they maintained that they might decide to reinterview certain individuals at a later date. On June 28, 2005, Senators Richard Durbin (D-IL), Edward Kennedy (D-MA), and Russell Feingold (D-WI) wrote a letter to the new Secretary of the U.S. Department of Homeland Security, Michael Chertoff, stating their belief "that Special Registration was ill-conceived, badly executed, and ultimately counterproductive." Further, they urged Chertoff "to terminate the Special Registration program in its entirety and to take steps to remedy the damage it did." So far, the courts have upheld the program and ruled that the U.S. Justice Department had the authority to enforce NSEERS.

In addition to these terrorism and homeland security–related concerns, the declining economy also diminished hopes for generous immigration reform measures and a significant increase in available green cards. With the start of the 108th Congress, Republicans and Democrats once again discussed significant immigration legislation. The first in a long line of bills was the Agricultural Job Opportunity, Benefits, and Security Act of 2003 (S. 1645). This bipartisan bill proposed a business-friendly reform of the H-2A visa program for agricultural workers and an earned legalization program. On July 31, 2003, Senators Orrin Hatch (R-UT) and Richard Durbin (D-IL) reintroduced the Development, Relief, and Education for Alien Minors (DREAM) Act (S. 1545), which was originally discussed in 2001 as H.R. 1918 and S. 1291 but quickly shelved after September 11, 2001. The DREAM Act wanted to make undocumented immigrant students eligible for in-state tuition and provide a path to legalization for immigrants who had entered the United States before the age of sixteen, had resided in the United States for a minimum of five years, and were of "good moral character." Even though both acts seemed to have bipartisan support in the beginning, they were soon criticized from both ends of the political spectrum and discussion stalled.

On January 7, 2004, President George W. Bush asked Congress to join forces in an effort to pass a comprehensive immigration reform bill that would simultaneously protect our borders, American workers, American businesses, and legal immigrants. In his press release on "Fair and Secure Immigration Reform," Bush stated that he did not "support amnesty because individuals who violate America's laws should not be rewarded for illegal behavior and because amnesty perpetuates illegal immigration." Instead, he proposed a Temporary Worker Program that would be open to prospective workers who were still abroad as well as to undocumented immigrants who were already present in the United States. He argued that these individuals should eventually be eligible for legalization as well as citizenship. His rhetoric was immediately dismissed by immigration opponents, who claimed that this was yet another amnesty provision, while proimmigration activists criticized the idea that undocumented immigrants who came forward to apply for a temporary visa would face a significant risk of deportation (e.g., if no more temporary work permits were available). In light of this opposition, President Bush eventually abandoned his plans to introduce a formal immigration reform bill, and the 108th Congress ended without passing any immigration reform legislation.

Bush's second term in office was characterized by more controversy over immigration. This time, however, the debates were not limited to Congress; millions of proimmigration activists started to voice their dissatisfaction with restrictive enforcement-only bills. The first bill of the session—the REAL ID Act of 2005—was still relatively uncontroversial and was signed into law on May 11, 2005. The passage of the Border Protection, Antiterrorism, and Illegal Immigration Control Act of 2005 (H.R. 4437), on the other hand, drew a lot of public criticism. H.R. 4437, which was originally introduced by Representative F. James Sensenbrenner (R-WI) on December 6, 2005, contained a number of highly controversial provisions: Not only did it turn unlawful presence in the United States into a felony and propose a penalty of up to five years in prison for those individuals and organizations who assisted an undocumented immigrant in any way, but it also introduced new expedited removal procedures, mandated a seven hundred–mile border fence and increased border patrol, and authorized state and local law enforcement to enforce federal immigration laws. The House passed the bill by a slim margin (239–182) on December 16, with 82 percent of Democrats opposed and 92 percent of Republicans in support of the bill.

The passage of the Sensenbrenner bill served as the catalyst for an unprecedented wave of proimmigration activism. A growing coalition of grassroots organizations and well-established immigrant and human rights groups spoke out against the proposal to criminalize and deport millions of undocumented workers. In the spring of 2006, millions of protestors rallied in support of immigration, with more than five hundred thousand in Los Angeles alone. As a response to the growing unpopularity of this highly restrictive, enforcement-only approach, Senator Arlen Specter (D-PA) introduced the Comprehensive Immigration Reform Act of 2006 (S. 2611), which opposed mass deportations of undocumented workers and instead called for an orderly legalization process for deserving individuals. In addition, this act would establish a new visa category for "guest workers" (H-2C), increase the cap on H-1B visas from 65,000 to 115,000, and require the United States to build a 600-mile border fence and develop new border security initiatives. State and local law enforcement officers would be prohibited from helping the federal government enforce immigration violations. S. 2611 passed the Senate on May 25, 2006, by a comfortable margin (62–36). Due to the widely differing provisions in the two bills (H.R. 4437 and S. 2611) and the approaching presidential election campaign, neither bill passed the conference committee, and the 109th Congress eventually failed to ratify a comprehensive immigration reform bill.

In 2007, the 110th Congress started another round of discussions about immigration reform. In response to pressures from a vocal proimmigration movement and the continued activism of anti-immigration groups such as the Federation for American Immigration Reform (FAIR) and the American Immigration Control Foundation (AICF), Senators McCain (R-AZ) and Kennedy (D-MA) negotiated a compromise bill that was supposed to appeal to both sides. The Secure Borders, Economic Opportunity, and Immigration Reform Act of 2007 (S. 1348) was the result of a bipartisan effort to pass comprehensive immigration reform. As introduced, the bill allowed undocumented immigrants who had resided in the United States for more than five years, had no criminal record, and were willing to pay a fine to adjust their status to legal permanent residency. The bill also contained the former DREAM Act in its entirety and determined that those undocumented immigrants who had entered the

United States as children could convert to permanent resident status if they graduated from high school and continued on to college. They would then be eligible for student loans and federal work-study programs but not Pell Grants. S. 1348 also provided for an additional 1.5 million temporary visas for the next five years after enactment, mandated the development of new border security measures and an electronic employment verification system, and determined that all aliens who attempt to enter the United States illegally shall be detained until removed or admission is granted. In addition, citizens of those countries that will not allow their citizens to be deported from the United States will be categorically ineligible for visas in the future.

This compromise bill was officially introduced on May 9, 2007, and the bill was debated on nine full days. During this time period, over three hundred amendments were filed and thirty-one were voted on. On June 7, 2007, an initial vote to invoke cloture failed due to the lack of support by Republican Senators (46 rejected the cloture motion, 1 abstained). After the second attempt to end debate failed (45–50; 15 votes short of the required 60), Senate Majority Leader Harry Reid (D-NV) announced, "We are finished with this for the time being." Senator Arlen Specter (D-PA) was slightly more optimistic in his assessment that immigration reform "is on life support, but it is not dead." A few days later, President George W. Bush expressed his continued commitment to immigration reform and promised to lobby Republican senators in an effort to garner more Republican support. In a bipartisan meeting on June 13, 2007, several key senators agreed on a deal to revive immigration legislation. Key aspects of their compromise involved increased funding for worksite enforcement and border security and a new rule that required all undocumented immigrants to return to their home country before they could adjust their status to legal permanent residency. Five days later, on June 18, Senators Kennedy (D-MA) and Specter (R-PA) introduced the new version of the bill as The Unaccompanied Alien Child Protection Act of 2007 (S. 1639). After much disagreement and several postponements, the Senate passed a cloture motion on June 26, with sixty-four Senators in support of the bill. On the same day, however, the House Republican Conference passed a resolution introduced by Pete Hoekstra (R-MI) that expressed opposition to the Senate immigration bill by a wide margin (114–21). On June 28, S. 1639 finally failed by a vote of 46–53, with 37 Republicans, 15 Democrats, and 1 independent voting against the cloture motion. After this second defeat of comprehensive immigration reform, Congress agreed to postpone further discussion until after the presidential elections in 2008.

Soon after President Barack Obama took office, Congress started to discuss a variety of immigration reform bills, most of them focusing on a specific group of immigrants or a reallocation of existing visas. On February 12, 2009, for example, Representative Jerrold Nadler (D-NY) and Senator Patrick Leahy (D-VT) introduced the Uniting American Families Act (H.R. 1024 and S. 424), which opens up the family reunification category to permanent partners of U.S. citizens and legal permanent residents, thus ending discrimination against gay and lesbian couples under immigration law.[54] The 111th Congress also saw much controversy over how to balance the three historical principles underlying the U.S. immigration system: family reunification, admitting immigrants with needed skills, and ensuring diversity.[55] In October 2009, Representative Issa (R-CA) proposed legislation to eliminate the diversity visa program and reallocate those visas to employment-based immigrants with advanced degrees (H.R. 3687). In addition, some immigration reform advocates pushed for a reduction in family reunification in an effort to increase the availability of green cards for the "best and the brightest." However, support for these measures was complicated by the ongoing economic crisis, and it remained questionable whether additional qualified workers needed to be recruited from abroad to remain competitive in a worldwide market. In the end, the 111th Congress failed to even get close to passing a comprehensive immigration reform law.

In response to Congress's inability to pass a comprehensive immigration reform law, numerous states started to discuss their own immigration bills to show their discontent. First in a long line of similar bills was Arizona's Support Our Law Enforcement and Safe Neighborhoods Act (Arizona SB 1070), which gave local law enforcement officers the right to stop, detain, and arrest a person suspected of being an undocumented immigrant. It also required every officer to check a person's immigration status if they were stopped or arrested for a non-immigration-related offense (e.g., during a routine traffic stop). If a person failed to produce the relevant immigration documents to prove their legal status, they would be charged with a misdemeanor. Even though the bill officially prohibited racial profiling, it was unclear how else a police officer might reasonably suspect someone of being an "illegal alien." This new procedure represented a clear divergence from the long-established rule that state and local police officers were barred from enforcing federal immigration laws. Arizona's SB 1070 was signed into law on April 23, 2010. Yet after much public controversy, the Department of Justice filed a motion for a preliminary injunction, which was issued the day before the law was scheduled to take effect.

Notwithstanding the fact that anti-immigration forces have failed to have the injunction removed and that this law would undoubtedly increase the occurrence of racial profiling, Republican as well as Democratic contenders in the 2010 election started to push for similar legislation in other states. According to a widely cited press release by Americans for Legal Immigration (ALIPAC), "national and local polls indicated that 60–81% of Americans support local police enforcing immigration laws" as of spring 2010. Perhaps even more troubling is the fact that seventeen other states introduced similar legislation in the weeks following the passage of Arizona's SB 1070 and that many of those states were neither close to the U.S.–Mexico border nor known to have an immigration "problem."[56] Despite a vocal alliance of proimmigration activists who criticized this meanspirited, enforcement-only approach and demanded comprehensive reform measures, most politicians seemed reluctant to address the need for a realistic solution that went beyond criminalizing undocumented immigrants.

In May 2011, in a "Blueprint for Building a Twenty-First Century Immigration System," President Obama "reiterated his deep commitment to fixing the broken immigration system." In this blueprint, he expressed his desire to "strengthen . . . our economic competitiveness by creating a legal immigration system that reflects our values and diverse needs." As part of this plan, President Obama proposed to encourage highly trained individuals to stay in the United States after they finish their education and develop legal avenues for agricultural laborers to migrate to the United States temporarily. He also spoke out in support of creating a pathway to legal status for some undocumented immigrants—a suggestion that was immediately criticized as another amnesty provision. The "Blueprint" also wants to hold businesses that knowingly hire and exploit undocumented workers accountable. In response to these guidelines, Senator Robert Menendez (D-NJ) introduced the latest version of a comprehensive immigration reform package on June 22, 2011: the Comprehensive Immigration Reform Act of 2011 (S. 1251). This bill contained both the DREAM Act and AgJobs, a proposed law that would have provided agricultural employers with a stable, legal labor force and included a path to legalization for the most deserving undocumented immigrants. Yet despite the broad-based consensus on the need for reform, recent history vividly illustrates the difficulties inherent in finding common ground when it comes to specific policy suggestions. Especially in light of the current economic crisis and consistently high unemployment rates, the possibility of passing a comprehensive immigration reform act seems further out of reach than ever.

Conclusion

The 104th Congress passed three majors pieces of legislation that, as a whole, had a detrimental impact on the lives of all noncitizens. Each of these three acts primarily focused on a different subgroup: while the IIRIRA targeted undocumented immigrants, the PRWORA limited the welfare eligibility of recently arrived legal immigrants, and the AEDPA restricted the rights of and increased the penalties for noncitizens who supported terrorist organizations. Yet in addition to these more obvious focal points, each act also contained provisions that affected other immigrants as well. As mentioned before, the final version of the *Illegal Immigration Act* was not limited to illegal immigrants—despite the fact that, after lengthy debates, both the House and the Senate had agreed to examine the legal immigration system separately. Similarly, the *Antiterrorism* Act had serious repercussion for a number of "alien criminals" who were not terrorists, and the PRWORA included several provisions that regulated immigration procedures and were not directly linked to an immigrant's ability to receive welfare (e.g., income requirements for potential sponsors).

Taken together, the congressional debates that led to the passage of these three acts represent a complex discursive field. Regardless of the specific context, the discourse kept coming back to a few central questions. On the most basic level, Congress struggled to determine which immigrants were desirable, which potential candidates should be kept from entering the United States, and which immigrants had forfeited their right to live in the United States. In this regard, the congressional debates in 1995–96 are a continuation of historical trends. As the first section of this chapter demonstrated, the United States has a long history of excluding immigrants who were likely to become a public charge, had a criminal history, or did not conform to heteropatriarchal family values.

Yet by the mid-1990s, the situation had become more complicated. Congress was expected to balance competing objectives, such as the concern about national security, the intention to improve America's economy, and the general tendency to enforce heteropatriarchal family values. Meanwhile, they also reacted to the public's anxieties about immigrants' racial characteristics, religious beliefs, culture, and class status. Under the new neoliberal doctrine, which generally subordinates political and social criteria to economic rationale, it had become increasingly difficult to address these anxieties. In some cases, Congress was able to make explicit connections to public concerns and contend that their reform measures would not only have a positive economic effect but also help alleviate other concerns. With regard to the AEDPA, for instance, Congress argued that their bill would guarantee the smooth operation of U.S. society and the economy in a cost-effective manner while protecting the life and safety of law-abiding citizens. Widespread security concerns were thus used to reinforce the economically oriented logic. In other cases, however, it was much more difficult to make these connections, and politicians offered conflicting interpretations. Welfare benefits for undocumented children, for example, presented a complex dilemma. While the proponents of generous policies believed that these children were innocent victims, they struggled to prove that their policy recommendations were in accordance with the larger neoliberal project. Their opponents, on the other hand, knew they had to couch their restrictive proposals into a humanistic rhetoric about more deserving U.S. citizen children to convince the larger public.

Throughout the immigration reform discourse in 1995–96, Congress employed a variety of rhetorical strategies to justify their neoliberal reform measures. Not only was this discourse different from earlier congressional debates; as this chapter demonstrated, the resulting policies represented a new phase in the long history of restrictive immigration legislation. In accordance with neoliberal doctrine, the 104th Congress introduced a variety of risk-management strategies to assess immigrants and admit only the most promising individuals. In the course of these reform measures, Congress reorganized the legal immigration system along economic lines, eliminated the social safety net, and excluded individuals who had violated the social contract. The following two chapters will examine two specific issues: the discourse about family reunification and the conflict about undocumented workers. By analyzing the debates that surrounded these two subjects, I will explain how Congress negotiated various concerns and tried to balance conflicting objectives.

2

Family Values and Moral Obligations

The Logic of Congressional Rhetoric

In June 1995, the U.S. Commission on Immigration Reform sent its second interim report, "Legal Immigration: Setting Priorities," to Congress.[1] In her introductory letter, Chair Barbara Jordan wrote that "the Commission recommends a significant redefinition of priorities and a reallocation of existing admission numbers to fulfill more effectively the objectives of our immigration system." According to this bipartisan commission, the U.S. government had not only admitted too many immigrants; it had also failed to adapt admission criteria to the changing demands of the labor market.[2] While the commission was mindful of America's historic commitment to family reunification, it was concerned about the negative impact that elderly and unskilled immigrants had had on the U.S. welfare system. Consequently, the commission recommended far-reaching reforms that advocated the use of economic objectives to streamline admission criteria.

Over the course of the 1995–96 immigration reform debate, numerous politicians came back to these initial recommendations. In a direct reference to Barbara Jordan's work, Senator Edward M. Kennedy (D-MA) reminded his fellow senators of the significance of immigration reform: "As we consider immigration reform today, we must be mindful of the important role of immigration in our history and our traditions. Immigrants bring to this country a strong love of freedom, respect for democracy, commitment to family and community, fresh energy and ideas, and a strong desire to become a contributing part of this Nation. . . . If we ever closed the door to new Americans, our leadership in the world would soon be lost" (United States Congress, Senate, April 15, 1996). Senator Kennedy added that America could only stay true to this heritage if it moderately reduced overall levels of immigration, gave preference to immediate family members and skilled workers, and protected unskilled American laborers from unfair competition. After all, America was not just a country of immigration but also a country devoted to protecting its own citizens. Accordingly, Senator Kennedy promoted a compromise solution that attempted to do justice to both sides—U.S. citizens as well as potential immigrants.

Congressional records indicate that the "America is a nation of immigrants" trope was not only popular but also flexible. While politicians like Senator Kennedy reasoned that it was in America's best interest to keep its borders open to attract a select group of promising individuals, others added that the United States also had a moral obligation to maintain its generous immigration policy.[3] Representative Louis Stoke (D-OH), for instance, claimed that restricting the number of legal immigrants "clearly violates the basic tenets of fairness and justice upon which our Nation, a nation of immigrants, was founded [and] that America must honor its pledge of being a nation that will reunite families" (United States Congress, House, March 21, 1996).

In contrast, proponents of more restrictive immigration laws alleged that even though "we are a Nation of immigrants, and immigrants have made great contributions to our country," Congress needed to determine "what level of legal immigration is most consistent with our resources and our needs" (Richard C. Shelby [R-AL]; United States Congress, Senate, April 25, 1996). According to this logic, the United States could not afford to admit large numbers of immigrants regularly because, as John J. Duncan (R-TN) phrased it, "too much of any good thing can become harmful, even destructive" (United States Congress, House, March 19, 1996). The supporters of more restrictive immigration laws argued that immigrants had started to become a burden on U.S. society. Not only did these politicians claim that the immigrant population was too large to benefit the nation; numerous speakers also argued that the preference system had failed to select the "best and the brightest." Consequently, Congress faced the difficult task of balancing a historical commitment to immigrants against the economic, cultural, and social interests of contemporary American citizens.

This extensive debate about the optimal structure of a legal immigration system for the twenty-first century was part of a larger "discursive formation." In *The Archaeology of Knowledge and the Discourse on Language*, Michel Foucault argues that "a discursive formation is not . . . an ideal, continuous, smooth text that runs beneath the multiplicity of contradictions. . . . It is rather a space of multiple dissensions; a set of different oppositions whose levels and roles must be described" (Foucault 1972,

155). As such, a discursive formation draws on a wide variety of issues and connects them in complicated and sometimes contradictory ways. A discursive formation can thus be understood as a complex network of multiple "discursive strands" that circulate around an issue like immigration. Each discursive strand highlights a particular aspect and helps us interpret the information and decide what is particularly important, who is deserving of welfare or immigration benefits and who is not, and how we assign blame for social problems.

From a sociological perspective, the concept of a discursive formation is very closely related to the idea of "framing." According to sociologist Erving Goffman, framing is a discussion of "what would otherwise be a meaningless aspect of the scene into something that is meaningful" (Goffman 1974, 21). Public discourse represents an important factor in policy formation. Social problems are always fabricated. There are no natural or objective criteria to decide what qualifies a social problem (Yoo 2008). Instead, the structure of the discourse, whether we think of it as discursive strands or interpretative frames, helps the public compartmentalize information and form judgments (Chavez, Whiteford, and Howe 2010, 13). Discourse thus influences public opinion based on the aspects of the debate that are covered, how these stories are represented and whose voices are included, and the language that is used in the articles.

Instead of examining the entire formation of immigration discourse, this chapter will focus on one particularly important discursive strand/frame: the controversy about family reunification. Throughout the larger debate, Congress made a few attempts to abolish the diversity lottery or reduce the number of work visas, especially for unskilled laborers.[4] However, most of the debate focused on the merits of the family preference system. Politicians fought over the total number of family-sponsored immigrants, discussed different preferences for certain family members, and offered conflicting definitions of a "nuclear family." Most importantly, though, they struggled to fit a humanistic rhetoric about family values and moral obligations into a discourse that was largely dominated by economic considerations.

By focusing on a specific example, this chapter will demonstrate how politicians from both ends of the political spectrum managed to combine these seemingly conflicting objectives. In contrast to James G. Gimpel and James R. Edwards, who contend that, unlike earlier discussion about immigration reform, "consensus had all but disappeared," I will show that there was actually a bipartisan consensus that the U.S. immigration system had to be streamlined to meet the demands of the labor market and select out the most promising neoliberal subjects (Gimpel and Edwards 1999, 4). Perhaps not surprisingly, there was almost no explicit opposition to the idea that the U.S. immigration system should be as economically profitable as possible. Yet, at the same time, the persistent emphasis on family values could be interpreted as a sign that some politicians were uncomfortable with the idea that immigration policy should be based exclusively on neoliberal criteria. Therefore, numerous politicians used personal anecdotes and remarks that expressed their concern for immigrants and their families to humanize the impersonal economic logic that drove the debate.

The discursive strand about family reunification also serves as a reminder that neoliberalism had reached a new phase by the mid-1990s (Cornwall 2008; Grewal 2005; Griffin 2007; Melamed 2011). In its earliest origins, neoliberal thinking was primarily focused on economic reforms such as freeing the market from government regulations and decreasing tax rates to foster economic growth. By the mid-1990s, however, neoliberalism had grown into an all-encompassing socioeconomic system, and its reach had expanded exponentially. According to Jodi Melamed, "neoliberalism, far more than a purely economic system, is also a world-historical configuration of governance and biological and social life, premised on the belief that the market is better than the state at distributing resources and managing human life" (Melamed 2011, 39). As part of this larger configuration of biological and social life, neoliberal discourse normalizes certain kinds of behaviors and identities, while others are dismissed as irrational and irresponsible. Gender identity, sexuality, and family structure emerged as key ingredients for responsible neoliberal citizenship.

According to neoliberal political ideology in the mid-1990s, the emphasis on free trade, open markets, and personal merit was not only inherently race and gender neutral but was actually designed to further antiracist and antisexist politics. This was an important deviation from mainstream political arguments during the Reagan administration, which denied that racial and gender inequality were even still a problem (Melamed 2011, 147). A closer examination of the immigration reform and family reunification discourse, however, calls these claims to antiracism and sexism into question. According to Penny Griffin's work on the sexual configuration of the global political economy, "the heteronormative reproduction of gender identity/identities is crucial to/in neo-liberalism because it allows for the maintenance of a particular neo-liberal vision of economic activity, one that is both masculinised and ethnocentric" (Griffin 2007, 221). The following analysis will show how the neoliberal discourse about family reunification reproduced heteronormative notions of gender identity and family structures.

This chapter will examine the neoliberal logic behind various attempts to restructure the family preference category. While I will make periodic references to specific laws or amendments, I am primarily interested in the language that was used to justify certain positions. Following Foucault's definition of discursive formation, I will identify key issues—issues that kept coming up in different contexts—and interrogate their relationship to one another and to the larger issues at stake in this debate. First, I will critically examine the claim that family-sponsored immigrants are particularly desirable because they remind Americans of the importance of traditional family values. Second, I will examine the controversy over a particular group of family-sponsored immigrants: elderly parents. Third, I will discuss the widespread concern among some politicians that immigrants admitted through the family preference system would be somehow inferior to past generations of immigrants. Finally, I will examine how politicians negotiated issues of race and ethnicity among family-sponsored immigrants.

In Support of the Nuclear Family: Continuing America's Historical Commitments

Politicians were generally eager to prove that their particular reform plans were not only suited to meet the economic needs of contemporary Americans but also consistent with America's historical commitment to immigration and immigrants. Most notably, politicians repeatedly cited their own immigrant ancestry as a way to establish credibility and prove that they were aware of the positive impact immigrants have had on this country. While numerous speakers made vague references to immigrants' cultural and social contributions, the majority of comments focused on financial considerations, such as tax payments, job-market effects, and the usage of public benefits. Immigrants' cultural and social contributions were usually only mentioned to underline economic arguments.

With regard to immigrants' economic impact on the United States, we can distinguish two positions: On the one hand, immigration opponents used personal anecdotes to illustrate fundamental differences between their ancestors and contemporary immigrants. According to their examples, the current generation of immigrants had little potential to succeed in an increasingly competitive job market. On the other hand, there were numerous politicians who detected a fundamental similarity across generations. They reasoned that past generations of immigrants were even poorer, less skilled, and less educated than present-day immigrants. However, through hard work and willpower, these people were able to succeed and ensure a better future for their children and grandchildren.

Senator Phil Gramm (R-TX), for instance, gave a lengthy account of his wife's Asian grandfather, who came to the United States as an indentured servant.[5] After he had worked off his contract, he married a young woman that he had picked out in a picture book (a so-called picture bride). His son was "the first Asian American ever to be an officer of a sugar company in the history of Hawaii" (United States Congress, Senate, April 25, 1996). Over several generations, Senator Gramm's in-laws had contributed to this country in many ways. Most importantly, though, Senator Gramm argued, "America is not a great and powerful country because the most brilliant and talented people in the world came to live here. America is a great and powerful country because it was here that ordinary people like you and me have had more opportunity and more freedom than any other people who have ever lived on the face of the Earth. And, with that opportunity and with that freedom, ordinary people like us have been able to do extraordinary things" (United States Congress, Senate, April 25, 1996). Similarly, Senator Mike DeWine (R-OH) reasoned that one of America's greatest strengths is its openness to change and its willingness to take risks. In his account of his grandfather, "a dirt poor Irishman," Senator DeWine stresses the fact that his grandfather "came here with guts and with ambition, but probably with very little else. He took a chance on America, and America took a chance on him because America back then thought big thoughts about itself and what great riches lay in the ambition—in the ambition of people who are willing to take risks. That is the kind of America we need to be, not a closed America that views itself as a finished product but an America that is open to new people, new ideas, and open to the future"(United States Congress, Senate, April 15, 1996). Gramm and DeWine were both reluctant to change the family reunification preference system for legal immigrants. According to their personal anecdotes, an immigrant's race, nationality, educational background, work experience, and financial resources did not necessarily determine whether he or she would become an economic success. Instead, they both cited abstract factors such as guts and ambition and an eagerness to make the best possible use of the opportunity and freedom America has to offer as much more important.[6] Preselecting certain individuals was thus rejected not only for being inconsistent with America's tradition but also because it was an ineffective mechanism to choose the most promising individuals.

Whereas some people were concerned that the emphasis on family reunification would deskill the current generation of new immigrants, others were quick to point out that this was not necessarily the case. Senator Gramm, who was one of the most outspoken proponents of a generous family reunification system, stressed the fact that some of the most successful individuals had entered the United States through a family sponsor. Specifically, Gramm focused on Indian immigrants, who had managed to surpass even native-born whites when it came to their level of education and their per-capita income. Using his legislative assistant, Rohit Kumar, as an example, Gramm praised the accomplishments of this particular Indian family. According to this narrative, Kumar's parents were original immigrants who became successful medical doctors shortly after their arrival:

> They then started the process of bringing their family to America. They brought their brother. He became a doctor. . . . He brought his wife, who became an interior designer. They brought their nephew, who is a computer engineer. . . . If we add up the combined Federal income tax that was paid 10 days ago by the people who came to America as a result of this first Kumar who came in 1972, this little family probably paid, at a minimum, $500,000 in taxes. Our problem in America is we do not have enough Kumars, working hard and succeeding. We need more. (United States Congress, Senate, April 25, 1996)

Clearly, Senator Gramm was not only critical of the claim that most contemporary immigrants represent a drain on the U.S. economy; he was also categorically opposed to the idea that those immigrants who had entered the United States through family members were, on average, lesser qualified than those people who had taken advantage of the employment-based immigration system. Instead, he strongly believed that the current immigration system served America's interests much better than reform proposals targeting the preference system.

Interestingly, both Senators Gramm (R-TX) and DeWine (R-OH) later insisted that it was necessary to practice some kind of risk management. DeWine, in particular, repeatedly noted that family reunification was an important tool in the fight against poverty and welfare dependency. Even though he admitted that his perspective was not based on empirical data, DeWine was convinced that legal immigrants "care very much about their families and have intact families and work very, very hard. The fact is that they are on welfare less than native-born citizens" (United States Congress, Senate, April 25, 1996). He strongly believed that one of the main reasons for America's high poverty rate was the fact that so many U.S. citizens no longer lived in traditional, "two-married-parents" family homes. Immigrants, on the other hand, were described as people who had continued to uphold family values and rely on the family as a support structure, rather than taking advantage of public welfare. Senator DeWine thus thought that "at a time when Congress has acted to rein in public assistance programs, I do not believe we should deprive people the most basic support structure there is, their immediate family" (United States Congress, Senate, April 15, 1996).[7]

A generous family reunification system was thus advantageous for a number of reasons. On one level, family ties represented an additional safety net. In an attempt to downsize the government apparatus and decrease federal spending, politicians were eager to activate informal support systems and shift responsibility from the state to the individual or, in certain cases, the family unit. Some commentators actually showed a clear understanding of the way family values and neoliberalism work together. For example, Karen K. Narasaki, executive director of the National Asian Pacific American Council, reasoned, "Families are the backbone of our nation. Family unity promotes the stability, health and productivity of family members and contributes to the economic and social welfare of the United States" (United States Congress, House, June 29, 1995).[8]

However, a continuation of the family preference system was also attractive because the profamily rhetoric that accompanied this discussion would send a positive message to other nations and encourage desirable immigrants to join our national community. Representative Luis Gutierrez (D-IL), for instance, justified the emphasis on family reunification with the following words: "We send a clear signal that we value keeping family members united and together, that we value a policy of fairness . . . that we value the history and character of our Nation and that the United States values inclusion and understanding and opportunity, rather than exclusion, blame, and fear" (United States Congress, House, March 20, 1996). Even though Gutierrez emphasized the historical significance of family values without making a direct reference to families' economic importance, this comment also complements the neoliberal logic of speakers like Senator DeWine (R-OH). After all, families who stay "united and together" are expected to support each other so that the government would not have to provide assistance.

Frequently, immigrants were described as positive role models who could make an important cultural contribution by promoting a return to conventional family values. John Swenson, the executive director of Migration and Refugee Services of the Catholic Church, argued, "Many immigrant groups represent cultures which place a premium on family ties. . . . It is important that, as a nation, we recognize the importance of affirming family within the immigration context as a means of . . . affirming the family in the U.S. in general" (United States Congress, House, June 29, 1995). While it is hardly surprising that a spokesperson for the Catholic Church would focus on the importance of traditional family values, a similar rhetoric was advanced by delegates from various organizations and politicians from both ends of the political spectrum. For the most part, politicians and expert witnesses claimed that immigrants' adherence to traditional family values represented an important contribution to a society facing high divorce and teenage pregnancy rates. Immigrants were thus seen as desirable because they could potentially remind U.S. citizens of the significance of a strong family unit and showcase that intact families are also productive families.

However, these depictions of the immigrant population were problematic for a number of reasons.[9] First, the aforementioned family-values rhetoric portrayed immigrants as a conservative force that could help the United States return to traditional values. Immigrants were classified as a group of people who were less corrupted by the dislocations typical of advanced capitalist societies. According to this logic, immigrants could help to reinvigorate a society that was too preoccupied with the distractions and indulgences of modern life and initiate a return to heteropatriarchal values. Second, this simplistic portrayal glossed over the fact that immigrants represent an increasingly diverse group of people from a variety of cultural backgrounds. The claim that *all* immigrants honored the importance of family networks was thus factually incorrect. While certain immigrants undoubtedly attached great importance to the nuclear family unit, others defined family and kinship in different terms, and yet others were just as individualistic as many native-born U.S. citizens.

Finally, this notion of the family was also an indicator of the heteronormative logic behind immigration reform. When politicians argued that immigrants should be allowed to enter the United States because of their eagerness to live in traditional two-parent families, they also implied that those people who did not adhere to this norm were less desirable. At no point in my research did I find a politician argue for a more inclusive definition of the family unit that would include unmarried couples, gay and lesbian couples, or transgender people. Even though the outright exclusion of gay and lesbian immigrants had been abolished in 1990, politicians were not only reluctant to take any affirmative steps toward allowing homosexual immigrants to take advantage of the family reunification system, but they were apparently hesitant to even acknowledge the fact that not all immigrants lived in traditional two-parent families. This unwillingness to include nonheteronormative families also indicates that the "family reunification" category was not primarily concerned with reuniting people who loved and supported each other—or, as Shani King calls them, "functional families" (King 2010, 510). Quite to the contrary, politicians made it very clear that the traditional heteropatriarchal family was the only social unit that was evidentially stable enough to provide long-lasting support. In short, heteronormative family values could be easily integrated into the neoliberal agenda, while other forms of family and kinship systems were not necessarily interpreted as an indicator of guaranteed financial stability and economic success.

This explicit commitment to a very narrow version of family also serves as a reminder that policy decisions are often "illogical from the perspective of policy effectiveness" (Schneider and Ingram 1993, 338). If the main objective of family reunification was to construct a social safety network for immigrants and keep them off of public welfare, the "family" category should undoubtedly be extended to other meaningful relationships that do not necessarily fit into the narrow heteronormative paradigm. Legal scholar Nora Demleitner argues that while "family" appears to be a self-explanatory concept in popular discourse, "the terms 'family' and 'marriage' are culturally based concepts, shaped through a variety of experiences, including cultural and legal" (Demleitner 2003, 273). Our dominant model of "family" continues to imply a household that consists of a married couple and their biological children. Even in a U.S. context, this stereotypical family is no longer the norm, even in the mid-1990s. With the dramatic increase in single-parent households and alternative child-care arrangements that involve grandparents, for example, the heteronormative family unit is on the numerical decline. Yet with the passage of the Immigration and Welfare Reform Acts as well as the Defense of Marriage Act in 1996, the U.S. government made a concerted effort to preserve and reward traditional family values.

While the focus on immigrants' traditional family values might not be logical from a cost-saving standpoint, this strategy makes a lot of sense in the context of the larger discourse and from a political perspective. Schneider and Ingram argue that the social construction of target populations represents an important political phenomenon that helps us understand why certain policies are passed with relative ease. This social construction involves popular images and representations of "groups whose behavior and well-being are affected by public policy. These characterizations are normative and evaluative, portraying groups in positive or negative terms through symbolic language, metaphors, and stories" (Schneider and Ingram 1993, 334). Social constructions are stereotypes that define groups as deserving versus undeserving, hardworking versus lazy, and so on. Based on these images, politicians have a much easier time pushing for reform measures that will benefit groups who are constructed in a positive way and who thus appear deserving of support. Policy that is directed toward the "deviants" will usually be punitive in nature and place additional burdens on these individuals. Accordingly, politicians had a much easier time justifying generous family reunification policies for traditional nuclear families, which were already portrayed in a very positive light in other policy debates (e.g., debates about the Defense of Marriage Act [DOMA] and the Personal Responsibility and Work Opportunity Reconciliation Act [PRWORA], which explicitly stated that "marriage is the foundation of a successful society").

(Re)Defining the Nuclear Family: The Controversy about Elderly Parents

While the entire terrain of immigration discourse was structured around neoliberal ideas, certain discursive strands emphasized the connection between neoliberal objectives and other related discourses. The discursive strand about the costs and merits of family reunification, for example, made explicit connections between immigrants' cultural contributions, their adherence to traditional Judeo-Christian family values, and the positive effect that these characteristics had on their ability to become productive neoliberal subjects. The rhetoric about family reunification tapped into public anxieties about the breakdown of the traditional family and moral decay, which can be traced back to concerns about the countercultural movements of the 1960s. Yet, while this discursive strand resonated with public anxieties about moral decline, politicians and the media also argued that strong family values were an integral aspect of the larger neoliberal project because strong families offer security and stability and lessen the need for public welfare. Traditional heteronormative family values were thus commonly praised as a cornerstone of a successful society.

Supporting family values and family reunification made political sense. When it came to immigration reform, the question was not *whether* Congress should support immigrant families, but *which* families it would support. If Congress wanted to ensure that immigrant families were indeed self-supportive and able to start contributing to society immediately, which family members should be allowed to immigrate? Which services represented a good investment? And what benefits would attract the "wrong" kinds of immigrants—people who were not eager to act like responsible neoliberal subjects but who might potentially be attracted to the so-called welfare magnet. In debates about these issues, politicians stressed the need to develop mechanisms to ensure that "family reunification does not create financial burdens on the taxpayers of this country" (Alan K. Simpson [R-WY]; United States Congress, Senate, April 15, 1996). Quite to the contrary, the right kind of family reunification policy would further the neoliberal agenda and ensure self-sufficiency.

One particular concern was immigrants' use of public benefits. While there was little evidence that working-age immigrants were, on average, more likely to receive Temporary Assistance for Needy Families (TANF), Medicaid, food stamps, or other public benefits, numerous expert witnesses indicated that refugees and elderly immigrants made excessive use of Supplemental Security Income (SSI) and had thus caused skyrocketing expenditures for this particular program.[10] One of the most hotly debated topics in the immigration reform discourse in 1995–96 was the rising number of poor, elderly immigrants who had been sponsored by immediate family members. As the following examples will show, the discursive strand that focused on elderly immigrants was much more explicit in its concern about financial considerations and risk-management strategies than the debate over family reunification in general.

Poor, elderly immigrants represented the ideal target for the public wrath about "undeserving foreigners" abusing the U.S. welfare system. Elderly immigrants were portrayed as the exact opposite of responsible neoliberal subjects. Not only were they supposedly undeserving of assistance because they had not already contributed into the system, but they were also commonly accused of fraudulently obtaining cash assistance by hiding their sponsors' assets. Instead of furthering the neoliberal agenda, not only did family reunification policies involving elderly parents result in a net loss for U.S. taxpayers, but overly generous welfare policies had also destroyed family values in immigrant families where children were traditionally responsible for taking care of their elderly parents. The discursive strand about elderly parents is not only important in this context because it represents a prime example for how Congress negotiated concerns about the economic efficiency of public assistance programs, but it also demonstrates how the discourse constructed a particular group as undeserving.

On February 6, 1996, the Senate Judiciary Committee called a special meeting to discuss the "Use of Supplemental Security Income and Other Welfare Programs by Immigrants." Expert witnesses Jane L. Ross, the director of the Health, Education, and Human Services Division; Carolyn Colvin, deputy commissioner for Programs, Policy, Evaluation, and Communications of the Social Security Administration; and Susan Martin, the executive director of the U.S. Commission on Immigration Reform, testified about the precarious financial situation of the SSI program. According to their statements, Congress had initially intended SSI to serve as a supplement to the Social Security program. U.S. citizens and legal permanent residents who were either sixty-five years of age or blind/disabled and did not have sufficient Social Security coverage or other forms of income/assets could apply for SSI.[11] Since elderly immigrants and refugees had limited work histories in the United States and were thus much less likely to receive funds from the Social Security program than native-born citizens who had worked in the United States their entire lives, they were overrepresented on the SSI rolls. By 1995, noncitizens represented about 12 percent of all SSI recipients, nearly one-third of aged SSI recipients, and about 5.5 to 6.2 percent of disabled recipients.[12] Put differently, roughly 3 percent of all noncitizens received SSI compared with 1.8 percent of U.S. citizens. Yet once Susan Martin, the new executive director of the U.S. Commission on Immigration Reform, further qualified this number by age, the statistics were perceived as even more alarming: "According to Census Bureau data, 23 percent of the noncitizen foreign born population [65 years of age or older] receive SSI, as compared to 7 percent of naturalized citizens and 4 percent of citizens by birth" (United States Congress, Senate, February 6, 1996).

Faced with this disproportionately high number of noncitizen SSI recipients, the Senate Judiciary Committee discussed various options that might help reduce federal spending for this particular group of immigrants. In his opening statement, Chairman Alan K. Simpson (R-WY) reminded his colleagues, "This edict that America's newcomers must be self-sufficient is central to America's historic immigration policy. . . . Our laws contemplate, and the public expects the newcomers to work or to receive any needed support from the relatives who brought them here, period" (United States Congress, Senate, February 6, 1996). While Senator Simpson is certainly correct with his claim that sponsors are expected to support their newly arrived family members, historical records indicate that these provisions were never meant to be applied indiscriminately.

The Immigration Act of 1917 was the first act to declare that a person who was deemed likely to become a public charge could only be admitted if a sponsor posted a bond on their behalf. Interestingly, though, immigration officers did not usually expect sponsors to post a bond. If sponsors were able to prove that they had the financial resources to provide for an immigrant and were willing to sign a so-called affidavit of support, the INS was satisfied. As a result, the Appellate Division of the New York State Supreme Court ruled that "the affidavit of support imposed only a 'moral' obligation on the defendants" and was not legally enforceable (Sheridan 1998).[13] Yet even though affidavits of support did not represent a legally binding contract, the Social Security Administration (SSA) nonetheless expected sponsors to provide sufficient financial support for a period of three years.[14] If a sponsored immigrant fell on hard times and applied for SSI, the SSA "deemed" a portion of the sponsor's income and assets to be available to the immigrant, even if the sponsor did not actually provide support to the needy immigrant. Most recently arrived immigrants were thus considered ineligible for SSI.[15] As soon as the deeming period was over, however, a significant number of needy immigrants applied for SSI benefits.

The Senate Judiciary Committee concluded that this provision was too expensive and in violation of a neoliberal agenda that encouraged self-sufficiency, especially in immigrants. Politicians were particularly concerned about the fact that the numbers as well as the proportion of noncitizens on SSI had been continuously on the rise for the past few years. Even though the aforementioned statistics had shown that the vast majority of elderly immigrants did *not* receive SSI—or any other form of public support—several experts suggested that there was reason to believe that "the United States welfare system is rapidly becoming a deluxe retirement home for the elderly of other countries" (Robert Rector, senior policy analyst at the Heritage Foundation; United States Congress, House, June 29, 1995, and Senate, February 6, 1996).[16] In addition, Norman Matloff, a professor of computer science at the University of California at Davis, claimed that contemporary immigrants no longer conceived of the welfare system as a last resort. Instead, elderly immigrants routinely entered the United States with the prior intention of applying for SSI. According to Matloff, the Chinese immigrant community, in particular, had developed networks and strategies to disseminate information about the U.S. welfare system to not only members of their own community but also Chinese citizens abroad. Allegedly, Chinese seniors viewed welfare as a "normal benefit of immigration, whose use is actually encouraged, like a library card" (United States Congress, Senate, February 6, 1996). Ironically, elderly Chinese immigrants were now chastised for their eagerness to abandon traditional Confucian values and adopt a much more consumer-oriented mind-set.[17]

This particular discursive strand offered an interesting variation on the racial, gender, and class politics surrounding the welfare and immigration reform discourses. In the larger discourse about welfare reform, the image of the welfare queen—a single African American mother of numerous children—informed the public imagination and was frequently used to explain why the system was in need of reform. According to this popular image, African American women's out-of-control sexuality and lack of traditional family values, morals, and ambition had caused them to become dependent on welfare. Welfare payments, not structural inequalities such as a lack of education, marketable job skills, or the unavailability of affordable child care, had prevented these women from developing into responsible neoliberal actors in the marketplace. Other depictions of welfare abuse commonly focused on poor Mexican and South American women strategically entering the United States to give birth to U.S. citizen children and gain access to welfare benefits (Fujiwara 2005, 80). In contrast, Congress—and the expert witnesses that testified before Congress—framed SSI abuse/overuse by immigrants as an issue that was particularly prevalent among elderly Asian immigrants, a group that was usually known for their strong family values and their higher economic status.

Not only did Norman Matloff's testimony about welfare abuse by elderly immigrants focus exclusively on elderly Chinese immigrants, but Robert Rector of the Heritage Foundation also contributed to this debate on multiple occasions. In a 1995 report entitled "America Is Becoming a Deluxe Retirement Home," Rector and his colleague William Lauber argue that "many individuals now immigrate to the United States specifically to obtain welfare benefits that far exceed those available in their own countries" (Rector and Lauber 1995, 58). According to Rector and Lauber, this is specifically true for Asian immigrants; prior to migration, many elderly Asian immigrants have access to a Chinese-language publication about life in America that provides a thirty-six-page guide to SSI benefits. Once in the United States, they can access "the largest-circulation Chinese language newspaper in the United States, *Shijie Ribao* (World Journal), [which] runs a regular Dear Abby–style advice column on SSI and other immigration-related matters" (Rector and Lauber 1995, 58). The popularity of these publications was presented as evidence that elderly Asian immigrants enter the United States with the prior intention of relying on SSI benefits and not on their children for support. The mainstream media in the United States confirmed this assumption. In her research on the role that editorial pages played in shaping public perceptions of welfare, Grace Yoo found that 42.1 percent of editorial pieces portrayed elderly immigrants as undeserving of welfare. Furthermore, "their adult children were depicted as financially able, but irresponsible in the care of their ageing parents, having left the responsibility to American taxpayers" (Yoo 2001, 57). The adult children are able to shy away from supporting their elderly parents because the federal safety net is available to them. By eliminating SSI for immigrants, these financially stable Asian immigrants would be forced to reclaim their traditional obligations, support their parents, and save the United States some money.

While politicians and expert witnesses seemed to agree that the current situation was unsustainable, there was considerable controversy about the ideal solution to the perceived problem. My analysis of congressional debates indicates that there were at least three different approaches:[18] First, Alan K. Simpson (R-WY) and several of his colleagues argued that it would be sufficient to strengthen existing public charge provisions and deport immigrants who made excessive use of public benefits. In accordance with the larger neoliberal project, they reasoned that the U.S. government should attempt to shift responsibility from state welfare programs to individual sponsors wherever possible. Instead of developing specific restrictions for elderly immigrants and other high-risk groups, it would be much more effective to keep a tight rein on all immigrants. As a first step in this direction, Senator Simpson advocated an income requirement for potential sponsors, the introduction of a legally enforceable affidavit of support, and an extended deeming period for all immigrants who were sponsored by family members.[19] This way, most immigrants would be ineligible for public support. For the small number of immigrants whose "deadbeat sponsors" were unable or unwilling to provide assistance, the state would provide short-term support.[20] However, if an immigrant received more than twelve months of welfare in five years, he or she would be subject to deportation under the public charge provision.[21]

Second, in addition to discussing elderly parents in the context of generally applicable affidavits of support, the U.S. Commission on Immigration Reform also advocated special restrictions for elderly parents. Even though the commission was reluctant to categorically exclude parents, they believed "that admission of an elderly parent who would otherwise be denied entry as a public charge should be contingent on a commitment of lifetime support because it is highly unlikely that the parent will become self-supporting after entry" (Susan Martin, executive director of the U.S. Commission on Immigration Reform; United States Congress, Senate, February 6, 1996). While all sponsors would be required to sign a legally binding affidavit of support, the document's scope would be limited for children and young adults. Since young immigrants had the potential to become self-supporting, they should be allowed to "earn their way into our generous network of social support" (Alan K. Simpson [R-WY]; United States Congress, Senate, February 6, 1996). Elderly parents, on the other hand, were highly unlikely to ever become net contributors.

Therefore, the U.S. Commission of Immigration Reform argued that they should be permanently denied all access to public support.

Susan Martin, the executive director of the U.S. Commission on Immigration Reform, also cautioned that this financial responsibility should not end when an elderly immigrant naturalized. In order to explain her reasoning, Martin offered the following comparison: "Just as a parent's responsibility for a child is irrespective of the child's citizenship, the sponsor's responsibility for a parent whose entry is conditioned on a contractual arrangement specified in the affidavit is irrespective of future naturalization" (United States Congress, Senate, February 6, 1996). Susan Martin, who appeared as an expert witness on multiple occasions, was always eager to point out that the commission's stance represented a rational and evenhanded compromise: instead of denying elderly immigrants the right to immigrate, they attempted to develop a risk-management strategy that would transfer costs from the federal and the state budgets onto individual sponsors. If immigrants really put such a high premium on family values and desired to sponsor a parent, they would certainly be willing to pick up the tab.

On a similar note, Robert Rector added, "Elderly and near elderly foreigners should be permitted to enter the U.S. only as guests of American relatives who sponsor them. Such elderly 'guests' would not have the option of becoming citizens and thereby becoming a future burden on the U.S." (United States Congress, House, June 29, 1995, and Senate, February 6, 1996). Since it would be unconstitutional for the U.S. government to deny naturalized citizens access to SSI, Rector reasoned, the United States should keep elderly immigrants from becoming U.S. citizens in the first place. Interestingly, both of their proposals emerged as family-friendly alternatives. Martin and Rector's recommendations also developed actuarial strategies that limited the financial risks and responsibilities of the federal government.

A third group, however, did not stop at limiting access to welfare and citizenship. Instead of trying to restrict elderly parents' access to SSI and other public benefits, these politicians argued that it had become necessary to significantly reduce the number of elderly immigrants. Early on in the debate, Robert Rector explained that the reasons behind these proposed restrictions were purely economic and completely in line with the government's larger objectives. He reasoned, "An advanced welfare state has to be very careful in designing its immigration policy. A welfare state will place great strains on its taxpayers if it encourages the immigration of large numbers of 1) elderly and near elderly persons; or 2) low-skilled persons" (United States Congress, House, June 29, 1995). Even though the majority actually agreed with this way of thinking, many politicians added that lower immigration levels and a priority system that favored spouses and children under the age of twenty-one would also be more appropriate to ensure that nuclear families could be reunited in a timely fashion.

On January 5, 1995, Senator Richard C. Shelby (R-AL) became the first member of the 104th Congress to suggest a comprehensive immigration reform bill. His Immigration Moratorium Act of 1995 (S. 160), which sought to provide relief for the American taxpayer, would have cut the amount of legal immigration from about one million to 325,000 immigrants per year for the next 5 years. This number would have included 175,000 spouses and minor children, 50,000 refugees and asylum seekers, 50,000 highly skilled workers, and 50,000 other relatives of U.S. citizens. Parents thus represented one of the lowest priorities. The House version of the Immigration Moratorium Act of 1995 (H.R. 373), which was sponsored by Bob Stump (R-AZ), would have reduced immigration levels even further. H.R. 373 ruled that, for the next 5 years, only 10,000 visas should be allotted to immediate family members per fiscal year.[22] Parents were explicitly prohibited from obtaining a visa through sponsorship by their children.[23] The Immigration Reform Act of 1995 (S. 1394), which was introduced by Senator Alan K. Simpson (R-WY) on November 3, 1995, wanted to reduce the annual level of legal, nonrefugee immigration to about 540,000. This number would have included 90,000 employment-based visas, 150,000 visas to reduce the backlog of people who had already applied, and 300,000 visas for immediate family members, which S. 1394 defined as spouses and unmarried minor children of U.S. citizens and legal permanent residents.

Later proposals contained provisions that would have made a very limited number of visas available to parents.[24] Spencer Abraham (R-MI), for example, offered an amendment to the Immigration Control and Financial Responsibility Act of 1996 (S. 1664), which would have allowed parents to receive immigrant visas only if the more immediate family categories did not need all of them (United States Congress, Senate, April 15, 1996).[25] As several representatives pointed out, though, this provision was unlikely to ever take effect since, in the past, there had always been more applications than visas.[26] Despite dramatic numerical differences and slight variations in the exact nature of the preference system, the aforementioned bills (S. 160, H.R. 373, S. 1394, and S. 1664) would have effectively denied parents of U.S. citizens and legal permanent residents an opportunity to immigrate in the United States.[27]

Even though politicians were generally eager to express their own commitment to family values and, as we have seen in the previous section, repeatedly praised immigrants' dedication to their families, these concerns were outweighed by economic considerations. However, it is also important to acknowledge that the discourse gradually shifted from economically oriented proposals that contained sharp limitations for family-sponsored immigrants to comparatively more generous proposals. The immigrant rights movement started to publicly question the logic that excluding certain groups of immigrants or denying them access to services would automatically lead to greater self-sufficiency. For example, alternative representations that described elderly immigrants as worthy of assistance because they had migrated legally and played by the rules emerged throughout the debate and became progressively more influential once "refugees and immigrants from Asia were committing suicide in the face of losing their benefits" (Fujiwara 2005, 79). This shift away from categorical exclusions to other generally applicable risk-management strategies is also indicative of the larger tendency to combine economic objectives with other, more palatable considerations. In order to make bills more appealing to representatives from both ends of the political spectrum, the final reform proposals made almost no outright exclusions. Instead, they assigned less economically desirable groups—such as elderly parents—a low priority and thus limited their admission numbers indirectly.

Despite the fact that all the major legal immigration reform bills contained provisions that would have negatively affected parents' chances to immigrate, the final version of the law (Pub. L. No. 104–208) did not make substantial changes to the family preference system. Up to this day, U.S. immigration policy holds that children, spouses, and parents of U.S. citizens are classified as "immediate relatives" and are thus not subject to numerical limitations.[28] In addition, the U.S. government did not pass any risk-management provisions that specifically applied to elderly immigrants (e.g., mandatory health insurance). Instead, the Illegal Immigration Reform and Immigrant Responsibility Act (IIRIRA) made the affidavit of support legally enforceable,[29] required sponsors to provide evidence that they could maintain the sponsored immigrants at an annual income no less than 125 percent of the poverty line, and ensured that the affidavit was enforceable until a sponsored immigrant had naturalized or until he or she had worked forty qualifying quarters of coverage as defined under title II of the Social Security Act.[30] The U.S. government had thus successfully shifted financial responsibility from the state to the individual sponsor without singling out a particular group of immigrants. Especially in the case of elderly immigrants, whose naturalization rates have always been fairly low, sponsors were likely to make a lifetime commitment when they signed an affidavit of support.

The affidavit of support could thus be expected to reduce the number of elderly SSI recipients for four interrelated reasons: First, new arrivals would be ineligible for a minimum of five years. Second, even if an immigrant became eligible for public support, he or she might be reluctant to take advantage of this opportunity because of the likelihood that they would be deported as a public charge or, more likely, denied reentry if they ever left the United States for an extended period time to travel. Third, many potential sponsors would be unable to demonstrate that they had an income at or above 125 percent of the federal poverty line. And fourth, even if a sponsor had the necessary financial resources, he or she might be hesitant to sign a legally enforceable contract for an elderly parent who would be unable to support himself/herself.[31] Consequently, a legally enforceable affidavit of support represented an ideal mechanism to reduce federal spending, while—at least rhetorically—upholding a commitment to family values.

The repeated reference to family values thus served a number of important discursive functions. The bill's proponents convincingly argued that this reform measure was neither biased nor meanspirited. Sensing that the economically oriented logic behind the new immigration policy might be controversial among certain groups, these politicians portrayed the affidavit of support as a generous compromise that allowed immigrants to bring additional family members into the United States. If immigrants continued to put such a high premium on family ties, they should be willing to accept some additional financial responsibilities. At the same time, those people who were unwilling to sign an affidavit of support were apparently not particularly committed to their family members and thus not worthy of family reunification visas.

Contemporary Immigrants: Prime Examples of Successful Nuclear Families?

As the previous section demonstrated, the discourse surrounding elderly parents accentuated economic considerations. In accordance with the larger neoliberal project, elderly immigrants were seen as less desirable because they had little potential to develop into net contributors. The ideal immigrant, on the other hand, was described as a self-sufficient neoliberal subject whose financial contributions outweighed his or her usage of public services. In addition, politicians praised heteronormative family structures as a meaningful support network that could help shift responsibility from the state to the individual family unit. In some cases, neoliberal and family values mutually reinforced each other. Other discursive strands, however, demonstrate that there was also a productive tension between these two aspects and that immigrants were oftentimes forced to choose between living with their nuclear family and maximizing their economic potential. As the following discussion will show, even politicians who generally insisted that immigrants act like rational neoliberal subjects and invest in their abilities did not hesitate to criticize them for abandoning their families in an effort to strategically improve their own economic status.

In particular, the proponents of lower immigration levels indicated that some immigrants did not actually place much importance on the nuclear family. Senator Richard C. Shelby (R-AL) reasoned that "when an immigrant comes to this country, leaving behind parents, brothers, sisters, uncles, aunts, and cousins, it is the immigrant who is breaking up the extended family" (United States Congress, Senate, April 25, 1996). Accordingly, the U.S. government had no obligation to reunite a family that was broken up by the immigrant himself/herself. John Bryant (D-TX) also believed that immigrants had to accept the negative consequences of their own decisions. According to Bryant, every potential immigrant had to make a simple choice: "If you do not want to leave your brothers and sisters and do not want to leave your adult children, then do not leave them" (United States Congress, House, March 21, 1996). If immigrants were truly attached to their extended family, they would simply stay in their home country.[32]

Congress also struggled to reconcile profamily rhetoric with their unwillingness to support "chain migration." On March 21, 1996, for instance, Lamar Smith (R-TX) warned that "the admission of a single immigrant over time can result in the admissions of dozens of increasingly distant family members. Without reform of the immigration system, chain migration of relatives who are distantly related to the original immigrant will continue on and on and on" (United States Congress, House, March 21, 1996). Later in the debate, Senator Alan K. Simpson (R-WY) painted an even more frightening picture. On April 15, 1996, he asserted that he had heard of cases where a single U.S. citizen or legal permanent resident successfully petitioned "30, 40, 50, 60, or 70 relatives" (United States Congress, Senate, April 15, 1996). Ten days later, he proclaimed, "the all-time record was 83 persons on a single petition" (United States Congress, Senate, April 25, 1996).[33]

Several politicians offered evidence to prove that the concern about uncontrollable chain migration was unfounded. In the vast majority of cases, an immigrant sponsored a select few immediate family members (usually a spouse and children) who then had to wait patiently for a green card to become available. However, within the larger discourse, it is almost impossible to refute these dramatic individual cases and anecdotal evidence by offering a rational rebuttal that relies on statistical data and legal/procedural information. After all, Senator Simpson's aforementioned story about the eighty-three people that a single immigrant petitioned for was most likely true and certainly much more memorable and newsworthy than the cautionary remarks by other politicians. Nonetheless, numerous politicians attempted to counter these stereotypical representations that were based on isolated cases by painting a broader and more complex picture.

Senator Spencer Abraham (R-MI) reminded his colleagues that the aforementioned examples were "more fiction than fact and so should not drive our policy decisions. It takes an immigrant an average of 12 years before he or she sponsors even the first relative for entry into the U.S. At that slow pace any stampede of family related immigrants is impossible" (United States Congress, Senate, April 10, 1996). Throughout the debate, Xavier Becerra (D-CA) was another outspoken critic of the chain migration thesis. On March 21, 1996, for example, he said, "This issue of chain migration is a false one. By the time you have someone come into this country, it usually takes 12 to 13 years before that individual can then petition to have anyone who is an immediate relative—not a distant relative—come into this country. . . . There is no chain migration" (United States Congress, House, March 21, 1996).[34]

Yet even though these critical voices repeatedly corrected exaggerated statistics and alarmist examples, the concern about chain migration not only influenced policy decisions but also validated several problematic assumptions: Simpson and Smith's remarks seemed to suggest that most immigrants had large families with multiple children, siblings, cousins, aunts, and uncles. Even though they did not explicitly comment on cultural differences in this context, both speakers clearly implied that the U.S. government needed to be concerned about "uncontrolled Third World sexuality." Many politicians also firmly believed that all these family members would actually come to America if given the chance. In addition, they implied that distant family members not only were undeserving but also would put a burden on U.S. society. Congressional debates set up a false dichotomy between family members and skilled workers and ignored the fact that many family-sponsored immigrants had a high level of education and professional experience.

As the aforementioned examples have shown, the discourse tended to combine specific economic concerns with general anxieties about the social and cultural impact of a large, ethnically diverse immigrant population. Arguments about the threat posed by contemporary immigrants not only tapped into widespread anxieties about race, ethnicity, and cultural difference but also connected the immigration reform discourse in the mid-1990s to earlier discourses. In his analysis of Peter Brimelow's hugely popular anti-immigrant treatise *Alien Nation*, Kevin Johnson argued that "Brimelow's racially-tinged arguments and alarmist tone are disturbingly reminiscent of past nativist appeals," such as the targeting of Chinese immigrants in the late 1800s and Mexican workers during the Great Depression (Johnson 1996, 117). Using immigrants as the scapegoat for society's fears and frustrations, including everything from labor market competition, concerns about public spending, and the changing racial and ethnic makeup of the country, is thus far from new. What is new, however, is the way that these fears played into the discourse and how they affected proposals for reform. During earlier immigration reform discourses, politicians quickly resorted to racially specific measures that would target the immigrant group that was deemed particularly problematic at the time. The Chinese Exclusion Act and the deportation of Mexican immigrants during the Great Depression are just two examples for racially specific initiatives.

In the 1990s, however, very few mainstream politicians, journalists, and intellectuals advocated a return to quota laws or other racially specific measures. Explicit mention of race and racial difference was left up anti-immigration advocates like Peter Brimelow. Instead, Congress attempted "to achieve racial goals through facially neutral means" (Johnson 1996, 113). Legitimate, race-neutral concerns about the economic impact of generous family reunification policies masked the racial impact that these changes would undoubtedly have and the racial anxieties that motivated them. In the 1990s, Congress developed a complex rhetoric that suggested contemporary immigrants had failed to succeed not because of their race but because they had *refused* to assimilate to mainstream American culture. This failure was especially apparent in immigrants who had sponsored entire extended families and stayed within their own cultural group instead of interacting with the mainstream culture. In accordance with the economic reasoning of the larger neoliberal project, politicians downplayed the importance of inherent characteristics—such as race and ethnicity—and instead focused on the negative choices made by certain individuals. Hence poor Mexicans were perceived as less desirable not because they were poor or of Mexican descent but because they had supposedly failed to act like responsible, neoliberal subjects (i.e., like law-abiding, middle-class U.S. citizens—who just happened to be overwhelmingly white).

In this context, politicians also made a sharp distinction between the public and the private realm. In an interesting twist on the outdated but still very popular notion of America as a melting pot of different cultures, Alan K. Simpson (R-WY) argued that it was still essential "to promote our national unity, [because], without American unity, we will have no democracy" (United States Congress, Senate, August 3, 1994). According to Simpson, "terms like 'assimilation' and 'Americanization' should not be 'politically incorrect'" (United States Congress, Senate, November 3, 1995). Multiculturalism was a great thing, as long as it was practiced in the confines of a person's own home or in their ethnic community. On the condition that immigrants respect the American flag and use the English language in public, "we don't care what you do in your private culture. If you want go home at night and worship the great eel, that is your business" (United States Congress, Senate, August 3, 1994). In keeping with the larger political climate, no one suggested that contemporary immigrants should be forced to abandon their own private values and beliefs.

At the very least, however, Senator Simpson's sarcastic comment suggests some of these cultural practices and beliefs were too bizarre to be taken seriously by the American public. In continuation of a long history of anti-Catholic sentiments, Mexican Catholicism was included in this group of bizarre religious practices that, according to mainstream U.S. standards, bordered on the occult. If we read this comment in the context of the underlying concern about immigrants' out-of-control sexuality, Senator Simpson's reference to the "great eel" can be read as a sexual innuendo as well. By equating immigrants' sexuality with a quasi-religious practice, Simpson stresses the cultural divide that separates the traditional Judeo-Christian values of U.S. families from the uncontrolled, pagan sexuality that is supposedly practiced by Third World immigrants.

In addition, it was argued that diversity and multiculturalism were only desirable to a certain degree. While even the most conservative politicians agreed that the United States had benefited from the rich cultural backgrounds of past generations of immigrants, they tended to be much more critical of current immigrants. After nostalgically acknowledging America's roots as a nation of immigrants, many politicians concluded that it was no longer acceptable, or even desirable, for immigrants to hold on to their traditions. To buttress their arguments, these speakers also insisted that former immigrants would agree with this assessment. Jon Kyl (R-AZ), for example, delivered the following speech: "My grandparents emigrated here from Holland. My grandmother hardly spoke English. I am very proud of my Dutch ancestry and the traditions that we have maintained, but I think that my grandparents, who assimilated into our society and became Americans, would be rather shocked and somewhat disappointed at the way that the system has grown over recent years. My guess is that they would be supporting attempts of people like Senator Simpson to try to bring the right kind of balance" (United States Congress, Senate, April 25, 1996).[35] On one rare occasion, Senator Richard Shelby (R-AL) actually said that European immigrants were more desirable because "our domestic population's cultural and ethnic heritages were more similar to those of new immigrants" (United States Congress, Senate, April 25, 1996). For the most part, though, the proponents of more restrictive immigration laws left their comments about the optimum racial and ethnic ingredients of a diverse society intentionally vague.

What emerged from the 1995–96 congressional debates was a general concern about the increasing number of different nationalities and cultures that were present in the United States. Early on in the debate, Governor Lawton Chiles (D-FL), one of the most fervent supporters of lower immigration levels, painted a particularly frightening picture. He claimed that, in Florida, "many of our public school teachers are in classrooms which resemble a UN general assembly of children. Imagine—one teacher faced with handling children of as many as 14 nationalities, languages and cultural differences." He went on to say that in the waiting room at Jackson Memorial Hospital in Dade County, "we have people with diseases often unknown in the U.S.; people who have not seen a medical professional in years; people who have no medical records or history and certainly no insurance" (United States Congress, Senate, June 22, 1994). Despite the fact that Governor Chiles was most likely referring to Haitian and Cuban immigrants, who had migrated from areas that are geographically close to the United States and Florida, his comment about "unknown diseases" seems to imply that the current immigrant population was composed of people from more remote areas of the world. Yet regardless of the specific reference, Governor Chiles believed that too much diversity posed a visible threat to U.S. society.

Even though politicians tended to voice their concerns in race-neutral terms, the aforementioned examples demonstrate that race and ethnicity were clearly an issue in the immigration discourse. Looking at recent census figures, not only is Florida's proportion of foreign-born residents higher than the national average (12.9 percent versus 7.9 percent in 1990 and 16.7 percent versus 11.1 percent in 2000), but Miami Dade County was also the only county in the United States in 2000 where the 1.1 million foreign-born residents outnumbered native-born residents (United States Census Bureau 2003, 6). Furthermore, the racial and national makeup of the immigrant population in Florida is also quite distinct from U.S. averages. According to census figures, in 1990, the top three countries of birth of the foreign born in Florida were Cuba (29.8 percent), Haiti (5 percent), and Jamaica (4.6 percent), while the top three immigrant groups in the entire United States consisted of Mexico (21.7 percent), the Philippines (4.6 percent), and Canada (3.8 percent). In light of these figures, it is pretty obvious that Bill Martini's (R-NJ) complaint about an inferior new brand of immigrants and Governor Chiles's concern about unknown diseases were not directed toward European immigrants but specifically targeted Latinos and Latinas.

Yet, despite the clearly discernible racial undertones in the immigration debate, most politicians were reluctant to mention, much less discuss, the fact that the contemporary generation of immigrants was mainly of Latin American and Asian descent. Instead, they used the public controversy over multiculturalism as a way to talk publicly about race. Within this larger discourse, multiculturalism was oftentimes portrayed as a concept that, instead of integrating Americans of diverse backgrounds into one unified society, had further divided the U.S. population into small, and sometimes hostile, factions. Building on this commonly accepted depiction of multiculturalism as a divisive force, numerous politicians argued that the U.S. government should make an increased effort to encourage recently arrived immigrants to assimilate to U.S. society. For example, Alan K. Simpson (R-WY) argued that the American public was "annoyed by the Government programs that are seemingly intended not to promote Americanization, as in all of the history of our past high immigration eras, but rather to actually inhibit assimilation and promote divisiveness, often in the name of multiculturalism" (United States Congress, Senate, March 14, 1995).

On other occasions, politicians argued that America's current emphasis on multicultural programs had made "assimilation often much more difficult and slower. Instead of following our traditional course of enhancing our strengths by melding a common American culture out of immigrants' diversity, multiculturalists now push to retain newcomers' different cultures" (Richard C. Shelby [R-AL]; United States Congress, Senate, April 25, 1996). This argument is problematic on a number of levels. First, Senator Shelby ignores the fact that America has never truly melded all immigrants' traditions into a larger American culture. If there was ever such a thing as a melting pot that combined different cultures, this was a highly selective process that prevented most cultures from contributing. Second, this type of reasoning fails to acknowledge the continued importance of racial characteristics. For instance, even if an Asian immigrant eagerly adopts American culture, as a visible racial minority, he or she will always remain outside of the national community to a certain degree. Third, and most important, Senator Shelby also implied that "multiculturalists" encourage minorities to position themselves in opposition to the majority culture.[36] However, research on immigrants' roles in U.S. society has clearly demonstrated that most immigrants are eager to engage with the majority culture and claim membership in U.S. society. For instance,

William Flores and Rina Benmayor have argued that, while Latinos have established a distinct social space for themselves, they also perceive themselves to be part of the larger society. Even more important, they argue, "this country is strengthened, not weakened, by the vibrancy brought to it by immigrant and non-white communities" (Flores and Benmayor 1997b, 5). Clearly, immigrants can aspire to become part of a larger national community while retaining important elements of their own culture.

As part of a larger backlash against race-specific services, affirmative-action policies, and programs that promoted different cultures, values, languages, and religions, U.S. Congress started to question the desirability of an immigration system that primarily attracted Asian and Latin American immigrants. However, in accordance with the larger neoliberal project, politicians focused on immigrants' behaviors and lifestyles. Immigrants were described as less desirable if they refused to assimilate to U.S. culture, take on Judeo-Christian values, and use the English language at work as well as in the privacy of their own homes. The neoliberal rhetoric seemed to suggest that these aspects were merely a matter of personal choice and individual merit, not a question of an immigrant's racial and/or ethnic background. At the same time, discourse participants were very well aware of the fact that this seemingly race-neutral rhetoric targeted primarily poor, nonwhite immigrants from Asia and Latin America, who evidentially had a much harder time living up to this neoliberal ideal.

This tendency to evade an open debate of complex and controversial issues such as U.S. race relations and family values is representative of the larger neoliberal discourse. Instead of critically interrogating the notion of an economically profitable "nuclear family," for example, politicians based their reform proposals on definitions that had already been established by other, related discourses, such as the debate about welfare reform and the Defense of Marriage Act. This reluctance to engage with the complexities of the matter is indicative of a general belief that politicians should be concerned with their constituencies and the U.S. government's perspective, not with immigrants (or other minorities) themselves. Immigrants were judged by their ability to navigate the U.S. labor market and their eagerness to become a part of mainstream culture. Accordingly, if immigrants struggled to succeed by U.S. standards, this was interpreted as their own fault, not as the result of racism or discrimination.

While the issue of multiculturalism in general caused considerable controversy, expert witnesses and politicians were even more concerned about the future of the English language.[37] As one possible reaction to the growing linguistic diversity in the United States, Charles T. Canady (R-FL) proposed an amendment that would have required future immigrants to pass an English language proficiency exam before they entered the United States.[38] Even though there was no evidence to indicate that immigrants were unwilling to learn the English language once they arrived in the United States, Representative Canady insisted that the current immigrant population showed a lack of initiative.[39] In support of the Canady Amendment, Toby Roth (R-WI) added that the language requirement was not meant as a punishment, but that "by giving people an incentive to learn English . . . it is really helping the immigrant" (United States Congress, House, March 20, 1996). English language exams were thus not only described as an excellent opportunity to preselect certain talented individuals, but they supposedly encouraged immigrants to take responsibility and make an investment in their future.

In addition, several representatives pointed to the fact that the English language was much more than a simple tool to communicate. Instead, the English language was described as "one of the wonderful melting ingredients in the melting pot" (Toby Roth [R-WI]; United States Congress, House, March 20, 1996). Newt Gingrich (R-GA) took this rhetoric even further. In an attempt to highlight the importance of the Canady Amendment, Gingrich suggested, "You are not born American in some genetic sense. You are not born American in some racist sense. This is an acquired pattern. English is a key part of this" (United States Congress, House, March 20, 1996). While the first part of this statement is certainly a correct depiction of American culture and society, Gingrich's seemingly positive message stands in direct opposition to the intentions behind the proposed amendment. Instead of allowing immigrants an opportunity to join the national community, Representative Canady intended to preclude certain individuals from entering the country. In contrast to the official rhetoric, which portrayed this amendment as an attempt to level the playing field and invest immigrants with more power and responsibility, the amendment was clearly biased in favor of educated European, Indian, and Filipino immigrants, who were more likely to have an advanced knowledge of the English language. Notably, Representative Robert A. Underwood (D-Guam), a strong opponent of the Canady Amendment, was the only person to point to this racial bias. He described the amendment as "a backdoor attempt that introduces an ethnic element into the discussion of immigration policy" (United States Congress, House, March 20, 1996).

Negotiating the Importance of Race and Ethnicity

Throughout the debate, several speakers made it clear that restrictive family reunification provisions represented thinly veiled attempts to continue America's history of racially exclusive immigration acts. Representative Patsy Mink (D-HI), for example, compared reform plans to the 1924 Exclusion Act, which had tried to prevent Asian family members from entering the United States (United States Congress, House, March 20, 1996), and Karen K. Narasaki, the executive director of the NAPALC, reminded the Judiciary Committee that "it is no secret that the history of this country's immigration laws has been fraught with racial bias." Narasaki not only was concerned about the fact that the elimination of certain preference categories—such as adult married children, siblings, and parents—would have had a disproportional impact on Asian immigrants, but she also advised Congress that this discussion would, "however inadvertently, add to the xenophobia and bigotry that has already begun to take their toll" (United States Congress, House, June 29, 1995). Representative Patsy Mink and Karen K. Narasaki thus dismantled the myth that immigration reform was a color-blind attempt to select individuals who held the most potential to become economically profitable.

Contrary to these critical voices, however, many politicians were adamant in their claims that stricter immigration control measures and rigorous selection criteria were neither unfair nor racially discriminatory. Instead, they argued that immigration was not a right but a privilege that the U.S. government accorded to a select group of promising individuals. In an interesting twist on the rhetoric about the law's discriminatory impact, Senator Richard C. Shelby (R-AL) asserted that "our current legal immigration law is fundamentally flawed [because] the selection criteria are discriminatory and skewed so as to disregard what's in our country's overall best interests" (United States Congress, Senate, April 25, 1996). Instead of looking at the effect immigration laws had had on potential immigrants, Senator Shelby was more concerned about shortchanging U.S. citizens. In his opinion, politicians "have a moral obligation to take care of American citizens first" (United States Congress, Senate, April 25, 1996).[40]

Other politicians joined Senator Shelby in his belief that U.S. citizens' interests should outweigh immigrants' needs. Representative Brian Bilbray (R-CA), for instance, proclaimed, "it is not only our right to have an immigration policy for the good of the American national interests, it is our responsibility as Members of Congress to make sure our decisions on immigration are for the good of America, and America first" (United States Congress, House, March 21, 1996). In an even more alarmist tone, Representative Lamar S. Smith (R-TX) asserted, "Congress must act now to put the national interest first and secure our borders, protect lives, unite families, save jobs, and lighten the load on law-abiding taxpayers" (United States Congress, House, March 19, 1996). While it is certainly correct that U.S. politicians need to answer to their constituents' demands, it is interesting that many representatives chose to construct America's national interests as diametrically opposed to a generous immigration system.

It remains unclear what the phrase "America's national interest" actually references. While some politicians were more concerned about immigrants' impact on certain industries (e.g., agriculture), others were eager to protect native-born workers from additional competition for scarce job opportunities, and yet others were referring to the effect high levels of immigration had on certain states and their budgets. Despite the fact that each position called for dramatically different measures, all these sides were simply subsumed under the collective banner of serving America's national interest. This ambiguity was no accident; it actually served an important rhetorical purpose. As the designated representatives of their constituencies, politicians were sworn in to look after their voters' interests and protect them from undue competition and unnecessary expenditures. On the surface, the rhetoric about serving America's national interest thus seemed reasonable enough, and it was hard to argue with this basic objective. Even more important, the alarmist rhetoric about reverse discrimination was emotionally appealing to many U.S. citizens. Although there was little factual evidence that immigrants actually displaced other workers and used more public services than native-born citizens, scapegoating a vulnerable population without political rights turned out to be a successful strategy. In the end, many people believed that Americans were the victims of overly generous immigration policies.

In addition, politicians seemed to think that as long as they couched their concerns in racially neutral terms, there was no reason to accuse them of racism or discrimination.[41] Senator Chuck Grassley (R-IA), for example, reasoned that immigration reform proposals could not possibly be "a xenophobic sort of thing" since he did not "hear at least spoken resentment toward aliens" (United States Congress, Senate, February 6, 1996). Politicians also implied that profit-oriented selection criteria could not be dismissed as racist, even if they happened to have a differential impact on certain nationalities and/or racial and ethnic minorities. According to the neoliberal logic behind various reform measures in 1995–96, the state was only interested in a person's ability and willingness to develop into a responsible, self-sufficient neoliberal subject. This neoliberal discourse not only belied the lasting impact a person's race, class, gender, and sexuality might have on his or her chances to succeed, but it actually implied that an economically oriented set of rules leveled the playing field for all competitors. If a person failed to comply with this basic rule, it was his or her own fault, not the fault of the system.

Representative Howard L. Berman (D-CA) took this argument to the next logical level. In keeping with the general tendency to blame immigrants for their failure to succeed, Representative Berman argued that it was immigrants' fault that Californians passed Proposition 187 (which limited undocumented immigrants' access to public education, health care, and social services) by an overwhelming margin. According to Berman, "it is wrong to conclude that the people who voted for Proposition 187 are racist or xenophobes. They are people who are looking at what has happened" (United States Congress, House, September 25, 1996). Politicians from both ends of the political spectrum added that it was high time to respond to these concerns. "If Congress fails to act to address these very real and reasonable concerns of the American people," argued Senator Alan Simpson, "there is a very strong possibility [that] we will lose our traditionally generous immigration policy" (Senator Alan K. Simpson [R-WY], United States Congress, Senate, April 15, 1996).[42] Simpson thus implied that the proposed changes in the immigration law would actually protect immigrants from even harsher measures. Since immigrants had started to abuse America's generosity, the American public was rightfully concerned and demanded change. Excluding the most undesirable subjects was thus necessary to alleviate the tension between immigrants and native-born citizens and protect those people who were slightly more desirable.

In order to strengthen the claim that the American public's desire to reduce current levels of legal as well as illegal immigration could not possibly be an expression of racist sentiments, several people cited evidence that African Americans and Hispanics supported these reforms.[43] Yet while it is correct that many domestic racial and ethnic minorities championed immigration reform, it is important to understand the nature of their concerns. There is evidence to suggest that high levels of immigration in general (and illegal immigration in particular) have affected low-skilled African American workers.[44] Poor African Americans were thus rightfully concerned about increased job competition. In addition, several expert witnesses pointed out that African Americans had no reason to be particularly supportive of immigrants. Expert witness Dr. Frank L. Morris, past president of the Council of Historically Black Graduate Schools, reminded the House Judiciary Committee that the United States had a long history of providing preferential treatment to recent immigrants over African Americans.[45] Even though he acknowledged that immigrants "did not bring about the state of Black America," Morris understood that "the patience of African Americans wears thin when America welcomes and provides . . . a better opportunity to achieve the American dream" to immigrants (United States Congress, House, June 29, 1995).

In the ensuing debate, numerous politicians complimented Morris on his testimony and expressed their concerns for American workers "in our inner cities" (Lamar Smith [R-TX]). Most politicians were reluctant to talk openly about the importance of race and the reasons behind African Americans' precarious economic situation. Instead, they repeatedly asked Morris to clarify his stance and admit that immigrants were directly responsible for African American's high poverty and unemployment rates. Apparently, politicians felt that such a statement would carry a different weight if it came from an African American expert witness. After Morris admitted that job displacement of unskilled African American workers was even more pronounced in regions that had a high ratio of immigrants, politicians gladly responded that they would do everything to protect vulnerable domestic minorities from the negative influences of immigrants.

In addition, many U.S.-born Latinos were concerned about the fact that Americans failed to distinguish between their positive contributions and the negative actions of a small minority of undocumented immigrants. In the immediate aftermath of Proposition 187, U.S. citizens of Hispanic descent had already experienced increased levels of discrimination and outright hostility. On several occasions, Latinos in California were asked to provide documentation in public schools, hospitals, at traffic stops, and even in grocery stores. In one case, which caused a short-lived media frenzy, two INS officers almost arrested the Latino mayor of Pomona, a city in Southern California. He was driving home from work in his pickup truck when he was pulled over by INS officers who, based on the man's physical appearance, his casual clothes, and the fact that he was driving a pickup truck, suspected him of being an illegal immigrant. They threatened to arrest and deport him until he was able to produce a badge that proved that he was an elected government official.[46]

Clearly, for members of certain racial and ethnic minority groups, immigration reform is not just an abstract economic issue. Past experiences have shown that high levels of immigration have led to increased hostility toward non-Anglo-looking-and-sounding individuals. However, exclusionary laws and the accusatory rhetoric that usually accompany them have also led to even more intolerance, discrimination, and outright hostility.[47] Latinos, in particular, have thus been careful to take a stance and suggest a compromise solution. Raul Yzaguirre, president of the National Council of La Raza (NCLR), and Cecilia Muñoz, NCLR's deputy vice president, appeared before Congress on several occasions. While they agreed that the United States had the right to enforce their borders and crack down on undocumented immigrants, they were also among the most outspoken critics of legal immigration reform. According to NCLR, "the country has benefited mightily from its tradition of welcoming those who enter our borders legally." In view of that, "NCLR takes the position that the principal focus of the nation's legal immigration policy must be the reunification of American families" (United States Congress, House, June 29, 1995).

Members of all racial and ethnic groups supported immigration reform. However, delegates from Latino and Asian American organizations were usually particularly careful to not lose sight of the fact that immigrants were human beings, not just potential additions to the U.S. labor force. Politicians, on the other hand, were oftentimes reluctant to recognize the importance of the human aspect of immigration control. Senator Alan K. Simpson (R-WY), for example, admitted, "I know full well that the numbers represent human beings—human faces." However, at the same time, he was also convinced that "we must keep focused always on the ultimate issue of what will promote the long-term best interests of the American people—those of us here" (United States Congress, Senate, November 3, 1995). Apparently, achieving this goal was only possible if politicians were willing to follow an actuarial strategy that reduced human beings to statistics in the name of equitable treatment. This way, politicians could avoid the complications of moral reasoning.[48]

Conclusion

As this chapter demonstrated, the discourse about family reunification was characterized by a productive tension between different values and objectives. As Michel Foucault argues in *The Archaeology of Knowledge and the Discourse on Language*, discourse is always "from beginning to end, historical—a fragment of history, a unity and discontinuity in history itself, posing the problem of its own limits, its divisions, its transformations" (Foucault 1972, 117). As such, a discursive formation consists of multiple discursive strands, which, even though they are interconnected, are characterized by different foci, concerns, and opinions.

With regard to the immigration reform discourse in 1995–96, most discursive strands drew on neoliberal concerns and economic considerations. For the most part, the underlying neoliberal framework went unchallenged. In the debate about elderly parents, for example, politicians did not even try very hard to hide the fact that they were primarily concerned about the costs and benefits associated with this particular group. In other cases, Congress took great pains to mask some of their concerns. Throughout the debate, politicians insisted that issues of race, gender, and sexuality were not relevant in this neoliberal system and did not warrant an in-depth discussion. The political discourse was grounded in the belief that neoliberalism's market logics were inherently antiracist and antisexist because an individual's success was predicated on their willingness to invest in their own abilities and act responsibly. However, as the previous analysis demonstrated, the neoliberal immigration reform discourse was not only far from race- and gender-neutral; it was actively involved in the (re)creation of identity categories.

This process is particularly relevant in debates about family reunification. While politicians tried to normalize the notion of "family" as a universal, self-explanatory category that bears economic relevance, I suggest that this connection is produced through the immigration reform discourse itself. The previous sections critically examined how this idealized notion of heteronormative families emerged from the immigration reform discourse and other related discourses (e.g., debates about welfare reform and DOMA). Despite rapidly changing family structures in U.S. society, the only families that were worthy of protection under immigration—and, I would add, welfare—legislation, were heterosexual couples that were married and adhered to traditional gender roles. The discourse normalized sexuality that happened within the confines of heterosexual marriage and that was channeled into childbearing. Furthermore, it presented heteronormative family structures as normal, natural, and appropriate for the economic survival of the family unit and, eventually, for society at large. This essentialized notion of "family" effectively prevented further debate about more far-reaching reforms of the family reunification system, such as the ability to sponsor same-sex partners.

Similarly, discourse participants were so invested in the belief that neoliberal reform measures represented the panacea to social ills and inequalities that the discourse "disguised the reality that neoliberalism remains a form of racial capitalism" (Melamed 2011, 42). The few instances that actually inspired a brief discussion of race remained on a very general level and were also meant to reassure Congress that its policies were indeed color-blind and thus unproblematic. Perhaps not surprisingly, the discourse about the reform of the family preference system was only concerned with the effects that these policies would have on society at large. No one even attempted to discuss the effect of neoliberal policies on families and ethnic/racial minorities.

3

Dehumanizing the Undocumented

The Legislative Language of Illegality

The previous chapter examined congressional discussions of the legal immigration system. In particular, the analysis focused on one noteworthy discursive strand: the controversy about family reunification. In accordance with a neoliberal project designed to impose economic rationale on governmental policies, many politicians felt that the U.S. immigration system should give preferential treatment to immigrants who had acted like self-sufficient neoliberal subjects and had the potential to develop into "net contributors" to the American economy. At the same time, politicians were also careful to buttress this economically driven logic with a humanistic discourse about heteronormative family values and moral obligations. Family-sponsored immigrants were described as particularly desirable because the nuclear family unit could function as an informal support network and alleviate the financial responsibilities of federal and state governments. Family-values rhetoric was used to both support and humanize the impersonal economic logic that drove the debate and deflect criticisms that dismissed the proposed reform measures as meanspirited and overly punitive.

While Congress was eager to portray legal immigrants as responsible, hardworking, community-minded individuals who lived in traditional nuclear family units, they were reluctant to acknowledge that undocumented immigrants were anything but lawbreakers and low-cost laborers. In an effort to justify his reform proposal, Lamar S. Smith (R-TX), for example, admitted that "illegal aliens are not the enemy. . . . Most have good intentions." However, he quickly added, "We cannot allow the human faces to mask the very real crisis in illegal immigration" (United States Congress, House, March 19, 1996). In contrast to the discourse about legal immigration, which weighed humanistic concerns against economic considerations, Congress was quite comfortable to discuss undocumented immigrants' economic impact without much regard to the human side of the issue.

A comparison of the two Jordan Commission reports to Congress effectively illustrates these dramatic differences between the perception of legal and illegal immigrants. In their 1995 report on the legal immigration system, the U.S. Commission on Immigration Reform made it clear that "a properly regulated system of legal immigration is in the national interest of the United States" (U.S. Commission on Immigration Reform 1995, i). The committee members emphasized the fact that legal immigrants create new businesses, revive neighborhoods, and "strengthen American scientific, literary, artistic and other cultural resources" (U.S. Commission on Immigration Reform 1995, i). Legal immigrants were desirable not only because of their economic contributions but also because diversity was hailed as an "important [component] of good schools and strong communities" (U.S. Commission on Immigration Reform 1995, i). Without a doubt, similar arguments could have been made with regard to undocumented workers. However, the Jordan Commission—and, as the following analysis will show, U.S. Congress—failed to acknowledge that unauthorized workers have also made important social and cultural contributions. In those rare instances when the commission recognized that "the presence of illegal aliens in those same communities has not, however, always been of such concern to public officials, employers, or the general public," they still claimed that these immigrants were only tolerated because "many private citizens and businesses have taken advantage of the presence of illegal workers and have effectively encouraged their migration by employing them at low wages" (U.S. Commission on Immigration Reform 1994, 110). Apparently, undocumented immigrants' only meaningful contribution to U.S. society was of an economic nature.

In contrast to this rather simplistic representation of undocumented immigrants' positive contributions, the U.S. government had a long list of complaints and concerns about this particular population. As the following analysis will demonstrate, congressional debates tied economic considerations to concerns about national security and crime rates and underlined these arguments with alarmist rhetoric about undocumented immigrants' "uncontrolled sexuality" and extensive use of public services. Despite the fact that several overriding concerns—such as welfare eligibility and immigrants' effect on the school system—connected the discourse about undocumented immigrants to the debate about the legal immigration system, these issues were discussed differently in each context. Whereas politicians were careful to weigh economic considerations against concerns about the well-being of documented immigrants, the discourse about undocumented immigrants was highly unsympathetic and portrayed these people as a threatening, undesirable, and unassimilable underclass.

This chapter will provide an analysis of the discourse on undocumented immigrants. I will compare the rhetoric about undocumented immigrants to the way that politicians portrayed legal immigration. The next three sections will examine three key concerns that dominated this discursive strand. First, I will take a look at the concern about sexuality, birthright citizenship, and the multifaceted discussion about undocumented children. Then I will interrogate the rhetorical connection between illegal immigration, crime, and terrorism—a concern that would become even more relevant after the terrorist attacks on September 11, 2001. Finally, I will provide a brief analysis of the discourse about employment verification and unauthorized workers' impact on the U.S. labor market.

While the previous chapter demonstrated how politicians reconciled their neoliberal agenda with a popular rhetoric about family values, the following sections will examine the discursive connection between illegal immigration, crime, and terrorism. I will argue that politicians criminalized undocumented immigrants to establish that these individuals were unfit to join the national community and access the rewards a neoliberal state had in store for responsible and motivated legal immigrants. In accordance with the neoliberal emphasis on individual characteristics over structural factors, politicians argued that undocumented immigrants had forfeited their right to reside in the United States because they had violated U.S. laws and social norms. Not only were undocumented immigrants portrayed as lawbreakers and terrorists, but they were also described as a burden on the U.S. taxpayer and, in certain instances, an irrational mass of people that was drawn to the U.S. welfare or education "magnet."

In addition, the following sections will also discuss a few instances where politicians struggled to reconcile this accusatory tone with their concern for undocumented children and their desire to appease constituencies that had become dependent on a cheap and easily exploitable labor force. In the end, however, Congress agreed that undocumented immigrants represented a problem population that had already proven that they were unfit to become full-fledged members of society. Politicians were willing to make some concessions—such as allowing "innocent" children access to public schools and developing a new visa program for unskilled workers—but all these reform initiatives included strict temporal limits and other restrictions.

Alarmist Depictions: Flood Imagery and the Welfare Magnet

One of the most striking features of this discourse is the alarmist rhetoric used to portray undocumented workers and the impact they have had on U.S. society. Politicians did not hesitate to express their lack of interest in individual stories and personal motivations. Dana Rohrabacher (R-CA), for example, admitted that "those millions of illegal immigrants that have come here, they may be fine people," but what really counted was the fact that "they are consuming resources and benefits that are meant for the people of the United States of America" (United States Congress, House, September 25, 1996). Instead of examining specific examples and acknowledging that immigrants were illegal due to a number of different circumstances, politicians relied heavily on generalizations and metaphors that described undocumented immigrants as a homogeneous mass. To use legal scholar Stephen Legomsky's words, the discourse failed to account for the fact that there are "degrees of moral and legal guilt" and that "one should not accept unflinchingly the premise that all undocumented immigrants are wrongdoers" (Legomsky 1995, 1468f).[1] Yet instead of painting a multifaceted picture that did justice to the complexity of the situation, the discourse focused almost exclusively on a race-, class-, and gender-specific stereotype of an "illegal alien": a young, unskilled, brown-skinned man who had crossed the U.S.–Mexico border without proper documentation. This stereotypical representation not only failed to apply to visa overstayers but also failed to include women as well as undocumented immigrants from other national and racial backgrounds (Johnson 1995, 1544f).

Throughout history, many have failed pay adequate attention to the diversity within the "illegal alien" population. In her research on the rhetorical construction of "illegal aliens" in the 1920s and 1930s, Lisa Flores found that the same negative images have dominated the immigration reform discourse over the course of time. More specifically, her research reveals that two competing images of Mexicans, in particular, have informed the immigration reform discourse since the early twentieth century: the image of Mexicans as a docile labor force and the fear of a Mexican problem population with a "purported penchant for criminality" (Flores 2003, 374). Mexicans were increasingly constructed as criminals who became all the more threatening as they entered the United States in large numbers.

By the mid-1990s, the emphasis on masses of illegal aliens still played a significant role. Flood images and comparisons to various natural disasters were of particular importance in this context. Analyses of the European (anti-)immigration discourse show that this linguistic phenomenon is not unique to the United States. Jäger and Link (1993) and van Dijk (1997, 1999, 2000), for example, have noted that the European media makes frequent use of flood metaphors to portray immigrants as a large, homogeneous mass of people. While numerous U.S. politicians utilized flood metaphors, "immigrant floods" were of particular concern to representatives from border states such as California, Arizona, and Florida. Dana Rohrabacher (R-CA), for example, proclaimed that "in California and elsewhere, we have a mammoth tide, a wave of illegal immigration, sweeping across our country," and Bill Young (R-FL) added that "Florida has long been overburdened by the flood of illegal immigration" (United States Congress, House, March 20 and 21, 1996, respectively).[2] Sometimes, these metaphors portrayed undocumented immigrants as an uncontainable force of nature that threatened to destroy U.S. civilization. Governor Lawton Chiles (FL), for instance, compared undocumented immigrants to Hurricane Andrew. Chiles declared, "As surely as the winds and rains of Hurricane Andrew assaulted south Florida in a crisis that forever changed it, there is another storm—illegal immigration—that is battering our shores today, unleashing yet another crisis" (United States Congress, Senate, June 22, 1994). By comparing undocumented immigrants to natural disasters, politicians implied that the effects of illegal immigration are purely negative—maybe even life threatening.[3]

Yet, while these comparisons were certainly dehumanizing, they also implied that the migrants themselves could hardly be blamed for their harmful effects on U.S. society. After all, it is impossible to hold hurricanes or floods accountable for the damage they cause. A similar claim can be made with regard to the popular rhetoric about different kinds of magnets—such as the "employment magnet," the "welfare magnet," and the "education magnet." Politicians argued that citizens of poor, disadvantaged nations were attracted by the superior services and opportunities available in the United States. Unable to resist, migrants entered the United States without proper documents. Taken together, these portrayals seem to suggest that undocumented immigrants do not have the ability to make conscious decisions and take responsibility for the effects of their actions. In short, illegal immigrants were commonly described as people who did not have the potential to develop into responsible neoliberal subjects who choose to adhere to U.S. laws, norms, and societal expectations. Whereas the reform of the legal immigration system was meant to ensure that newly arrived immigrants were self-sufficient and ready to contribute to the U.S. economy, the frequent employment of flood and magnet metaphors strategically disregarded solutions that discussed undocumented immigrants as anything but a homogeneous mass of people driven by their desire to take advantage of the generosity of the U.S. welfare state, health care, and the public school system.

In contrast to this widespread belief that it was the "mass" of undocumented immigrants that had hurt the United States, some politicians focused on individual immigrants' intention to harm. Brian Bilbray used the following example to illustrate that there was nothing "natural" or "unconscious" about undocumented immigrants' desire to enter the United States: "There was a woman from the interior of Mexico who had actually taken the time to write three letters to the school district to make sure that her children could get a public education in the United States even if they were illegal . . . She waited three times to get an answer back that says, 'If I bring my children here, from Mexico, do I have to show they're legally here?' And they said 'No you have no problem at all getting them educated in this country'" (United States Congress, House, March 20, 1996). According to Representative Bilbray, undocumented Mexican immigrants thus arrive with the conscious desire to use as many public services as possible. While this comment seems to recognize that undocumented immigrants possess agency and have the potential to make rational choices, Representative Bilbray does not regard this woman's behavior as evidence that she would make an efficient neoliberal subject and an involved, ambitious parent. Due to the fact that this Mexican mother is undocumented, her eagerness to receive a free education for her children is not interpreted as a smart cost–benefit analysis, but as a sign that she is trying to exploit the generosity of the U.S. school system.

Numerous other politicians argued that undocumented immigrants' attempts to benefit from the education, health care, and welfare systems not only were harmful to the state but should also be regarded as an attack against U.S. citizens and legal immigrants. Oftentimes, it was not even necessary to develop elaborate justifications or to give specific examples, but the language that was used to portray undocumented immigrants clearly demonstrated these negative perceptions. For example, Henry J. Hyde (R-IL) argued, "Today, undocumented aliens surreptitiously cross our border with impunity. Still others enter as non-immigrants with temporary legal status, but often stay on indefinitely and illegally" (United States Congress, House, March 19, 1996). Notably, this was one of the few examples where a politician explicitly mentioned the fact that not all undocumented immigrants had crossed the border illegally. However, the use of adjectives clearly demonstrates that it is the undocumented border crosser, who is referred to as a "surreptitious alien," who causes the real concern.

In accordance with a larger tendency to focus almost exclusively on those crossing the border illegally and ignore those staying on expired visas, many speakers used the act of crossing the border as an illustration for undocumented immigrants' dishonorable motives. On March 19, 1996, for example, Randy Tate (R-WA) complained, "hundreds of thousands sneak across our borders in the dark of the night without conscience" (United States Congress, House, March 19, 1996).[4] Yet other politicians quoted even more alarmist instances. On February 26, 1996, California Assemblyman Jan Goldsmith expressed the following concerns: "We have constituents in my district who are fearful at night as they hear gunshots in the night and they hear screams and yells and people talking in their yards and their areas, in rather remote areas, and they are scared. They are scared because they have literally hundreds of people in the evening coming across their property, destroying their property, banging on their doors, looking into their windows, and they're in an isolated area. It is a disaster waiting to happen" (United States Congress, House, February 26, 1996). On a similar note, Randy (Duke) Cunningham (R-CA) described what his wife, who is a school principal in San Diego county, and her colleagues have to go through on a daily basis. "We have many of the illegals living in the canyons. . . . They are coming up at night, they are defecating on the lawn, they are using the water systems because they do not have showers down in the canyons, and the teachers are literally afraid to go into the classrooms at night" (United States Congress, House, March 20, 1996). While some residents of border regions might have been rightfully concerned about their own security, it is obvious that there were other factors involved. Goldsmith and Cunningham not only described undocumented immigrants as public nuisances, who behaved quite disrespectfully, but their examples also implied that, due to their improper socialization, Mexicans and other illegal border crossers might be unable to assimilate into mainstream culture.

If we look at these and similar comments, it becomes quite obvious that undocumented immigrants did not simply raise economic concerns, but that their existence sparked much more complex and deep-seated anxieties. Even though politicians were reluctant to openly discuss legal immigrants' racial and ethnic backgrounds as well as the effects of the changing racial makeup of the immigrant population on American attitudes toward immigration, they were usually eager to emphasize that legal immigrants had made meaningful cultural contributions that had enriched and rejuvenated U.S. culture. Legal immigrants were portrayed as individuals that came from a variety of racial, national, and class backgrounds. With regard to undocumented immigrants, however, the discourse focused almost exclusively on unskilled and uneducated Mexicans who had crossed the border without proper documentation. Even though mainstream politicians did not explicitly say that they were particularly apprehensive toward undocumented Mexicans, the larger discourse produced a highly racialized image of the illegal immigrant population and implied that undocumented Mexicans did not represent a welcome addition to "our" society but were rather a threat to national unity.

The immigration reform discourse made a sharp distinction between documented and undocumented immigrants. After Senator Spencer Abraham (R-MI) proposed an amendment to split S. 1394, which combined legal and illegal immigration reform, into two separate bills, numerous politicians felt compelled to stress the differences between legal immigrants, who were generally described in much more favorable terms, and undocumented immigrants.[5] In support of his own amendment, Abraham argued, "there is a very big difference between dealing with folks who break the rules and break the laws and seek to come to this country for exploitative reasons, and dealing with people who want to come to this country in a positive and constructive way to make a contribution, to play by the rules" (United States Congress, Senate, April 25, 1996).[6] Other politicians used rather creative analogies to illustrate the qualitative difference between legal and illegal immigrants. Steven LaTourette (R-OH), for example, came up with the following analogy: "You could argue that the work of a brain surgeon and a barber both involve the human head, yet no one would think of going to a barber for brain surgery or a brain surgeon for a haircut. This is precisely the type of ill-conceived logic we employ if we attempt to lump illegal and legal immigration into one reform package" (United States Congress, House, March 21, 1996).

Contrary to factual evidence that clearly proved undocumented workers had little or no access to public benefits—except for short-term emergency assistance—many politicians were convinced that undocumented laborers were not only poor and unskilled but were also more likely to receive federal and state benefits. Senator Edward M. Kennedy (D-MA), for example, claimed, "When you are talking about illegals, you are talking about people who are breaking the rules, talking about unskilled individuals who are displacing American workers, you are talking about a heavier incidence in drawing down whatever kind of public assistance programs are out there. . . . When you are talking about legals, you are talking about individuals who, by every study, contribute more than they ever take out in terms of the tax systems" (United States Congress, Senate, April 25, 1996). Congress not only believed that undocumented immigrants were inferior to legal immigrants (with regard to their level of education, job qualification, and their willingness to adhere to laws and societal norms), but they also portrayed undocumented immigrants as a group whose behavior reflected badly on other noncitizens. As a result, Congress felt that legal immigrants should have a vested interest in drastically reducing the rising number of undocumented migrants. Numerous politicians either who were immigrants themselves or whose parents or grandparents had migrated to the United States thus felt compelled to speak out against illegal immigration. Chief among them was Representative Jay Kim (R-CA), who declared, "As one of the few first generation legal immigrants in Congress, I am offended by the merging of the initiatives to combat illegal aliens with legal immigration reform" (United States Congress, House, March 21, 1996).[7] As I discussed in the previous chapter, it was not unusual for politicians to cite their own immigrant ancestry as a way to establish credibility and prove that they were sensitive to these issues. On one level, a similar claim can be made with regard to Robert Menendez (D-NJ), who repeatedly stressed that he was "an American-born son of legal immigrants," and Jay Kim's insistence on distinguishing between his own family and that of an undocumented immigrant. However, it is certainly noteworthy that the only two representatives who deemed it necessary to establish that their families were indeed *legal* immigrants were of Cuban and Korean descent. Even though the neoliberal rhetoric that was used to justify immigration reform actively denied that race continued to be an important factor, Kim and Menendez's comments reveal that politicians were very well aware of the fact that the debate was far from race neutral or color blind.

Due to the hostile tone of the debate, many legal immigrants also felt that they had to choose their battles and make sacrifices to protect their own rights and opportunities. By spring of 1996, opinion polls, media representations, and congressional debates had made it increasingly clear that the American public needed a scapegoat for high unemployment, poverty, and crime rates, and the well-publicized collapse of the welfare system. In the early days of the 104th Congress, many politicians had directed their reform proposals against undocumented and documented immigrants. After much debate, politicians realized that it would be difficult to pass a comprehensive anti-immigration bill that also targeted legal immigrants, who had successfully assembled an influential coalition of supporters and lobbyists. Proponents of more restrictive laws gradually started to cut their losses and shift their attention to a sole culprit: undocumented immigrants. In order to strengthen their argument, they created a false sense of competition and loudly proclaimed that, as Elton Gallegly (R-CA) phrased it, "the greatest potential threat to legal immigration is illegal immigration" (United States Congress, House, September 25, 1996). In the end, Congress passed a bill that severely limited the rights and protections of undocumented immigrants, without limiting the number of family reunification and employment visas.

Sympathetic Figures: Children of Undocumented Immigrants

Even though the discourse on undocumented immigrants was characterized by a lack of compassion, there was one particular group that caused some politicians to rethink their emotionally detached, economically oriented logic: children. Children's well-being was discussed on numerous occasions and in connection to a wide variety of issues, including welfare eligibility, health care, and parents' ability to obtain a waiver or suspension of deportation. At the most basic level, Congress agreed that all children deserved to be protected from abuse, neglect, hunger, and life-threatening illnesses. At the same time, many politicians implied that there was a fundamental difference between children who were legal permanent residents and U.S. citizens and undocumented children. For the most part, politicians insisted that the latter group should only be able to access emergency assistance, while the full array of social services should be limited to children who were legally in the country.

Throughout the debate, politicians also expressed concern about the increasing number of "mixed status families." With Congress generally unwilling to provide long-term help to undocumented immigrants, politicians struggled to find a way to support the large number of citizen children who had been born to undocumented parents. Since these children were U.S. citizens, they were eligible for the whole range of public services, including Temporary Assistance for Needy Families (TANF), food stamps, public housing assistance, and Medicaid. Yet, as long as these children were minors, their assistance checks had to be issued to their undocumented parents. In its first report to Congress, the U.S. Commission on Immigration Reform stated that this practice had a number of "undesirable side effects. Some illegal aliens will benefit from the resources made available to citizen members of their household, but denying the citizen members access to the assistance would be inequitable and illegal" (U.S. Commission on Immigration Reform 1994, 125).

One particularly interesting response to this perceived problem came from Elton Gallegly (R-CA), who proposed to create a complex welfare distribution system that made it more difficult for mixed status families to receive welfare for their U.S.-born children. In particular, Gallegly wanted to prevent undocumented parents from cashing in their children's welfare checks. Instead, local governments should be forced to create a costly guardianship system to manage and allocate benefits for these citizen children.[8] Ultimately, Gallegly's proposal would have increased public expenditures and led to more state bureaucracy—a result that would have been in clear violation of a neoliberal reform project that called for a rigorous downsizing of the welfare state. Hence it is not surprising that this amendment was met with opposition. On March 20, 1996, Nydia Velazquez (D-NY) and Lucille Roybal-Allard (D-CA) proposed to strike the Gallegly Amendment, which they perceived as "a costly and an unworkable, unnecessary, unfunded mandate that serves absolutely no legitimate national interest" (United States Congress, House, March 20, 1996). Most representatives agreed with this assessment and admitted that the Gallegly Amendment did not represent a workable solution.

However, the Velazquez/Roybal-Allard Amendment also triggered a larger debate about the merits of birthright citizenship. While the majority was ready to defend the Fourteenth Amendment, a small but vocal minority insisted that it was high time to rethink the limits of birthright citizenship. Not only did these politicians argue that the Fourteenth Amendment was never intended to include the children of undocumented persons, but they also asserted that "illegal immigrants have found a way to abuse this right," as Marge Roukema (R-NJ) put it (United States Congress, House, May 24, 1995). This controversy about the Fourteenth Amendment was hardly new. Since the amendment's ratification in 1868, the nativist movement had attacked the comparatively generous citizenship regulations on a number of occasions. In contrast to many other First World nations, the United States offers three basic means of obtaining U.S. citizenship: by being born on U.S. soil (*jus soli*), by having parents who are U.S. citizens (*jus sanguinis*), and through naturalization. With the passage of California's Proposition 187 in 1994, the calls to strip away automatic birthright citizenship became once again louder. Anti-immigration activists portrayed birthright citizenship as a "magnet" that attracted young couples and provided them with backdoor access to social services. Yet legal scholars argue that the denial of citizenship to the U.S.-born children of undocumented immigrants was not only "in clear conflict with America's social values, the Judeo-Christian ethic, and many of the nation's most closely held beliefs" but would also "clearly contradict the wishes of the founding fathers" (Shulman 1995, 709f). Furthermore, such a drastic change would require a constitutional amendment, not a mere section in an immigration reform bill.

Throughout the debate, politicians were adamant in their claims that female immigrants strategically timed their delivery to make sure that their children would get U.S. citizenship. In a particularly extreme example, Dianne Feinstein (D-CA) proclaimed, "Many people reportedly get on planes coming from Asia, get Medicaid, give birth to their children, get citizenship, and return" (United States Congress, Senate, June 22, 1994). Most other politicians focused on Mexican and Central American women who crossed the border shortly before they were scheduled to give birth.[9] Allegedly, these female migrants not only knew that they were eligible for short-term medical services and neonatal care but also hoped to gain access to other benefits by giving birth to a U.S. citizen. Nathan Deal (R-GA) pejoratively referred to this phenomenon as "booty-strapping." He testified, "We have all . . . heard the traditional description of bootstrapping your way into a benefit. This is booty-strapping. This is a situation in which, by virtue of the act of illegal entry on the part of a parent, the birth of the child gives the right to benefits from the taxpayers' coffers" (United States Congress, House, March 20, 1996).[10]

The negative perception of female migrants' desire to take advantage of the U.S. medical and welfare system was oftentimes connected with exaggerated concerns about their uncontrolled sexuality. Throughout the debate, politicians and expert witnesses implied that, due to their outrageously high birth rates, undocumented immigrants were trying to take over certain parts of the country, most notably California. And even though no one explicitly mentioned undocumented immigrants' racial and ethnic background, it was fairly obvious that Congress was also concerned about the fact that Latinos would soon outnumber non-Hispanic white residents and citizens in certain parts of the country.

In this context, the use of statistics is of particular importance. On February 26, 1996, Harold W. Ezell, U.S. Commission on Immigration Reform, testified that "almost 70 percent of the babies in L.A. county hospitals are born to illegal alien parents, almost 70 percent" (United States Congress, House, February 26, 1996). Tellingly, Ezell conveniently neglected to indicate that most wealthy white women preferred to deliver their babies in private hospitals outside of L.A. county and were thus not included in these statistics. Furthermore, since hospitals were not required to collect information on their patients' citizenship or immigration status, these numbers qualify as little more than guesswork.[11] Within the larger discourse, however, it hardly matters that these numbers were taken out of context; these statistics are not representative of the nation at large. These alarmist examples from one of the regions with the highest percentage of Latinos were cited because they resonated powerfully with widespread anxieties about Latino/a sexuality. And due to that fact that Ezell's numbers were based on actual research and statistics, they seemed to validate these fears and make them appear rational and objective.

Significantly, childbirth and neonatal care were not the only medical services that Congress was concerned about. Throughout the larger debate, politicians repeatedly questioned whether the U.S. government should change anything about their commitment to provide emergency medical services to every human being, regardless of their legal status. Not surprisingly, the proservices side focused almost exclusively on the well-being of women and children. On April 29, 1996, Edward M. Kennedy (D-MA) argued, "We should . . . support the care for expectant mothers because it is the right thing to do. We ought to be supporting the care for the children because it is the right thing to do" (United States Congress, Senate, April 29, 1996). However, he was also careful to underline this humanistic argument with several other concerns. For example, Kennedy reminded his colleagues that these services would not only benefit undocumented immigrants but that "emergency medical care, immunization, treatment for infectious diseases . . . benefit all, because they relate to the public health and are in the public interest" (United States Congress, Senate, April 15, 1996). Hence the comparatively small costs for emergency medical services and immunizations represented an excellent investment that could prevent much more costly problems.

In light of the overwhelming evidence that certain forms of medical benefits were necessary to protect the general public, very few representatives suggested eliminating these services. However, some politicians were not satisfied with these elusive long-term benefits. Instead, they called for much more immediate results. One of the most popular suggestions in this context was Ed Bryant's (R-TN) amendment, which required medical facilities to report any undocumented person who had received free emergency medical treatment from a public hospital.[12] This way, we would continue to provide emergency care to all human beings, but we could also make sure that "the Federal Government [gets] something in return for its payment of taxpayer dollars" (United States Congress, House, March 20, 1996). According to Bryant, compassion is a good thing, as long as we never forget that "an illegal alien, healthy, sick, or injured, is still an illegal alien" and thus a lawbreaker who "should expect to suffer the consequences if caught" (United States Congress, House, March 20, 1996).

His opponents did not accept his premise that everyone would continue to receive emergency medical care under this amendment. In response to Ed Bryant's (R-TN) assertion that this was "not about a denial of medical care to illegal aliens," Xavier Becerra (D-CA) pointed out that Bryant's amendment "would cause a dramatic chilling effect within our medical care system. What we would have is a situation where people may in fact not go for treatment or take a family member for treatment for fear of what would happen as a result of trying to approach a hospital" (United States Congress, House, March 20, 1996).[13] According to Becerra and several other representatives, Bryant's amendment would create a climate of fear and undocumented persons would be rightfully afraid to seek medical treatment. Therefore, the amendment would risk lives, facilitate the spread of contagious diseases, and lead to increased harassment of foreign-looking patients who seek treatment at public hospitals. In the end, Congress decided that the negative consequences would outweigh the desired effects. On March 20, 1996, Congress rejected the Bryant amendment by a recorded vote of 170 yeas to 250 nays.[14]

In addition to the controversy over medical services, undocumented immigrants' access to public education was another cause for extensive debate. On March 20, 1996, Elton Gallegly (R-CA) offered an amendment that authorized states to deny public education benefits to immigrants who were not lawfully present in the United States. According to Gallegly, expenditures for education had skyrocketed in those states that had a large population of undocumented immigrants—most notably California. Even though it was impossible to provide reliable statistics, Gallegly strongly believed that "California alone spends more than $2 billion each year to educate illegal immigrants" (United States Congress, House, March 20, 1996).[15] At the same time, Gallegly maintained that "the dollars and cents are only part of the story. Equally important is the fact that illegal immigrants in our classrooms are having an extremely detrimental effect on the quality of education we are able to provide to the legal residents" (United States Congress, House, March 20, 1996).

Yet even though representatives from both ends of the political spectrum agreed that the U.S. education system was in desperate need of reform, most politicians were reluctant to pin blame on the children of undocumented immigrants. Opponents of the Gallegly amendment employed several different rhetorical strategies to explain their stance. Numerous politicians argued that the amendment was immoral, inhumane, meanspirited, and downright cruel. On September 25, 1996, for example, Enid Greene (R-UT) argued that "educating the children in our communities is . . . as important as protecting them from physical harm." Martin Frost (D-TX) reminded his colleagues, "Whether these children should or should not be in this country is really beside the point. The fact is that every child, no matter his or her race, creed, nationality, religion, or immigration status should have a desk in a school. Every child living in this Nation should be entitled to an education. Denying the children of illegal immigrants access to education will not solve the problem of illegal immigration and seal our borders" (United States Congress, House, September 25, 1996).[16]

In addition, a number of politicians emphasized the need to distinguish between "guilty parents" and "innocent children." Ileana Ros-Lehtinen (R-FL), for example, testified, "The children did not choose to be in the United States illegally. They do not deserve, therefore, to be punished for the actions of their parents" (United States Congress, House, March 20, 1996). A few months later, Patrick J. Kennedy (D-RI) posed the following rhetorical question: "Are we as a body going to reduce ourselves to mistreating little children because we are angry that their parents have not complied with our laws?" (United States Congress, House, September 25, 1996).[17] All the aforementioned statements were difficult to argue with. After all, no politician was prepared to stand up and proclaim that he or she was indeed trying to punish elementary school students.

Furthermore, numerous politicians reminded their colleagues that this amendment would turn teachers and school officials into quasi-INS agents. Without proper training and meticulous guidelines, there was a high risk that these individuals would single out students of color and ask them to provide documents that established their legal status. In this context, Patrick J. Kennedy (D-RI) told his colleagues, "It sickens me to think of the discrimination that will inevitably result as parents will be forced to prove that their children are indeed legal. Unfortunately, those children who look foreign will be forced to prove that they are, in fact, Americans. Be assured that the children whose ancestors are Irish, or British or Dutch or French won't be asked to prove their legality—they can easily pass as American" (United States Congress, House, September 25, 1996). Earl Pomeroy (D-ND), the adoptive parent of two Korean children, added that "the fear that my children might be pulled out of a classroom because of an inane act of Congress . . . is too horrible to contemplate" (United States Congress, House, September 25, 1996). Undoubtedly, Earl Pomeroy's concerns resonated with many politicians. By directing his colleagues' attention away from undocumented students to his own children, Pomeroy was able to create a much more compelling image of an innocent victim in need of protection.

Opponents of the Gallegly amendment were also prepared to underline this emotional rhetoric with a number of economic arguments. Since Elton Gallegly (R-CA) and his supporters repeatedly referred to the high costs associated with the obligation to educate *all* children, the opposition countered that, as Ileana Ros-Lehtinen (R-FL) phrased it, "the cost to us as a nation would be far greater by excluding these children from our schools" (United States Congress, House, March 20, 1996). The antici-pated costs, in this context, were not limited to direct financial expenditures. Anthony C. Beilenson (D-CA) warned that the Gallegly amendment "would contribute to crime, to illiteracy, to ignorance, to discrimination," Bill Richardson (D-NM) expressed concern over the "community health and safety hazard," and Sheila Jackson-Lee (D-TX) cautioned that "many of these children will be left with nothing to do during the school hours, pos-ing a danger to themselves and others" (United States Congress, House, March 20 and September 25, 1996, respectively). Above all, politicians were concerned about the fact that hundreds of thousands of undocu-mented children might eventually join gangs and commit crimes. In their view, a balanced cost–benefit analysis needed to take into consideration the increased expenditures for local law enforcement, incarceration, and emergency health care that resulted from denying education to the chil-dren of undocumented workers. In short, the Gallegly amendment would have far-reaching effects that were in clear violation of the neoliberal objective to make the governing of certain risk groups more effective and economically efficient.

In addition, the aforementioned examples helped to create a climate of fear. Numerous politicians implied that many, if not all, undocumented children would develop into dangerous predators if they were denied access to public education. At first glance, this alarmist rhetoric stands in opposition to the repeated attempts to depict undocumented children as innocent victims who needed to be protected at all costs. In the context of the larger discourse, though, both of these arguments were used to rein-force the negative portrayal of undocumented adults. According to this logic, parents' decision to bring their children with them proved that they were selfish, neglectful, and disregarding of their children's needs. In short, since undocumented immigrants were seen as a dangerous underclass, the U.S. government needed to step in to protect immigrant children, educate them, and expose them to mainstream values, beliefs, and expectations. The argument suggested that if Congress denied these children access to the public school system, they would start to manifest the same undesir-able character traits that their parents already exhibited.

In addition to comments that combined various types of "costs," sev-eral politicians advanced a fairly straightforward cost–benefit analysis that focused exclusively on the financial aspects of illegal immigration. Not only did they emphasize the fact that the Gallegly amendment was likely to increase spending on law enforcement and security measures, they also called attention to the costly bureaucratic measures that would be necessary to determine which students possessed legal permanent resident status and which did not. Esteban Edward Torres (D-CA), for example, concluded that the Gallegly "amendment will cost—not save—money for state and local governments and public schools" (United States Congress, House, March 28, 1996). Furthermore, neoliberal logic dictated that public expenditures should be used as investments in promising individuals who were likely to turn into net contributors in the future—a principle several politicians applied to the controversy over undocumented children's access to public education. Nancy Pelosi (D-CA), for example, reasoned that it was "short-sighted and inhumane" to "deny anyone the opportunity to be educated. If undocumented children cannot be educated, they will have nowhere to go but the streets. These children will not just go away if we continue to deny them benefits. They will be sent reeling into the cycle of poverty that we are seeking to end" (United States Congress, House, March 20, 1996). Yet while numerous politicians from both parties dismissed the Gallegly amendment as cruel, discriminatory, and overly punitive and argued that its effects would be in conflict with the larger neoliberal agenda, several Republican representatives believed that this policy was an effective way to solve the "illegal immigration problem."

Gallegly's supporters focused on the same aspects as their opponents. However, they stated that the denial of public school benefits to undocumented children was economically sensible and claimed that their amendment was intended to protect U.S. citizen children who live in impoverished communities and share classrooms and resources with undocumented students. Instead of assessing the effects the amendment might have on undocumented immigrants, they shifted their focus to the sons and daughters of U.S. citizens and legal permanent residents and implied that these children had suffered extreme hardships in the public school system. According to this logic, there was a direct connection between the number of undocumented immigrants in a particular school district and the difficulties that that district experienced. Supposedly, the U.S. education system had reached a state of crisis because undocumented children consumed so many resources that other students were no longer able to receive the kind of education they should be entitled to. In order to illustrate the gravity of the situation, numerous politicians painted a frightening picture of the public school system. Elton Gallegly (R-CA), the author of the amendment that banned undocumented children from public schools, testified, "The Nation's education system is in crisis. Classrooms are over-crowded. Teachers are in many cases overburdened and resources are in short supply. . . . When illegal immigrants sit down in public school class-rooms, the desk, textbooks, blackboards in effect become stolen property, stolen from the students rightfully entitled to those resources" (United States Congress, House, March 20, 1996). Instead of focusing on the larger structural and political changes, such as highly publicized cuts in property taxes, which had led to the deterioration of the public school system in California, Gallegly advanced a one-sided explanation that scapegoated one of the most vulnerable populations in the United States. According to his statement, undocumented children were in direct competition with other students and had taken something that rightfully belonged to legal residents and U.S. citizens.[18]

Other politicians added that the children of legal residents and U.S. citizens were not only more deserving of our scarce resources, but they were also more worthy of our sympathy and compassion. In response to the common accusation that the denial of public school benefits was meanspirited and inhumane, Dana Rohrabacher (R-CA), one of the most outspoken champions of the Gallegly amendment, argued, "We care about the children of people who live in foreign countries. But that does not mean we are going to allow everybody in the world to bring their children here and break down our education system so our kids cannot get an edu-cation. . . . We care about the American people, and we have no apologies for that" (United States Congress, House, March 19, 1996). In a similar fashion, other politicians expressed their beliefs that this provision was good public policy because it authorized states "to put the needs of their own citizens above those of illegal aliens" (Frank Riggs [R-CA], United States Congress, House, March 20, 1996).[19]

Gallegly's supporters were not only convinced that undocumented stu-dents had already harmed their fellow classmates, but they also implied that the situation would further deteriorate if the U.S. government did not take immediate action. Even though there was little factual evidence that access to primary and secondary education was a significant factor in par-ents' decision to overstay their visas or enter the United States without documents, numerous politicians believed that public school benefits had "proved to be a powerful magnet or open invitation," as Marge Roukema (R-NJ) put it (United States Congress, House, March 20, 1996). Congress also painted a frightening picture of the unintended effects that this "magnet" might have in the future. Dana Rohrabacher (R-CA) warned his colleagues, "If we keep educating everybody in the world who can sneak across our border and bring their families, anybody who cares about their children throughout the entire planet will do everything they can possibly do to get their kids into our country" (United States Congress, House, March 20, 1996).[20] Since a free public education was easily available to everyone, regardless of his or her legal status, it supposedly encouraged undesirable behavior and deterred potential immigrants from going through a lengthy and complicated legal immigration process. According to the neoliberal agenda, the U.S. government thus needed to develop a system that selectively rewarded only those individuals who played by the rules.

In addition, Gallegly's supporters demonstrated that the expenses for undocumented children's education did not represent a sensible investment either. Since these students did not possess a work permit and were not likely to get one in the near future, American society was unlikely to benefit from their academic achievements.[21] In view of these factors, the Gallegly amendment was commonly described as a rational, economically efficient measure that would help redirect money to worthy recipients who not only had the potential to develop into net contributors in the long term, but who were also deemed to be more deserving in the first place. Hence Gallegly's supporters praised his amendment as a sensible and evenhanded way to further neoliberal objectives, discourage undesirable behavior, and eliminate expenditures for individuals who were unlikely to develop into self-sufficient neoliberal subjects.

In contrast to the common tendency to downplay the importance of race and class, Gallegly and his supporters also made a point of showing that their amendment would actually help to protect poor students of color. In an attempt to counter the accusation that this amendment would increase discrimination against foreign-looking children, Gallegly's supporters tried to convince their colleagues that the current policy had had particularly disastrous effects on low-income families, many of whom were people of color. Brian Bilbray (R-CA), for instance, insisted, "This is not an issue that affects the rich, white people of this country. This is an issue that hits the school districts of the working class in this country" (United States Congress, House, March 20, 1996).[22] While Bilbray is certainly correct in his assessment that a high number of poor, undocumented students do put a burden on the underfunded local districts that provide educational services, this does not mean that their exclusion would result in any fundamental changes. Disparities in the public school system, especially in California, were not primarily caused by undocumented immigrants, but the desolate funding situation was the product of decades of antieducation policies—tax cuts, devolution, and reduced federal spending. At best, the Gallegly amendment would have provided short-term relief for school districts with a high percentage of undocumented students.

Immigrants as a Security Risk: Terrorists, Drug Dealers, and Criminal Aliens

In addition to cultivating widespread concern that undocumented immigrants, including their children, were taking something that rightfully belonged to U.S. citizens, politicians and expert witnesses also exploited the public's recently awakened fear of terrorist attacks. For the longest time, Americans had firmly believed that terrorist attacks only happened in other, less stable parts of the world. With the bombing of the World Trade Center on February 26, 1993, and the ensuing destruction of the Alfred P. Murrah Federal Building in Oklahoma City, however, this certainty came to a sudden end. Quickly, the American public not only came to the painful conclusion that they were not invincible; they also zeroed in on a common enemy: terrorists.

Early in the debate, some politicians acknowledged that not all terrorists were members of an extremist Islamic organization. On May 25, 1995, for example, Orrin G. Hatch (R-UT) argued, "We must resolve that anarchistic radicalism, be it from the left or from the right, will not prevail in our freedom-loving democracy," and Joseph R. Biden (D-DE) added, "Responding to this risk means standing against those who seek to destroy our democratic form of government, whether they come from the left or the right, from home or abroad" (United States Congress, Senate, May 25, 1995). However, the majority seemed to subscribe to the belief that the young, white U.S. citizen who had committed the Oklahoma City bombing represented a rare exception to the general rule that terrorists were almost exclusively Islamic fundamentalists. Accordingly, many politicians favored provisions that designated these radical Islamic groups as terrorist organizations to make sure that they would be cut off from funding, that active members would be deported, and that surveillance would be increased.

This notion of "Islamic terrorism" has a long history in the United States and was already "deeply embedded in the broader cultural, institutional and discursive structures of Western society" (Jackson 2007, 397). In his analysis of the discursive construction of "Islamic terrorism," Richard Jackson argues that this concept emerged from a variety of related discourses. On a scholarly level, analyses of Islamic terrorism are rooted in a larger study of religious terrorism (Rapoport 1984). Even though experts were careful to clarify that terrorism was in no way exclusive to Islam, they still helped to establish an explicit connection between terrorism and one particular religion: Islam. For example, "Walter Laqueur, a respected terrorism expert, suggests that while there is 'no *Muslim* or *Arab* monopoly in the field of religious fanaticism . . . the frequency of *Muslim- and Arab-inspired terrorism* is still striking'" (cited by Jackson 2007, 403, his emphasis). This scholarly discourse meshed well with a long tradition of negative media representations and cultural stereotypes depicting Muslims as violent and fanatic or as the exotic Other in Orientalist discourse. Recent events could thus be used as a confirmation of these negative images of Muslims, and the terrorism narrative quickly became the dominant discursive frame for portrayals of Muslim immigrants.

Throughout the debate about a more effective antiterrorism policy, Congress seemed to agree that the concern for public safety justified far-reaching and invasive measures. At the same time, politicians were also careful to present their reform plans as necessary and carefully balanced risk-management measures. While the neoliberal initiative to reform the legal immigration system was careful to identify characteristics that could help the U.S. government assess immigrants' potential to develop into productive neoliberal subjects, the debate about terrorism was founded in a belief that "Muslim heritage" represented a meaningful risk factor for a person's propensity to engage in terrorist activities. Hence the constant focus on Muslim organizations and immigrants from Muslim nations was portrayed as a rational examination of a particular risk group, not as a prejudiced attack against a religious minority.

On March 13 and 14, 1996, Congress convened for a general debate of the Effective Death Penalty and Public Safety Act of 1996 (H.R. 2703). The original version of the bill, which had been introduced by Henry J. Hyde (R-IL), contained a provision that made it illegal to raise funds for certain terrorist organizations, most notably Hamas, Hezbollah, and as Hyde put it, the "Islamic Jihad." If a person was found guilty of donating money, services, or, in some cases, merchandise to one of these organizations, he or she was subject to expedited deportation without opportunity for judicial review. A number of politicians were opposed to this stipulation and rejected the idea that all Muslims who had ever joined or supported such an organization could be described as potential terrorists.[23] However, there was significantly less concern about the idea that most terrorists were indeed radical Muslims. Throughout the divisive and highly emotional debate about the Hyde Bill and the Barr Amendment, which was repeatedly interrupted by comments about innocent victims and letters from grieving family members, the term "terrorist" was gradually turned into a code word for Middle Easterners who belonged to extremist Muslim organizations.

Initially, politicians still deemed it necessary to qualify their remarks and name specific groups. Bill McCollum (R-FL), who was strongly opposed to the Barr Amendment, proclaimed, "The next time we have some major foreign organization, a state from Libya, Iran, Iraq, or Hamas or whoever come over, bomb a building, kill a lot of people, we are going to be the ones to blame for it, not somebody else." Charles E. Schumer (D-NY) expressed his concern that the Barr Amendment was "anti-law enforcement" because "Hamas will be allowed to continue to raise funds here," and John Conyers (D-MI) added that Bob Barr (R-GA) "would allow the Islamic Jihad to come into the United States and not be denominated a terrorist organization in his bill" (United States Congress, House, March 13, 1996).[24] However, these references to specific countries and organizations were the exception, and most politicians tended to make vague references to terrorist activities in general. Olympia Snowe (R-ME), for example, supported "provisions to combat international terrorism, to remove aliens, to control fundraising for foreign terrorists." Bill Bradley (D-NJ) described the bill as "a strong, adequate response to the serious problem of terrorism, [which] will provide the United States with the necessary tools to respond to the international and domestic terrorist threats." Larry Craig (R-ID) stated, "I abhor and condemn terrorism in any form. Our Nation cannot tolerate terrorism . . . and our Nation's law enforcement must have the tools it needs to fight this menace" (United States Congress, Senate, June 7, 1995). Notably, none of the aforementioned speakers made explicit connections to Islam or explained who exactly qualified as a terrorist.

Because of this lack of specificity, one might conclude that these statements were intended to be inclusive and were made in reference to a range of different organizations and individuals who all posed a threat to the United States. However, I contend that it is essential to examine this vague rhetoric in the context of the larger discursive formation. In *The Archeology of Knowledge and the Discourse on Language*, Michel Foucault argued that a discursive formation can be characterized as a complex system of interdependent statements. In order to understand a discursive formation "what one must characterize and individualize is the coexistence of these dispersed and heterogeneous statements; the system that governs their division, the degree to which they depend upon one another, the way in which they interlock or exclude one another, the transformation that they undergo, and the play of their location, arrangement, and replacement" (Foucault 1972, 34). Each individual statement is thus inextricably linked with other statements that are part of the same discursive field. Accordingly, speakers are able to rely on a general frame of reference that allows them to omit certain details; if the audience is familiar with the larger discursive formation, they can be expected to fill in the gaps on their own. In the context of the antiterrorism discourse in 1995–96, it had already been established that the enemy was a Middle Eastern man who belonged to an extremist Muslim organization. In the later stages of the discourse, speakers could thus evoke a very specific image by the mere mentioning of the term "terrorist."

Another noteworthy feature of a discursive formation is the fact that it does not exist in isolation. Each discursive formation is not only automatically connected with related discourses, but speakers are also able to establish links and call to mind certain concepts and/or judgments that have been made in different contexts. During the debate about undocumented immigrants, politicians repeatedly implied that there was a link between a person's legal status, their propensity to commit certain crimes, and their susceptibility to join a terrorist organization. This link, however, only existed on a discursive level. Throughout the 104th Congress, there was not a single expert witness who was able to prove that there was an actual connection between terrorist activities and organized crime, such as international drug trafficking, and that the same people were involved in numerous illegal activities. Even more important, research has shown that undocumented immigrants are particularly careful to do everything by the rules and not draw the police's attention toward them (Chavez 1998). Knowing that they are subject to deportation, undocumented individuals are usually careful drivers; stay away from bars, the local drug scene, and other heavily patrolled areas; and are oftentimes hesitant to become politically active or join any kind of public organization, much less a terrorist one.

Throughout the discourse about "criminal aliens," however, numerous politicians insisted that the threat posed by foreign terrorists was inherently connected to the fact that a disproportionate number of federal prisoners were non-U.S. citizens. By making this discursive connection, politicians deployed the terrorism discourse as an effective way to legitimize other political projects (Jackson 2007, 422). Similar to Congress's attempt to frame antiterrorism measures as a rational attempt to monitor and, if necessary, exclude a certain risk group, the discussions about "criminal aliens" made it clear that the U.S. government had the obligation to identify and deport noncitizens who had committed a crime in the United States. All these noncitizen criminals had violated the rules—whether they were convicted for tax fraud or murder. Hence they had forfeited their right to reside in the United States and benefit from the services and opportunities that were offered by their host country. In accordance with the larger neoliberal project, politicians argued that noncitizen criminals should be denied the rewards that the United States had in store for those individuals who respected the law and played by the rules. In the course of the 104th Congress, however, the debate about "criminal aliens" became increasingly intertwined with the general concern about undocumented workers, and Congress rarely discussed the fact that most of these noncitizen criminals were indeed legal immigrants.

Statistical evidence for undocumented immigrants' high crime rates reinforced existing anxieties and further justified strict new policies. During a preliminary meeting of the House Subcommittee on Immigration and Claims, for example, expert witness T. Alexander Aleinikoff, who served as the General Counsel of the INS, testified that, as of January/February 1995, "69,926 foreign-born nationals are . . . incarcerated in state correctional facilities" and "27,938 foreign-born nationals are currently incarcerated in Federal institutions" (United States Congress, House, March 23, 1995). A few months later, in June, Senator Spencer Abraham (R-MI) cited significantly lower numbers: "More than 53,000 crimes have been committed by aliens in this country recently enough to put the perpetrators in our State and Federal prisons right now. An estimated 20 to 25 percent of all Federal prison inmates are noncitizens" (United States Congress, Senate, June 7, 1995). By the beginning of 1996, politicians commonly believed that this estimate—25 percent—applied specifically to undocumented immigrants, not to foreign-born individuals in general. On March 19, 1996, for example, Gerald Solomon (R-NY) began his testimony by citing "a few facts. No. 1: Nationwide more than one-quarter of all Federal prisoners are illegal aliens" (United States Congress, House, March 19, 1996).[25] Throughout the day, numerous other politicians repeated this "fact."[26] By the end of the legislative period, this statistic was not only commonly accepted but also made it into the conference report on H.R. 2202.[27] In that report, Lamar Smith (R-TX) asserted, "Illegal aliens should be removed from the United States immediately and effectively. Illegal aliens take jobs, public benefits, and engage in criminal activity. In fact, one-quarter of all Federal prisoners are illegal aliens" (United States Congress, House, September 25, 1996).[28]

The *Sourcebook of Federal Sentencing Statistics*, a publication that is issued yearly by the U.S. Sentencing Commission, indicates that these last statements are mere fabrications.[29] The 1996 yearbook demonstrates that 11,372 of the 41,608 individuals who were sentenced to a federal prison term between October 1, 1995, and September 30, 1996, were noncitizens. In other words, 27.3 percent of the newly sentenced inmates were not U.S. citizens. Since the U.S. Sentencing Commission does not collect data on inmates' legal status, the noncitizen category includes legal permanent residents, temporary visa holders, as well as undocumented immigrants. It is thus simply impossible to make a definitive statement about the percentage of "illegal aliens" in federal prisons. In addition to circulating this blatant misinformation, politicians and expert witnesses also omitted another important piece of information: the type of offense that led to people's incarceration. A comparison of the citizen and noncitizen category reveals that there are significant differences in the kind and severity of the offense. With regard to the citizen category, 11,525 (38 percent) of new offenders had been convicted of drug trafficking, 5,151 (17 percent) of fraud, 2,353 (7.8 percent) of firearms violations, and 2,111 (7 percent) of larceny. Noncitizens, on the other hand, were primarily sentenced for drug trafficking (4,611 individuals, or 40.5 percent) and immigration violations (4,436 cases, or 39 percent). Obviously, immigration-related offenses are much more common among noncitizens (a mere 322 U.S. citizens were convicted for these offenses), but they hardly fit the bill of a dangerous criminal who poses a threat to the general public. In addition, U.S. citizens were overrepresented in all the violent crime categories: 97.7 percent of all convicted murderers who served time in a federal prison, 90.6 percent of inmates found guilty of manslaughter, 98.2 percent of sexual offenders, and 91.8 percent of inmates who were found guilty of assault were U.S. citizens.

Contrary to the image presented in these statistics, numerous politicians painted a frightening picture of the criminality of undocumented immigrants. Early on in the debate, Charles E. Schumer (D-NY) proclaimed, "The repeated violence and costly burden of criminal aliens is one of the most vexing problems of our criminal justice system. . . . Here we have tens of thousands of violent criminals, repeat offenders of the worst kind, many of them who entered the country illegally, all of them have forfeited their right to reside here, and yet our system is paralyzed; it doesn't promptly deport these violent criminals" (United States Congress, House, February 23, 1994). Similar statements can be found in nearly every discussion about undocumented immigrants. Two years after this initial hearing, during a debate about the conference report on H.R. 2202, fellow–New Yorker Benjamin A. Gilman (R-NY) praised the immigration bill because it is "directed at these serious threats from criminal aliens, engaged in both the illicit drug trade as well as international terrorism." According to Gilman, Congress has "a strong obligation in protecting our citizens from illegal criminal aliens, who prey on them with drugs and other crime-related activity" (United States Congress, House, September 25, 1996). What is particularly interesting about Gilman's statement is the fact that he juxtaposes dangerous undocumented workers with innocent U.S. citizens who need to be protected. This type of rhetoric not only ignores the aforementioned statistical evidence but also fails to acknowledge that undocumented immigrants are often victims as well.[30]

In light of these alarmist statements, it is hardly surprising that the 104th Congress extended the definition of an "aggravated felony" for immigrant offenders, created special removal procedures, and severely limited the individual liberties and legal rights of noncitizens. Evidence suggests that Congress based their decisions on faulty statistics and one-sided representations. However, it is no coincidence that Congress did not make an effort to gain access to more reliable statistics and better-informed expert witnesses. Under the actuarial logic of the neoliberal state, which sought to develop a "rational" reward system for particularly deserving individuals, it was much more important to create a system that would protect U.S. society from all "criminal aliens," regardless of their actual number and the crimes they had committed or were likely to commit. On January 9, 1995, Toby Roth (R-WI) summarized this underlying logic in the following words: "I hope we can all agree that there is no place in this country for people who come here and commit serious crimes. Criminals are one commodity we do not need to import" (United States Congress, Senate, January 9, 1995). While this assessment was certainly correct—and I think it is self-evident that every nation would like to protect itself from violent criminals—the implications were highly problematic.

Roth, for example, claimed that there was only one effective solution to this problem. According to him, "our Federal criminal alien deportation laws . . . set out an irrational, lengthy and overly complex process that prevents us from deporting criminals as rapidly as we should be." As a result, he introduced the Criminal Alien Control Act of 1995 (S. 179), which "simplifies existing law by eliminating the confusing array of crimes for which criminal aliens are deportable. Under my legislation, any alien who commits any felony is deportable—period" (United States Congress, Senate, January 9, 1995). While Representative Toby Roth (R-WI) was probably more concerned about the fact that his bill would be tough on criminals, a strategy that would prove popular with many voters, there was a clear neoliberal subtext to his argument. Consistent with the neoliberal objective to streamline governmental procedures and reduce federal spending, Roth's bill eliminated the lengthy appeal process, removed all forms of discretionary relief, and eradicated the distinctions between violent criminals who posed a public threat and individuals who had been convicted of minor, nonviolent offenses such as fraud, tax evasions, forgery, and immigration-related offenses.[31] Since all these individuals had forfeited their opportunity to develop into valuable assets to U.S. society, they were undesirable and had proven that they were undeserving of rights and protections that were routinely awarded to U.S. citizens.[32]

Even though the 104th Congress eventually passed a very restrictive law, there was a vocal minority that was strongly opposed to these provisions. In particular, several Democrats disagreed with the idea of connecting antiterrorist stipulations to widespread concerns about rising crime rates in general and extending invasive measures to all noncitizens, especially since there was no proven connection between terrorists and "regular" criminals. Joseph R. Biden (D-DE), for instance, challenged the common perception that the law should make a distinction between citizens and noncitizens and limit immigrants' access to basic rights and legal protections. On May 25, 1995, he declared, "My lord, I do not want to be part of anything that establishes that kind of Star Chamber proceeding. Technically, they may be right; philosophically, it is dead wrong" (United States Congress, Senate, May 25, 1995). A few days later, Russ Feingold (D-WI) warned his colleagues, "In the haste to respond to a national tragedy, we may be making mistakes that will be difficult to undo. . . . Suddenly, habeas reform has become a tool for fighting terrorism. I find that a stretch of the imagination. What we have is a classic, political move to get another agenda wrapped into an emotionally charged, moving vehicle" (United States Congress, Senate, June 7, 1995). Ultimately, the opponents of these restrictive provisions were unable to gather sufficient support. Since convicted criminals were not exactly sympathetic figures, several politicians tried to remind Congress that this bill had much broader implications and that friends and families would be affected as well.[33] At the end of the day, however, these appeals to fairness, equality, and compassion were fruitless and Congress decided that they "should err on the side of protecting America, not the convenience of foreign nationals" (Olympia Snowe [R-ME], United States Congress, Senate, June 7, 1995).[34]

Even though, on a factual level, concerns about rising crime rates, anxieties about foreign terrorists, and widespread opposition toward undocumented immigrants were separate issues, the discourse about immigration reform tended to conflate these three problems. Whereas neoliberal reform initiatives tried to adapt the legal immigration system in such a way that it met the demands of the U.S. economy and excluded those few individuals who had supposedly little potential to develop into law-abiding, hardworking members of society, the proposed treatment of undocumented immigrants took the opposite approach. Instead of identifying the few undesirable subjects, Congress created a scenario that portrayed all undocumented immigrants as potential criminals and terrorists. According to this dominant logic, undocumented immigrants had already proven that they were willing to break the law and disregard the rules and demands of U.S. society. Because they had violated immigration laws, "illegal aliens" were described as a risk group that needed to be monitored and, if necessary, excluded.

Economic Considerations: Immigrants' Impact on the U.S. Labor Market

As the previous sections have demonstrated, congressional debates in 1995–96 criminalized undocumented workers in a number of ways. Not only did Congress describe undocumented immigrants as criminals who had deliberately violated U.S. immigration laws; the discourse also intertwined—and sometimes even conflated—concerns about crime, terrorism, and illegal immigration. From the very beginning of the legislative period, Congress put a pronounced emphasis on the role of "criminal aliens"—a small fragment of the illegal immigrant population that had committed crimes other than overstaying a visa or crossing the border without a permit. Once the discourse had established both that undocumented immigrants had disregarded immigration laws and that a certain portion of that population was also incarcerated for other crimes, it became increasingly difficult to discuss undocumented immigrants in more positive terms. Throughout the 104th Congress, debates about undocumented immigrants were almost exclusively framed as an effort to control a problem population, which should be excluded from the rewards the neoliberal state had to offer to those responsible individuals who played by the rules.

Throughout these debates, Congress was particularly concerned about illegal border crossers. While those with expired visas caused a certain degree of anxiety and were sometimes mentioned in passing, poor and uneducated Mexicans and South Americans were usually perceived to be the real threat. Therefore, numerous politicians deemed it necessary to increase the number of border control officers, erect physical barriers, and install high-tech surveillance technology to prevent these undesirable individuals from crossing the border without proper documentation. However, this type of selective enforcement, which only targeted a fraction of the undocumented immigrant population, was not met with unanimous approval. The opponents of these enforcement-only measures were concerned about the racist implications of this approach. Jerrold Nadler (D-NY), for example, was convinced that H.R. 2202 was "more responsive to hysteria and prejudice than to reason and fact. Let there be no mistake: This Nation has every right and obligation to control our borders and to enforce our immigration laws. But absurd boondoggles, like building a giant fence . . . and good old-fashioned Xenophobia have nothing to do with legitimate protection of our borders" (United States Congress, House, March 19, 1996). In addition, numerous politicians pointed out that increased border control efforts would have no effect on visa over-stayers, who were much more likely to be non-Hispanic whites and Asians than undocumented border crossers.[35]

Several politicians thus argued that the United States needed to develop a reliable and convenient employment verification system that allowed employers to check on applicants' work authorization. Since employment opportunities represented one of the main attractions for undocumented immigrants, Congress believed that these workers would refrain from entering the United States if they could not expect to find an employer who was willing to hire them.[36] Undoubtedly, employment was one of the major factors that needed to be considered in the immigration reform discourse. At the same time, however, employment was also one of the most controversial topics that divided Congress in several clearly distinguishable fractions. This division was not only based on politicians' conflicting beliefs about the labor market and the proper form of governmental regulation; it was also connected to the fact that many individuals, businesses, and entire sectors had benefited immensely from the presence of large numbers of low-wage workers who did not enjoy any effective legal protections.

In contrast to the debate about "criminal aliens" and welfare recipients, where it was relatively easy to vilify undocumented immigrants, the discourse about employment options was more nuanced. While congressional debates had created an image that portrayed undocumented immigrants as an undesirable underclass of poor and uneducated individuals who were prone to crime and unlikely to develop into responsible neoliberal subjects, politicians were also aware of the fact that their constituencies were, in many cases, dependent on this cheap and flexible labor force. In addition, protectionist policies, which categorically excluded large numbers of foreign workers, were difficult to reconcile with a neoliberal agenda that, in theory, favored the globalization of trade as well as labor.

Interestingly, the debate about immigration reform in the mid-1990s failed to make meaningful connections between the recent passage of the North American Free Trade Agreement (NAFTA) and its impact on migration. This reluctance to link free trade to labor migration mirrored the earlier decision not to discuss the potential opening of the U.S.–Mexico border to people as well as commerce. When the United States, Canada, and Mexico first began negotiating a trade agreement in the late 1980s, this stirred up a good deal of controversy in the United

States. While free trade proponents immediately embraced the idea of a trade agreement between the three neighboring countries, a coalition of organized labor, environmentalist groups, and politicians who feared that firms would relocate their business to Mexico opposed the deal. Some of these NAFTA opponents questioned the commonly held belief that a trade agreement would keep jobs and workers in Mexico and would thus help to prevent future migration. Instead, they argued that the passage of a free trade agreement necessitated more restrictive immigration laws that would force the Mexican government to prevent their citizens from migrating north in pursuit of better jobs and higher wages.

The neoliberal logic that sustained free trade "might call for a breaking down of immigration barriers among the member nations, thereby facilitating a freer flow of labor" (Johnson 1993–94, 955). However, Kevin Johnson's research demonstrates that the political climate in the United States did not allow for such a move. The popular consensus in the United States in the early 1990s called for stricter immigration reform measures that would curb illegal immigration and increase border control measures. To complicate matters even further, U.S. and Mexican interests were diametrically opposed when it came to the issue of labor migration. "Political exigencies in the United States demanded provisions limiting illegal immigration from Mexico. Mexico, however, indirectly benefits from the migration of some of its poorest citizens" (Johnson 1993–94, 958). If Congress had tried to discuss immigration in the context of free trade, they would have jeopardized the passage of NAFTA. Instead, NAFTA authorized all three member nations to take steps necessary to curb immigration. According to Article 1607, "no provision of this Agreement shall impose any obligation on a Party regarding its immigration measures" (Article 1607, NAFTA).

Three years later, U.S. politicians were no closer to advocating for an open border policy and applying the free trade logic to migration. Since debates about NAFTA had already successfully disconnected issues of free trade from concerns about migration, the immigration reform discourse in 1995–96 continued this trend and refrained from a potentially messy discussion of the effects that NAFTA had had on illegal immigration. An analysis of congressional debates demonstrates that the issue of free trade was hardly ever mentioned. Quite to the contrary, the discourse reinforced a deeply held stereotype that had informed immigration reform matters for decades—the idea that Mexicans migrate north because in Mexico they are forced to live in substandard conditions and work for extremely low wages. The more recent reasons behind these dramatic differences in the standard of living (e.g., NAFTA and the devaluation of the Mexican Peso) were not discussed.

Instead of engaging in this larger and much more complex debate, politicians narrowly focused on U.S. interests and tried to justify two seemingly conflicting objectives: convince the public that their measures were tough on crime and welfare abuse, while ensuring that labor-intensive sectors—such as agriculture—would have easy access to a continued supply of cheap labor. As the following analysis will demonstrate, politicians argued that U.S. immigration policies should try to maximize the positive effects of labor migration, while eliminating the risks associated with admitting millions of undocumented workers who were not screened for their potential. In accordance with the larger neoliberal project, politicians thus developed a number of different economically profitable suggestions that would enable businesses to hire unskilled, low-wage workers for a limited period of time. While some politicians suggested that employers should try to rely on unemployed U.S. citizens, others claimed that it would be necessary to import these laborers from other countries. Even though there seemed to be an overwhelming consensus that these individuals were not suitable candidates for full membership in a neoliberal state, several reform proposals acknowledged that it might be beneficial to turn the current population of undocumented workers into *temporary* laborers. Other discursive strands about crime and welfare abuse had already established that it would be irrational to reward these undeserving individuals with access to legalization and the benefits associated with legal permanent residency and, eventually, citizenship. Hence temporary work permits seemed to represent a rational response that would undoubtedly further neoliberal objectives.

Even though the discourse about undocumented immigrants as laborers was far from positive, it was certainly less accusatory than other discursive strands. This was also one of the rare instances where politicians acknowledged that undocumented immigrants were not the only ones who should be blamed for the current situation. Even some of the most outspoken critics of undocumented workers, such as Marge Roukema (R-NJ), admitted, "Illegal immigrants may be the lawbreakers in this equation, but U.S. employers are often their accomplices, turning a blind eye and deaf ear to the issue" (United States Congress, House, May 24,

1995).[37] Congress had no illusions about the fact that some unscrupulous employers knowingly hired undocumented immigrants. Expert witness Michael Fix testified that, in many cases, domestic workers were not even asked for a work permit, and Robert L. Bach, the executive associate commissioner of the INS, made it very clear that some of the fake documents were so poorly made that any layperson would be able to determine that those papers were not legitimate.[38]

Despite these expert testimonies, however, some politicians continued to defend employers. Restaurant-owner Sonny Bono (R-CA), for example, felt that employers were the real victims of the proposed employment verification system. He emphatically asked, "Why us? . . . Why do I have to deal with all this and why am I the bad guy? I don't want to be a bad guy. . . . All I want to do is sell pasta" (United States Congress, House, March 30, 1995). On a similar note, Ed Bryant (R-TN) proclaimed that "the majority of U.S. employers make every effort to ensure that they are complying with the law." If they accidentally hired an undocumented worker, it was not their fault. In this opening statement, Bryant also defended the common practice of performing selective background checks on Asian American and Latino workers. He argued that "after having the wool pulled over his or her eyes a few times by an illegal immigrant masquerading as a legal citizen, you can begin to understand why an employer might tend to discriminate against those who fit the profile of an illegal immigrant" (United States Congress, House, March 3, 1995). In an interesting twist on the widespread concern about discriminatory hiring practices, Bryant implied that the immigrants themselves—and not the biased employers— were to blame for this situation.

Additionally, a bipartisan coalition from rural states such as Idaho, Oregon, Washington, North Dakota, Arkansas, and Georgia insisted that many agribusinesses were unable to attract documented immigrants and U.S. citizen workers. According to Representative Mac Collins (R-GA), the reason for this shortage of farm labor was obvious: "until we break the cycle of dependency on the Federal Government, there will continue to be a great need for seasonal agricultural labor."[39] His colleague Jack Kingston (R-GA) agreed with this assessment and added that "in Glennville, GA, a small town in the First District that I represent, an onion farmer told me recently that he pays $9 an hour for people to pick Vidalia onions, but he cannot get Americans to do the work because they make too much money enjoying the public largesse that we call welfare reform" (United States

Congress, House, March 21, 1996). Undocumented immigrants, on the other hand, had not yet been corrupted by the welfare state and were thus still willing to do hard physical labor for low wages. Therefore, undocumented farm workers were sometimes portrayed as the ideal neoliberal subjects. They were eager to accept any job that was being offered, flexible about moving from one position to the next, and even more important, ineligible for all forms of long-term assistance. Due to these undeniable qualities, these mostly Mexican farm workers were perceived as economically desirable.

Representatives from farming states also believed that U.S. agribusinesses would not be internationally competitive without the cheap labor provided by undocumented workers.[40] Since agriculture was the biggest industry in many parts of the country, representatives from these regions were adamant that Congress needed to listen to their concerns and protect this sector from an uncertain future. According to these politicians, agriculture's needs were a top priority. Senator Ron Wyden (D-OR), for example, argued, "first, we have to make sure that the U.S. agriculture industry is internationally competitive, and second, we have to make sure that American farm workers are not displaced by foreign workers" (United States Congress, Senate, April 29, 1996).[41] Wyden was not convinced that higher wages and welfare reform measures that forced recipients to work would solve this problem. He argued, "We have to be realistic that if we want to keep a competitive agricultural industry, these temporary, seasonal jobs are never going to make a person a millionaire; these jobs are always going to involve tough, physical labor, and they most likely aren't going to be filled by out-of-work engineers" (United States Congress, Senate, April 29, 1996). Realistically speaking, agriculture and several other labor-intensive sectors needed a cheap and easily exploitable workforce to generate the same high revenues into the future.

While Congress unanimously agreed that the U.S. government had a vested interest in keeping U.S. agriculture competitive, they were split over the ideal solution. As part of the neoliberal reform package, subsidies and other protectionist interventions were out of the question. Instead, Congress needed to find a way to create a flexible system that would regulate itself without much further governmental involvement. Yet in contrast to the widespread practice of hiring cheap workers without a work permit, this system should be officially authorized and there should also be a strict procedure to dispose of those workers who were no longer needed. For many politicians, a guest-worker program represented the ideal solution.

On March 21, 1996, Richard W. Pombo (R-CA) thus introduced the "Temporary Agricultural Worker Amendments of 1996," which established a new temporary visa category for unskilled agricultural workers (H-2B visas). According to the Pombo Amendment, agribusinesses would be allowed to petition for foreign workers after they established that they had been unable to hire an "able, willing, and qualified United States worker." Employers had to pay "not less than the prevailing wage for similarly employed workers." However, the Pombo Amendment clarified that this provision "does not require an employer to pay by the method of pay in which the prevailing rate is expressed" (United States Congress, House, March 21, 1996). In other words, employers were allowed to pay a piece rate, deduct money for housing expenses, and charge their workers for the food that they received. Even more important, employers had to establish a so-called trust fund to assure that the temporary workers would return to their home countries after their work permit expired. Each employer was expected to withhold 25 percent of the worker's wages. This amount would only be made available to the worker after he had returned to his home country. As an additional insurance against possible problems and additional expenditures, Representative Pombo made it clear that H-2B workers would not be allowed to bring family members, were not eligible for public services, and were even expected to reimburse the government for any emergency medical services that they had received.[42] In short, the Pombo Amendment wanted to make sure that temporary workers did indeed behave like ideal neoliberal subjects who contributed to the system without ever burdening the U.S. taxpayer.[43]

Many politicians were appalled. Even though the majority actually agreed that, without some kind of guest-worker program, H.R. 2202 had the potential to cause a widespread labor shortage for agriculture and certain other sectors, not everyone was prepared to create a new class of disenfranchised workers. Kika de la Garza (D-TX), for example, admitted, "Under ordinary circumstances, I would be interested in supporting an amendment of this nature. . . . But in the spirit in which we are dealing here today, to me it is insulting, it is demeaning. These will be indentured servants in the United States of America, indentured to individuals who will withhold under law 25 percent of their pay, maybe or maybe not get housing or be charged for housing or forced to buy it at the ranch store or the company store" (United States Congress, House, March 21, 1996).[44] Howard L. Berman (D-CA) took this rhetoric, which compared guest workers to indentured servants, a step further. In particular, he was concerned with the reasoning behind the guest-worker program. According to Berman, the arguments that had been advanced by Pombo and his supporters "are the same arguments that were given to justify slavery before the Civil War. If we could find American, or in that case, free people, to do the work, we would not need to rely on slaves" (United States Congress, House, March 21, 1996). Hiring cheap unskilled workers, exploiting them for a short period of time, and discharging them as soon as the seasonal work was done, might be economically sensible, but for Berman it was an improper way for a wealthy First World nation to treat workers.

Several politicians felt that Pombo had taken the neoliberal logic a step too far. Ed Pastor (D-AZ), for example, believed that "the motive . . . is greed. That is the motive, greed. Right now with undocumented people, we are keeping the wages on the fields low. Once they are gone, we want to bring in guest workers to keep the wages low. It is greed" (United States Congress, House, March 21, 1996). However, the majority of Pombo's opponents tried to prove that his amendment was in direct violation of some of the most important facets of the neoliberal reform project. These representatives were particularly troubled by the fact that the Pombo Amendment encouraged the government to privilege one specific sector—agriculture—without affording the same rights and opportunities to other struggling industries. Esteban Edward Torres (D-CA) was not alone in his belief that agribusinesses had been the driving force behind this amendment. Torres claimed that "agribusinesses want to circumvent the market system by carving out a giant government loophole in the immigration system. . . . Instead of allowing them to bring in foreign workers with virtually no rights, agricultural employers should turn to market methods for recruiting American workers" (United States Congress, House, March 21, 1996). Other politicians added that a guest-worker program was inappropriate not only because it showed partiality toward the agricultural sector but also because this kind of government intervention was in violation of the free market doctrine. According to Thomas M. Barrett (D-WI), it was "ironic that the proponents of this program who are pushing so hard do not want to rely on the time-tested notion of using the free market. This is a capitalistic society. If there is a shortage of workers . . . pay them more. Pay them more money, and they will come" (United States Congress,

House, March 21, 1996). In an effort to illustrate that these protectionist measures were inconsistent with the neoliberal rhetoric about free markets, Representatives Torres and Barrett actually turned the Republican free-market doctrine against them and argued that Republican reform proposals had violated their own free-market agenda.

In addition, numerous politicians felt that Pombo's eagerness to import 250,000 unskilled workers called the entire reform process into question.[45] For the last year and a half, Congress had attempted to find ways to reduce the number of immigrants in general and unskilled workers in particular. By March 1996, Congress had finally reached a point where the majority was ready to sign off on a costly reform bill. The Pombo Amendment rendered all these anticipated expenditures moot. After all, it made little economic sense to spend billions of dollars on border enforcement only to develop an expensive guest-worker program that would bring in the same people the INS was trying to keep out.[46]

On top of this questionable cost–benefit ratio, the Pombo Amendment also cast a damning light on politicians' ulterior motives and made them look hypocritical. Earl Pomeroy (D-ND), for example, voiced the following criticism: "There have been some in favor of immigration reform that want to have it both ways: Crack down on immigration, triple fence the border, but by golly, do not disrupt our ability to get that cheap supply of unskilled labor up from south of the border. They want to have it both ways, but you cannot have it both ways" (United States Congress, House, March 21, 1996).[47] Many politicians were also concerned what their electorate might think about this debate. George Miller (D-CA) believed that "this amendment must be rejected because it simply is ludicrous on its face. The American public watching this debate must wonder if we have lost our minds" (United States Congress, House, March 21, 1996). After a long, contentious debate, the majority thus decided that a guest-worker program did not represent the ideal solution to the anticipated labor shortage in certain industries.[48]

Conclusion

Even though the discourse about undocumented immigrants was inextricably linked with the debate about legal immigration reform, both of these discursive strands were characterized by different concerns and a different type of rhetoric. Even more important, politicians made a concerted effort to portray documented and undocumented immigrants as not only fundamentally different but also fierce competitors for the same jobs and benefits. In 1996, Congress passed a neoliberal reform package that reorganized the immigration system in such a way that it would conform to economic objectives. With regard to legal immigrants, however, Congress was careful to justify these reform measures with a positive-sounding rhetoric about historical commitments and family values. Undocumented immigrants, on the other hand, were not treated with the same kind of respect and understanding. For the most part, Congress did not hesitate to express their negative perceptions of undocumented immigrants in the most extreme terms. Throughout the debate, politicians described undocumented immigrants as welfare freeloaders, lawbreakers, dangerous criminals, terrorists, and public health risks. In short, undocumented immigrants were consistently characterized as an unassimilable, undesirable underclass.

Yet as the last section illustrated, unauthorized workers also filled jobs that many Americans were unwilling to do. Not only did immigrants' hard physical labor for extremely low wages allow agribusinesses to thrive; many of these workers had also paid taxes, purchased goods, and helped to boost the economy. In many ways, unauthorized workers thus represented ideal neoliberal subjects. When discussing potential employment verification systems and guest-worker programs, Congress thus faced a dilemma: On the one hand, politicians had developed an intricate rhetoric that criminalized undocumented workers and explained why the U.S. government had a vested interest in excluding these individuals who were supposedly unfit to become full-fledged members of the neoliberal state. If Congress wanted to remain true to their word and reduce the population of undocumented immigrants, they needed to consider a combination of different enforcement mechanisms, instead of solely focusing on border enforcement. On the other hand, Congress was also very well aware of the fact that agribusinesses and other labor-intensive industries would be extremely discontented if immigration reform eliminated their cheap labor force. Even though the Immigration Reform Act of 1986 had already established penalties for employers who violated immigration laws, the INS had rarely enforced these provisions, and the business lobby intended to keep it that way.

In the end, Congress caved in to these concerns. Yet instead of passing the Pombo Amendment, which would have taken the neoliberal reform project to its logical extreme, Congress chose a different route. The conference report on H.R. 2202 decreased employer sanctions and made it even more difficult to take legal action against companies who hired unauthorized workers. By establishing a new "intent standard," which required the state attorney to prove that a company had *knowingly* hired a person who did not possess the necessary work permit, Congress effectively created a new loophole for the business community. In light of these provisions, it is difficult to believe that the 104th Congress was truly committed to reducing the number of undocumented immigrants.

Yet even though the discourse about undocumented immigrants did not produce coherent reform measures that were committed to reducing the total number of undocumented workers, Congress did actually pass a bill that furthered the neoliberal reform agenda, while satisfying their constituencies. Throughout the legislative period, politicians created an image that made it very clear that undocumented Mexican, Central, and South American border crossers represented the real problem population. These individuals were portrayed as criminals, public health risks, and a threat to those law-abiding U.S. citizens who happened to live close to the U.S.–Mexico border. People staying on expired visas, who were much more likely to be non-Hispanic whites and Asians, were not targeted in the same fashion. Without explicitly talking about race, Congress eventually managed to pass a reform measure that selectively targeted Latinos through increased border control. Many voters were thus convinced that the new immigration law, which eliminated legal protections and mandated the creation of highly visible border control efforts, would effectively exclude risk groups such as Muslim terrorists and Latino criminals, while continuing the economically profitable practice of labor migration.

4

Manufacturing the Crisis

Encoded Racism in the Daily Press

In November 1996, Annette Ha of San Leandro, California, sat down to express her growing frustration with the "hysterical, mean-spirited scapegoating" that informed political debates and media representations of immigrants (*San Francisco Chronicle* [*SFC*], November 9, 1996). In a letter to the *San Francisco Chronicle*, she wrote,

> I am an immigrant. According to many opponents of immigration who have received extensive coverage in the media: I am lazy; I refuse to speak English; I suck up welfare benefits; I am ungrateful; I am violent; I am uneducated. Basically, I contribute nothing to this country while taking much away from it. In reality, I am none of these things. I'm a college student. I follow the laws. I pay my taxes. . . . Unfortunately, I and millions of other law-abiding immigrants get lumped together in a faceless horde upon which American [*sic*] can place blame for any and all social and economic problems. (*SFC*, November 9, 1996)

Instead of repeating the same stereotypical images, groundless accusations, and xenophobic attitudes, Annette Ha argued, politicians and journalists need to make a conscious effort to foster a debate that was "rooted in rationality, common sense and compassion" (*SFC*, November 9, 1996). Ha was not alone in her call for a more rational and evenhanded immigration discourse. By November 1996, newspapers across the nation had received a surge of letters and editorials that condemned the growing anti-immigrant climate.

At the same time, news media representations oftentimes reinforced negative perceptions of immigrants in general and undocumented workers in particular. In the aforementioned letter to the editor, Annette Ha used herself as an example to demonstrate that the ubiquitous anti-immigrant rhetoric was one-sided and, at least in her case, incorrect. As a tax-paying, law-abiding naturalized citizen, she was offended that the mainstream media frequently equated people like herself with the "faceless horde" of undocumented immigrants who had somehow failed to reach a similar level of personal achievement. To correct these common misperceptions and distinguish people like herself from less successful immigrants, Ha called for "a national study" and "real statistics" to produce "firm, unbiased numbers" (*SFC*, November 9, 1996).

As part of a concerted effort to decrease public expenditures, many experts tried to determine if immigrants represented a drain on the economy and the welfare system. Their methodology identified "risk factors" such as age, family status, education level, and financial assets, which could be used to predict an individual's chances of developing into a net contributor to American society. Based on these criteria, many studies identified Latin American immigrants as a problem population. Due to the fact that this classification was backed up by statistical data, the results were commonly accepted as impartial and nondiscriminatory. Even Annette Ha, who was adamant in her claim that not all immigrants represented a drain on the economy, never questioned the underlying belief that it was not only possible but also desirable to identify and punish those immigrants who had failed to live up to the neoliberal ideal of an active citizen who seeks to invest in his or her abilities and conduct his or her life as an enterprise. Ultimately, Ha's rhetoric validated the general tendency to blame immigrants for their poverty and to downplay the importance of larger structural factors.

In *Brown Tide Rising*, linguist Otto Santa Ana demonstrates that texts like Annette Ha's letter to the editor were characteristic of anti-immigrant discourse in the mid-1990s. His analysis of *Los Angeles Times* coverage between 1992 and 1998 revealed that immigrants from Latin American countries were commonly equated with dangerous waters (tide, flood, wave, etc.), described as animal-like, as invaders, as a disease, or as a threat to America's national identity. Even articles that explicitly condemned racism, xenophobia, and meanspirited anti-immigrant measures—like Ha's letter to the editor—tended to employ the same types of metaphors. They thus reinforced the public's negative perceptions of immigrants and left deep-seated stereotypes and anxieties unchallenged. According to Santa Ana, it is important to acknowledge that "these metaphors are not merely rhetorical flourishes, but are the key components with which the public's concept of Latinos is edified, reinforced, and articulated" (Santa Ana 2002, xvi).

In contrast to Santa Ana's analysis, my study of mainstream newspapers will extend beyond the scope of studying metaphors. Even though I agree with his assessment that "everyday metaphor . . . is a crucial measure of the way that public discourse articulates and reproduces societal dominance relations," I argue that his focus on the ubiquity of dangerous water, animal, and disease metaphors misses the more subtle strategies that make this discourse so powerful (Santa Ana 2002, 21). In particular, my analysis will demonstrate that the neoliberal discourse on immigration of the mid-1990s created a new, seemingly raceless way of talking about immigrants, while drawing on earlier overtly racist discourses. Journalists at respectable mainstream newspapers made a conscious effort to appear nondiscriminatory and frame immigration reform measures as necessary attempts to make a costly system more economically efficient. Although I agree with Santa Ana's claim that "contemporary U.S. public discourse on minority communities is oppressive," I will demonstrate how the media discourse disguised its racist effects by mostly refraining from the personalized attacks and overt racism that characterized earlier immigration discourses (Santa Ana 2002, 11).

Instead, the immigration reform discourse of the mid-1990s was based on the belief that neoliberal reform measures are "the key to a postracist world of freedom and opportunity" (Melamed 2011, 42). In contrast to earlier liberal notions of race, which insisted that racism was primarily a moral issue that could be overcome by educating white people and dispelling prejudiced beliefs, neoliberal discourse presented a very different solution. It was no longer deemed necessary to confront biases and develop state interventions into racial inequality. According to neoliberal discourse, race had ceased to be a meaningful determinant for success and failure; a person's status in society was the logical result of his or her ability and eagerness to abide by the rules of the free market. This image of the United States as a postracist society was buttressed by stories about particularly successful immigrants of color, such as wealthy Asian businessmen acting as "global citizens" or young Muslim immigrant women who adhere to U.S. standards of beauty, happily consume luxury goods, and enjoy their newfound freedom.

The discourse drew a sharp distinction between the beneficiaries of neoliberal reforms, who are valued as "multicultural, reasonable, law-abiding, and good global citizens," and the dispossessed, who are devalued "as monocultural, backward, weak, and irrational—unfit for global citizenship because they lack proper neoliberal subjectivity" (Melamed 2011, 44). Within this framework, it appears perfectly logical for governments to treat populations differently, depending on their worth and their ability to act like proper neoliberal subjects. This approach is supposedly not racist—even if some racial groups benefit more than others—but it will eventually teach everyone to exercise their economic freedom and act as rational consumers. Privatization and market-like structures are thus lauded as inherently antiracist and ideally suited to redistribute resources and reward proper behavior (Melamed 2011). By drawing attention away from structural inequalities and highlighting individual deficiencies, neoliberal discourse deracializes inequality.

This chapter and chapter 5 will examine the mainstream media discourse on immigration and immigrants in 1995 and 1996—the same years as the congressional debates analyzed in the first two chapters. My analysis will focus on three major newspapers: the *New York Times, San Francisco Chronicle*, and *Houston Chronicle*. This chapter looks at the way the mainstream media discourse, as exemplified in the *New York Times, Houston Chronicle*, and *San Francisco Chronicle*, interacted with the congressional discourse. Chapter 5 will focus on the use of human-interest stories and the role that these stories played in the larger discourse. In the first section of this chapter, I will look at the media coverage of immigrants' access to public education and the controversy over immigrant-specific programs such as bilingual education. Since this discursive strand was explicitly concerned with federal as well as local policies, articles oftentimes contained an explicit commentary on congressional debates and local politicians' opinions. In addition, the education controversy represents a prime example of the neoliberal logic that was used to disguise the power relation that underlay the deployment of these policies and the social inequalities that would be produced by these seemingly impersonal reform measures. The second section will examine the media discourse about racism, discrimination, and the role of language. I will show how several editorial pieces provided a thoughtful analysis of the immigration discourse and, in some cases, explicitly criticized politicians' anti-immigrant rhetoric. The chapter concludes with an examination of the media backlash against a local politician who neglected to frame her anti-immigrant sentiments in racially neutral terms.

The Immigration Discourse in Different Local Contexts

According to Otto Santa Ana, discourses are deeply grounded in "the articulated social order to which people are normally oblivious" (Santa Ana 2002, 18). In the context of immigration, most Americans believed that it was common sense that the United States protect its border and select only the best and the brightest immigrants. Even though there were conflicting suggestions for how exactly the U.S. government should translate these fundamental beliefs into public policy, the discourse rarely questioned the general validity of these commonsense beliefs. Michel Foucault has discussed this basic understanding of the social order as the discursive production of "truth."[1] According to Foucault, a society's fundamental beliefs about the social order are linked in a circular relation with the discourse itself. Hence there is an inherent connection between truth, power, and discourse. Foucault wrote, "There are manifold relations of power which permeate, characterize and constitute the social body, and these relations of power cannot themselves be established, consolidated nor implemented without the production, accumulation, circulation and functioning of a discourse. There can be no possible exercise of power without a certain economy of discourses of truth which operates through and on the basis of this association" (Foucault 1980, 93). Foucault's work shows how historically specific bodies of knowledge are produced and circulated. Importantly, political practice cannot simply overthrow these established "truths"; it only invests them with new meanings, cites new evidence, and produces new connections. Practices of government are not simply informed by specific bodies of knowledge, but governments use discourse as a technology of power that categorizes, manages, and shapes subjectivities.

While Foucault was primarily concerned with the production of truth in specific historical contexts, such as the development of the French penal system in the early nineteenth century, Nikolas Rose uses Foucault's theories to examine how neoliberalism linked various bodies of knowledge, "integrating them *in thought* so that they appeared to partake in a coherent logic" (Rose 1999, 27). Rose is primarily interested in the larger political rationalities that inform a variety of reform initiatives in the present historical moment. According to Rose, these rationalities can be described as "discursive fields characterized by a shared vocabulary within which disputes can be organized, by ethical principles that can communicate with one another, by mutually intelligible explanatory logics, by commonly accepted facts, by significant agreement on key political problems" (Rose 1999, 28). This neoliberal—or, as Rose labels it, *advanced liberal*—logic seeks to restructure social government along economic lines. Under neoliberalism, the conception of the citizen is transformed. In particular, citizens are expected to behave as consumers. An ideal neoliberal subject "was to conduct his or her life, and that of his or her family, as a kind of enterprise, seeking to enhance and capitalize on existence itself through calculated acts and investments" (Rose 1999, 164).

My analysis of congressional debates applies Nikolas Rose's work on neoliberalism to a specific reform initiative in order to demonstrate how a neoliberal consensus framed the 1995–96 immigration discourse. Not only did politicians make policy recommendations intended to further neoliberal objectives; they also couched their support as well as their opposition to certain provisions in neoliberal terms. In short, policies were desirable if they made the immigration system more economically profitable and undesirable if they privileged immigrants with little potential to develop into self-sufficient neoliberal subjects. Both Democrats and Republicans thus subscribed to the same neoliberal framework and presented their policy suggestions in neoliberal terms (Agrawal 2008; Giddens 1998; Peck and Tickell 2007). Sometimes, this neoliberal logic was backed by a variety of other "truths"—such as the insistence that immigrants adhere to heteronormative family values and the concern about potential threats to our national security—but the underlying neoliberal framework was never explicitly questioned or discussed.

While the mainstream media discourse on immigrants and immigration replicated similar neoliberal arguments, it simultaneously expanded neoliberal logic and made connections to other widely accepted truths and objectives. As one of the most important sources for the public's understanding of politics, the economy, and changing social relations, the news media are expected to produce factual, many-sided, and nondiscriminatory coverage. Highly regarded newspapers like the *New York Times, San Francisco Chronicle*, and *Houston Chronicle*, in particular, are known for their relatively moderate positions. However, newspapers not only provide up-to-date information; they also attempt to package the information in a way that is interesting and entertaining for readers. Events, issues, and political developments that are deemed to be of interest to many readers are thus covered much more extensively than those issues that do not allow for engaging stories.

Not surprisingly, then, mainstream media coverage did not necessarily focus on those aspects of immigration that elicited the most controversial debates in Congress. For instance, even though immigration reform measures received widespread media attention in 1995–96, there was almost no coverage of the controversy over sponsors' escalating financial responsibilities, the restructuring of the family preference category, and the increasingly harsh treatment of "criminal aliens." In contrast, all three papers published dozens of articles, editorials, and special reports about asylum claims by African women who had escaped female genital mutilation—a topic that elicited comparatively little debate in Congress. The U.S. media thus actively participated in the process of framing the immigration reform debate and shaping public opinion.

As discussed earlier, politicians tend to frame social problems in such a way that fits their political agenda. The most attractive policy suggestions punish powerless people who are already depicted in a negative way and have little control over the political agenda. According to political scientists Anne Schneider and Helen Ingram, "negative social constructions make it likely that these groups will often receive burdens even when it is illogical from the perspective of policy effectiveness" (Schneider and Ingram 1993, 337). For example, denying undocumented students access to higher education opportunities thus makes political sense even though it is highly unlikely that this policy would either save money in the long run or even reduce the number of undocumented immigrants in the United States. As long as politicians package these measures as a way to protect vulnerable U.S. citizen students and offer them privilege over a group of students that has been constructed as undeserving and outside of the national community, voters will most likely support these anti-immigrant measures.

Similar to politicians' concerns about voter demands, mainstream media outlets are concerned about their consumers. They organize information to meet their readers' interests and political opinions and produce a paper that informs and entertains at the same time. Legalistic debates about the restructuring of the family preference system would yield little public interest. Graphic descriptions of asylum seekers fleeing from female genital mutilation, on the other hand, make for a much more interesting story. Ultimately, journalists raised the same concerns as Congress: their stories invited readers to think about issues such as personal responsibility, the availability of social services, and adequate risk-management strategies that would help exclude those immigrants who had little potential to develop into contributing members of U.S. society. Even more important, even though most journalists examined different case studies than politicians, their coverage used similar neoliberal frames and reinforced the validity of the underlying neoliberal ideology. The media thus not only influenced public opinion through their selection of newsworthy stories but also helped to shape discourse through the way they presented the stories.

Based on local interests and the readership for each paper, there were considerable regional variations and stylistic differences between the three newspapers. As mentioned before, my analysis will focus on the *New York Times, San Francisco Chronicle,* and *Houston Chronicle.* I selected these particular papers because of their locations and their wide circulation. As one of the most widely distributed newspapers in the nation, the *New York Times* reaches a large and comparatively diverse audience across the United States.[2] It is based in New York, the largest city on the East Coast and home to the largest number of immigrants outside of California and Texas. According to the 2000 U.S. Census, metropolitan New York had 9,314,235 inhabitants, 33.7 percent of whom were immigrants from a wide variety of countries. Approximately 23.5 percent of New York City's immigrants came from Asia, 20.2 percent from Europe, 14.1 percent from South America, 8.9 percent from Central America, and 29 percent from the Caribbean. Due to the diverse nature of this immigrant population and to the fact that 42.2 percent of those immigrants had arrived within the last ten years, it was to be expected that the *New York Times* would contain extensive coverage of local and national immigration-related concerns.

In comparison, the immigration coverage in both the *San Francisco Chronicle* and the *Houston Chronicle* had a much more regional focus. The *Houston Chronicle* was selected because it is the local newspaper in Texas's most populous city with the largest and most diverse immigrant population.[3] In contrast to San Antonio and El Paso, where Mexicans constitute, respectively, 73.2 percent and 92.1 percent of the immigrant population, metropolitan Houston is home to almost one million immigrants from all over the world. Even though Mexicans represent the largest proportion (50.6 percent), 12.5 percent of all foreign-born Houstonians migrated from other Central American countries, 21.1 percent are Asian, 5.2 percent are European, and 2.3 percent are of Caribbean descent. A remarkable 48 percent of those immigrants moved to Houston, one of the nation's fastest-growing metropolitan areas, within the previous decade. California, on the other hand, has long served as a destination for immigrants. By 1995, however, California had also experienced a violent backlash against undocumented immigrants—especially those of Mexican descent. Proposition 187, which would have denied undocumented immigrants in California access to public schools and other publicly funded services, and the media frenzy that surrounded its passage in November 1994 made national headlines and continued to influence the immigration discourse in 1995–96. Much of the immigration discourse in Southern California, where Mexican nationals constituted the largest immigrant group by far, was thus focused on the controversy surrounding undocumented immigrants from Mexico.[4] Yet since my analysis is interested in the way that national, racial, gender, and class differences between different immigrant groups informed the discourse, I decided to concentrate on San Francisco, rather than Los Angeles or San Diego.[5] Due to its historical ties with Asia, San Francisco was home to a much more diverse immigrant population than metropolitan areas in the southern part of the state. According to the 2000 U.S. Census, Asians constituted 51.7 percent of the foreign-born population in San Francisco, including 124,511 Chinese, 75,571 Filipinos, and 20,771 Vietnamese immigrants. An additional 14.6 percent of immigrants in San Francisco came from Mexico, 10.6 percent from other Central American countries, and 14.2 percent from Europe.

As the most widely read of the nation's papers of record, the *New York Times* contained the most extensive and varied coverage on immigrants and immigration reform measures. According to a keyword search on LexisNexis, the *New York Times* published more than 2,500 articles, editorials, and letters that dealt with some aspect of immigrants' lives and their impact on U.S. society in a matter of two years (between January 1995 and December 1996). Congressional politics, presidential elections, and candidates' opinions about immigration reform were of particular importance. Not only did the *New York Times* provide factual information about bills and amendments; journalists oftentimes commented on the political discourse itself. The *New York Times* coverage of congressional and presidential politics was not only interested in *what* was said but also in *how* it was said. For example, when Representative John L. Mica

(R-FL) compared welfare recipients to alligators and Barbara Cubin (R-WY) added a story about "the wolf welfare program," the *New York Times* immediately pointed to the fact that "today's debate featured a veritable menagerie of animal imagery" (*New York Times* [*NYT*], March 25, 1995).[6] The *New York Times* also questioned *why* politicians were so keen on taking a tough stance on immigrants and portraying them in such a negative light. Journalists argued that lobbyists and public-opinion polls exerted influence over individual politicians and party platforms. In addition, the *New York Times* coverage showed how politicians focused their efforts on divisive issues, such as immigration reform, to win public approval. On rare occasions, the *New York Times* even commented that political debates were linked to and informed by the media discourse. Interestingly, several politicians participated in the *New York Times* discourse on immigration. Then Governor George W. Bush (R-TX), Senator Joseph E. Lieberman (D-CT), Congressmen Elton Gallegly (R-CA) and Pete Wilson (R-CA), and Jack Kemp, a former Republican representative and housing secretary, authored editorials. Texas Senators Phil Gramm (R-TX) and Kay Bailey Hutchison (R-TX) and Representatives Peter T. King (R-NY), Robert G. Torricelli (D-NJ), and Nydia M. Velázquez (D-NY), among others, wrote letters to the editor.

In addition to this explicit focus on congressional politics, the *New York Times* printed a significant number of articles that showed how immigration and immigrant policies were put into action. The *New York Times* was particularly concerned about immigrants' access to public education, terrorism, and the emergent industry of private detention centers, which were used to detain asylum seekers as well as "criminal aliens." Other topics that received a fair amount of attention in the *New York Times* included human trafficking, cases of involuntary servitude in sweatshops and brothels across the nation, as well as organized crime in certain immigrant communities.

Even though there was a lot of overlap with the immigration-related coverage in the *San Francisco Chronicle* and the *Houston Chronicle*, these two papers set different priorities. Unlike the *New York Times*, which is sold to readers across the United States, the *Houston Chronicle*, in particular, is mostly aimed at readers in the greater Houston area and was thus more interested in Texas-specific concerns and local matters. For example, the Houston Livestock Show and Rodeo's decision to deny noncitizens the right to apply for their scholarship program and a Texan immigration court's refusal to grant political asylum to a group of Sikhs were discussed in dozens of articles. Naturally, border-patrol efforts, the proposed border-crossing fee, and Americans' relationship with their Mexican neighbors warranted extensive coverage in Texas. In addition, the *Houston Chronicle* was concerned about Texas's dependence on immigrant labor. A significant number of articles focused on employment verification efforts, which were usually dismissed as impractical and overly invasive, and on local reactions to the increasing number of day laborers.

The *Houston Chronicle*'s reports on immigrants, even more than the coverage in the other two papers, was also characterized by a fundamental ambivalence. On the one hand, Texans were clearly apprehensive of the influx of poor, unskilled, nonwhite immigrants who used public services and sent their children to public schools. On the other hand, the *Houston Chronicle* also acknowledged that immigrants, even those without work permits, represented an integral part of the local economy and, at least to some extent, the community. The *Houston Chronicle* was much more inclined to support measures that granted amnesty to undocumented workers and allowed low-skilled workers to enter the United States under a new guest-worker program. This seemingly generous position, however, did not necessarily reflect progressive attitudes or journalistic integrity. Instead, it might be read as a probusiness agenda that mitigates an otherwise conservative approach to social issues and welfare policies. In comparison to the *New York Times* and the *San Francisco Chronicle*, the *Houston Chronicle* also contained the highest percentage of human-interest stories about undocumented immigrants and workers who had been legalized under the 1986 Immigration Reform and Control Act. The majority of these articles were sympathetic to their plight while reinforcing the notion that undocumented immigrants represented an unassimilated underclass in American society.

The *San Francisco Chronicle* published comparatively few articles that dealt with immigrants and immigration. In this twenty-four-month period, there were only about five hundred articles, editorials, and letters to the editor. Most of these texts were also significantly shorter and less analytical than the reporting in the two other papers. There were fewer than a dozen human-interest stories about individual immigrants and their families and very few examples of the impact that immigrants had had on local communities. Coverage of congressional debates and legislative changes was brief and factual, with little commentary or additional information. With two noteworthy exceptions—its explicit condemnation of racism and discrimination and its generous attitude toward homosexual immigrants—the *San Francisco Chronicle* rarely took a firm stand on controversial issues. Articles about these two issues, however, contained some important commentary on society's prejudices and the way that these prejudices informed people's attitudes, legislative decisions, and the media discourse on immigration.

Media Coverage of the Education Controversy

By the mid-1990s, many Americans firmly believed that their public education system had reached a crisis point. Parents across the nation complained about overcrowded classrooms, apathetic teachers, and disappointing test scores. Whereas inner-city schools faced the consequences of decades of underfunding, many historically white, middle-class school districts had just started to experience an increasing influx of minority families and reacted with a combination of fear and anger. In Hartford, Connecticut, for example, white parents protested racial balance laws that required schools to become more "integrated" (*NYT*, January 23, 1995); in Aptos, California, wealthy white parents tried to split their school district into two parts, "one 80 percent white and enjoying plenty of elbow room, the other 85 percent minority and severely overcrowded" (*SFC*, January 18, 1996); and in Westbury, Long Island, a frustrated teacher was sent to jail after he had purposely closed the classroom door on a Haitian student, who lost part of his finger in the incident (*NYT*, January 8, 1995). A multitude of similar confrontations and the extensive coverage they received in the local and national news media heightened the sense that there was a widespread education crisis.

Under Keynesian welfare policies, the United States had developed an educational system that was supposed to address social injustice and, at least to a certain extent, redistribute resources and lead to greater social equality. According to the neoliberal political agenda, it had become necessary to examine the effectiveness of this educational system, which was widely regarded as an inefficient bureaucratic structure that was unresponsive to both individual and economic needs (Hursh 2005; Robertson 2000). Instead, neoliberalism stressed the privatization of the public sector—including education—and advocated the development of a market-like educational system that gave individual students and their families more choice. According to Susan Robertson, "parents were constructed as the customers of educational services" (Robertson 2000, 174). By increasing the range of available educational options, this neoliberal logic suggested, we would develop a competitive market-like structure that would enable parents to adequately address their children's needs and improve their quality of education. "Neoliberal policy makers have skillfully packaged the reforms to make it appear that they are promoting equality" (Hursh 2005, 5). In reality, neoliberal governments desire to reduce overall funding for education, but it is highly questionable whether this market-like structure will lead to greater equality for everyone. Recent developments—and the disastrous effects of "No Child Left Behind"— have demonstrated that the neoliberal educational reforms of the last two decades have promoted inequality and further defunded already struggling schools without developing better options for the majority of students in those districts.

In the context of the immigration reform discourse of the mid-1990s, however, blaming parents and immigrant students for overcrowding successfully obscured the effects of funding cuts and education privatization. The mainstream media unanimously agreed that overcrowded schools posed a problem. Based on the testimony of various experts—such as teachers, administrators, and parents—the media constructed an alarmist image of this crisis. Every once in a while, critics questioned whether the severity of the education crisis had been blown out of proportion. Mayor Rudolph W. Giuliani, for instance, told the *New York Times* that "there were misconceptions about school overcrowding in New York City" and admitted that "the number of children without desks was not nearly as substantial as reported by news organizations" (*NYT*, September 15, 1996). Yet, even this type of analysis, which was the rare exception in the larger discourse, did not question the idea that there was indeed a crisis; it only attempted to adjust some relatively minor details. The media took it for granted that the United States was experiencing an education crisis and also agreed that immigrant students represented one of the primary culprits.

By 1995, it was no longer even necessary to provide evidence for these widely accepted "truths." Instead, authors matter-of-factly claimed that "the crunch . . . resulted from a combination of higher birth rates and expanding immigration to the city" (*NYT*, January 31, 1995) and that "enrollment growth, mostly due to immigration, continues to outpace school construction" (*NYT*, September 5, 1995). This factual language seems to leave little room for disagreement and obscures the fact that there is no natural cause-and-effect relation between increasing numbers of immigrant students and overcrowded schools. After all, more residents also meant more tax revenues; more funding for schools; more job opportunities for teachers, administrators, and staff; and an opportunity to create newer and better schools with more foreign-language options. Potentially, everyone could have profited from the newly arrived immigrants.

Yet once a combination of seemingly objective data and expert testimony had established that immigrant students were not an asset but a burden on the nation's school system, the media continued to reinforce this perception with a series of articles about students without desks, classes in stairways, and offices in boys' lavatories. This focus on the most extreme cases of school overcrowding was underlined by alarmist language that routinely described the influx of immigrant students as "surges," "streams," and "floods."[7] According to Otto Santa Ana, who identified similar quotes as "dangerous water" metaphors, this semantic has serious implications: "Treating immigration as dangerous waters conceals the individuality of the immigrants' lives and their humanity. In their place a frightening scenario of uncontrolled movements of water can be played out with *devastating floods and inundating surges* of brown faces" (Santa Ana 2002, 77, his emphasis).

While my sample confirms the claim that water images played an important role in the media coverage of immigrant students, I did not find evidence to substantiate Santa Ana's thesis that these metaphors specifically targeted Latino immigrants. Admittedly, these differences in representation might be, at least in part, based on geographical differences. Since Santa Ana focused exclusively on the *Los Angeles Times*, it is hardly surprising that his data contained more references to Latino immigrants in general and Mexican Americans in particular than the *San Francisco Chronicle* or *New York Times*. However, I contend that Santa Ana's narrow focus on metaphors ultimately prevented him from recognizing the complexity of the immigration discourse, and I believe the mainstream media discourse was much more subtle in its racism than Santa Ana's analysis suggests.

Among other things, Santa Ana's approach cannot account for the frequency in which journalists commented on racial differences quite explicitly, without relying on metaphors. In all three papers, journalists commented on specific nationalities that were described either as "model minorities" or, at the other end of the spectrum, as unprepared and maybe even incapable of succeeding. Not all students were described as part of a faceless and potentially homogeneous "flood" of immigrants; some were described as individuals who were judged by their ability to live up to neo-liberal ideals and invest in their potential and act as responsible neoliberal subjects. *New York Times* writer Doreen Carvajal, for instance, juxtaposed desirable and undesirable immigrant groups: "There are suburban school districts that smoothly absorb immigrants, particularly wealthy students with advanced skills, like many Japanese in Scarsdale or Iranians in Great Neck, L.I. Westbury also had few difficulties with earlier Haitian arrivals, many of whom had been through elite schools in their country. Then came the most recent group, impoverished students from El Salvador or Haiti, who frequently did not know how to read or write in their own languages" (*NYT*, January 8, 1995). Through articles like these, the news media made it clear that it was not immigrant students per se who had caused the current education crisis but lower-class newcomers from Latin America and the Caribbean. Stories about neighborhood conflicts, redistricting efforts, and resistance to bilingual programs focused almost exclusively on students from Mexico, Haiti, the Dominican Republic, and El Salvador. In contrast, positive examples of overachievers and families who were committed to a strong work ethic and willing to invest in their children's education most frequently cited Asian immigrants. The *New York Times*, for example, reported on the flourishing industry of elitist "cram schools," which prepare Asian American students for Ivy League universities (*NYT*, January 28, 1995), and the *Houston Chronicle* published numerous articles on the Houston Livestock Show and Rodeo's new citizenship requirement for their scholarship program, which resulted in the denial of a $10,000 award to an Asian honors student (*Houston Chronicle* [*HC*], March 23, 1996, and April 12, 1996).[8]

While these distinctions reinforced existing racial stereotypes, they also assumed a new function within the emerging neoliberal immigration discourse. Doreen Carvajal's comment, for instance, emphasized the interconnections between nationality, class, and education and the effects these factors had on different communities. In many ways, her portrayal represented a fairly accurate assessment of the social inequalities that characterized the U.S. education system. Due to persistent residential segregation along race and class lines, there were immense funding differences between individual school districts. It is thus hardly surprising that a few well-educated immigrant students coming into wealthy suburban school districts were much easier to deal with than a lot of poorly educated immigrants coming into overcrowded, underfunded inner-city schools.

Yet despite these obvious racial inequalities, the media tended to frame this "problem" in such a way that it understated the importance of race and structural inequalities. In accordance with the larger neoliberal project, Carvajal implied that the "impoverished students from El Salvador or Haiti" had failed to succeed because they were inadequately prepared for the intellectual tasks they were asked to perform. In the context of the larger neoliberal logic, this assessment seemed to make a lot of sense. Supposedly, Asian students succeeded because their parents had ensured that they were on a path to success and received the necessary help—oftentimes in form of "cram schools"—to excel. The parents of students from El Salvador and Haiti, on the hand, failed to make a similar investment in their children's education, and as a result, they could not compete with other, better prepared students. Even though Carvajal mentioned two specific nationalities, her focus on individual merit and lack of schooling disguised the role that social inequalities played in this context, and there was no further analysis of the fact that the unsuccessful students were described as both impoverished and Latino/a.

In contrast, wealthy Iranian and Japanese students were portrayed as particularly desirable because they were equipped with not only skills necessary to succeed but also a particular mind-set that drove them to work even harder. Hence they were seen as deserving of additional resources and support. This positive portrayal was firmly embedded in the larger discursive framework and its understanding of the proper allocation of financial resources. The dominant neoliberal framework required that funds be made available to those people who had the most potential to develop into self-sufficient neoliberal subjects. In other words, the state should invest in those people who would eventually return the investment with considerable interest. The selection of these promising individuals was backed with statistics and scientific research that measured indicators for success. Within this neoliberal logic, selection criteria were commonly described as racially neutral and nondiscriminatory. If certain groups outperformed others, this was not the system's fault but the logical result of a group's superior abilities and efforts.

Even though newspapers sometimes acknowledged that discrimination might play a role in a student's chances for success, these concerns were usually outweighed by the belief in a framework that stressed individual merit over structural factors. The mainstream media's tendency to focus on individual stories discouraged journalists from interrogating the validity of this interpretative frame. Even though special reports and personal testimonies of successful immigrant students were meant to add a human perspective and emphasize some laudable achievements, they had another, much more problematic effect in the context of the larger discourse.[9] By providing a multitude of personal success stories without much reference to the structural factors that had enabled these particular students to thrive, the mainstream media fostered the belief that scholastic performance was only determined by individual merit. By focusing on specific groups, most notably Asian Americans, the news media also validated the existing belief that some groups were more prone to success than others.

Polls demonstrate that many readers already believed that Asian immigrants were less threatening, more successful, and thus ultimately more desirable than Latinos. As part of a special ten-part series about immigrants who had gained amnesty in 1986, for example, the *Houston Chronicle* conducted a series of telephone interviews of 828 adult Texans. The results are interesting on a number of levels. While authors Thaddeus Herrick and James Pinkerton asserted that most Texans had a fairly positive attitude toward immigrants and immigration, they also found that there was a huge gap between Texans' perceptions of Asian and Hispanic immigrants. According to their interviews, "nearly half of all Texans say Hispanics are 'very or extremely likely' to cause higher taxes . . . while one-quarter say the same about Asians. Similarly, Texans are more likely to believe Hispanics, rather than Asians, cause an increase in crime and cause the quality of education to decline" (*HC*, October 20, 1996).[10] Yet, despite these striking differences, Texans did not think of themselves as prejudiced or even racist. To the contrary, the majority portrayed themselves as open minded and welcoming of other cultures. Asked whether the growing number of Hispanics would improve American culture and add positive ideas and customs, for instance, 77.6 percent responded that this was at least somewhat likely.[11]

This type of reasoning is symptomatic of the larger discourse about immigrants and immigration. While American citizens, their elected officials, as well as the media were willing to celebrate diverse cultures and commend the increasing availability of ethnic restaurants, festivals, and music styles, they were much more reluctant to accept fundamental change and translate this abstract appreciation to other areas. Immigrants were expected to *add* their unique contributions to dominant culture, not transform it. Oftentimes, even the most celebratory articles made it clear that immigrants needed to adapt to American culture and adopt "our" customs, traditions, and most importantly, the English language.

One particularly interesting discursive strand focused explicitly on the future of the English language. Encouraged by the widespread anti-immigrant climate, numerous states had started to discuss English-only laws. These laws would declare English the official language, which would have been little more than a symbolic act, but some also contained provisions to terminate bilingual education programs and prevent the publication of official documents in languages other than English.[12] Proponents of these English-only bills justified their proposals with a rhetoric that intertwined economic considerations, assimilationist arguments, and an appeal to many people's fears about a racially, ethnically, and linguistically diverse group of new immigrants. From this perspective, it was not sufficient for immigrants to learn English; they were expected to abandon their own language in the process. The "problem" was not that certain parts of the immigrant population did not make enough of an effort to learn English, but that they continued to use their first languages in their daily interaction with people of their own nationality. To support this view, English-only advocates repeatedly invoked the problematic "melting-pot" metaphor and claimed that the English language served as a "glue" to hold this nation together. Consider the following examples:

1. Most Republicans contended that the United States, a melting-pot nation of immigrants, was becoming dangerously segregated into linguistic ghettos that the federal government increasingly accommodated with documents, ballots, and classes in languages other than English (*NYT*, August 2, 1996).
2. Toby Roth (R-WI) contended that, for generations, immigrants had by choice or necessity learned English and turned the United States into a "melting pot." Now, he says, the United States is turning into a "salad bowl": "We want to keep our nation one nation, one people. . . . We need to keep our commonality, our common glue" (*HC*, September 10, 1995).

3. Bob Dole said, "Insisting that all our citizens are fluent in English is a welcoming act of inclusion, and insist we must. . . . We need the glue of language to help hold us together" (*NYT*, September 5, 1995).

4. A *New York Times* editorial suggested, "Let us adopt a national language law. It will serve as the glue to hold together our culturally and racially diverse society" (*NYT*, November 30, 1995).

These quotes were based on a number of problematic assumptions. On the most basic level, the authors implied that the United States did indeed have an easily identifiable common culture that was holding the nation together and that needed to be protected against foreign influences. Since this was accepted as a "truth" that had been established by related discourses, no one deemed it necessary to provide further explanation. Interestingly, this insistence on a shared culture was not commonly perceived as a racist comment. Even though the context made it fairly clear that these remarks targeted Spanish-speaking immigrants from Central and South America, the neoliberal discourse made a distinction between "racist" comments, which attacked *people* of color, and those remarks that attacked foreign *cultures* and *languages*.

In addition, those people who wanted to preserve Western cultural hegemony were usually in denial that this was essentially an effort to protect white privilege. Presidential candidate Bob Dole (R-KS), for instance, emerged as one of the most outspoken critics of bilingual as well as multicultural education. Quoting his address at the Seventy-Seventh National Convention of the American Legion, the *New York Times* wrote that Dole had called for a stop to "the practice of multilingual education as a means of instilling ethnic pride or as a therapy for low self-esteem or out of elitist guilt over a culture built on the traditions of the West" (*NYT*, September 5, 1995). The article continued: "Somewhat in the same vein, Mr. Dole also condemned history courses that heavily emphasize national shortcomings, particularly past treatment of minorities" (*NYT*, September 5, 1995). Dole's insistence on fairness and balance was a particularly effective strategy to produce racist effects with seemingly neutral language. Dole's comments dismissed his political opponents' efforts to develop a more inclusive and multifaceted history education as propagandistic; he also portrayed his own approach as racially balanced and nondiscriminatory.

This type of rhetoric not only impressed the conservative audience at the American Legion convention but also resonated well with many voters who were anxious about a perceived loss of privilege. What is remarkable about white Americans' belief that they had become an oppressed minority is the fact that this attitude was not just limited to the far right of the political spectrum but also included people who were actually opposed to Bob Dole's views. In response to the aforementioned article about the American Legion address, for example, Thomas L. Friedman wrote that it was unfortunate that Senator Dole had raised "a hot-button issue to revive his campaign" (*NYT*, September 10, 1995). According to Friedman, Dole's choice "to play on the patriotism of the American Legion and the fear of new immigrants" would only further divide the country (*NYT*, September 10, 1995).

Yet despite this call for moderation, Friedman's personal examples helped to validate Dole's claim that white men were under attack and needed to defend themselves. Friedman wrote that he had been approached by many teachers who complained about the fact that "it was not 'politically correct' for them to [criticize multilingual education] at their schools because multicultural extremists, pushing diversity as an end in itself, were the dominant trend" (*NYT*, September 10, 1995).[13] After noting that this situation "is sad," Friedman concluded that "we should oppose a notion of diversity that becomes an end in itself, a diversity that becomes a substitute for neighborhood and community, where Hispanics, blacks, Asians and Jews have their corners, separate but equal" (*NYT*, September 10, 1995). Borrowing the same type of civil rights rhetoric, Congressman Peter T. King (R-NY) wrote a letter to the editor, claiming that "bilingualism creates two societies both separate and unequal" (*NYT*, December 5, 1995). Whether these two societies were actually equal or, more realistically, unequal, both authors agreed that too much cultural diversity was a threat to national unity.

While these arguments preyed on fear and prejudice, they also in some ways reflected a realistic assessment of the situation. Undoubtedly, widespread bilingualism would in fact change American society. From the perspective of the white middle class, who were concerned about their declining social and economic status, a shift to a multilingual society might contribute to their further marginalization. However, even though this concern about the increasing importance of foreign influences was inextricably linked with anxieties about the large number of nonwhite people who had brought these new languages and cultures to the United States, the discourse tended to make a distinction between these two issues. In an effort to appear nonracist, the dominant discourse did not couch these concerns in terms of racial/ethnic fear but in a much more subtle debate about cultural differences and linguistic traditions. Yet, despite this emphasis of cultural difference over biology, race worked as an unspoken subtext in the dominant discourse.

A number of articles also defended English-only laws in economic terms. These articles were characterized by an unmistakable "us" versus "them" mentality that pitted newly arrived immigrants against native-born citizens in a fight for scarce resources. In accordance with the neoliberal project, several authors insisted that U.S. citizens should not have to finance immigrant-specific services such as bilingual education or printing government documents in languages other than English. If immigrants needed to access these services, they could not expect U.S. citizens to cover part of the costs. Instead, immigrants had to act like all customers—pay a fair price or forego the service. Advocates also insisted that this system was neither unfair nor discriminatory, but a necessary part of a market-driven economy. Representative Randy Cunningham (R-CA), for instance, reportedly said that his proposal to eliminate all government documents in languages other than English was actually a fairly generous provision, "because if I were mean-spirited, I would say, 'Stay where you are'" (*HC*, August 2, 1996).

Other commentators insisted that this market-oriented logic had even broader implications. From their perspective, immigrants should not only pay the literal costs for the services they obtained, but the right to immigrate carried a price tag as well. Since a residence permit was a valuable commodity, it was only logical that the U.S. government make its receipt dependent on a number of terms and conditions. Robert P. Watson's letter to the editor, for example, illustrated this underlying logic with the following argument: "We don't have to feel guilty about it. Immigrants are here to enjoy the benefits that their country didn't provide. One of the costs of enjoying the benefits of America is the use of the English language" (*NYT*, January 21, 1996). According to Watson, the United States should not waste time and resources on bilingual education. Instead, he argued, "total immersion . . . is the best way to help them assimilate and be successful. They don't have to be spoon fed" (*NYT*, January 21, 1996).

The latter argument was particularly popular in the debate about the merits of bilingual education programs. A number of journalists insisted that once a child moved to a new country, learning a foreign language was a natural process that did not warrant additional expenditures. Pointing to past generations of immigrants, who had managed to learn the English language without bilingual programs that were tailored toward their specific needs, these authors claimed that it was beside the point whether these costly programs were more efficient and helped students master the new language more quickly.[14] Instead, "those questions seem to have been overtaken by concerns about whether bilingual programs yield the returns that would justify their cost" (*NYT*, October 15, 1995).[15]

Some commentators even referred to bilingual education programs as "linguistic welfare." In a letter to the editor, Peter T. King (R-NY), for example, insisted that "nearly three decades of linguistic welfare have discouraged new Americans from learning English and barred their access to the American Dream" (*NYT*, December 5, 1995). In the context of the larger antiwelfare discourse, this analogy was not only possible but also actually fairly common. By December 1995, the idea that welfare benefits created dependency and discouraged recipients' own initiative had become firmly embedded in the minds of many Americans. Based on this general perception, it was apparently only a small step to transfer this thesis to bilingual education programs and argue that these courses actually harmed immigrant students, instead of encouraging them to learn English as quickly as possible.[16] Hence ending bilingual education would not only benefit the U.S. taxpayer but also assist immigrant students. Representative Peter T. King (R-NY), for instance, repeatedly claimed that he did not see English-only laws "as a partisan issue but as a practical, commonsense step that will benefit our nation in the long run" (*NYT*, December 5, 1995). This line of argument, which described anti-bilingual-education laws as "fair" and "commonsensical" measures, was particularly effective within the larger discourse.

Yet not everyone accepted this analogy between welfare recipients and students in bilingual education programs. In response to King's remarks, one person pointed out that his bilingual-education-as-linguistic-welfare analogy was rather unconvincing. Amy Storrow, a writer-in-residence at an elementary school in Houston, wrote, "Representative Peter T. King's Dec. 5 letter rests on a flawed premise. He implies that mastery of a second language is comparable to an unearned handout, to laziness and sloth. To compare bilingual education to a (Republican) vision of welfare makes no sense" (*NYT*, December 7, 1995). In her experience, students in bilingual education programs "are industrious and eager to learn." Not only does their English proficiency improve quickly; they also retain their ability to speak their first language fluently. According to Storrow, the fact that these students grow up bilingually can only be regarded as an asset in an increasingly competitive global economy.

Numerous articles agreed with Storrow's claim that expenditures for bilingual education programs represented a sensible investment that was likely to pay off in the future. In addition, they reminded the public that true bilingual programs were not intended to become holding pens for immigrant students who did not know enough English to follow "regular" classes. According to Lourdes Burrows, the project director of the Newcomers Academy for New Americans, it was important to keep in mind that "the term 'bilingual' means use of both languages. Bilingualism is a skill needed in today's international work force" (*NYT*, March 30, 1995). Successful bilingual instruction thus served several different yet related purposes: not only did bilingual classes help immigrant students learn English, but they also encouraged these students to use their native languages and, ideally, teach their American peers a second language. After a few years of bilingual education, both native-born Americans and immigrant students would graduate with an ability to speak two—or, depending on the location and situation, even more—languages fluently. Representative Nydia M. Velázquez (D-NY) strongly agreed with this positive assessment of bilingual education programs. In a letter to the *New York Times*, she wrote, "Multilingualism is a tremendous resource to the United States because it permits improved communications and cross-cultural understanding. Conversely, English-only measures undermine the economic competitiveness of the United States" (*NYT*, December 11, 1995).[17]

Even though some of the aforementioned articles and letters point to elusive advantages such as improved cross-cultural understanding, almost all bilingual education advocates explicitly emphasized the idea that these programs would also benefit the nation's economy in the long run. Reminiscent of the rhetoric that supported welfare-to-work programs, these articles claimed that it made economic sense to finance services that would help immigrants become self-sufficient by giving them the skills to succeed in a highly competitive job market and make an important contribution to a largely monolingual society. Taking this principle to its logical extreme, several New Yorkers not only promoted bilingual education programs; they also called for a number of additional short-term support services for newly arrived immigrant students. Contrary to the widespread tendency to eliminate group-specific services that could be perceived as welfare, New York City created a number of so-called newcomer schools, which catered to the needs of immigrant families. Yet even though this step might look like the polar opposite of the pronounced effort to save money by eliminating services, it was essentially based on the same neoliberal logic. Not surprisingly, the media also couched their support in a similar economically oriented rhetoric. In an article about the plan to create a newcomer school, for example, the *New York Times* argued, "With immigrants making up a third of the 153,000 new students in the city's schools last year, officials have calculated that spending about $400,000 to start a school that aims to integrate them and their families into city life is a wise investment" (*NYT*, September 7, 1995).

When it came to illegal immigrants, however, the mainstream media were much more reluctant to advance similar arguments. In his work on the construction of illegal immigrants as targets of government, Jonathan Xavier Inda distinguishes between two different strategies to manage subjects who had failed to live up to the expectations of a neoliberal—or, as he labels it, "postsocial"—society. On the one hand, the state employs so-called technologies of citizenship, which "endeavor to reinsert the excluded into circuits of responsible self-management, to reconstitute them through activating their capacity for autonomous citizenship" (Inda 2005, 19). We can see these technologies at work in the treatment of legal immigrant students. These students were generally perceived as a worthy investment. Even though they might not yet have the skills to succeed, they were certainly capable of learning the rules and becoming active citizens. Undocumented immigrants, on the other hand, were commonly regarded as a threat, whether cultural or economic, that needed to be contained. Instead of trying to help these individuals develop into productive members of society, they were subjected to "anticitizenship technologies," intended to contain and discipline them.

With regard to these two populations, the "problem" was constructed in two fundamentally different ways. The media portrayed documented immigrants as a population who faced some temporary challenges that could be overcome with assistance and an active commitment on their part. However, the media's stance toward undocumented immigrants was much more negative. According to Inda, the United States was not interested in "empowering or activating the self-governing capacities of marginalized subjects" but attempted to incapacitate these individuals (Inda 2005, 31). Tactics such as denial of welfare and health-care benefits, limited access to public education, and deportation were not only aimed at the current population of undocumented immigrants; these harsh measures were also intended to deter future migrants. The primary "problem" was thus neither the education of undocumented children nor the widely discussed education crisis in general. Instead, undocumented immigrants' presence in the United States was commonly described as the most pressing concern—one that justified the use of a wide range of increasingly harsh measures.

In this context, it did not even matter whether undocumented workers paid taxes and helped to finance the services that they used. Instead, most media reports made it clear that by entering the country illegally or overstaying their visa, undocumented immigrants had forfeited their right to expect access to even basic services. Undocumented immigrants' mere presence in the United States was described as an affront to law-abiding taxpayers. While politicians expressed their concern for American citizens during congressional debates, they were even more eager to emphasize their commitment to their constituencies in conversations with the media. Knowing that their voters would receive these messages, politicians actively attempted to cast the public-education issue as one of fairness toward U.S. citizens. Hence they could emerge as the defenders of Americans' rights and avoid charges of racism and anti-immigrant sentiments. By identifying problem populations rather than condemning specific "personal" characteristics like race, the discourse not only disguised its own racist effects but also represented policies as fair and balanced reactions to pressing social problems.

Elton Gallegly (R-CA), the author of a controversial amendment to end public education for undocumented children, and Pete Wilson (R-CA), one of the main supporters of California's Proposition 187, were among the most vociferous participants in the public discourse about illegal immigrants' access to education. In one of numerous editorials, Gallegly insinuated that President Clinton's reluctance to sign off on his amendment meant that the president was unable to "decide whether he cares more about illegal immigrants or American taxpayers, about law-breakers who should be escorted out of the country or the citizens saddled with providing them a free public education" (*HC*, May 16, 1996). This juxtaposition, which creates a stark contrast between deserving "citizens" and threatening "anticitizens," insists that there is only one real solution: denying undocumented immigrants the right to a free public education. Using a similar rhetoric, Pete Wilson (R-CA) emphatically stated, "It is time for Congress to end the 'magnetic lure,' to end the unfunded mandates, which are unfair and costly to state taxpayers and to the children of legal residents" (*NYT*, July 11, 1996).[18]

While these politicians believed that undocumented immigrants represented a problem population that needed to be deterred, they also tried to justify their policies with a rhetoric that appeared evenhanded and commonsensical. Knowing that the opposition would advance an emotional rhetoric that focused on the policy's adverse impact on innocent children, Gallegly's supporters made a conscious effort to emphasize the larger issues and draw attention away from sympathetic figures such as school-age children. One popular tactic in this context was centered on the argument that the character of illegal immigrants, as well as their goals and motivations, should not be taken into consideration in policy decisions. Donald Mann, the president of Negative Population Growth, for example, insisted, "Our support of such programs has nothing to do with the merit of illegal immigrants as individuals. Most are hardworking and industrious. We understand their wish to live here and their desire for better lives for themselves and their children" (*NYT*, June 19, 1996). The Gallegly amendment was thus portrayed as neither meanspirited nor punitive, but rather a logical reaction to immigrants' legal status.

Not surprisingly, all three papers ensured that their journalists did not cross the line into open hostility and immigrant bashing. Letters to the editor, on the other hand, provided one space within mainstream media for more extreme opinions. In contrast to the carefully edited comments by politicians and journalists, letters to the editor give us a glimpse of the virulent anti-immigrant subtext that underlay the public discourse. The controversial nature of this topic—undocumented children's access to public schools—sparked an emotional debate among readers. Since these letter writers did not have to worry about their public image and their chances for reelection, they made little attempt to cast the education question as an issue of fairness and deterrence. A number of contributors felt that there should not even a debate about undocumented immigrants' access to public schools: "If they were identified and deported, the problem of schooling would not exist because there would be no illegal immigrants living here permanently" (*NYT*, June 19, 1996). At the same time, however, even letter writers mostly avoided racial slurs and personal insults and sometimes even acknowledged that most undocumented immigrants were "hard working and industrious" (*NYT*, June 19, 1996).

However, in the same letter, Donald Mann also claimed that, while he "understand[s] their wish to live here and their desire for better lives for themselves and their children . . . Congress should be debating how to devise programs that would identify and deport every illegal immigrant in this country" (*NYT*, June 19, 1996). J. L. Dunlavey complained to the *San Francisco Chronicle*, "I've had it up to here with all the crying and moaning about the laws being changed to stop the free ride and the educating of the illegals' children. In this high technology age, it would be quite simple to identify and deport these people. By removing them you eliminate the problem" (*SFC*, July 24, 1996). Even though all three papers contained a fair number of these anti-immigrant statements, the *Houston Chronicle* attracted the most letters that advocated deportation and the denial of all services. Bill James, for example, stated matter-of-factly that "providing free education and benefits to illegal aliens defies logic. If a person is identified as an illegal alien, why is that person still here? Our laws state that she or he must be deported" (*HC*, July 13, 1996).[19] A few weeks later, another letter writer expressed his disappointment with Phil Gramm's (R-TX) and Kay Bailey Hutchison's (R-TX) refusal to vote for the public education ban. According to John Flatten, the senators' pronouncement could only be interpreted as "admittance that the U.S. government will not maintain a policy of locating and exporting [*sic*] illegals" (*HC*, July 28, 1996).

In September 1996, only weeks before the conference committee would reluctantly surrender to President Clinton's persistent request to eliminate the Gallegly amendment from the immigration bill, numerous readers expressed their strong support of the ban on public schooling. Even more important, they emphasized that the education crisis represented only one of a myriad of problems caused by the continued presence of "illegal aliens," "illegals," or as some writers phrased it, "these people." Bill Toney, for example, blamed illegal immigrants for the education crisis, high public expenditures for social services, and rising crime rates. According to his letter, large-scale deportation represented the only sensible solution to these pressing problems. Toney wrote, "Many of these crimes can be

avoided by simply returning the potential violators. The education of illegals is complicated by language and culture differences which could also be
avoided by returning them to their homelands" (*HC*, September 5, 1996).
While this type of rhetoric was rejected by some readers, Toney's tendency
to conflate a multitude of immigrant-related issues into one seemingly
crushing problem was extremely popular among Gallegly's supporters.[20]

In contrast, Gallegly's opponents tended to advance a rhetoric that
distinguished between different problems and called for less drastic solutions. While almost everyone agreed with the basic premise that illegal
immigrants did indeed pose a serious problem, the proeducation lobby
was convinced that the Gallegly amendment was not the right solution.
The Gallegly amendment would not force undocumented immigrants
to depart, and it wasn't realistic to expect the number of future entries
to drop as a result of the ban. According to these writers, a ban on public education was unwarranted because it "won't do diddley about illegal
immigration" (*HC*, September 28, 1996). Even though this assessment is
probably correct, it is important to acknowledge that the supporters of the
education ban had based their arguments on a slightly different idea of
how the state should govern illegal immigrants. They were convinced that
the state needed to promote zero-tolerance policies. As mentioned before,
the pro-Gallegly side insisted that all illegal immigrants represented
"anticitizens" who were undeserving of public support. Accordingly, the
denial of education benefits was part of a larger effort to "get tough" on
undocumented immigrants, not a specific method to encourage voluntary
departures and deter additional migrants.

The mainstream media never explicitly questioned the need to "get
tough." Since the American public was already convinced that there was
a crisis and, even more important, that undocumented immigrants had
caused this crisis, it was difficult to challenge this widely accepted "truth."
Yet not everyone agreed with Gallegly's response. Citing a long list of concerns about children's physical well-being, crime rates, and gang violence,
Gallegly's critics maintained that the social costs of denying education to
the children of undocumented immigrants would almost certainly outweigh the elusive benefits. Even if undocumented immigrants did not
exactly adhere to the ideal of the active, law-abiding, neoliberal subject,
many Americans were reluctant to classify young children as "anticitizens" and withdraw all support. In particular, the media was appalled that
Congress was willing to target children before they had made the slightest

attempt to enforce labor standards and discuss an employment verification system. Journalist Debra Saunders, for example, wrote, "If the day should come when the government has to deny children access to an education, so be it. But surely that day cannot have arrived if Congress . . . doesn't feel a need to ensure that employers obey the law" (*SFC*, March 25, 1996). A few days later, a *San Francisco Chronicle* editorial used even more descriptive language to express dissatisfaction with Congress's approach. The editorialist exclaimed that he or she was "deeply trouble[ed]" that Congress had passed "an idiotic policy [which] would result in a dramatic increase in gang membership, youth crime and youth victimization" (*SFC*, April 12, 1996).

Even conservative critics such as the Federation for American Immigration Reform (FAIR) and economist George Borjas articulated their frustration with Congress's skewed priorities. On March 25, 1996, the *San Francisco Chronicle* reported that FAIR "was so disgusted with what the Reps and Dems did last week . . . that it withdrew its support for the two major bills in Congress" (*SFC*, March 25, 1996). FAIR's belief that Congress had the right to pass tough measures remained unshaken. But in the same article, spokesman Ira Mehlman explained that FAIR's main concern was that "they decided to get tough with school kids before they got tough with employers, which is where they really need to start" (*SFC*, March 25, 1996).[21] According to FAIR, the "getting tough" principle did not justify punitive measures that would do little to solve the underlying problem.[22]

In addition to pointing out that the education ban represented an ineffective strategy to combat the perceived immigration crisis, George Borjas also reasoned that Elton Gallegly (R-CA) and his supporters were very well aware of the fact that "this policy is not a serious attempt to curtail the illegal alien flow, for it is unlikely ever to be enforced" (*NYT*, July 11, 1996). Borjas was not alone in his assessment. A number of journalists argued that the Gallegly amendment served a very specific political purpose: the Republican Party in general and California's representatives in particular wanted to ensure that middle-class voters believed that they were getting tough on illegal immigrants, while big businesses could rest assured that Congress would not eliminate their supply of a cheap and easily available labor force with little access to legal protections.

Even though their political opponents had made similar complaints during congressional debates, these remarks tended to amount to little more than curt comebacks and snide remarks. Similar accusations in the mainstream media, however, had the potential to be more damaging to individual candidates and entire parties—especially since the public-school controversy unfolded only months before the presidential election. One particularly popular weapon, in this context, was sarcasm. Editorials in all three papers used sarcasm to illustrate politicians' hypocrisy and their willingness to target children in an effort to further their own political motives. Both because of the quality and the quantity of their writings, Arthur Hoppe, who contributed to the *San Francisco Chronicle* for more than forty years, and Pulitzer Prize winner A. M. Rosenthal of the *New York Times* are particularly interesting in this regard.[23] Only days after the House passed the Gallegly amendment, Arthur Hoppe began to question the motives behind this move. He wrote,

> By denying education to the children of illegal immigrants, we will create a new generation of poor who are even poorer than the present poor. This will not only fill the need for an increasing number of even poorer people created by the widening gap, but it will appeal to every red-blooded patriot. After all, someone has to be at the bottom of the heap. Someone has to scrub the motel's toilet bowls. Someone has to change diapers for $4 an hour. Someone has to bend double over the strawberries in the summer heat. Someone has to scrounge the dumpsters for the family meal. How far better, everyone who loves this country will agree, that it be a foreigner rather than an American. (*SFC*, March 25, 1996)

Politicians' claim that the Gallegly amendment was supposed to deter future immigrants was dismissed as entirely unconvincing. Instead, Hoppe argued that the education ban could only be interpreted as a nod toward the upper class in general and big businesses in particular. Notably, Hoppe's cost–benefit analysis mocked the underlying neoliberal rationale. In addition to the aforementioned commentary on illegal immigrants' economic contributions, Hoppe also compared Congress's rhetoric in support of the education ban to arguments made by proslavery advocates in the nineteenth century. Specifically, Hoppe wrote the following:

> Slavery has admittedly garnered a sullied reputation. None would condone enslaving a freedom-loving American citizen. But these people are foreigners. Without education or welfare benefits or, in

most cases, even a rudimentary knowledge of our language, they cannot hope to rise much above the beasts of the field. How far better for them and for us, if they were given good homes with caring masters who would adequately clothe and feed them and perhaps even offer them rudimentary schooling in letters and numbers. Laws could easily be passed banning the past abuses that gave slavery a bad name. (*SFC*, March 25, 1996)

This sarcasm also hints at an ethical dimension that had been foreclosed by neoliberal thinking. Even though Hoppe did not explicitly articulate his ethical concerns, his slavery analogy made it clear that Americans should be suspicious of a rhetoric that described these measures as fair and evenhanded reforms that would eventually benefit the entire nation. His analogy demonstrated that immigration reform was not just about numbers and weighing elusive costs against hard-to-define benefits. Instead, immigration reform represented an attempt to manage and control human beings.

Rosenthal's critique was slightly different. Despite the fact that he exposed Congress's interest in sustaining a docile, uneducated labor force, his critique was primarily concerned with the "social costs" involved in the public-school ban. In particular, Rosenthal compared undocumented immigrants to "real criminals" and suggested that their children could easily be subjected to the same treatment. He wrote, "If the 650,000 children of parents who have just committed the civil offense of illegal entry can be kicked out of school, or better, blocked from ever entering, then for Heaven's sake what are we doing letting children of real criminals sit there, bothering teachers with questions and using our school toilets?" (*NYT*, September 17, 1996). Ultimately, the existing crime problem would undoubtedly escalate. In conclusion, Rosenthal "reassured" his readers that "if these illiterate thugs wind up in prison you can bet that decent Americans like Mr. Dole won't allow any mollycoddling like teaching them how to read and write, which would be plain ridiculous after kicking them out of school when they were little kids using up chalk" (*NYT*, September 17, 1996). Confronted with this depressing chain of events, the reader is left to wonder why Congress passed a provision that would clearly only contribute to the problem it pretended to solve.

Rosenthal's editorials usually come back to the same succinct explanation: politics. With the presidential election coming up, both parties tried to maintain a public image that appealed to their voters. In particular, Republicans and Democrats knew it was political suicide to speak out against a highly popular immigration reform law. For the entire legislative period, both parties had contributed to an immigration discourse that was dominated by a sense of urgency. Politicians and the media had constructed a frightening notion of the illegal immigrant as a threat to the economy, the welfare system, national security, public health, and a number of other areas. In short, by September 1996, it was commonly accepted as "truth" that there was an immigration crisis that warranted immediate attention. Not surprisingly, both parties were eager to get credit for the passage of an immigration reform law.

Due to this eagerness to emerge as the party that "got tough" on illegal immigration, candidates were forced to make sacrifices—sometimes against their better judgment. In particular, Rosenthal accused vice-presidential candidate Jack Kemp of opportunism: "Barely a day passed before Mr. Kemp turned in a badge of honor he had often pointed to—intelligent, thoughtful support for immigrants. Without any embarrassment he announced he was supporting the California movement to throw children of illegal immigrants out of school, an idea he had ridiculed before" (NYT, October 15, 1996). Yet, even though Kemp's change of heart drew some criticism, Bob Dole, Bill Clinton, and all the other presidential candidates were equally willing to rethink their priorities if the political gain seemed to outweigh the costs. In most cases, these shifts were perceived as fairly minor and were barely mentioned in the news media. This is no coincidence. Since reform measures were described as impersonal responses to a quantifiable problem, mainstream politicians were able to cite new evidence and adjust their solutions. The neoliberal logic driving immigration discourse, coupled with a discourse on "fairness" that eschewed overt racism, made it possible for politicians to rethink their priorities without appearing too obviously opportunistic to most voters.

Language and Discrimination

As the previous section demonstrated, education emerged as one of the most hotly debated issues in the media discourse on immigration reform. Bilingual education, English-only laws, and especially Elton Gallegly's (R-CA) proposed ban on primary and secondary education for undocumented children generated summary accounts and feature stories, critical analyses, emotional letters, as well as justifications by politicians involved in the legislative process. In one way or another, all these texts contributed to the public discourse about immigrants and immigration reform. Yet, in addition to these issue-oriented contributions, a number of journalists embarked upon a critique of the discourse itself. This section will focus specifically on the mainstream media's commentary on the prejudices inherent in immigration reform discourse.

Based on their experiences with Proposition 187's campaign rhetoric, which had successfully tapped into Californians' fears and anxieties about undocumented Latino immigrants, the *San Francisco Chronicle* was particularly sensitive to the power of discourse to shape immigration policy. In an editorial entitled "Keep Politics Out of Immigration Policy," the author cautioned that Proposition 187 "has shown that there are many people—including leaders who foment divisiveness for political advantage—only too willing to fan the flames of xenophobia in the name of immigration reform" (*SFC*, September 10, 1995). Even more problematic, the author noted, was the fact that a number of Californians took this anti-immigrant rhetoric to the next level and used it "as an excuse to discriminate against and harass Hispanics and Asians" (*SFC*, September 10, 1995).

With these incidents in mind, *San Francisco Chronicle* journalists tried to use their own influence to prevent another surge of hate crimes and harassment. In response to the widespread anti-immigrant rhetoric, *San Francisco Chronicle* journalists made repeated attempts to expose politicians' campaign tactics and alert readers to the discourse's real-life effects. On a local level, for example, the *San Francisco Chronicle* was quick to condemn the so-called Save-Our-State II initiative, which collected signatures for a constitutional amendment to deny citizenship to U.S.-born children of illegal immigrants. The *San Francisco Chronicle* warned, "First, there will be the fear-mongering propaganda. . . . As happened during the debate on Proposition 187, some especially ignorant people will feel the initiative effort gives them license to taunt and harass 'foreign-looking' people" (*SFC*, May 28, 1995). In conclusion, the article appealed to readers' reasonableness and sense of fairness, "rather than resort to hypocrisy and heightened xenophobia" (*SFC*, May 28, 1995).

In a similar fashion, the *San Francisco Chronicle* criticized federal politicians' attempts to play into their electorate's fears and anxieties. One particularly persuasive article, for example, focused on the popular campaign tactic of attacking minorities for political gain. Citing research by political scientist Michael Rogin, writer Robert B. Gunnison explained, "Demonizing is a natural extension of negative campaigning and take-no-prisoners partisan politics. But it goes even further: It transforms its subjects into monsters who pose exaggerated threats and raises the prejudice and fear of the targeted audience" (*SFC*, February 19, 1996). Even though Gunnison used Pete Wilson's presidential campaign as a specific example, he maintained that demonizing was a highly effective tactic that was used by Democrats and Republicans alike.[24]

A few days later, another *San Francisco Chronicle* editorial underlined the fact that demonizing and scapegoating were not just popular with political extremists.[25] In addition, the editorialist pointed out that hateful rhetoric had a long list of negative repercussions: not only did it lead to harassment and discrimination, but "voters who have been encouraged to blame any deterioration in their well-being on immigrants, corporate executives, other ethnic groups or foreign countries will be looking for retribution—not healing—from the White House" (*SFC*, March 3, 1996). To solve economic and social problems, political leaders needed to end "the politics of blame" and provide a "vision for better times" (*SFC*, March 3, 1996).

While numerous journalists condemned politicians—and presidential candidates in particular—who resorted to fear-mongering rhetoric to advance their own careers, they were much more reluctant to interrogate the media's role in the larger discourse. Ironically, articles and editorials that explicitly criticized politicians' campaign rhetoric oftentimes perpetuated the same negative images of immigrants. The aforementioned *San Francisco Chronicle* editorial from May 1995, for example, voiced opposition to the "rancor and hate that will accompany" the Save-Our-State II initiative in no uncertain terms. Yet, only a few lines later, the editorialist advocated fast, expedited deportations for "criminal illegal immigrants" immediately after their release from jail and praised President Clinton's "legislative package that makes clear that stemming the tide of illegal immigrants is a high priority" (*SFC*, May 28, 1995). These articles and editorials thus confirmed the perception that there was indeed an immigration problem and ultimately reinforced the negative image of undocumented immigrants that they had set out to critique.

On rare occasions, however, journalists wrote introspective pieces that took a critical look at the role of the media and journalistic language itself. In an attempt to illustrate the power of the media, for example, *San Francisco Chronicle* editorialist Jon Carroll showed that white Americans, who gathered much of their information about nonwhite minorities from mainstream media sources, routinely believed that the United States was much more diverse than it actually was.[26] Carroll wrote, "There is a perception of a flood, but there is no actual flood. There has been a change, yes, and all change is unsettling, but a change is not the same as a flood. We are not being inundated by immigrants" (*SFC*, March 27, 1996). In addition to these investigative approaches, other editorialists tried to counter common prejudices with factual information. A *Houston Chronicle* editorial, for example, emphasized a recently published Immigration and Naturalization Service (INS) study that established that the "bulk of the United States' population of illegal immigrants is now being supplied by some unexpected sources: . . . Poland, Haiti, the Philippines and the former Soviet Union are topping the list" (*HC*, January 14, 1996). According to the short editorial, these findings illustrated that the media had constructed an image of the illegal immigrant that was neither fair nor accurate. Instead, the INS study showed "that too much of the immigration debate too often falls into a search for too-easy answers based on too-simplified stereotypes" (*HC*, January 14, 1996).

Some journalists who commented on the prejudiced nature of the media discourse also made a conscious effort to provide more positive, multifaceted portrayals. These efforts to address the complexity of the immigrant community, however, met a lot of resistance. Richard Rayner's feature story about Maria T., an undocumented Mexican mother of four young children, represents a prime example. This feature-length article—provocatively titled "What Immigration Crisis?"—appeared in the Sunday edition of the *New York Times*. British immigrant Richard Rayner, who was married to a Finnish wife, used Maria T. as an example to discuss the current anti-immigrant climate. He expressed sympathy for her struggles and illustrated the difficult challenges she had been forced to overcome since she entered the United States illegally.[27] However, he also emphasized the fact that Maria T. "receives $723 in cash and $226 in food stamps" for her U.S. citizen children (*NYT*, January 7, 1996). Based on this evidence, Rayner admitted that, in many ways, Maria T. "represents the nightmare scenario—an illegal immigrant who's sucking money from the system and putting nothing back. Even so, it's not clear that she's a villain. She hopes one day to go to work herself. She hopes and believes that her bright children will become outstanding" (*NYT*, January 7, 1996).

After this case study, Rayner discussed the larger immigration discourse. He came to the conclusion that "the anti-immigration forces have done an excellent job of creating an atmosphere of crisis in which the debate has focused on how to slow the 'flood' of immigration, legal and illegal. But illegal immigration should not be folded over to scapegoat legals as well. The real point is that there isn't any immigration crisis" (*NYT*, January 7, 1996). Even more important, Rayner examined how media representations helped to perpetuate a problematic image of the illegal immigrant, while legal immigrants from Europe, like he and his wife, were discussed in entirely different terms. He concluded that race was one of the main factors: "One of the problems with the immigration issue is that it does impinge on the race issue, and thus appeals temptingly and dangerously to the worst side of all of us" (*NYT*, January 7, 1996).[28]

Even though most people were reluctant to admit that they had internalized these racist stereotypes, it was next to impossible to escape the influence of the larger media discourse. Rayner even admitted that he had been in situations where he inadvertently thought in the same racist terms he tried to defy in his writings. Rayner used his twenty-two-year-old Mexican nanny as an example. After he explained that "the only white applicant for the job was a disturbingly energetic 30-something woman with great rifts in her curriculum vitae, a self-confessed graduate of '12 Steps,'" Rayner said that he and his wife "went the safe route" and hired a young and highly qualified Mexican nanny with a two-year-old U.S. citizen daughter (*NYT*, January 7, 1996). He admitted that he had found himself "sympathetic and friendly one moment, a paranoid patron the next, questioning her stability, her hygiene, her habits. I can't imagine that Pete Wilson himself would be any crankier than I was when Christine came back with the stroller and told me that while she'd been walking our baby a man on the street had asked her for a date" (*NYT*, January 7, 1996).

This self-indulgent "confession" of white guilt is illustrative of the ambiguity that characterizes the entire story. On the one hand, Rayner was critical of the role that the media had played in the current anti-immigrant climate. In particular, he argued that the current immigration discourse had the power to influence the electorate, change policy decisions, and cause even deeper social divisions precisely because "the debate is more emotional than informed. It's all temper tantrums and red-hot sound bites" (*NYT*, January 7, 1996). While I agree with his assessment that the discursive effect of most coverage of illegal immigration from Mexico is to reinforce racial stereotypes, I do not think the debate was "more emotional than informed." Quite to the contrary, the media discourse was powerful, especially because it was able to use neoliberal rationale to obscure racist effects. This neoliberal framework actually enabled people like Rayner to publicly confess his own prejudices and still think of himself as a compassionate liberal. What is perhaps even more problematic about this article is Rayner's decision to focus on Maria T., an abused, Mexican, welfare mother. Her portrayal played directly to American prejudices in ways that even the most conservative politicians did not feel secure enough to do.

Clearly, this feature story did not attempt to glorify undocumented immigrants. On the contrary, Rayner was very outspoken about the fact that Maria T. consumed public services and had little chance to develop into a "net contributor" anytime soon. But since Rayner's story challenged some basic "truths" about illegal immigrants, *New York Times* readers attacked the article on a number of different fronts.[29] In particular, readers were disturbed by the fact that Rayner did not cite the usual criticism about unauthorized immigrants' negative impact on the economy. Jeffrey Bates, for example, wrote, "By casting the debate on illegal immigration as one about values, Rayner ignored the fundamental complaint many Americans have on this topic. After a lifetime of employment, and the subsequent financing of numerous social programs via taxes on our incomes, we now question who really benefits" (*NYT*, January 28, 1996).[30]

Other readers took their objections to a much more personal level. Consider the following example: "Another 'illegal immigrants are good for the country' story. As an American, I really don't have any rights, except to pay my taxes, serve in time of war and keep my mouth shut for fear of being called a racist" (*NYT*, David Harris, January 28, 1996).[31] This comment about the writer's "fear of being called a racist" represented another fairly common reaction to racial anxieties. While people like Rayner felt that admitting to their own prejudices would absolve them from suspicions that they were indeed a racist, this writer chose the opposite strategy. He insisted that the current political climate prevented a white man like himself from expressing his feelings and opinions. The underlying assumptions were clear: while David Harris maintained that white men had become victimized by the discourse's insistence on political correctness, he also implied that there were indeed (negative) things that needed to be said about racial minorities.

The reaction to Richard Rayner's article was not an isolated case. All three newspapers received and published similar letters whenever they attempted to provide a multifaceted portrayal of an undocumented immigrant that challenged commonly held "truths." In some cases, these letters were dismissive of the author's arguments and openly hostile toward immigrants. In response to a *San Francisco Chronicle* editorial about immigrant rights, for example, Annette Christensen sent the following letter: "Here we go again with another bleeding heart liberal's whine. . . . I am sick and tired of hearing how America 'benefits' from immigrants. Granted, there is a small percentage where our society does benefit from some immigrants; however, immigrants cause more damage than good. How do we benefit from immigrants when the majority come here and take over certain neighborhoods, do not interact with our society, do not take part in our American culture, only stay within their own circle, will not/cannot/ do not speak English. You tell me how our culture benefits from that?" (*SFC*, August 15, 1996). In most other cases, however, the letter writers expressed their dissent in more polite terms. A *Houston Chronicle* feature story about Asusena, a twenty-seven-year-old mother from Honduras, for example, generated a response by Robert A. Wallis, the district director of the INS for the U.S. Department of Justice in Houston. In his opinion, "the story read like an open invitation to those considering crossing our borders in violation of law. It profiled undocumented immigration as an acceptable, beneficial and at times necessary activity" (*HC*, February 3, 1995). Interestingly, Wallis explicitly objected to writer Mike Tolson's refusal to reiterate the dominant discourse. Wallis complained, "The story paid hardly any attention to the current national debate regarding illegal immigration which centers, not on its benefits, but on its tremendous social and economic costs" (*HC*, February 3, 1995). Other *Houston Chronicle* readers disagreed with Wallis's assessment. A few days later, Nestor Rodriguez pointed out, "The story did not read like an open invitation to undocumented immigrants, nor did it parade undocumented immigrants as triumphant entrants into our society. It appears to me that the story attempted to go beyond the anti-immigrant rhetoric and survey other views on current immigration" (*HC*, February 9, 1995). Yet compared to the large quantity of angry letters, these civil exchanges were fairly rare.

Articles that challenged commonly held beliefs about undocumented immigrants were oftentimes perceived as a provocation. In response, readers felt compelled to defend their beliefs and restore the commonly accepted image of the illegal immigrant. Yet even though many readers were reluctant to accept complex portrayals that depicted undocumented immigrants in a more positive light, they were equally shocked by openly hostile and racist remarks. The dominant neoliberal discourse had created the impression that the United States was a color-blind society that valued personal responsibility and hard work. In the process, racial anxieties had not disappeared. Instead, they were well concealed and continued to inform the discourse on immigration, affirmative action, welfare reform, and a host of other issues.

If a public persona violated this rule of political correctness and openly expressed their animosity toward certain groups, the repercussions were immediate and severe. One example of this discursive rule is the controversy over Democratic Councilwoman Julia Harrison's hostile remarks toward Asian Americans. On March 31, 1996, the *New York Times* reported that two Asian American candidates—Ethel Chen and Chun Soo Pyun—were running for the New York City Council. The author, Cecilia W. Dugger, thought that their candidacy was a newsworthy event because "no Asian-American in the city has ever been elected to the Council, the State Assembly, the State Senate or the United States Congress" (*NYT*, March 31, 1996). What was even more interesting about their campaign, however, was the fact that both candidates cited exactly the same reason for their decision to run for office: they wanted to beat seventy-five-year-old Councilwoman Julia Harrison, who had repeatedly insulted the Asian American community in Flushing. Dugger quoted Harrison's anti-Asian comments at length. Dugger wrote, "When Mrs. Harrison, 75, describes what Asian immigrants have meant to Flushing over the last decade, she talks about criminal smugglers and Asian robbers. . . . She talks about rude merchants and illegal aliens who depress the wages of American working people" (*NYT*, March 31, 1996). In addition, Harrison publicly proclaimed, "They were more like colonizers than immigrants. They sure as hell had a lot of money, and they sure as hell knew how to buy property and jack up rents of retail shops and drive people out. . . . The money came first. The paupers followed, smuggled in and bilked by their own kind" (*NYT*, March 31, 1996). In conclusion, Harrison remarked, "It's very discombobulating, very upsetting. We all recognize that change is part of life, but it doesn't sit well" (*NYT*, March 31, 1996).

Even though it is certainly remarkable that an elected official felt comfortable to express her anti-Asian feelings so explicitly, it is even more noteworthy that the *New York Times*'s initial article seemed to endorse her opinions. Throughout the article, Dugger not only left Harrison's racist remarks unexplored; she even attempted to justify white residents' hostile stance toward immigrants. Her reporting made it clear that she sympathized with Harrison's "elderly white constituents, who say they have come to feel increasingly out of place in their own neighborhood as growing numbers of Asian-Americans have settled there, speaking languages the old-timers don't understand and selling foods they have never tasted" (*NYT*, March 31, 1996).[32] This remark, as well as Dugger's repeated usage of terms such as "old-timers" and "original residents" clearly implied that elderly white constituents did indeed have a right to defend "*their own* neighborhood."

In addition, Dugger validated white people's sense of displacement by portraying Asian immigrants as a force that was likely to take over the city in the near future. Dugger referred to Asian Americans as "the city's fastest-growing immigrant group," alerted readers to "an influx of thousands more Asian immigrants," "the sheer magnitude of the Asian influx," and most notably, the "huge bubble of citizenship seekers," which was likely to "explode" in the near future. Along the same lines, Flushing was referred to as a "teeming Asian hub," "the city's leading magnet for Asian immigrants," and as the "home to an ever-growing concentration of Taiwanese, Koreans and Indians." This language created a sense of urgency and imminent danger.

While Dugger used this alarmist language throughout her lengthy article, she went to considerable trouble to interview a variety of immigration experts, politicians, and residents in order to adhere to the rules of fair and balanced reporting. Nevertheless, this approach ultimately helped reinforce negative stereotypes of Asian Americans. Despite the fact that Dugger talked to a number of Asian Americans, she did not grant them an opportunity to explain their perspectives on the racial tensions in Flushing. Instead, Asian Americans were asked to explain why they were not as politically active as other ethnic groups. White residents, on the other hand, were encouraged to comment on Flushing's changing racial makeup. While several elderly white residents agreed with

Councilwoman Julia Harrison's stance, others expressed concern over her reactionary attitude. They described Flushing's changing racial makeup in more positive terms. What linked all these comments, however, was a clearly identifiable prejudice against Asian Americans. After quoting numerous white residents who complained about Asian marketplaces and "exotic foods," the article concluded with a remark from Sol Nachemin, an eighty-two-year-old son of Russian immigrants. Nachemin, who was described as one of the more welcoming individuals, went on the record with the following comment: "I have a sneaking admiration for them. They're hard-working. They're good business people. At the library, I see all these Oriental kids sitting around the table doing their homework. It reminds me of the Jewish kids of my generation" (*NYT*, March 31, 1996).

This article caused an immediate uproar. In a matter of a few days, readers wrote dozens of letters to the editor. On April 2, 1996, for example, David Kraut called attention to the fact that "Mrs. Harrison's remarks are repugnant and misinformed. I hope that like the racists of 100 years ago, she will lose her fight to keep immigrants out" (*NYT*, April 2, 1996). A few days later, Michael I. Rhee, a member of the Conference on Asian Pacific American Leadership, corrected Harrison's misperceptions about an "Asian invasion," and Josephine Chung, president of the New York chapter of the Organization of Chinese Americans, demanded a public apology from Julia Harrison. What was missing from the public discourse, however, was a critical interrogation of the *New York Times*'s coverage. Not a single letter to the editor complained about the clear bias of Dugger's article and the discriminatory language that she used to discuss Asian Americans. The only letter that explicitly commented on the article itself—and not solely on Julia Harrison's remarks—was written by Nancy Sciales, M.D., and William J. Sciales, M.D., two elderly residents of Flushing. These two individuals were clearly disturbed by Dugger's failure to report that there were many people in Flushing who perceived the new immigrants as a welcome addition to their community. They wrote, "Years ago we eagerly visited the first Korean restaurant in Flushing. Today we are regulars at many of the Chinese and Korean restaurants here. We are fortunate to be able to purchase superb fruits and vegetables from local Asian markets. . . . Our new neighbors may not look like us, but we share many ideals: a strong work ethic reinforced by strong religious convictions, devotion to family and reverence for education" (*NYT*, April 6, 1996). Before long, the coverage of Julia Harrison's remarks had consequences beyond the news media level. In reaction to the public controversy, concerned Asian Americans formed the "Asian American Alliance," which rebuked Harrison's allegations and demanded a public apology. Their fight was soon joined by a host of public officials, including Governor George E. Pataki, Mayor Rudolph W. Giuliani, and county Democratic leader Thomas J. Manton, who called Harrison a "disgrace to the Democratic Party" (*NYT*, April 14, 1996). A mere month after the first article, more than two thousand concerned citizens rallied outside city hall to call for Harrison's resignation. Nonetheless, Julia Harrison was reluctant to admit any wrongdoing. Instead, "she called her detractors 'a pack of yapping hyenas' and likened their denunciation of her to gang rape" (*NYT*, April 14, 1996). In response to the mounting pressure by her own party, however, she finally decided to read a public apology at a city council meeting. In her brief comments, she announced that her intention "was not to insult a hard-working and proud community but to speak about the changes in and integration of an entire community. . . . Those who know me and my record do not perceive me as anti-Asian, racist nor even as a bigot" (*NYT*, May 3, 1996). Obviously, Harrison's only regret was that she had failed to obey the rules of public discourse and mask these concerns in racially neutral terms.

Conclusion

Julia Harrison's remarks represented a rare moment of slippage, when all the careful pretenses of mainstream immigration discourse slipped enough to let the racism peek through. For the most part, the neoliberal discourse on immigration reform focused on apparently objective measurements— cost–benefit analysis, actuarial tables, and statistics—to make arguments appear scientific and rational, rather than emotional. Hence the discourse disguised the underlying racial anxieties and obscured the negative and racist effects of the policies it generated. Overtly racist discourse, on the other hand, exposed the workings of power and introduced human "feelings" into the discursive field. Both results were ultimately undesirable and therefore needed to be suppressed.

The 1990s media discourse on immigration hid its racist subtext quite well. Proponents of immigration reform were careful to describe their reform measures as necessary responses to quantifiable *problems*, not efforts to target specific *populations*. One highly effective strategy, in this context, was the media's attempt to discuss reform measures in terms of "common sense" and "fairness." With regard to the Gallegly amendment, for example, proponents argued that it made "common sense" that the U.S. government did not reward undocumented immigrants by allowing their children to get a public education. This type of rhetoric refuted charges that the education ban was meanspirited and overly punitive and separated the underlying motivations from the desired effects. Since the ban on public education was supposedly fair and equitable, it was no longer important whether this measure would actually deter future immigrants.

Yet even though the mainstream media and its interlocutors were careful to express their concerns in nonracist terms, its coverage also confirmed already existing stereotypes and reinforced negative perceptions in numerous ways. It is important to acknowledge that many readers were familiar with the fairly overt racist discourse on immigration that took place on conservative talk radio and was publicized by organizations such as STOP IT (Stop Out of Control Problems of Immigration Today), the Border Patriots, or the Minuteman Civil Defense Corps. Since these discursive strands worked intertextually, it was not even necessary for politicians and journalists to make racist remarks; they could count on the fact that sympathetic audiences would read their commentary in light of these much more explicit sources.

In addition to these discursive effects, the mainstream news media also supplied readers with many examples that seemed to verify their fears and anxieties. As the previous examples demonstrated, the media tended to focus on Asian immigrants when they praised scholastic achievements and Latinos when they discussed poverty, welfare usage, and other social problems. This racialization of different immigrant groups is even more evident in human-interest stories. Chapter 5 will focus on a variety of human-interest stories about undocumented day laborers, pregnant teenagers, and "criminal aliens." In particular, this analysis will demonstrate how human-interest stories combined personal stories and public anxieties about immigrants' race, gender, and sexuality with the underlying neoliberal logic that informed the entire discourse.

5

Entrepreneurial Spirits and Individual Failures

The Neoliberal Human-Interest Story

In spring 1996, the *Houston Chronicle* devoted dozens of articles to Adela Quintana, a fourteen-year-old Mexican immigrant who was pregnant by her twenty-two-year-old husband. A few months later, the *San Francisco Chronicle* caused a public outcry with a story about a twelve-year-old Iraqi immigrant, whose family had arranged her marriage to thirty-year-old Mohammed Alsreafi. In October 1996, the *Houston Chronicle* ran a ten-part series about four immigrant families from Mexico and El Salvador. During the same month, the *New York Times* published a six-part series, entitled "Housing's Hidden Crisis," which focused on New York City's poorest tenants, many of them undocumented immigrants, who were "forced by deepening poverty and a dwindling supply of inexpensive rentals into apartments that are cramped, squalid, illegal or even dangerous" (*New York Times* [*NYT*], October 7, 1996).

At a time when the print news media were facing increased competition from the twenty-four-hour news coverage on television and the Internet, newspapers had to make an effort to reemphasize their strengths and distinguish their coverage from that of their competitors. Specifically, newspapers banked on their ability to tell complicated stories. Patti Valkenburg et al. argue that, in an increasingly competitive news market, "journalists and editors are at pains to produce a product that captures and retains audience interest. Framing news in human-interest terms is a way to personalize, dramatize, and emotionalize the news" (1999, 551). Robert A. Logan, director of the science journalism center at the Missouri School of Journalism, agrees that human-interest stories play a particularly important role in cultures that value *infotainment*. Logan defines a human-interest story as "a feature story in which the focus of the article centers on the personality, characteristics, demeanor, lifestyle, and habits of a featured source, or the ambiance surrounding a featured source's

195

work" (Logan 2006). The human-interest frame thus provides a context for understanding, identifying, and labeling the information in a way that is inherently different from other commonly used frames—such as presenting a story in terms of conflict, attribution of responsibility, or economic consequences (Valkenburg et al. 1999).

In respectable newspapers, human-interest stories represent well-researched accounts of the featured source's struggles and accomplishments. Yet while these individual stories are undoubtedly true in the sense that they accurately portray the lives and emotions of the few central figures, they oftentimes portray a "truth" that is partial at best. Bill Ong Hing argues, "Anecdotal evidence is almost always small enough to be intrinsically irrefutable and yet it is only one person's story that obscures the larger picture and nearly erases the possibility of multiple pictures" (Hing 1998, 159). In the context of the larger discourse, these emotional and dramatic stories oftentimes validated existing stereotypes that had already been established by the larger discourse. For example, many readers of the aforementioned articles had probably already encountered numerous accounts of immigrants' nonnormative sexuality, including portrayals of arranged marriages between Muslims and stories of Latina immigrants having too many children at an extremely young age. Consequently, these dramatic stories are not usually processed as particularly extreme examples; in the absence of conflicting data about each group, they are regarded as accurate depictions of cultural norms and traditions.

Human-interest stories tend to manipulate the reader's emotions and blur the line between fact and fiction. The news media—and human-interest stories in particular—"have the capacity not only to tell the public *what* issues to think about but also *how* to think about them" (Valkenburg et al. 1999, 567). Valkenburg's research on how different news frames affect readers' thoughts and influence their ability to recall information outlines two important differences between human-interest stories and other news frames: (1) readers of human-interest stories are much more likely to focus on emotional and individual implications, and (2) "news framed in terms of human interest, often used to make a story more interesting and compelling, can diminish rather than enhance the recollection of information" (Valkenburg et al. 1999, 566). There are some potential explanations for this diminished ability to recall the core information: some indicate that emotional stories disrupt readers' information-processing capacities or induce cynicism, which in turn encourages readers to discount the information presented in the story (Valkenburg et al. 1999). Many readers thus walk away with an emotional response that informs *how* they think about a particular issue, without them actually knowing *what* the underlying problem is. These effects are particularly problematic if certain discursive strands rely almost exclusively on the use of human-interest frames instead of also discussing the underlying conflict.

According to Stephanie Shapiro, human-interest stories are a particularly influential news genre because they attract a wide variety of readers, including those who are fairly uninformed and generally reluctant to follow complex political, social, or economic debates. For instance, many Americans were not interested in housing code violations and housing inspectors' efforts to navigate New York City's convoluted bureaucracy. At the same time, these readers were probably fascinated by the story of Juana Castillo, an undocumented Mexican immigrant who shared a dark, dank tunnel space with her three small children and relied on grunts, shrieks, and gestures to communicate.[1] On the one hand, human-interest stories have the potential to raise public awareness and encourage otherwise uninformed readers to empathize with individuals like Juana Castillo. On the other hand, these stories tend to oversimplify the problem and ignore complications that might detract from the narrative flow (Shapiro 2006). If readers are unable to supplement individual case studies with additional information and conflicting evidence, they often walk away with a one-sided version of the larger issue the story was intended to illustrate.

In addition, Stephanie Shapiro warns that some human-interest stories are more voyeuristic than informative. These stories tend to focus on particularly sensationalistic examples, and they make little attempt to use these case studies as a means to illuminate the underlying problem and explain the factors that have caused so much personal misery. In the case of Juana Castillo, for example, the *New York Times* wrote extensively about Castillo's sense of desperation, her abusive boyfriend with alcohol problems, and their children's isolation, which had "left emotional and intellectual scars" (*NYT*, October 9, 1996). These descriptions were painfully explicit, with many gruesome details about their living conditions and the abuse and neglect the children, in particular, had been forced to endure. The story concluded that "for Miss Castillo, the immigrant mantra has grown hollow, sullied by too many rat-infested rooms, sunless mornings, melancholy children" (*NYT*, October 9, 1996). Yet, due to the fact that the story included next to no information beyond the personal level, Juana Castillo ultimately emerged not as an example of immigrant dreams gone sour but as a flawed individual who made some bad choices for herself and her children.

In many cases, this type of coverage reinforced existing stereotypes. Human-interest stories about Latino immigrants invariably focused on poor, uneducated, and undocumented families who were struggling to make ends meet. Their extreme poverty was usually also linked to other factors such as domestic violence, crime, as well as the fact that most of these women had multiple children—oftentimes from different partners. The very fact that all three newspapers contained a large number of these negative depictions of Latino immigrants helped paint a one-dimensional picture. What is even more problematic is the fact that there were almost no alternative representations of Latino immigrants. Not only did most human-interest stories depict poverty and neglect, but the few positive examples of successful immigrants focused almost exclusively on Asian immigrants.

In addition to human-interest stories about individual families' struggles with poverty and domestic violence, journalists also focused on "cultural clashes" between native-born U.S. citizens and recent immigrants. In particular, all three newspapers were interested in conflicts caused by so-called day laborers, unskilled workers who gather on street corners and in parking lots to secure short-term jobs doing construction, yard work, and other types of physical labor. On the one hand, newspapers acknowledged that day laborers represented a vital addition to the labor market. Not only did they work hard for extremely low wages; they were also exceptionally flexible, willing to perform a range of jobs and move to wherever their labor was needed the most. Some journalists even conceded that day laborers faced harsh discrimination and were oftentimes exploited by their employers and harassed by the police. On the other hand, most human-interest stories portrayed day laborers as an unassimilable underclass. Even though day laborers might represent an economic asset, they were also perceived as a threat to public safety and middle-class values. I will demonstrate how this tension was tangible in the news media coverage of day laborers and how it also informed policy decisions and influenced the treatment of day laborers in different localities.

This chapter will compare three different types of human-interest stories and explain how these stories functioned within the larger immigration discourse. First, I will focus on stories about individual families and their struggle with poverty, adverse living conditions, and domestic violence. Specifically, I will examine one of the most ambitious, complex, and reflective journalistic projects: *Houston Chronicle*'s ten-part series, entitled "Out of the Shadows." Second, I will examine the newspaper coverage of the marriage and pregnancies of two young girls from Mexico and Iraq. Third, I will demonstrate how human-interest stories about day laborers and neighborhood conflicts stimulated racial anxieties and contributed to a social climate that polarized native-born Americans and immigrants.

Taken together, this chapter will examine how these stories, which were oftentimes more expressive than informative, functioned within the larger neoliberal discourse, which emphasized hard data and cost–benefit analysis. I contend that human-interest stories represented an integral part of the neoliberal project, especially since they foreclosed the debate of structural inequalities and other problems that were generated or at least reinforced by neoliberal economic forces. In particular, I argue that the dramatic examples of immigrants' apparent inability to escape poverty and adhere to heteronormative family values were used to validate the discourse's focus on individual deficiencies. This strategy was especially effective because the mainstream media juxtaposed these negative examples of individuals who had failed to live up to the neoliberal ideal of an active citizen with stories of successful immigrants whose entrepreneurial spirit had ensured economic stability and happiness for their families.

In addition, human-interest stories represented a covert way to introduce race into the larger discourse. In accordance with the general preference for "color-blindness," mainstream newspapers did not comment explicitly on the importance of race. As previous chapters have demonstrated, neoliberal rhetoric tended to disguise racist effects behind economically oriented arguments. Human-interest stories followed the same strategy. While these stories praised successful immigrants for their entrepreneurial spirit, their exceptional work ethic, and their eagerness to adhere to heteronormative family values, the authors made it equally clear that less successful individuals had not tried hard enough to live up to the ideals of neoliberal citizenship. Yet as the following analysis will establish, the stories' subjects were also highly racialized and, especially in the case of Latinas, sexualized. For the most part, human-interest stories suggested that Latino/a immigrants' cultural background represented one of the main obstacles on their road to responsible, self-sufficient neoliberal success. According to this logic, an immigrant's potential to thrive was based on his or her willingness and ability to assimilate to U.S. culture and adopt mainstream ideals and values. Even though journalists were reluctant to comment explicitly on the importance of an immigrant's racial background, their fascination with cultural differences represented a covert way to talk about race.

"Focus on the Family"

Houston Chronicle's "Out of the Shadows" series was an ambitious journalistic endeavor that combined historical information about U.S. immigration legislation, statistical data, profiles of five of the leading immigration experts, and most importantly, detailed reports on four immigrant families.[2] Between May and September 1996, journalist Thaddeus Herrick chronicled the lives of two Mexican families in San Antonio, while his colleague James Pinkerton spent his summer with a Mexican and a Salvadoran family in Houston. The four families were selected after a series of interviews with various immigrants in both metropolitan areas. The final report, which documented the day-to-day challenges faced by these four families, was published in both English and Spanish (online). In addition, the stories were accompanied by a photo essay. The pictures showed the report's featured families at home, at work, at school, in their neighborhoods, and in front of American flags and a variety of other patriotic symbols. The final product was a remarkably complex and well-researched piece of journalism that has received a lot of critical acclaim since its initial publication. The series was also turned into a website that brought together the stories and a wide variety of photographs.[3]

In contrast to most other human-interest stories, the report's creators were also up-front about their agenda and the purpose behind their decision to focus on these Latino immigrant families. Instead of letting the stories speak for themselves, the authors included a prologue, which provided context and background information, as well as an epilogue, which reflected on the lessons to be learned from the individual stories. Both pieces emphasized the fact that immigration reform was a complex issue that was inextricably linked to American culture, society, politics, and the economy. In particular, Herrick and Pinkerton argued that politicians should consider the effects of the Immigration Reform and Control Act of 1986 (IRCA) in their attempt to develop better immigration policies. According to these two authors, the IRCA's residency requirements, deadlines, and guidelines for acceptable documentation resulted in an artificial division between those undocumented workers who were deemed eligible for amnesty and those who were subject to deportation. Ultimately, the IRCA's provisions thus illustrated "America's ambivalence toward immigration. We are hopeful and fearful, sentimental and xenophobic. We see ourselves as a nation of immigrants, and we see immigrants as a threat—to our culture, to our jobs, even to our security" (*Houston Chronicle* [*HC*], "Out of the Shadows—Prologue," October 20, 1996). It is thus hardly surprising that the amnesty provision did not represent a solution to structural inequalities, discrimination, and a lack of economic opportunities.

While some individuals had been able to attain a modest level of success and gain access to jobs that were unavailable to undocumented workers, many workers legalized under amnesty were still "trapped in the other America, where homes often are without telephones and savings are scarce. . . . Two of five families are without private health insurance. . . . Few own homes or cars. Even basic nutrition is beyond the means of many" (*HC*, "Out of the Shadows—Prologue," October 20, 1996). Compared to immigrants without legal documentation, however, these legal permanent residents were at least able to access various government services, enjoy legal protections, and most importantly, live without the constant fear of detection and possible deportation. The stories about the four families, three of whom had taken advantage of the amnesty provision, were supposed to illustrate these differences and "put a human face on the larger immigration debate" (*HC*, "Out of the Shadows—About This Report," October 20, 1996).

Even more important, the authors insisted that their stories should be read in the context of the current immigration reform effort. Interspersed with the four personal accounts, Thaddeus Herrick and James Pinkerton offered their interpretations and hinted at the lessons that could be learned from these stories. Most of these comments, however, were embedded in the actual story line and could thus be easily missed. In order to ensure that readers understood the stories' larger implications, the authors added an interpretative epilogue that clarified the connection between these four examples and the current immigration discourse. In their epilogue, Herrick and Pinkerton repeatedly claimed that the United States lacked the will to stop illegal immigration. They were clearly dissatisfied with the latest immigration reform efforts, which would neither stop undocumented immigrants from coming to the United States nor provide them with the means to succeed. While the two authors acknowledged that "America has given these immigrants an opportunity," they also reminded readers that "in order for them to succeed, to fully participate in the kind of life so many Americans take for granted, the country may need to give them even more" (*HC*, "Out of the Shadows—Epilogue," October 20, 1996). Their series clearly distinguished between those families and individuals who possessed the right kind of entrepreneurial spirit that had helped them prosper and those who had been unable to achieve a comparable level of success. Yet, even though this emphasis on personal merit echoed the general neoliberal logic, their examples were also careful to point out that this success was not merely based on individual factors but also the result of government programs that specifically targeted these immigrants' need to learn English, get an education, and find a job that would enable them to become self-supportive. Herrick and Pinkerton contended that successful immigration reform needed to move beyond the current trend to downsize government and cut immigrant-specific services. Instead, their series recognized that immigrants were part of a larger system, where success was based on more than individual merit.

Yet, even though the authors were critical of the U.S. government's implementation of the neoliberal project, their rhetoric reproduced that same neoliberal logic. For example, the interpretative sections as well as the four narratives discussed immigration reform in terms of costs and benefits. Herrick and Pinkerton stated that U.S. citizens were rightfully concerned about the possibility that "the most recent tide of immigrants, increasingly poor and unskilled, cost the country" (*HC*, "Out of the Shadows—Epilogue," October 20, 1996). They confirmed the widespread concern that "Latin Americans bereft of educational and economic advantages [were] more likely than native-born Americans to live in poverty and collect welfare" (*HC*, "Out of the Shadows—Prologue," October 20, 1996). And, in conclusion, Herrick and Pinkerton asserted that "impoverished, uneducated Latin Americans" who lived an "unprotected, easily exploitable way of life" were "assimilating into San Antonio's voracious inner-city culture" (*HC*, "Out of the Shadows—Epilogue," October 20, 1996). This alarmist language not only reinforced the perception that undocumented Latin American immigrants represented a particularly problematic population but also insinuated that some of these immigrants were "anticitizens" who needed to be policed, controlled, and possibly removed.

Yet, in contrast to this fragment of the immigrant population, which had generated more costs than benefits, Herrick and Pinkerton insisted that there were also some positive examples of successful immigrants. As the following sections will demonstrate, the report made a clear distinction between the two success stories and the two families whose lives were characterized by poverty, gang activity, drugs, and violence. While the latter were reprimanded for their seeming inability to make the "right" decisions, the former group was praised for their constant effort to overcome obstacles and live up to neoliberal ideals. On one level, the portrayal of Mari Hernandez's "near-heroic climb from maid to migrant to entrepreneur" and Maria Ortiz's ability to work "her way up from cleaning toilets to overseeing the hotel restaurant" merely replicated the dominant neoliberal rhetoric.[4] At the same time, however, it is important to recognize that the report focused exclusively on immigrants who had entered the United States without proper documentation. As previous chapters have demonstrated, the immigration discourse typically portrayed all "illegal aliens" as undeserving "anticitizens" who represented a threat to society, public safety, the economy, as well as the school system. "Out of the Shadows," on the other hand, interrogated this categorical distinction between legal and illegal immigrants and suggested that at least some of these illegal immigrants might be worth the investment and deserving of legalization programs.

The narrative structure of the report helped to underline the fact that undocumented—or, in this case, legalized—Latino immigrants were a heterogeneous group. Instead of dividing the report into four separate sections with a specific focus on each individual family, the authors decided to intersperse the four story lines and organize the narrative around a number of important issues, such as interpersonal relationships, education, work, and the English language. In many cases, a particularly negative example was followed immediately by an account of a person who had successfully mastered the same challenge. The third installment, for instance, started with a brief glimpse into the Reyes family's life, which was characterized by alcoholism, domestic violence, and "rickety rentals deep in the barrio" (*HC*, Part IV, October 20, 1996). Without a transition, the story line switched to Mari and Erasmo Hernandez, who had "two insured cars, credit cards and a small savings account. With luck, they would soon be in their own home" (*HC*, Part IV, October 20, 1996). Because of this narrative mode, the reader was oftentimes left with the impression that a family's level of success was not at all connected to structural factors but primarily based on their ability to conform to the neoliberal ideal of self-help.

In addition to comparing and contrasting these families' achievements and failures, the authors included frequent explanatory comments that guided the reader's response and encouraged a specific interpretation of the more descriptive passages. With regard to the two families who had reached a modest level of success, the authors were particularly interested in the personal characteristics, behaviors, and values that had enabled them to reach their position. Mari and Erasmo Hernandez, in particular, were consistently lauded in terms that represented them as ideal neoliberal subjects. When the authors introduced Mari for the first time, they described her as an "entrepreneur and one-time illegal immigrant, beneficiary of amnesty and soon-to-be first-time homeowner" (*HC*, "Out of the Shadows—Part I," October 20, 1996). The story recounts her journey from Mexico to Brownsville, where she cleaned houses for middle-class whites and met her soon-to-be husband Erasmo, a hard worker who is highly motivated to get ahead in life. Once legalized, the couple moved to Houston. Erasmo accepted a physically demanding job in a nearby plant, and Mari entered a government-sponsored training program for beauticians. After successful completion of the program, Mari decided to take a risk and open her own business, the H and L Beauty Salon, which has thrived ever since.

According to the authors, Mari and Erasmo's unfaltering will to make the most of the few chances they were offered had turned them into "examples of a government program that worked" (*HC*, "Out of the Shadows—Part III," October 20, 1996). The subsidized training program had proven to be a good investment. This exemplary progress, however, would not have been possible without a number of other factors. On the one hand, the story focuses on both Mari and Erasmo's willingness to work extremely hard and supplement their low income with temporary jobs. Instead of enjoying the fruits of their labor, the couple continues to make personal sacrifices and prioritize work over family life. On the other hand, the authors also implied that the Hernandezes' modest success was at least partly based on chance or, rather, on their inability to have children. They wrote, "Add a couple of children—the Hernandezes had tried for years to have a baby—and Erasmo's salary would be poverty level for a family of four. With Mari's income and no kids, however, the couple avoided that trap" (*HC*, "Out of the Shadows—Part IX," October 20, 1996).

In line with the larger discourse about immigration and welfare reform, Herrick and Pinkerton insisted that a couple's adherence to neoliberal family values was the key to their success. Since financial stability was commonly accepted as the ultimate goal in a neoliberal society, poor people were expected to delay or even abandon their desire to have children if they aspired to escape their poverty. For low-income families like the Hernandezes, children represented a stumbling block to financial security and middle-class living standards. Mari Hernandez's wish to have children, despite her fragile financial situation, was thus dismissed as irrational, and the authors made little attempt to mask their disapproval. Instead, a woman's reproductive choices needed to be governed by rationality and self-control.

In contrast, the Ortizes were praised for their unfaltering commitment to their two young children and their determination to provide them with the best possible education. Thirty-five-year old Maria Ortiz, who had fled the civil war in El Salvador in the early 1980s, was described as a role model for other parents: "She worried about her daughter's education. . . . She wanted to protect her daughters as best she could from the American fast lane, allowing them to finish high school, get a scholarship and have a career. 'Nothing too big,' Maria would say. 'But a better life'" (*HC*, "Out of the Shadows—Part IV," October 20, 1996). In order to achieve this goal, Maria was an active parent who volunteered at her daughters' schools and communicated with administrators and teachers regularly. As a result of her efforts, eleven-year-old Nathalie was accepted into a competitive fine-arts magnet school and Marisol, a kindergartner, attended one of Houston's best elementary schools. According to the authors, Maria's drive and commitment were a direct result of her own upbringing. They wrote, "Maria's high school education gave her an advantage in seeing 'the good way,' as did her middle-class Salvadoran upbringing" (*HC*, "Out of the Shadows—Part II," October 20, 1996). From a neoliberal perspective, Maria thus represented a particularly desirable immigrant because, without further expenditures, U.S. society would be able to profit from the money the Salvadoran government had already invested in her education.

Maria's upbringing was also described as one of the main factors that had taught her to stay away from the U.S. welfare system. In contrast to many of her coworkers, who supposedly went on welfare because they refused to clean offices, hotel rooms, and bathrooms daily, she had never shied away from hard or dirty work. From her perspective, it was disgraceful for an able-bodied adult to accept government assistance. In addition, Maria had kept close to her extended family.[5] In times of need, she could always rely on her parents and siblings. They helped each other with child care; assisted each other when they bought, renovated, and moved into their own houses; and perhaps most importantly, were able to understand each other's struggles. Maria's extended family thus represented a valuable informal support network. In short, Maria was described as a desirable immigrant because she came from a "culture" of hard work and unfaltering family values.

In the course of the series, Maria Ortiz emerged as the model immigrant. Not only did her ambition, intelligence, and strong work ethic help her succeed in a competitive job market; her commitment to her family and her ability to rely on their support had turned her into an exemplary neoliberal subject. As undocumented immigrants, Maria and her relatives had never signed an affidavit of support. Nonetheless, they regarded it as self-evident that family members would support each other, instead of taking advantage of the welfare system. Hence Maria's story seemed to confirm a number of concerns and suggestions that had dominated the legislative discourse. As previous chapters have demonstrated, Congress's goal was to decrease government expenditures and turn financial obligations over to individual immigrants and their sponsors. Maria's exemplary success suggested that this was the right—and maybe even the only— solution to the "immigration crisis."

At the same time, the story's stark contrasts between the individual families made it clear that immigrants like Maria were economically desirable and much more acceptable members of U.S. society than those legalized immigrants who had failed to live up to neoliberal ideals. Whereas all the other adult protagonists were unable to communicate in English and continued to socialize with Spanish-speaking individuals only, Maria had mastered the English language and passed the naturalization exam in record time. Perhaps not surprisingly, she was the one and only person in this series who had regular contact with native-born Americans and navigated American culture, society, and politics almost effortlessly. In other words, she had successfully assimilated into mainstream America. The authors thus used Maria as their focal point. She was the person readers could identify with: her concerns about her daughters' education corresponded to the readers' own worries, and her dream to buy a house in the suburbs resonated with readers as well.

The editorial about the series, which was published a few days after the last installment, confirmed this fundamental distinction between potential U.S. citizens and those immigrants who represented a burden or, even worse, a threat: the stories "told of successes and tentative steps toward the American dream with small business enterprises and home ownership. They told of the kind of difficulties that many American families face with rearing children and choosing good schools for them. And the stories recounted, in real, human terms, some behaviors and circumstances that so irk citizens, who feel they are bearing the financial and social burdens of illegal immigration. Recounted were brushes with the criminal justice system, welfare fraud, some cases of complete unfamiliarity with the English language and teen-age parents who had their babies at state expense" (*HC*, "In the Shadows—Editorial," October 29, 1996).

The story left little doubt as to which family fell into which category. In contrast to the two glowing representations of the Ortizes and the Hernandezes, the authors expressed little understanding for the struggles of the Reyes family and for Roberto and Teresa, two undocumented immigrants who had failed to apply for amnesty in 1986. The Reyeses, in particular, were depicted as the epitome of an undesirable immigrant family. Throughout the narrative, the authors repeatedly emphasized the fact that Victor and Marcelina Reyes had seven children and two grandchildren. The introductory passage of the first installment, for instance, explained that "Rey's mother and father, his brother, five sisters and 2-month-old niece were halfway to Piedras Negras, Mexico," while Rey, his girlfriend Gloria, and their little daughter Kimberly—"two 16-year-olds and their baby"—were watching *Menace II Society* (*HC*, "Out of the Shadows—Part II," October 20, 1996). In the third installment, the reader learned that the family was on their way back from Mexico: "At 4 a.m. June 17, the day after Father's Day, Victor and Marcelina and their six children, one grandchild and three Mexican relatives—a total of 12—piled into the Ford and headed home to San Antonio" (*HC*, "Out of the Shadows—Part III," October 20, 1996).[6] This image of twelve family members who "piled" into an old and unreliable car resonated powerfully with readers' preconceived notions about Mexican Americans.

Since this story was published in a respectable newspaper, each of these passages was probably an accurate description of the Reyes family. Yet, in the context of the larger immigration discourse, this particular representation of the Reyes family also had another, much more problematic function. As previous chapters have shown, the anti-immigrant discourse was constructed around a number of powerful images. One of the images, which caused much anxiety among many native-born U.S. citizens, was the figure of the poor, overly fertile Latina immigrant, who—due to her large number of children—had become trapped in a culture of poverty, crime, and violence. This negative image undoubtedly informed readers' interpretation of "Out of the Shadows" and helped them classify the information they received about the Reyes family.

This portrayal of Latina mothers also needs to be read in the context of debates about "welfare mothers," which occurred almost simultaneously and helped to construct a negative image of women on welfare and poor women in general. According to the welfare reform discourse, "the stereotypical welfare mother is a symbol of the supposed irresponsible, sexually promiscuous, and immoral behavior of the poor" (McCormack 2005, 660). Not surprisingly, the larger neoliberal framework suggested that these women had fallen on hard times because of the poor choices they had made—choices about their education, employment, partners, and having children out of wedlock. Single motherhood emerged as one of the major explanations for poverty. "Welfare mothers" were supposedly poor and "dependent" on welfare because they were sexually promiscuous. Their irresponsible behavior was seen as a threat to not just their own economic survival but traditional family values and domestic stability. This image was far from race neutral: "Embedded in the notion of the welfare mother are powerful ideologies of race, class, and gender that . . . portray women, particularly Black and Hispanic women, as inadequate mothers; and view nontraditional family forms as pathological" (McCormack 2005, 660). Political debates and media representations in the mid-1990s were able to build on this negative image of "welfare mothers" and develop a similar racialized and hypersexual portrayal of poor Latina immigrant women.

In the study, Marcelina Reyes, in particular, emerged as a problematic figure. Married to an abusive husband who made less than fifteen thousand dollars per year, Marcelina had seven children in quick succession. Hence she had no opportunity to learn English, get an education, or take advantage of job training opportunities like Mari Ortiz or Maria Hernandez. It was not even necessary for the authors to connect these pieces of information. The larger discourse only allowed for one possible explanation: Marcelina's seeming unwillingness to control her fertility had prevented her family from climbing up the social ladder. As a result, they were permanently "trapped in the other America." Her family had become part of "America's distinct and debilitating urban culture" (*HC*, "Out of the Shadows—Prologue," October 20, 1996). The story further implied that Marcelina's unrestrained sexuality and the family's resulting failure to leave the "barrio" had had devastating consequences for her children. Herrick and Pinkerton were particularly interested in the two children who had just become parents themselves. Brenda, Marcelina's oldest daughter, was described as an ambitious, intelligent student, who was determined to be the first in her family to graduate from high school and get a college degree. In short, Brenda had the potential to realize her dreams and create a better future for herself and maybe even for her family. During her senior year, however, she became pregnant and stopped attending school regularly. Her grades dropped, and she scored in the bottom 10 percent of the SAT. In the end, it was unclear whether she would even try to attend junior college.

According to the story, Brenda was caught between two conflicting forces. On the one hand, several dedicated teachers who had recognized her untapped potential tried to instill a strong work ethic and a sense of personal responsibility into this young second-generation-immigrant student. On the other hand, however, Brenda had grown up with no positive role models. Her parents, who had not even finished the seventh grade, had consistently failed to act responsibly themselves. In the end, Brenda was apparently unable to live up to her teacher's expectations and escape her parents' negative influence. This simplistic portrayal, which ignored other factors (such as access to sex education, birth control, and health-care services, more generally) and failed to take Brenda's own perspective into account, reinforced the common perception that it was Mexican immigrants' lack of self-control that made it impossible for them to advance beyond unskilled, minimum-wage jobs.

The representation of Brenda's brother Rey further confirmed this thesis. As opposed to his sister, Rey had never even made an effort to turn his life into a success. He had managed to get expelled from every single school he had ever attended—for stealing, fighting, and pulling knives on fellow students. When he was thirteen years old, Rey joined a gang of mostly Mexican American teenagers and now, at age sixteen, faced charges for possessing stolen goods. He was also thinking about breaking up with his girlfriend, who had just given birth to their daughter, Kimberly.

According to the authors, Rey's life story was far from unique: "In many ways, he is not unlike your average 16-year-old. He dresses like one, talks like one, shares the same interests. The difference is that Rey, isolated by poverty and deprived of the special guidance a troubled kid needs, is more vulnerable to the pitfalls of urban America" (*HC*, "Out of the Shadows—Part I," October 20, 1996). What is implied in this passage, of course, is that Rey is not unlike your average Mexican American teenager, or just another brown or black resident of "urban America." The story offered vivid descriptions of his clothing, which included baggy pants, T-shirts, and green bandanas, as well as his physical appearance: "His head was shaved around the sides, a stubbly 'wedge' left on top and a 'rattail' dyed reddish blond in the back" (*HC*, "Out of the Shadows—Part I," October 20, 1996). Obviously, this image corresponded with the reader's idea of a violent, drug-dealing gang member. For the most part, however, the authors refrained from such explicit rhetoric and let the image speak for itself.

Instead, the authors relied heavily on the use of metaphors and code words and insisted that Rey's story represented "a vivid illustration of the enormous challenges facing young inner-city Hispanics" (*HC*, "Out of the Shadows—Part VII," October 20, 1996). On one level, these allusions to "urban America" and "inner-city" problems seemed to acknowledge that social inequalities, poverty, and racial segregation obviously had an effect on many young Latinos and Latinas. Yet, since the story neither attempted to interrogate the specific nature of these problems nor explained why these problems afflicted so many young Latinos and Latinas, the aforementioned comments did little but confirm existing racial stereotypes.

In contrast to Marcelina Reyes's apparent failure to ensure a better future for her children, Teresa's story was much more ambivalent. Teresa, an undocumented mother of six children between the ages of one and sixteen, was described as an active parent who made every effort to protect her children from the "urban culture" that had supposedly ruined the lives of the Reyes children. In their poor, predominantly Mexican American neighborhood, her two sons, ten-year-old Guillermo and twelve-year-old Jesus, stood out: "Not only were they lighter-skinned than most of the children at Cassiano, they dressed differently. Teresa allowed no baggy shirts or pants. Teresa also frowned upon wedge haircuts and rattails" (*HC*, "Out of the Shadows—Part VI," October 20, 1996). Even though Teresa had almost no formal education, she was described as smart and eager to learn. Her actions and comments proved that she had clearly identified the potential obstacles that could prevent her children from getting ahead in life. Teresa recognized that gangs might seem appealing to her young sons, while pregnancy was the primary obstacle for her daughters.

Compared to Marcelina, Teresa not only was depicted as a better, more caring mother but also emerged as a person who had gained more insight into the intricate social norms and divisions of U.S. society. In many ways, however, Teresa merely reproduced the dominant discourse about welfare dependency and recipients' lack of personal responsibility. For instance, Teresa was critical of legal immigrants who received welfare benefits and adamant in her claims that her family did not deserve to be "stuck at Cassiano Homes amid welfare moms and their gang-banger children" (HC, "Out of the Shadows—Part II," October 20, 1996). By juxtaposing Teresa's antiwelfare rhetoric with her repeated efforts to gain access to food stamps, free school supplies, and free immigration counseling, the story also implied that Teresa's negative attitude toward federal welfare benefits might be a direct result of her own lack of eligibility. Yet her feelings also illustrated the pitfalls of the national discourse on welfare reform. While the abstract rhetoric about a cycle of poverty and the need to help recipients become self-sufficient sounded convincing to many Americans, it was easy to forget that these reforms would not put an end to poverty. Teresa, for instance, had apparently internalized the dominant rhetoric, but she also realized that her children's immediate needs outweighed her desire to conform to these norms. More fundamental reforms were needed before she could pass up an opportunity for valuable goods and services.

Herrick and Pinkerton, however, had a different and much more simplistic explanation for Teresa's difficult situation. They wrote, "Teresa felt hobbled by her secret. In truth, her illegal status was just one of several obstacles. She was raising six children, two of them no more than 2 years old" (HC, "Out of the Shadows—Part II," October 20, 1996). To make matters worse, Teresa's hyperfertility and her struggle to take proper care of six children was complicated by domestic violence. Even though the authors were hesitant to blame Teresa for the fact that she had stayed in an abusive relationship for well over a decade, they made it clear that they could not understand her position. Initially, Herrick and Pinkerton explained that "though she describes her marriage as punctuated by bouts of Roberto's drunkenness and hostility, Teresa refused to leave her husband because, she said, 'He is all I've ever known'" (HC, "Out of the Shadows—Part IV," October 20, 1996). In later installments, they added that Teresa had stayed because "she needed Roberto's money and he needed shelter" and because "somehow she felt guilty in her marriage . . . no matter how poorly Roberto treated her" (*HC*, "Out of the Shadows—Part VIII," October 20, 1996). What they do not talk about is the fact that Teresa's options are extremely limited given her immigration status and her socioeconomic situation.

Despite the fact that this series represented an ambitious effort to portray immigrants as a diverse group of individuals who had achieved varying levels of success, the story ultimately reinforced the dominant neoliberal rhetoric. By juxtaposing two success stories with two particularly bleak examples of families whose lives were characterized by poverty, violence, and crime, the authors downplayed the importance of structural factors and emphasized the significance of individual ambition and an entrepreneurial spirit. In addition, the authors framed these immigrants' lives as a struggle between Mexican—or, in case of the Ortiz family, Salvadoran— cultural values and the influence of their host country's culture. While the two successful families had been eager to adapt to mainstream U.S. culture, the two other families had seemingly failed to assimilate. In the end, the series suggested, their lack of success was primarily based on their inability to see the problems inherent in their own cultural practices and belief systems. Even though the authors did not comment explicitly on the importance of race, this discussion about "culture" has a clear racial subtext.

This tendency to use cultural differences as a way to talk about race dates back to the liberal race paradigm, the Chicago School of Sociology, and the publication of Gunnar Myrdal's 1944 study *An American Dilemma*. Robert E. Park and his associates were among the first to challenge the predominant biological concept of race. According to their study of European immigrants in the late nineteenth and early twentieth centuries, race relations went through a four-stage cycle, with assimilation as the ultimate goal. The Chicago sociologists argued that the same model of cultural assimilation could be applied to nonwhite immigrant groups and other racial minorities, who would all eventually be incorporated into American society in essentially the same way as white ethnic groups. Gunnar Myrdal agreed that racial segregation and discrimination could not endure in the United States and that assimilation was the most desirable outcome for all groups. As long as African Americans were willing to follow the footsteps of European immigrants and assimilate to U.S. national culture, they would reach greater equality and acceptance and America would achieve its manifest destiny (Melamed 2006). This theory undoubtedly helped pathologize African American cultural norms and family structures, which were identified as one of the root causes of inequality. Myrdal's theory was also based on his unfaltering belief that African Americans were treated differently and did not have the same opportunities as white Americans. Racial inequality was not the result of biological differences but cultural differences, combined with structural inequalities such as employment discrimination and legal segregation.

While the current discourse about immigrants' culture as the primary obstacle to economic success certainly draws on these earlier discourses, it revises the liberal paradigm of race as culture in a number of important ways. I agree with Jodi Melamed's assessment that, in the new neoliberal version of race as culture, "'culture' no longer replaces older, biological conceptions of race; it displaces racial reference altogether" (Melamed 2006, 19). Neoliberal multiculturalism thus makes it almost impossible to engage in a critical analysis of persisting structural inequalities and their racist effects. If two of the four immigrant families in the "Out of the Shadows" series were able to act like neoliberal subjects and achieve personal success, there was clearly nothing wrong with the larger system. If immigrants fail to succeed, this failure is based on individual deficiencies and their unwillingness to assimilate to U.S. cultural norms and the dominant neoliberal mind-set. It is thus up to the individual immigrant—and not the U.S. government—to ensure success. This strategic focus on culture and individual traits, as opposed to race and structural inequality, will become even more obvious in the following section.

Teenage Pregnancy

In the course of the 1995–96 welfare reform movement, teenage pregnancy and out-of-wedlock births were identified as two of the major evils that had led to the so-called culture of poverty and the ensuing cycle of dependency that it supposedly produced. When anthropologist Oscar Lewis developed the "culture of poverty" concept in the late 1950s, he set out to explain how Puerto Rican families' lives were transformed by poverty. Lewis argued that poor children were socialized in such a way that made it difficult—if not impossible—for them to escape poverty. Supposedly, poor children's lives were characterized by absent fathers, drugs, violence, poor work habits, and perhaps most importantly, their mothers' obsession with sex. Hence Lewis separated poverty from structural causes such as a high unemployment rates, substandard housing, and a lack of access to quality education, and instead argued that poor people's choices and behaviors were the underlying cause of their dismal situation. While Lewis's theories asserted a strong influence on the "War on Poverty" in the mid-1960s, contemporary scholars questioned the validity of his claims and warned of the problematic implications that Lewis's theories have had for social welfare policies.[7]

Yet, despite these criticisms, the neoliberal reform movement in the mid-1990s was not only firmly grounded in the belief that success was a direct result of individual merit; it also suggested the poor people's lives were characterized by a common set of problematic behaviors and values that were continually passed on from one generation to the next. It was up to the government to break through this "cycle of poverty" and force poor people to abandon their erroneous ways. Teenage pregnancy and single motherhood, in particular, were perceived as two of the most pervasive problems. Title I, section 101, of the Personal Responsibility Act (Pub. L. No. 104-193) spelled out Congress's findings and concerns—among them statistics showing that teenage mothers were more likely to receive welfare. Congress claimed, "Children of teenage single parents have lower cognitive scores, lower educational aspirations, and a greater likelihood of becoming teenage parents themselves" (Pub. L. No. 104-193, title I, § 101, 9[I]). In conclusion, the law stated, "In light of this demonstration of the crisis in our Nation, it is the sense of the Congress that prevention of out-of-wedlock pregnancy and reduction in out-of-wedlock births are very important Government interests" (Pub. L. No. 104-193, title I, § 101, 10).

This explicit emphasis on individual choices and personal deficiencies is reflected in the decision to call the welfare reform act the Personal *Responsibility* Act. This name seemed like a logical description of a reform effort that dismantled the welfare state and blamed the poor for their own failings. According to the larger discursive field, overly generous welfare benefits had trapped recipients in a cycle of poverty and dependency and enabled them to continue their immoral and irresponsible behaviors. Instead of further supporting these poor choices, like single motherhood and teen pregnancy, the welfare reform act was designed to force poor people to achieve self-sufficiency and make responsible decisions. Demanding self-sufficiency from immigrants was seen as an even more important goal. Since immigration was not a right but a privilege (at least according to the immigration reform discourse of the mid-1990s), immigration reform measures set to develop better mechanisms for selecting the most productive individuals. To further this objective, newly arrived immigrants were explicitly excluded from all welfare benefits, and the Illegal Immigration Reform and Immigrant *Responsibility* Act embarked on a larger project to ensure that immigrants would be legally required to deliver their end of the immigration bargain by acting responsibly, working hard, paying taxes, staying out of trouble, and adhering to heteronormative family values.

According to the personal responsibility rhetoric that informed both the welfare- and immigration-reform discourse, poor citizens, and even worse, poor immigrants, failed to live up to neoliberal ideals. It thus became necessary for the U.S. government—through welfare and immigration reform—to force them to assume greater responsibility for their lives. This sense of crisis had been shaped and cultivated by the entertainment as well as the news media. Countless human-interest stories focused on single mothers and pregnant teenagers and offered vivid illustrations of their children's struggles and the insurmountable obstacles that they invariably faced. Since the underlying neoliberal logic foreclosed any attempt to engage in a serious debate about the role that race and ethnicity played in this discourse about sexuality and motherhood, stories tended to discuss teenage pregnancy in terms of "cultural differences." Yet, while most discourse participants were reluctant to talk openly about race, there seemed to be a consensus that teenage pregnancy and single motherhood were primarily black problems. Throughout the discourse, code words such as "welfare mothers" and "welfare queens" were used to signify a person's race, and the term "cultural differences" functioned as a covert way to talk about racial differences. Even though much of the discourse made no direct references to a person's race, there was a pronounced racial subtext that was easily understood by readers familiar with it.

The discursive images of the welfare queen and the teenage mother helped shape the general public's ideas about poverty and establish clear distinctions between those individuals who were deserving of public assistance and those who were personally responsible for their problems. According to Karen McCormack, "the stereotypical welfare mother is a symbol of the supposed irresponsible, sexually promiscuous, and immoral behavior of the poor" (McCormack 2005, 660). Poor single mothers were not only blamed for their poverty and discussed as a social problem; they were also commonly portrayed as inadequate mothers. The discursive field that produced these images fit nicely within the dominant neoliberal construction of productive citizens, good motherhood and healthy families, and personal responsibility. It is also marked by "powerful, taken-for-granted assumptions about the characteristics of moral citizens (as hardworking, independent, self-controlled, sexually monogamous)" (McCormack 2005, 663). Welfare recipients are positioned outside of the narrow boundaries of moral, neoliberal citizenship and blamed for their decision to have children out of wedlock and for their failure to support their children financially.

This discursive construction of bad motherhood was further complicated when the pregnant teenager was not a U.S. citizen but an immigrant from a different cultural background. The following section will look at two specific cases that received considerable media attention in 1996. The first case concerned Adela Quintana, an undocumented Mexican immigrant who had resided in the Houston area for the better part of her life. She came to the attention of the Children's Protective Services Agency (CPS) when she used a fake birth certificate, which her mother had obtained for her, to apply for welfare benefits for herself and her unborn child. According to the birth certificate, which was made out to "Cindy Garcia," Quintana was only nine years old, rather than fourteen, when she became pregnant. When the welfare agency became aware of the pregnant girl's age, Quintana was immediately taken into custody and placed into a children's shelter. Shortly afterwards, Quintana disappeared during church services and became the subject of a massive search. When the police located her three days later, Quintana was placed into temporary custody of CPS and her twenty-two-year-old boyfriend Pedro Sotelo, who admitted to having had sex with her, was arrested for sexual assault of a minor.[8]

For the next year and a half, the *Houston Chronicle* followed the case, from the birth of Quintana's son, who was born blind, to Sotelo's court case, the controversy over his amassed traffic tickets, and the eventual deportation proceedings for both parents. During this time, the *Houston Chronicle* published more than twenty articles and dozens of readers wrote indignant letters to the editor. Even after Pedro Sotelo was eventually deported, the case reappeared in the media periodically. On July 7, 2006, for example, the *Houston Chronicle* reported that Salvadoran immigrant Jose Lazo, a nationally known spokesman for displaced Enron workers, faced deportation proceedings because he had impregnated his thirteen-year-old girlfriend when he was seventeen years old. According to the *Houston Chronicle*, his situation was comparable to "Pedro Sotelo, a Mexican living in Houston who was 22 when he got his 14-year-old wife pregnant" (*HC*, July 7, 2006).[9]

The second case, which involved an Iraqi immigrant couple, did not receive the same degree of media attention. There were only three letters to the editor, written in response to an article titled "No Sex Charges in Case of Iraqi Girl's Marriage" (*San Francisco Chronicle* [*SFC*], August 7, 1996) and one follow-up story that appeared in print a few weeks later. However, the coverage of this unnamed eleven-year-old Iraqi girl, whose family had arranged a marriage with thirty-year-old Mohammed Alsreafi, expressed the same anxieties that had characterized the controversy about Adela Quintana. In particular, both stories portrayed the older men as dangerous sexual predators, who, to make matters worse, failed to understand why U.S. society regarded their actions as illegal and morally repugnant. In contrast, the girls were described as the victims of an oppressive, patriarchal culture that had so much power over them that they were incapable of resisting their abusers. For the most part, the stories implied that the U.S. government needed to rescue these young women and protect them from their own values and traditions. At the same time, a number of discourse participants insisted that these two young women were victims of a "cultural collision." According to this reading, it was not the immigrant community who needed to assimilate their beliefs to the dominant culture, but it was U.S. society that was insensitive and intolerant of other cultures and needed to learn to accept value systems that were different from their own. As the following analysis will demonstrate, both sides ultimately reinforced a problematic image of immigrants as a culturally different Other.

Both of the initial human-interest stories insisted that these cases were not just about two young teenagers who had sexual relations with older men; there were larger issues at stake. Specifically, the *San Francisco Chronicle* story about the Iraqi girl argued that her relationship was not an isolated case. Quite to the contrary, her arranged marriage to an older man was described as the logical consequence of her upbringing and her community's adherence to "Middle Eastern cultural values" that supposedly dominated the lives of Iraqi immigrants in the United States. To provide some explanatory background information, the *San Francisco Chronicle* asked numerous experts to explain Middle Eastern culture to

U.S. readers. Iyad Alqazzaz, an expert in Middle Eastern culture and history at California State University, noted that while it was not unusual for Iraqis to arrange marriages for their fifteen- or sixteen-year-old daughters, it was "extremely unusual for a twelve-year-old to marry" (*San Francisco Chronicle* [*SFC*], August 7, 1996). According to Alqazzaz, U.S. authorities should thus draw a clear line between those cases that are unacceptable in both cultures and those cases that are sanctioned by Iraqi cultural practices. Since evidence seemed to suggest that the Iraqi girl might have been older than the age listed on her immigration card, which indicated that she was eleven years old when she first allegedly had sex with Alsreafi, Alqazzaz's statement seemed to support Deputy District Attorney Susan Breall's decision to drop the sexual assault charges.

This image of Arabs, Muslims, and Middle Easterners—three distinct categories that are oftentimes conflated in popular discourse—as a menacing cultural Other has been a part of the U.S. cultural imagination for a long time. Drawing on Michael Omi and Howard Winant's theory of racial formations, Mehdi Semati explores how "today's imagery, narratives, and ideas about Muslims, the Middle East, and 'Islam' have their roots in Orientalist visions and narratives that the 'West' has produced for centuries" (Semati 2010, 258). According to Edward Said's work, artists, writers, and politicians all helped construct the "Orient" as an exotic Other—a place that is inherently and fundamentally different from the West and that, as a contrasting image, helps us define Western civilization. More recent political events, such as the 1967 Arab–Israeli war, the Arab oil embargo, and the first bombing of the World Trade Center, helped adjust the 1990s image of the "Muslim Other" from an embodiment of exoticism and inferior culture to something much more menacing. According to this new racial formation, which has become even more pronounced after the events of September 11, 2001, Muslim men are depicted as religious fanatics and potential terrorists who are permanently trapped in a belief system that is "immutable, fixed, frozen and static" (Semati 2010, 266). Muslim women, on the other hand, are commonly perceived as victims: victims of brutal men, an oppressive culture, as well as their own inability to find fault with their religion and culture. In short, Muslim women and, by extension, their children, need rescuing.

Even though the larger discourse had already firmly established an image of Iraqi culture as inherently violent and oppressive, it was apparently still necessary to cite independent experts who confirmed this commonly accepted "truth." As previous chapters have demonstrated, politicians and other public figures were well aware of the need to appear nondiscriminatory and abstain from openly racist language. If a person violated this unspoken rule, the consequences were immediate and severe. It is hardly surprising then that journalists as well as the law enforcement officers involved in this case tried to make sure that their reactions to this sensitive issue were endorsed by the leading experts. The story about this arranged marriage thus not only cited various experts but also emphasized the fact that Deputy District Attorney Susan Breall "said she arrived at [her decision to drop the charges] after a thorough investigation and consultation with an expert familiar with Iraqi culture" (*SFC*, August 7, 1996). Since this young girl was "married in the eyes of her culture and her community," who regarded their marriage as a "voluntary, consensual, sexual relationship," the prosecution would have effectively condemned the entire Middle Eastern immigrant community if they had taken this case to trial (*SFC*, August 7, 1996). Political correctness and cultural sensitivity clearly forbade such a course of action.[10]

Not everyone agreed with this assessment. Despite the fact that human-interest stories do not usually involve strong positions on the issues being discussed, this initial story about Mohammed Alsreafi clearly suggested that his actions should be illegal and were morally repugnant. And if his community was willing to accept and, in the case of the girl's parents, facilitate his abusive behavior, it supposedly deserved to be put on trial by U.S. authorities. To support this reading, the author framed the article as a story about lies, corruption, and sexual abuse. The article vividly portrayed the family's conflicting excuses and explanations. When first questioned, the girl's parents had supposedly claimed that their twelve-year-old daughter was not married. Yet, upon realizing that this explanation could lead to a lawsuit against Alsreafi, they had "said they were married and produced some video of the ceremony" (*SFC*, August 7, 1996). In addition, they insisted that their daughter was not twelve but eighteen years old. Meanwhile, Alsreafi kept changing his story as well. While he had initially admitted to having sex with a twelve-year-old, he later claimed that he was not aware of her age, had never had sex with her, and had lawfully married her a few months earlier. The story thus implied that Iraqis were secretive, dishonest, and had actively attempted to deceive U.S. authorities.

In the end, it remained unclear which version of the story was actually true and whether the young woman was twelve or eighteen years old. Even more important, the story seemed to suggest that finding the truth was not important since the same concerns would hold true in either case. From the very beginning, the author made it clear that this was most certainly "a case in which Middle Eastern cultural values collide with California law" (*SFC*, August 7, 1996). I contend that, judging from the accusatory tone of this human-interest story, this statement did not just reference the crime that had allegedly been committed by Mohammed Alsreafi. Instead, the article's opening line should be understood as a much more far-reaching commentary on Middle Eastern culture, traditions, and values in general. By juxtaposing Middle Eastern *culture* with California *law*, the author implied that there should not even be a debate over which system had precedence over the other.

By framing this controversy as a collision of cultural values and the U.S. legal system, the discourse obscured the racial subtext. At the same time, however, racial anxieties and prejudiced notions about Muslim culture informed this discourse. The neoliberal demand for a color-blind rhetoric prevented xenophobic remarks and obliged the media to appear open minded, at least to a certain extent. Yet this standard for political correctness was not accompanied by a more far-reaching interrogation of widely held beliefs about Muslim culture. As the aforementioned example demonstrated, the mainstream media was careful to frame their concerns in racially neutral terms. A racially specific subtext, however, made it perfectly clear that Muslim culture was not only deemed incompatible with mainstream U.S. culture but also perceived as highly problematic and oppressive of women. Since the larger immigration discourse had already established that it was necessary to protect "our culture" from harmful foreign influences and protect Muslim women from oppressive traditions, the story was able to tap into this general emotion without much explanation.

Interestingly, some readers felt that this implied reading was not quite obvious enough. In their letters to the editor, these readers explicitly stated that the United States had no obligation to endorse cultural traditions that were in clear violation of the dominant value system. On August 13, 1996, for instance, Laina Farhat wrote that "cultural sensitivity is a noble notion, but is not a blanket. . . . Why is child marriage all right just because her 'community' thinks it is all right? What are we thinking of? We should rescue that child!" (*SFC*, August 13, 1996). Two days later, Gary C. Cramer made a very similar point when he insisted that "not all cultural differences are worthy of the same respect in a Western society, and this is especially true when it comes to sex with children" (*SFC*, August 15, 1996). While most readers would certainly agree that preteen girls should be protected from adult males, it is important to keep in mind that there was no indication that other Iraqi immigrant parents arranged marriages for their eleven- or twelve-year-old daughters. Yet despite this lack of evidence, these letters implied that this one case was not an isolated occurrence but representative of the entire Iraqi immigrant community. The discourse thus not only highlighted cultural differences between Iraqi immigrants and native-born U.S. citizens but also suggested that immigrants were uncompromising in their cultural beliefs and unaware of U.S. laws and traditions. Notwithstanding the fact that this young girl had spent almost her entire life in the United States, the *San Francisco Chronicle* thus consulted a Middle East specialist, who referenced customs in "remote rural areas" in an effort to explain her behavior.

Given the fact that, in the mid-1990s, U.S. citizens were much more anxious about "waves" of Latino/a immigrants than the comparatively small number of Muslim immigrants, it is hardly surprising that Latinos' and Latinas' perceived inability to conform to a certain type of fertility received much more attention (as demonstrated by the popularity of the Quintana case). The larger discourse had already established a clear division between "normative" Anglo fertility and "nonnormative" Latina fertility. According to Leo Chavez's work on "Latina Reproduction and Public Discourse," Latinas' reproductive "behavior is held to be irrational, illogical, chaotic, and, therefore, threatening" (Chavez 2007, 70). Primary recurring themes in the media discourse about Latina reproduction include "high fertility and population growth; reproduction as a 'reconquest' of the United States; and immigrant overuse of U.S. social services" (Chavez 2007, 71). In the case of Adela Quintana and Pedro Sotelo and the discourse about cultural differences and their effect on Adela's abnormal sexual behavior and her resulting pregnancy thus fit nicely within the larger discourse about Latina fertility. While the *Houston Chronicle* was undecided about whether the young teenager's common-law marriage and her pregnancy were the result of Mexican cultural traditions or a consequence of her mother's negligence, Sotelo's court-appointed attorney specifically cited "cultural differences" to defend his client against aggravated sexual assault charges. In the third lengthy article, which was provocatively entitled "He Is Bewildered," Sotelo's attorney went on record with the following comment: "Pedro Sotelo, 22, charged with sexual assault for allegedly impregnating a 14-year-old, does not understand the controversy over his relation with the girl, his attorney says. 'It is a cultural collision,' said Sotelo's court-appointed attorney, Dick Wheelan. 'He is bewildered. Where he comes from, this is not uncommon. In his mind, he feels he is not guilty of anything. It's not quite the same situation as if these two people were born and raised in the United States'" (HC, January 27, 1996). Throughout the ensuing controversy, the Houston Chronicle periodically returned to this line of defense. On February 4, 1996, for example, the Houston Chronicle reported, "Dick Wheelan, Sotelo's attorney, said his client is a victim of a 'cultural collision' and that in Mexico, where Sotelo comes from, it's not an unusual situation" (HC, February 4, 1996). A few months later, the newspaper informed readers that "inadvertently helping the state, Sotelo never denied the allegation [that he had sexual relations with 13-year-old Quintana], he just denied that it was wrong." The article continued with another quote from Dick Wheelan who, once again, announced, "it was a cultural collision. . . . Where he comes from, this is not uncommon" (HC, June 17, 1996). While it remained unclear whether Sotelo advanced these justifications upon the advice of his lawyer or whether he was actually unaware of the fact that it was illegal in the United States for adult men to have sexual relations with thirteen-year-old girls, it is important to note that his attorney decided to use this perception of essential cultural differences in his defense.

The series of articles about Quintana's initial disappearance, her son's birth, and the ensuing deportation hearings for both parents kept coming back to this notion of cultural difference. Several stories also alluded to economic factors such as Quintana's lack of a formal education and Sotelo's efforts to provide for his family. In the first story about the case, for example, Quintana was described as a girl who "has not been to school since she was 8" (HC, January 24, 1996). A few days later, the Houston Chronicle referred to her as "the diminutive expectant mother, described by lawyers as a fourth-grade dropout" (HC, January 30, 1996). During her deportation hearings, Quintana had already returned to school and testified that she wanted to finish her education and get her GED.[11] Similarly, Sotelo repeatedly stressed that he would be a good husband and father. On April 1, 1997, for example, he told the judge that "he pays the family's bills by earning $250 a week installing air conditioners, but he acknowledged that [his son] Bryant, who receives a monthly Social Security supplement for his blindness, would need welfare programs all his life"

(*HC*, April 1, 1997). Both Quintana and Sotelo tried to convince the judge that they deserved a chance to remain in the United States with their disabled son, who was a U.S. citizen by birth. They portrayed themselves as hard workers and ambitious students who were eager to develop into self-supporting neoliberal subjects and adhere to heteronormative family values going forward. Interestingly, however, the stories did not really comment on this line of defense. While the *Houston Chronicle* quoted their statements at length, the authors did not elaborate on this neoliberal logic or attempt to assess whether Quintana and Sotelo had the potential to develop into desirable immigrants. Instead, the human-interest stories focused almost exclusively on cultural differences.

For the most part, letters to the editor followed the same logic and argued that Quintana and Sotelo's relationship was a result of their different cultural values. Several readers expressed their support of the young couple and argued that they should be allowed to hold on to their values and start a family. Delores Wigal, for example, wrote, "Sending this young man to prison is ridiculous. In their country (Mexico), their love for each other is perfectly natural," and George L. Lattie argued, "Their ages are not an uncommon combination in their homeland, or in much of the world. . . . To break up a family because of cultural prejudice would be terrible" (*HC*, February 1, 1996, and February 7, 1996, respectively). Mexican immigrant Clara Alicia Boggs agreed with this assessment. She insisted, "After discovering Adela was 14, not 10, and that her age difference with Pedro is accepted in Mexico, everyone should have gotten out of their lives" (*HC*, February 13, 1996). According to these readers, the United States needed to be more accepting of other cultures and traditions, instead of applying their own culturally specific standards to everyone.

The majority of letter writers, however, did not accept this argument. They claimed that this kind of cultural relativism was unacceptable, especially since it involved a pregnant teenager. These critical responses can be divided into two categories: On the one hand, numerous readers argued that, regardless of the desirability of accepting cultural differences, there were certain clearly definable legal standards of what was right and what was wrong. Susan Nenney, the communications director of Planned Parenthood of Houston and southeast Texas, for example, insisted that "protecting young girls from the sexual advances of adult men represented an unshakable rule that that no culture should be permitted to violate." She wrote, "It may be socially accepted elsewhere, but that doesn't make it right—in any culture" (*HC*, February 7, 1996). Milton E. Milstead not only agreed with this assessment but also added that Mexican culture's apparent acceptance of Sotelo's relationship with Quintana was just as deplorable as other social norms that were acceptable in some cultures, "including cannibalism, incest, head hunting, child abuse." Milstead concluded that "any man, regardless of his origins, who takes advantage of a 14-year-old girl is guilty of at least child abuse, if not statutory rape, and should be punished" (*HC*, February 15, 1996).

On the other hand, a number of letters insisted that it should not even matter whether Sotelo's relationship with a fourteen-year-old girl was acceptable under another cultural standard; the only meaningful standard that should be applied in this case was U.S. law. Larry Albert, for instance, wrote that he had "lived in several countries, and they all have their unique laws. They do not accept our home-country customs as an excuse to break their laws. Neither should we" (*HC*, February 8, 1996). Following a similar logic, Susie Alverson argued that this case should "be a lesson to all those who live in this country: Ignorance of the law will not exclude sexual offenders and others from prosecution, nor will the excuse that the 'practice' is readily accepted in the perpetrator's home country" (*HC*, March 18, 1996). Finally, Edward J. Sanchez took this line of reasoning to its logical extreme when he gave Sotelo the following choices: "If you wish to live in our country, please obey our laws. If you wish to obey your country's laws, please live there" (*HC*, June 26, 1996). While all these arguments are certainly in line with the larger neoliberal project that expected immigrants to fulfill certain expectations and develop as hardworking, law-abiding members of society, none of these letters touched on one of the main pillars of the neoliberal logic: the economic aspects of this case.

Yet, in addition to the aforementioned letters, there were a number of readers who made this connection and insisted that the court should unceremoniously deport these two undocumented workers because both of them had already produced more costs than benefits for U.S. society. Early in the debate, before Quintana gave birth to her U.S. citizen son, Alex Diaz suggested that the court should "save the taxpayers a lot of money: Send Adela Garcia and her boyfriend, Pedro Sotelo, back home. They are both from Mexico. If her child is born here, the welfare system will be supporting Garcia and her child for the rest of their lives and the justice system will be spending a lot of money on Sotelo. Two one-way bus tickets will be cheaper for taxpayers and best in the long run" (*HC*, February 1,

1996).[12] After it became publicly known that their son, Bryant, was born with visual impairment and faced mental-development problems, letters were worded more carefully. By the mid-1990s, it had become just as unacceptable to publicly criticize services for special-needs children as it was to make openly racist remarks. However, this rule did not keep readers from expressing their frustration about the added costs. F. Klepfer, for example, complained, "While I certainly feel compassion for any child with an impairment, I also am angry that much of the cost of this family's maintenance will come out of taxpayers' pockets" (*HC*, June 26, 1996). In the end, Immigration Judge Clarease Mitchell Rankin decided that Adela Quintana should be allowed to stay in the United States to care for her U.S.-born child. Pedro Sotelo, on the other hand, was deported in May 1997.

In contrast to the "Out of the Shadows" series, stories about these two Iraqi and Mexican immigrant girls did not spend much time discussing economic factors. Due to the controversial nature of these cases, reporters primarily focused on cultural differences and debates over what kind of behavior was acceptable for immigrants in the United States. At the same time, however, these stories were an integral part of the larger neoliberal discourse. According to Nikolas Rose, neoliberal governments expect their citizens to function as self-directed entrepreneurs. Instead of coercing their citizens to behave in certain desirable ways, neoliberal governments ensured that citizens were "not merely 'free to choose,' but *obliged to be free,* to understand and enact their lives in terms of choice" (Rose 1999, 87, his emphasis). The conduct of these free citizens was regulated and shaped through the invention of social norms that responsible neoliberal subjects "voluntarily" adhered to. I believe that this is precisely the reason these two cases caused so much anxiety. Not only had these two young women violated social norms and standards for normative sexual and reproductive behavior, but they refused to acknowledge that there was anything wrong with their choices. To make matters worse, neither the unnamed Iraqi girl nor Adela Quintana was willing to conceive of herself as a victim—the only other role that was available to them.

Day Laborers and Neighborhood Conflicts

Stories about day laborers and neighborhood conflicts between native-born citizens and recent immigrants expressed a similar anxiety about cultural differences. Between January 1995 and December 1996, all three newspapers published dozens of human-interest stories that explored how large cities, suburbs, and small towns dealt with an increasing influx of immigrants. Almost all these articles were framed as stories about cultural clashes. Native-born residents complained about the detrimental effects that immigrants had had on "their" neighborhoods and demanded that newcomers be policed and, if necessary, forced to adhere to U.S. cultural norms. In particular, residents were concerned about large groups of Latino men who congregated in parking lots and on street corners to secure employment as day laborers. In Oakland, California, for example, "local merchants consider [day laborers] a nuisance" (*SFC*, February 3, 1995). In Healdsburg, California, "drunkenness and disorderly conduct were the primary police concerns" (*SFC*, July 3, 1995). In Houston, Texas, "business owners and residents often complain about gambling, drinking, fighting and public urination by workers" (*HC*, August 15, 1995). In Mount Kisco, New York, "residents complained that too many Hispanic men were loitering on street corners, drinking and urinating in public and living in overcrowded housing" (*NYT*, December 1, 1996). This type of behavior, which was deemed disrespectful and unacceptable, was cited in almost every article about neighborhood conflicts and day laborers.

While most authors assumed that the reasons why communities would not tolerate immigrants loitering, drinking, fighting, and urinating in public were self-explanatory, a few stories explained why certain groups of immigrants were particularly objectionable. Residents of small towns and suburbs were especially outraged about the way immigrants had changed their predominantly white and wealthy communities. Even though most people were careful to express these concerns in racially neutral terms, there was an unmistakable racial subtext. In Storm Lake, Iowa, for example, an increasing influx of Laotian, Indian, and Mexican immigrants had caused a surge of nativist sentiments.[13] U.S.-born residents were alarmed by the demographic changes that their small university and farming community had experienced over the last two decades. By the mid-1990s, many people were convinced that immigrants were "taking over the place. . . . They have to broadcast school cancellations in three different languages. When you go to the clinic, their languages are posted all over. They're catering to them" (*NYT*, February 17, 1996).

Other rural communities across the nation voiced similar concerns. In Mount Kisco, New York, residents were even more outspoken in their anti-immigrant sentiments. In an open letter to the local newspaper, *The*

Patent Trader, "Linda Skiba and Beth Vetare Civitello wrote that they would risk being called prejudiced to draw attention to what they saw as the deterioration of 'the once bucolic Village/Town of Mount Kisco that we have always loved'" (*NYT*, December 1, 1996).[14] According to these two residents, police records proved that their accusations were not racially motivated but based on factual evidence.[15] Other Mount Kisco residents made it even clearer that Skiba and Civitello's dramatic plea ("we want our town back") referred to Latino immigrants, who were not welcome in "our town" (*NYT*, December 1, 1996): Martin McGrath, a retired contractor and longtime member of the Mount Kisco Planning Board, made the following statement in an interview with the *New York Times*: "The more you move into the village proper, you see people sitting on benches. . . . You see them walking around the village. You know they're not Mount Kisco people. They're Hispanic" (*NYT*, December 1, 1996). Not surprisingly, however, McGrath insisted that this comment was not based on racist sentiments, but was supposedly a reaction to the fact that "Hispanics" had caused increasing public expenditures. He said that Mount Kisco's U.S.-born residents are "all in good faith. We have our Christian image. Everyone's a human being. But I don't see that that gives them the right to overburden our facilities: water, sewage, garbage" (*NYT*, December 1, 1996). According to these three individuals, factual evidence proved that Latinos represented a burden on local taxpayers and a threat to public safety. Hence they felt justified in advancing a racially specific rhetoric that was directed against Latinos, in particular.

In addition, a number of stories described day laborers who congregated on street corners and in front of stores as a threat to other people and women in particular. In an interview with the *San Francisco Chronicle*, for instance, Joseph Brandon, the chief of investigations for the San Francisco district of the Immigration and Naturalization Service (INS), argued that it was essential to get day laborers off the streets: "The crowds of laborers, most of whom are men, often intimidate women and have prompted complaints from citizens in almost every city where they gather. . . . Many residents and merchants feel it is a real threat to their safety" (*SFC*, May 1, 1995). Other people painted an even more alarming picture. Richard Leggio, who owned a sneaker store in Glen Cove, Long Island, told the *New York Times*, "It was horrible. . . . I'd have 30 guys hanging out, and my girls would be afraid because they would make comments and customers don't like it. My store is recessed and so you get 40 Spanish guys and not too many ladies would come in" (*NYT*, July 8, 1995). Local immigrant rights groups took these fears very seriously and acknowledged that large congregations of laborers in parking lots were certainly not ideal, especially if they harassed customers. However, they were also concerned that this conflict brought out racial animosities between Glen Cove's predominantly white population and newly arrived dark-skinned Salvadoran immigrants, whose behavior was perceived as particularly inappropriate.

Stories about communities that had successfully solved their "immigrant problem" validated the belief that "peaceful coexistence" was only possible when immigrants adapted their behavior to U.S. expectations and kept a distance from white women. At first, many small towns tried a strategy of intimidation and harassment that was supposed to coerce immigrants to either act like responsible neoliberal subjects or, if they were unwilling or incapable of doing that, to move somewhere else. Glen Cove, Long Island, for example, passed an ordinance that attempted to ban Central American workers from their downtown area. The Houston Police Department started "a zero-tolerance effort to clean up the area. . . . Those who commit such violations as blocking the sidewalk, using profanity in public and disorderly conduct will be subject to prosecution" (*HC*, August 15, 1995). And in San Francisco and Mount Kisco, INS officers and housing inspectors raided factories and overcrowded housing complexes, deported undocumented workers, and issued tickets to those tenants who had violated the housing code.[16] Some of these actions against immigrants were executed like military operations. The housing raids in Mount Kisco represent a particularly frightening example. The *New York Times* reported that "around midnight, Mount Kisco police and building inspectors raided the gray clapboard house at 71 Maple Avenue, roused the 25 Hispanic laborers who lived there, photographed them in their beds, ordered them to pack and told them they could spend the night on the floor of a community center across the street. Their alleged offense: living in overcrowded housing. The punishment: a $1,000 fine or 15 days in jail" (*NYT*, December 1, 1996).

Ironically, the police used a statute that was intended to protect poor tenants as a form of official harassment against them. Instead of ensuring that landlords provided adequate living conditions and that buildings were safe, sanitary, and up to code, code-enforcement officers were primarily interested in making sure that renters were not in violation of the maximum occupancy code. In a federal class action suit against Mount

Kisco, the Immigrants' Rights Project of the American Civil Liberties Union asserted that the town had selectively enforced their housing code against Latino immigrants, while it ignored other violators.[17] According to the case docket for *Mount Kisco Worker's Project v. The Village/Town of Mount Kisco*, "village officials engaged in a systematic effort to drive immigrants out of town by conducting midnight housing raids on Latino homes, evicting Latinos from the public park and establishing a mandatory hiring site for day laborers" (IM-NY-0039). The case was eventually settled outside of court and the Village of Mount Kisco agreed to set forth reforms to protect immigrant workers' rights and cease enforcement of local law 6, which had mandated the establishment of a day-laborer hiring site.[18] All these operations were not simply troublesome and costly for immigrants; they also evoked traumatic memories for many individuals who had fled regions where these nightly raids were common.

At first glance, it seems like these forms of official harassment are hardly in accordance with a neoliberal regime that prefers to govern on the grounds of freedom, as Nikolas Rose has argued. Initially, however, these tough measures were politically effective with voters who felt threatened by their new neighbors. Because districts were careful that law-enforcement officers did indeed target those people who had broken the law, it was possible to frame these campaigns as necessary and nondiscriminatory attempts to restore law and order and police dangerous "anticitizens." In the long run, however, harassing nonwhite immigrants with housing raids and endless citations for minor violations represented a political strategy that was doomed to fail. Once communities realized that day laborers and other unskilled immigrants had become an integral part of the local economy and were not likely to go away in the near future, they were forced to find a more permanent and noninvasive way of policing this alleged "problem population." Even though police raids and similarly invasive measures did not accomplish their official goals, they created a climate of fear and successfully reminded immigrants of their vulnerable position.

Following the lead of major metropolitan areas such as Houston and San Francisco, a number of small towns reluctantly created so-called work stops or work centers for day laborers. As the bare minimum, these centers offered public restrooms and a space where day laborers could congregate and wait for prospective employers. The establishment of these centers immediately eliminated some of the most pressing concerns, including complaints about loitering, harassment of female passersby, and public urination. Many centers also offered services such as English classes, GED courses, and legal advice. Work centers thus helped many immigrants secure work, receive the agreed-upon wages, and improve their chances for obtaining more permanent positions. Even more important, they represented an integral part of the neoliberal endeavor to turn immigrants into responsible subjects who *chose* to respect social norms and adhere to commonly accepted behavior codes.

Tellingly, however, most Americans had little interest in integrating these new immigrants into their own communities and encouraging them to leave their vulnerable economic position. On the contrary, middle- and upper-class U.S. citizens had a vested interest in having a class of workers who were not only readily available and easily exploitable but also eager to adhere to U.S. laws and customs. Work centers and similar initiatives that were aimed at the effective and noninvasive monitoring and policing of immigrants' behavior were thus extremely popular in the mid-1990s. Most people were even willing to overlook the fact that about half of all day laborers did not possess a legal work permit. While some individuals acknowledged that "we're probably helping a lot of illegal (immigrants) that we shouldn't," the public was convinced that the tangible benefits of these services outweighed the costs and justified the unusual practice of offering assistance to undocumented persons (*HC*, August 15, 1995).

The mainstream media also repeatedly reminded readers that these measures were not meant to alter the relationship between middle-class Americans and unskilled immigrant laborers in any fundamental way. The *San Francisco Chronicle*, for instance, reported that, despite the fact that "the economic realities of the area dictate that the symbiotic relationship between the two communities will continue," efforts in Healdsburg, California, to assist day laborers did nothing to alleviate the "tensions between . . . Latinos and Anglos" (*SFC*, July 3, 1995). In an article about Glen Cove, which was described as "a reluctant pioneer for immigrant rights," the *New York Times* even conceded that many Americans promoted work centers specifically because they segregated day laborers from middle-class residents: "When the men are invisible from the main streets, there are fewer complaints, less pressure and more tolerance" (*NYT*, July 8, 1995). The *Houston Chronicle* found a different way to make essentially the same point: since the work stop in Gulfton had encouraged the mostly Latino workers to stay off the streets, the area's "overall appearance and atmosphere have improved" (*HC*, May 18, 1995).[19] Human-interest stories justified U.S. citizens' concerns about a predominantly male population of day laborers by illustrating their inappropriate and offensive behaviors in detail. These stories also reassured readers that even seemingly generous provisions were not intended to produce closer social interaction between immigrant laborers and middle-class residents.

Stories about other kinds of neighborhood conflicts, in contrast, suggested that some immigrants might actually have the potential to become full-fledged members of society. Oftentimes, authors distinguished between single men, who were described as a problem population, and more desirable immigrants who lived together as a nuclear family unit. A *New York Times* article about South Fork, Pennsylvania, for example, focused on a thirty-five-year-old Mexican immigrant named Juan, who had "worked day and night" to bring his wife and two children to the United States (*NYT*, February 25, 1996). According to the story, Juan's ability to help his family migrate after less than two months represented a major accomplishment that would certainly improve their chances to settle permanently and advance economically. Juan's family was described as one of about "20 percent of the Hispanic immigrants [who] are part of 'intact families' that are moving ahead." In contrast, "about half the Hispanic people . . . are 'people in transition,' people who live with three or four other men or women who are single or have left spouses and children behind" (*NYT*, February 25, 1996). While the article was critical of single migrants and the effects long-term separation had on young children, in particular, the author praised the remarkable accomplishments of immigrant children who had grown up in intact families. For example, the story also focused on Carolina Avendo, an Ecuadorian immigrant who did not speak a word of English when she first entered high school. Due to her hard work and her family's support, however, she was able to graduate as the class salutatorian.[20]

A lengthy *San Francisco Chronicle* story about Healdsburg, a small community in Northern California, stressed the importance of neoliberal family values even more explicitly. The author claimed, "No other North Bay community can point to such a significant—and relatively painless—shift in ethnic population ratios in such a short period of time. The smoothness of the transition, locals say, stems from the large number of immigrants from rural Mexico, people who have brought with them enduring family traditions and a strong work ethic" (*SFC*, July 3, 1995). In the late 1970s and early 1980s, on the other hand, when "the working

(Latino) population was largely seasonal, mainly single men, . . . drunkenness and disorderly conduct were the primary police concerns" (*SFC*, July 3, 1995). In reaction, white residents started to speak out against immigrants and put swastikas on cars that were owned by Latinos. Yet once immigrants started to settle down and bring their families, these problems decreased noticeably and white residents became more welcoming and open minded. The article concludes with the realization that racial tensions still persist to a certain degree, but it also claims that economic realities and immigrants' effort to adhere to neoliberal family values have enabled both groups to coexist peacefully.

Conclusion

In contrast to the news coverage of political debates and policy decisions, which I examined in the previous chapter, human-interest stories were much more interested in personal struggles and successes than larger economic issues. Yet, as this analysis demonstrates, all these stories represented an integral part of the larger neoliberal project. In some cases, articles instructed readers quite explicitly on how to interpret individual case studies. *Houston Chronicle*'s special report about four Mexican and Salvadoran immigrant families in Houston and San Antonio, for example, made specific connections to the underlying neoliberal logic. Instead of letting the stories speak for themselves, the authors decided to include an interpretive prologue and epilogue, which explained that the featured sources were representative of a larger immigrant population. Even more important, the authors contended that their four case studies illustrated the potential pitfalls of the immigration reform project in the mid-1990s. While the authors agreed with the basic premise of neoliberal reform measures, which were supposed to make the U.S. immigration system more economically efficient and shift financial responsibility to immigrants and their sponsors, they were critical of the way the government had implemented this neoliberal agenda. Contrary to the congressional discourse, which tended to vilify undocumented workers and endorse dramatic border control measures, the *Houston Chronicle* series insisted that it would be more beneficial for the United States to acknowledge that undocumented immigrants were already an integral part of the U.S. economy. Instead of wasting money on fences and additional border patrol officers, the United States needed to ensure that all immigrants, documented or not, turned into responsible neoliberal subjects like Mari Hernandez and Maria Ortiz, instead of joining "America's distinct and debilitating urban culture" (*HC*, "Out of the Shadows—Prologue," October 20, 1996).

Tellingly, almost all human-interest stories were framed as "cultural clashes" between recent immigrants and native-born U.S. citizens. This focus on cultural differences not only presented a strategy to introduce race into a discourse that was supposed to appear economically oriented and racially neutral but also enabled authors to talk about a number of other sensitive issues, such as immigrants' sexuality. Almost all the shocking stories about poverty, crime, and domestic violence focused on Latino families who had large numbers of children. Due to their parents' neglect, these children were seemingly unable to escape a debilitating "culture of poverty." In many cases, they followed their parents' negative example and had children while they were still teenagers. Taken together, these stories not only confirmed the perception that Latinas were personally responsible for their poverty but also implied that Latinas, in particular, were unable to control their sexuality and make smart reproductive choices.

The stories about Adela Quintana, a pregnant Mexican American teenager, and the unnamed Iraqi girl who was married to a much older man further emphasized the belief that immigrants' own cultural values hindered their ability to develop into neoliberal subjects. In both cases, the featured subjects had supposedly acted in accordance with "their own" cultural values and traditions. While authors were willing to concede that this might be an understandable behavior for a teenage girl, they were clearly disturbed by the fact that the two girls did not understand that there was anything wrong with their relationships, even after they had talked to a variety of social workers. Their behavior was thus seen as incompatible with the neoliberal demand for responsibility and a willingness to adhere to social norms. Ultimately, these stories questioned whether it was possible for some immigrants to escape their own culture and develop into self-sufficient neoliberal subjects.

The final section of this chapter examined how stories about day laborers weighed economic objectives against deep-seated "cultural" anxieties. Tellingly, none of these stories actually featured a day laborer and allowed him to explain his perspective. Quite to the contrary, stories usually portrayed day laborers as a "problem" that required an explanation and, eventually, a resolution. Journalists talked to store owners and U.S. citizen residents who complained about loitering, drinking, and public urination, and let them express their concerns. Day laborers emerged as a group of disrespectful and threatening individuals who needed to be policed and segregated from the rest of society. At the same time, the stories also implied that early attempts to openly harass workers were incompatible with the neoliberal objective to govern on the grounds of freedom. Instead, they demonstrated how less invasive measures, such as the construction of work centers, had created a system that contained a problem population in such a way that the economically profitable hiring process could continue seamlessly.

Conclusion
<hr>

Legacies of Failed Reform

Fifteen years after the passage of the Illegal Immigration Reform and Immigrant Responsibility Act (IIRIRA), it is difficult to ignore the fact that it never achieved the goals outlined by politicians in the mid-1990s. Most notably, the IIRIRA has failed to reduce the population of undocumented immigrants residing in the United States. Quite to the contrary, the approximate number of undocumented persons has more than doubled over the last decade and a half. The Immigration and Naturalization Service (INS) estimates indicate that the unauthorized resident population was roughly 3.4 million as of October 1992 and growing by about three hundred thousand persons a year. By October 1996, when the IIRIRA was signed into law, there were approximately five million unauthorized immigrants present in the United States. According to the Department of Homeland Security, this number grew at an unprecedented rate to an all-time high in 2007, when the unauthorized immigrant population reached 11.8 million. Mostly due to the economic recession, estimates indicate a slightly lower total of 10.8 million undocumented persons as of October 2010 (Hoefer, Retina, and Baker 2011, 2). The vast majority of these people entered the United States more than ten years ago (91 percent), and 3.6 million (34 percent) have called the United States home for more than twenty years (Hoefer, Retina, and Baker 2011, 3).

This increase is a direct result of the policies that were set into place in the mid-1990s. Instead of deterring undocumented migrants from entering the United States in the first place, increased border-patrol measures have discouraged return migration. Militarizing the border means that migrants have to take greater risks and pay more money to human smugglers. As a result, undocumented Mexicans, in particular, are no longer engaging in the same pattern of back and forth migration that has been characteristic of that population for decades; they are more likely to stay in the United States permanently to avoid costly and dangerous border crossings. Even more important, the IIRIRA did nothing to prevent people from overstaying their temporary visas. Since there is little risk of detection and since many businesses continue to overlook the fact that these individuals have no work permits or, in many cases, fraudulent documents, the number of immigrants living in the United States on expired visas has increased consistently.

I believe, however, that this remarkable difference between proclaimed goals and actual effects should not be interpreted as a sign that the IIRIRA is a failed policy. Instead, the IIRIRA has furthered neoliberal objectives, and its consequences have been highly advantageous for politicians, business owners, and at least to a certain extent, the U.S. welfare state. In the course of the discourse, it has become a widely accepted "truth" that increased expenditures for border-patrol measures are a necessary and rational response to the threat posed by undocumented workers and, even more so, by terrorists and other "criminal aliens." Especially after the tragic events on September 11, 2001, it has become almost impossible for politicians to speak out against border fences and other border-patrol measures. While there is no evidence that these costly enforcement-only policies have lowered the number of undocumented immigrants or have led to the apprehension of any terrorists, they fulfill an important function within the discourse. By advocating for more border patrol, politicians show that they are committed to homeland security and keeping Americans safe. Not surprisingly, many politicians are still trying to pass measures that would militarize the U.S.–Mexico border even further.

As previous chapters have demonstrated, congressional debates (and to a lesser extent media representations) from the mid-1990s constructed undocumented immigrants as an undesirable underclass of lawbreakers that are uneducated, unskilled, low-wage laborers. In other words, undocumented workers were commonly portrayed as "anticitizens," who needed to be policed, detained, and if necessary deported. For the most part, politicians and the media have framed their concerns in neoliberal terms. They argue that, due to their lack of education and marketable skills, undocumented immigrants have no potential to develop into responsible neoliberal subjects and will likely represent a permanent unassimilable underclass. Building border fences and equipping border-patrol officers with high-tech gear thus seems to be a reasonable response to this threat.

In many cases, this neoliberal cost–benefit analysis was explicitly connected to anxieties about crime and terrorism. Based on the fact that many immigrants resided in the United States without proper paper work, the discourse frequently categorized them as lawbreakers, who would not hesitate to break other laws and harm innocent U.S. citizens. Even though there was little factual evidence for a connection between terrorism and illegal immigration, the immigration reform discourse in the mid-1990s successfully linked these concerns and concluded that stricter immigration laws were necessary to protect the United States from terrorist threats and potential attacks. Invasive immigration laws, which limited noncitizens' basic rights and legal protections, in combination with streamlined deportation procedures, were regarded as a rational and necessary response to perceived terrorist threats. After the terrorist attacks on September 11, 2001, this discursive strand became more prominent, and efforts to increase homeland security have proven extremely popular with many concerned citizens.

Shortly before the tragic events of September 11, immigrant rights advocates had succeeded in building broad support to "Fix 96" and address the worst injustices of the immigration, welfare, and antiterrorism acts. During his campaign in 1999, George W. Bush defined immigration reform as one of his national priorities. In an effort to get the support of Latino voters, Bush emphasized his personal connections to Mexico and the Mexican people—through his Mexican American sister-in-law, his ability to speak Spanish, and his track record as Governor of Texas and a strong supporter of bilateral cooperation and improved relations along the border. At least for a brief moment, the presidential rhetoric seemed to indicate a shift in discourse toward acknowledging that immigrants are more than low-wage laborers or criminals and an integral part of our society and culture, especially along the southern border. Once elected, President Bush traveled to Mexico in early February 2001 to meet with President Fox and discuss the establishment of a guest-worker program and a path toward legal permanent residency and eventual U.S. citizenship for undocumented immigrants in the United States. Discussions were supposed to continue at a summit in September 2001. This brief, hopeful moment came to a sudden end on September 11, 2001, and the discursive terrain shifted to a renewed emphasis on crime, terror, and the need to protect the United States.

The Bush administration declared war on terrorism and terrorists, both within the United States and internationally. According to the War on Terror discourse, it was the U.S. government's obligation to protect "us" (law-abiding and freedom-loving U.S. citizens) from "them" (the terrorists who were determined to destroy those freedoms). In his address to the nation on September 20, 2001, President Bush provided the following message: "Americans are asking, why do they hate us? They hate what we see right here in this chamber—a democratically elected government. Their leaders are self-appointed. They hate our freedoms—our freedom of religion, our freedom of speech, our freedom to vote and assemble and disagree with each other." While the contemporary terrorism discourse draws on previous rhetorical constructions of Muslims and Arabs as religious fanatics who are inherently undemocratic, the consequences of this rhetoric are more far reaching than ever. The discursive construction of Muslim terrorists as a threat to freedom, democracy, and homeland security was used to justify a whole range of increasingly invasive and extensive measures from "voluntary" interviews to mandatory registration for Muslim males and the passage of the USA Patriot Act of 2001. These measures affected both documented and undocumented immigrants, and U.S. citizenship no longer offered guaranteed protection under the law. Even U.S. citizens of Muslim and Arab heritage were subject to surveillance and detention.

The War on Terror opened a new chapter in the history of racial profiling. While the U.S. government had widely condemned the use of racial profiling in law enforcement since the mid-1990s, politicians increasingly embraced the idea that the new face of the terrorist threat had forced them to revisit the issue. Kevin Johnson argues that, in the wake of the terrorist attacks of September 11, "public opinion shifted and approved reliance on race, national origin, nationality, and religion as reasonable law enforcement tools in many national security measures" (Johnson 2004, 68). Furthermore, racial profiling and (I would argue) racism against Muslims and Arabs was increasingly constructed as a national security matter that appeared both rational and patriotic (Hiemstra 2010, 79f). This explicit emphasis on race, religion, and national origin represents an important transformation of the effort to appear race neutral and nonracist in the mid-1990s. Despite the fact that the Muslim and Arab population in the United States was both incredibly diverse and, in many cases, highly assimilated and characterized by remarkable educational and economic accomplishments, *all* members of the group—and individuals who fit the visual stereotype and "looked" Muslim—became subject to surveillance, harassment, and hate crimes. Actual facts, such as the lack of a criminal record and an oftentimes decades-long commitment to their communities and to democratic values, were dismissed as irrelevant. Muslims were constructed as indisputably different and as followers of a religion that was inherently violent and dangerous. Despite the pronounced effort to highlight religious and cultural differences instead of race, this depiction of culture as an immutable essence serves as a substitute for race and represents a "racial project" (Omi and Winant 1994) that transformed the social and legal positions of Muslims and Arabs in the United States.

The War on Terror discourse not only racialized Arabs and Muslims; it also affected immigrant rights more generally. Despite the fact that the attackers had entered the United States with valid (student) visas, politicians insisted that, in the name of homeland security, it was imperative to screen all individuals crossing the U.S.–Mexico border to ensure that no terrorist would ever be able to enter undetected. Terrorism and illegal immigration were constructed as part of the same larger problem: our inability to protect our borders and deny entry to criminals and potential terrorists. Illegality was far more than a simple lack of legal status, but the discursive emphasis on illegality helped to portray "immigrants in ways that marginalize, criminalize, and yet dangerously *include* immigrants in neoliberal imaginings" (Hiemstra 2010, 77). The rhetorical construction of "illegal aliens" framed the problem as primarily a legal one. Despite the fact that politicians and journalists use the term "illegal alien" so frequently that it has become an accepted, seemingly rational depiction, it is important to remember that this term is far from neutral. By framing these immigrants as criminals, we preclude other potential depictions that might emphasize their contributions to the labor market ("undocumented workers") or highlight the structural reasons that forced them to migrate to the United States ("economic refugees"). According to Nancy Hiemstra, "labeling a person 'illegal' is a subtle yet powerful tool for creating, marking and magnifying perceived difference and exclusion" (Hiemstra 2010, 78). The fear of terrorism only further justified the increased surveillance and criminalization of an already marginalized group.

In accordance with neoliberal ideology, the measures to control immigrant populations became more indirect and dispersed across various actors. These efforts included both state and, in an attempt to downsize government, private actors. Some examples for government-initiated efforts included the National Security Entry-Exit Registration System (NSEERS), which required male nationals from twenty-five primarily Muslim countries to report for fingerprinting, photographing, and interviews with federal officials. In addition, all individuals who were suspected to be undocumented immigrants were subjected to what Rachel Ida Buff refers to as the "deportation terror." Her research argues that the recent wave of deportation raids, which were carried out by the newly established Bureau of Immigration and Customs Enforcement (ICE), help create a climate of fear and silence among immigrant populations (Buff 2008). Yet, while both of these enforcement efforts are carried out by government agencies, they rely on information provided by concerned citizens. In the post-9/11 world, U.S. citizens are asked to scrutinize their friends, neighbors, and coworkers and watch out for questionable and potentially dangerous behavior. Furthermore, flight passengers are now encouraged to report suspicious activity to airport security. When Muslim passengers who were removed from their flight from Minneapolis to Phoenix threatened with a discrimination lawsuit, Congress quickly introduced legislation to "shield passengers from lawsuits because such lawsuits chill the flying public's willingness to report suspicious behavior" (Semati 2010, 256). The U.S. public is thus not only expected to scrutinize those individuals who fit the profile of a Muslim terrorist; they can also report them without fear of retribution and without expecting to be asked for any actual evidence. Apparently, membership in a particular racial group is enough justification.

The recent expansion of local government laws that target immigrants and limit their ability to obtain everything from housing to driver's licenses also represents an integral part of neoliberal governance. According to Philip Kretsedemas, between 2004 and 2008, approximately three hundred laws were passed in forty-three states that require government workers as well as private citizens to verify the legal status of local residents and report them if they lack the proper documentation: "This includes ordinances that require landlords to verify the legal status of their tenants, employers to verify the legal status of their employees, gun shop owners to verify the legal status of their customers, hospital workers to verify the legal status of emergency room patients, educators and social workers to identify unauthorized migrants within their client populations, and electoral workers to verify the legal status of voters" (Kretsedemas 2008, 556). These new governing strategies help the U.S. government manage populations in different ways: while some individuals are protected and nurtured, others are subjected to disciplinary techniques without much concern for their personal welfare and their right to privacy (Kretsedemas

2008). Without a doubt, immigrants are among the latter group. Persistent anti-immigrant anxieties and their accompanying racial projects cement this distinction and justify increasingly invasive measures that target groups who have somehow failed to live up to neoliberal ideals and are not deemed worthy of protection.

As previous chapters have demonstrated, concerns about immigration and undocumented immigrants, in particular, were also inextricably linked to anxieties about sexuality. Chapter 5, for example, demonstrated that proper neoliberal citizenship was contingent on not only economic contributions but also a certain type of fertility. In contrast to the general tendency to portray all undocumented immigrants as "anticitizens," these human-interest stories contained a few positive examples of individuals who developed into responsible neoliberal subjects by adhering to neoliberal family values. These success stories, which praised parents for their decision to have only one or two children and highlighted their attempts to invest in educational opportunities and instill a strong work ethic into their children, were juxtaposed with accounts of individuals who, because they had failed to restrain their sexuality, entered into a vicious cycle of teenage pregnancy, single motherhood, poverty, and in many cases, a host of other problems. According to the neoliberal model, these women had forfeited their right to access the rewards the state had in store for responsible individuals who made the right choices and invested in their future and the future of their family members.

In contrast to these negative depictions of undocumented immigrants, which were meant to justify new restrictions and more invasive policies, the discourse about documented immigrants was more multifaceted. In the beginning of the 1995 legislative period, many politicians and the media insisted that legal immigrants had become a burden on U.S. society. They had not only failed to develop into desirable net contributors (who paid more in taxes than they received in benefits) but also supposedly refused to assimilate into mainstream culture. In the case of legal immigrants, politicians were especially reluctant to engage in an open discussion about race. In accordance with the larger tendency to downplay the importance of race and develop seemingly color-blind policies that rewarded personal merit, politicians argued that the current generation of immigrants was less desirable than their own ancestors' generation because they did not display the same entrepreneurial spirit. At the same time, however, this explicit focus on immigrants' potential to assimilate into the U.S. economy and society also served as a technique to mask widespread anxiety about immigrants' changing national origins, as the percentage of white Europeans declined relative to other groups.

While early reform proposals contained provisions that would have decreased the total number of immigrant visas and eliminated entire visa categories (e.g., visas for adult siblings of U.S. citizens), politicians started to rethink this approach after a broad coalition of immigrant rights groups and business lobbies started to speak out against it. In its place, Congress developed a complicated system to ensure that the state would no longer bear the financial risk of admitting immigrants who would likely fail to develop into responsible neoliberal subjects. Instead of categorically excluding those immigrants who were at high risk of applying for welfare benefits and other costly services, Congress transferred financial responsibility onto immigrants and their sponsors. The IIRIRA made newly arrived immigrants ineligible for most welfare benefits, including Temporary Assistance for Needy Families (TANF), Medicaid, and Food Stamps and turned the affidavit of support into a legally enforceable contract. If immigrants failed to become self-supportive, sponsors had to bear the financial burden and provide the type of support formerly covered by welfare benefits.

As part of the dominant reform discourse, documented immigrants emerged as the polar opposite of undocumented immigrants. While many politicians and the media loudly proclaimed that the United States should honor its historical commitments to legal immigrants and their families, they were just as adamant in their claims that the United States had the right to enforce its laws and protect its borders. Increasingly, the discourse pitted undocumented against documented immigrants. Congress and the media argued that undocumented immigrants consumed resources that rightfully belonged to U.S. citizens and legal permanent residents, and even more important, they held undocumented immigrants responsible for the current anti-immigrant climate. Accurate or not, this rhetoric proved quite successful. While it is difficult for elected officials to justify supportive measures for undocumented immigrants under the best of circumstances, even immigrant and human rights organizations began to make sharp distinctions between deserving documented and undeserving undocumented immigrants. In an effort to prevent the highly controversial cutbacks in family reunification visas and other invasive measures that targeted documented immigrants, these organizations supported a split of the comprehensive immigration reform bill into two separate parts.[1] Whatever their intention, this approach ultimately validated the notion that undocumented immigrants did indeed represent an undesirable problem population.

This tendency to vilify undocumented immigrants and conflate concerns about illegal immigration, crime, and terrorism became even more pronounced in the wake of September 11, 2001. Yet, while many politicians and the media continue to make a sharp distinction between productive and desirable legal immigrants and "illegal aliens," who are commonly constructed as unwanted "anticitizens," a growing coalition of human rights and immigrant organizations remind the American public that undocumented immigrants are not only a diverse group of individuals but also human beings endowed with inalienable rights. Even more important, they are human beings who are no longer willing to remain silent in the face of retaliatory measures that criminalize them and make them subject to ever more invasive laws. Triggered by the introduction of H.R. 4437, the so-called Sensenbrenner bill, millions of undocumented immigrants and their supporters marched for their rights across the United States in the spring of 2006. At the outset, this nascent movement represented a reaction to the harsh measures that were part of the Sensenbrenner bill, which would have turned an undocumented immigrant's mere presence in the United States into a felony. Yet after the remarkable turnout at the first few marches, which were largely the result of grassroots activism by a loosely constructed network of various immigrant rights organizations, supporters "proclaimed that the marches represented 'the new civil rights movement'" (Johnson and Hing 2007, 100). The second wave of protests moved beyond the rejection of punitive immigration measures and instead sought justice and a path to legalization for undocumented immigrants. By the summer of 2006, however, the movement had visibly slowed down, and Congress eventually failed to pass a comprehensive immigration reform act.

Despite the fact that the marches did not result in the passage of immigrant-friendly legislation, they undoubtedly influenced public perception and the way the immigration reform discourse was framed. Acutely aware of the popular perception of "illegal aliens" as a dangerous underclass of lawbreakers, protesters made every effort to correct these stereotypes. All the marches were peaceful and law abiding. Protestors waved American flags and carried trash bags to pick up after themselves, and the overall atmosphere was jubilant, celebrating the contributions of undocumented immigrants. Popular signs read, "we are neighbors, not criminals" and "we are workers, not terrorists." The immigrant rights movement thus criticized the tendency to frame undocumented immigration as a fundamentally legal problem. The "illegal" frame dehumanizes undocumented immigrants and inflates the severity of their offense, while the marchers emphasized that they did not come here to commit crimes or turn into a threat or a burden. Instead, they offered a number of alternative frames. They came to the United States at great personal risk to work hard and make a life for themselves and their families. Their desires, backgrounds, and aspirations are identical to legal immigrants; they were just unable to access the narrowly constructed legal immigrant categories and obtain a coveted green card.

This emphasis on immigrant contributions to U.S. society and the economy became even more pronounced in the activism surrounding the DREAM Act, a piece of legislation that would provide undocumented immigrant students with access to higher education opportunities and a path to legal permanent residency. The DREAM Act, which was initially framed as a bipartisan, commonsense legislation with a very limited scope, was first introduced in 2001 by Senators Durbin (D-IL) and Hatch (R-UT). The bill seemed to align perfectly with neoliberal objectives: instead of calling for a general amnesty, the DREAM Act would draw a clear line between "illegal alien" parents, who had broken the law and should not be rewarded, and their children, who were not only portrayed as innocent victims but also lauded for their hard work and their efforts to become productive members of society. DREAM Act supporters framed the potential recipients as hardworking and gifted students who were highly assimilated and ready to contribute in a variety of ways, as doctors, scientists, and computer specialists. Providing them with a path to citizenship made economic sense. Instead of trapping these promising individuals in a world with limited opportunities, the United States should cash in on the investment they had already made in the form of a free elementary and secondary education and enable undocumented students to live up to their full potential and turn into self-sufficient neoliberal subjects.

The grassroots social movement that is dedicated to the passage of the DREAM Act in particular, and the activism surrounding immigrant rights more generally, is remarkable in a number of ways. First of all, we need to acknowledge that undocumented immigrants' willingness to speak out and demand rights represents an incredibly brave move and opens up a new chapter in the discourse around immigration reform. In the mid-1990s, immigrant rights organizations were forced to make a tough choice. Faced with the potential for far-reaching punitive reforms of the legal immigration system, they decided to advocate for legal immigrants' rights by emphasizing their positive impact and drawing a clear line between legal and illegal immigrants. "Illegal aliens," who were already widely perceived as undesirable and potentially dangerous, became the scapegoat for a variety of social ills from terrorism and crime to hyperfertility and the decline of traditional family values. Politicians eagerly followed this demarcation, and the IIRIRA targeted a population of powerless people who appeared to be the logical recipients of a punitive political agenda. The passage of the Antiterrorism and Effective Death Penalty Act, the Illegal Immigration Reform and Immigrant Responsibility Act, and the Personal Responsibility and Work Opportunity Reconciliation Act resulted in a climate of fear among undocumented immigrants, who were rightfully concerned about the potential consequences of public visibility and political activism. Yet, despite the fact that their voices had been silenced for so long and that the mainstream discourse had basically failed to even acknowledge them as human beings, undocumented immigrants started to advocate for human rights and social change. The wave of activism that followed began to forge a new public image of undocumented immigrants as political actors, workers, parents, and neighbors. In other words, the events in spring 2006 helped to reframe the discourse and introduce a more complex image of undocumented immigrants and their impact on the United States.

At the same time, many of the common arguments that were used by immigrant rights activists confirmed and maybe even strengthened the neoliberal agenda. This problematic effect is probably most pronounced in the rhetoric surrounding the passage of the DREAM Act. In their effort to depict undocumented students in a positive light, the DREAMers oftentimes aligned themselves with the ideology of meritocracy (Jefferies 2008). Activists highlighted stories of individual students who were uniformly presented as highly intelligent, hardworking, and eager to overcome seemingly insurmountable obstacles. After graduating as valedictorians, they were accepted into Harvard, Berkley, or the University of Michigan, only to find out that their lack of legal status would prevent them from fulfilling their dreams of higher education. Even though Ivy

League schools like Harvard were able to award privately funded scholarships to highly deserving undocumented students, these students still encountered a number of obstacles along the way. While scholarships might cover tuition, undocumented students would be unable to work legally to pay for their living expenses, get a driver's license, travel on airplanes to attend conferences, or accept internship opportunities. Yet perhaps even more important, they would have to live in constant fear of detection and cope with the knowledge that their diploma would not enable them to work legally.

This discursive framework portrayed the potential beneficiaries of the DREAM Act as exceptional individuals who were fighting an unjust system that denied them the opportunity to succeed. Immigrant students' educational accomplishments were the direct result of their own choices and their personal determination to excel. According to Julian Jefferies, "such individualist renderings obliterate the fact that structural factors, such as social and cultural advantages, unequal educational opportunities, and discrimination in all of its forms, are barriers to this success" (Jefferies 2008, 251). The pronounced emphasis on individual characteristics as the main determinant for success confirms a neoliberal agenda that downplays the importance of structural inequalities.

In reality, very few undocumented students were able to reach a comparable level of education, not because they were less intelligent or hardworking, but mostly because the structural barriers did indeed prove insurmountable. Research demonstrates that only 72 percent of undocumented students who arrived before the age of fourteen and 40 percent of youth who did not come to the United States until age fifteen complete high school (Gonzales 2011, 611). Due to constant funding cuts for public education, especially in poor neighborhoods and for immigrant-specific programs such as bilingual education, very few undocumented students would ever even qualify for conditional permanent residency under the DREAM Act. Not only did about half of all undocumented youth lack a high school diploma, the necessary minimum requirement to apply, but even with good grades and access to in-state tuition, college was still out of reach for the majority. The DREAMers' rhetoric thus played into the neoliberal agenda by stressing individualism and suggesting that access to legalization and permanent residency was all that undocumented students needed to succeed and become productive neoliberal citizens.

In addition to setting up a clear distinction between deserving immigrant students who had excelled through hard work and determination and those undeserving students who had failed to graduate high school, the DREAMer rhetoric also, in many ways, confirmed the negative portrayal of their parents and undocumented adults, more generally. DREAMers wanted to make sure that politicians realized that common stereotypes of illegality did not apply to them. They highlighted that, far from being criminals, they were innocent victims in the immigration dilemma. They had been brought to the United States by their parents, usually before they were even able to voice their opposition. Growing up, most undocumented youth were unaware of their lack of legal status and had considered themselves fully assimilated to U.S. culture. Finding out that they were illegal usually came as a shock to them (Gonzales 2011, 608). Yet, since they had grown up with American values and ideals, they also recognized the unfairness of the situation and fought for their right to access their piece of the American dream. Granting them the opportunity to become legal residents and get an education was portrayed as an act of fairness. While they might not be American on paper, their dreams and aspirations were identical to those of their American peers. They did not want to become low-wage laborers like their parents—or, even worse, be forced to return to a country that could hardly be called their home anymore. Instead, they distanced themselves from their parents and aligned themselves with their high-achieving, college-bound U.S. citizen peers. Instead of offering a more fundamental critique of the stereotype of "illegal aliens" as an uneducated, unassimilated underclass, DREAMers mostly insisted that these stereotypes simply did not apply to them.

While we can easily criticize this approach as insufficient and potentially harmful, undocumented students' decision to portray themselves as exceptionally deserving and different from the rest of the undocumented population is also understandable in light of the larger political climate. After years of unmitigated abuse, punitive reform measures, and an almost constant emphasis on personal responsibility, calls for a general amnesty provision for everyone seemed destined to fail. Proposing a narrowly tailored path to legalization for the most deserving individuals seemed to hold the best chances for success, especially if it was supported by an unabashedly neoliberal framework that highlighted students' eagerness to gain access to neoliberal citizenship. There is no question that these students should have the right to call the United States their home and access higher education and job opportunities. Of course they should—not because they have acted like exemplary neoliberal subjects, but because they are human beings. The real question is, How can we transcend beyond the limitations imposed on us by the neoliberal discursive framework? And how can we reenvision an immigration reform discourse that truly accounts for the complexities of the situation by investigating the effects of structural inequalities, race, gender, sexuality, international trade agreements, and the forces of globalization?

As long as the discussion remains narrowly focused on the specific nature of the measurable costs and benefits associated with immigration and particular groups of migrants, it is unlikely that the policy outcomes will change significantly. Instead, immigrant advocates need to interrogate the underlying neoliberal logic and the seemingly unquestioned belief that immigrants should only be allowed to enter the United States if they possess certain marketable skills and assets that enable them to succeed without any further assistance. Since the mid-1990s, the mainstream immigration discourse has fostered the belief that immigration visas should function primarily as a reward for highly skilled and motivated individuals who adhere to neoliberal family values. And, connected to this pronounced focus on personal merit, the discourse has made it very clear that if immigrants fail to succeed economically and integrate into U.S. society, this failure is the direct result of personal deficiencies, rather than a consequence of structural inequalities, discrimination, and a lack of temporary support measures such as language or job training opportunities. Contrary to the current tendency to decrease public expenditures by eliminating group-specific services, past experience has shown that it is much more beneficial for the U.S. economy and, even more important, for those urban centers and small towns that attract large numbers of new immigrants to improve the services available to newly arrived immigrants. At the very least, we need to make a conscious effort to end the highly problematic and ultimately useless cycle of blaming immigrants for the difficulties of succeeding in a highly competitive labor market. Instead, federal and state governments as well as local communities need to develop not just short-term measures to address existing problems; they also need to come up with long-term solutions to structural inequalities.

Similarly, immigrant advocates need to make a concerted effort to interrogate the discursive construction of undocumented immigrants as undesirable and potentially dangerous "anticitizens" who have willfully violated U.S. laws, taken advantage of the welfare system, and harmed innocent U.S. citizens. Instead, it is crucial to acknowledge that most of these individuals are risking their lives to work in the United States and support their families. Even more important, immigrant advocates need to emphasize the fact that undocumented workers did not *choose* to disregard U.S. immigration laws, but that the overwhelming majority would undoubtedly prefer to immigrate legally and enjoy the rights and privileges connected to legal permanent residency. Unfortunately, however, the current U.S. immigration system clearly privileges skilled workers, wealthy applicants, and candidates from nations with low immigration numbers. Consequently, many potential immigrants from Mexico and other Central and South American nations face long immigration backlogs and other insurmountable obstacles to enter the United States through legal channels. A workable immigration reform measure needs to acknowledge these undeniable problems, reduce visa backlogs, and develop new legal channels for future immigrants. However, I strongly believe that the creation of a guest-worker program that prohibits workers to bring their families and authorizes employers to exploit workers and retain part of their wages is a step in the wrong direction. Instead of solving existing problems, such a flawed guest-worker program would only help to continue a long history of abuse and exploitation.

Following Monisha Das Gupta's exciting new work on the challenges that radical South Asian immigrant activists pose to the neoliberal order, I argue that we need to start looking beyond the borders of our nation-state and demand transnational migrant rights. Instead of narrowly focusing on specific groups and evaluating their level of deservingness in light of neoliberal objectives, immigrant rights advocates should demand the recognition of inalienable human rights—the right to freedom, safety, work, fair wages, and so on. All these rights, which are currently contingent on a narrowly defined and hard-to-access category of nation-based citizenship, should be accessible to everyone, regardless of their formal citizenship or immigration status. The South Asian activists that Das Gupta studies "offer a new lexicon and, beyond that, a paradigm that frees rights from the conceptual prison of citizenship" (Das Gupta 2006, 256). We need to rethink citizenship—and, along the same lines, legal permanent residency—as a system of power, instead of regarding it as a privilege that the U.S. government is able to selectively hand out to a deserving few.

Most important, however, we need to interrogate some of the basic premises that have informed the mainstream immigration discourse for the last decade. As previous chapters have demonstrated, U.S. society's fundamental beliefs about immigration and immigrants are closely connected to the discursive production of "truth." In the course of the immigration reform debates in the mid-1990s, politicians and the mainstream media successfully constructed an alarmist image that maintains that large-scale immigration has had a detrimental impact on the U.S. economy, society, the quality of public education, the welfare and the criminal justice system, as well as a variety of other areas. In other words, the public was led to believe that it had become necessary to monitor immigrants more closely and establish stricter selection criteria, and many people deemed it necessary to close our borders and limit the total number of immigrants. Even though it is difficult to challenge widely accepted "truths," especially after the discourse has continued to reproduce them for an extended period of time, I think it is still crucial to remind the public that there is, at the very least, no definite evidence that it is necessary or desirable to close our borders to people who are eager to immigrate, work, and become a part of the national community.

Finally, I believe that immigrant advocates need to examine how this pronounced focus on economic objectives has disguised the racist effects of immigration laws and the discourse that surrounds them. In the current political climate, many immigrant rights organizations deem it more productive to frame their arguments in the same neoliberal terms that their opponents use. In an effort to preserve existing immigration quotas and protect immigrants' rights and legal protections, these advocates try to demonstrate how immigrants contribute to the economy and why they are deserving of our support. However, this approach ultimately confirms the underlying neoliberal logic and seems to validate the popular belief that neoliberal immigration reform measures are rational, color-blind responses to quantifiable problems. In contrast, I argue that it would be more beneficial to investigate why so many Americans are opposed to high immigration levels and, in many cases, anxious about the changing national and racial origins of the current generation of immigrants. In light of the fact that the politically correct color-blind rhetoric has obviously failed to decrease racism and inequality, it is essential to foster a critical debate about the continued importance of race and racial anxieties.

Acknowledgments

Many individuals contributed, directly or indirectly, to my completion of this manuscript, and I am extremely grateful for their support and encouragement along the way. Most important, I recognize the superb guidance of my dissertation advisor, Rob Buffington. Rob's scholarly insights and encouraging feedback and his willingness to comment on countless drafts helped to improve my project immensely. I thank Rob particularly for supporting my project and helping me clarify my thoughts and my writing.

I am also grateful for the invaluable input of the other members of my dissertation committee, Susana Peña and Ellen Berry. I thank Susana not only for her insightful comments on various chapter drafts but also for being a passionate teacher and mentor. Her classes prepared me to think about the intersections of race, ethnicity, class, gender, and sexuality. I thank Ellen for her confidence in the final product well before it materialized. Her passion about feminism and theory and her continued support throughout my graduate studies greatly benefited me.

I express special thanks to several people whose guidance and support made significant and lasting contributions to my academic success. First and foremost, I thank Eithne Luibhéid, an extraordinary person and a great teacher, whose enthusiasm and knowledge about the U.S. immigration system as a site for constructing and contesting sexuality inspired me to formulate my own dissertation project.

I am enormously grateful for the support of the "Sexualities and Borders" Research Cluster at the Institute for the Study of Culture and Society at Bowling Green State University. I thank Vibha Bhalla, Bill Albertini, Amy Robinson, Joelle Ruby Ryan, Erika Kubik, and Jamie Stuart, who generously volunteered their time to read my work. I also thank the staff at Jerome Library at Bowling Green State University, Ohio. Special thanks to Coleen Parmer, who spent long hours searching for hard-to-find transcripts of congressional debates and other government documents. I express my thanks to the American Culture Studies Program for providing continued financial support and awarding me a dissertation fellowship during my final year of writing.

At Indiana University South Bend, I have profited from the friendship and support of many colleagues. Special thanks to the Social Science Writing Group, and especially to Gail McGuire, who read and commented on drafts of various chapters and helped make sure that my dissertation would actually evolve into a book. Thank you also to Cathy Borshuk, David Blouin, Jen Colanese, Allison Foley, and Audrey Ricke. In the course of preparing this study for publication, I was fortunate to receive a faculty research grant at IUSB that enabled me to devote an entire summer to the project.

Many thanks to the editorial staff at the University of Minnesota Press for assistance at every stage of the process and to the two reviewers for helping me turn my manuscript into a better book.

Finally, I acknowledge the crucial role of my family and friends for never losing faith in the project and supporting me every step of the way.

Notes

Introduction

1. For example, see the Personal Responsibility and Work Opportunity Reconciliation Act of 1996 (PRWORA), the Antiterrorism and Effective Death Penalty Act of 1996 (AEDPA), the Workforce Improvement and Protection Act of 1998 (WIPA), the Defense of Marriage Act of 1996 (DOMA), and the REAL ID Act of 2005.

2. The Personal Responsibility and Work Opportunity Reconciliation Act of 1996 (Pub. L. No. 104-193) made an explicit connection between poverty, welfare, and family structures. In the introduction (§ 101), "Congress makes the following findings: (1) Marriage is the foundation of a successful society. (2) Marriage is an essential institution of a successful society which promotes the interests of children." In later sections, the act outlines how poor citizens—as well as immigrants—are expected to conform to these traditional notions of family to improve their economic situation.

3. Dan Stein, the executive director of the Federation for American Immigration Reform (FAIR), and Wayne Cornelius, a professor of political science at the University of California at San Diego, both discussed the connection between trade and migration and the importance of NAFTA when testifying in Congress.

4. According to the Department of Homeland Security, an estimated 5 million undocumented immigrants were living in the United States in 1986. Approximately 3.9 million of those were potentially eligible for legalization. Some 3 million unauthorized immigrants registered and tried to achieve legal status; 2.68 million of those were granted legal status. The main amnesty program was open to those people who could document continued physical presence in the United States since January 1, 1982. The second program was for "Special Agricultural Workers" (Rytina 2002).

5. Please note that Nikolas Rose prefers the term "advanced liberalism." According to Mitchell Dean, neoliberalism generally refers to "specific styles of the general mentality of rule," whereas advanced liberalism designates "the broader realm of the various assemblages of rationalities, technologies, and agencies that constitute the characteristic ways of governing in contemporary liberal democracies" (Dean 1999, 149f). Since my analysis is primarily focused on the rhetoric

used to justify certain measures, I will use the term "neoliberalism" throughout this book—even when I make references to Rose's scholarship.

6. The guests on the show included Rosa Rosales, the President of the League of United Latin American Citizens (LULAC); John Trasvina, the interim president of the Mexican American Legal Defense and Education Fund (MALDEF); Robert Rector, the President of the Heritage Foundation; Representative Michael McCaul (R-TX), a member of the Homeland Security Committee; Dan Stein, the president of the Federation of American Immigration Reform (FAIR); and Roy Beck, the executive director of Numbers USA.

7. This argument was apparently quite popular with Lou Dobbs. On April 2, 2006, Dobbs argued that "to say that anyone involved in this debate is a xenophobe or a racist seems to be the first thing uttered when they have run out of facts to support their view." In a conversation with Leo Chavez, a professor at the University of California and an author of several influential books about undocumented immigrants, Dobbs insisted that Hispanic organizations must have no convincing arguments for "illegal immigration" since "every time this issue is brought up, illegal immigration, [they] want to charge racism, or xenophobia."

8. In his introduction, Hanson explains that he will rely "almost exclusively on economic motivations for political opposition to immigration. I will leave unexplored the claim that opposition to immigration is rooted in conflicts over identity" (2005, 8).

1. Exclusionary Acts

1. This chapter focuses on voluntary immigration only. In addition to sixty million voluntary immigrants, approximately twelve million Africans were brought to America as slaves.

2. Please note that some scholars offer slightly different periodizations. LeMay and Barkan (1999), for instance, distinguish between a period of unrestricted admission (colonial period to 1880) and a period of unlimited immigration and limited naturalization (1880–1920). DeSipio argues that the Civil War should be used to mark the end of the second period (1841–60) and the beginning of the third period (1865–1920).

3. Please note that this discussion is limited to the legal immigration system. In contrast to the discourse surrounding the reform of the legal immigration system, the rhetoric about undocumented immigrants was much more focused on individual characteristics, undocumented immigrants' willingness to break the law, as well as their negative impact on the welfare state. Tellingly, the discourse largely ignored the fact that, for the most part, undocumented immigrants actually represented the quintessential independent, self-sufficient, and economically

minded neoliberal subject. (See chapter 3 for a more extensive analysis of the debate about undocumented immigrants.)

4. In 1790, all "free white persons" were allowed to naturalize after only two years of residency. In 1798, the Alien and Sedition Acts lengthened the residency requirement to fourteen years. However, there were no further requirements.

5. The Province Law of 1700 deemed the sum of five pounds sufficient to ensure that an immigrant did not become a public charge. On June 29, 1722, the bond was set at one hundred pounds. The Massachusetts Province Laws of 1756 confirmed this amount and specified the classes of persons included under the public charge provision. See LeMay and Barkan 1999 for additional information.

6. Samuel G. Morton (1799–1851) was a doctor who became famous for his systematic large-scale experiments on the differences in brain sizes. He measured the skulls of different people and came to the conclusion that Europeans had the highest brain capacity. The second rank went to the Chinese, third to Southeast Asians, fourth to American Indians, and last to the Australian Aborigines and Africans. His findings have since been proved wrong, but he is still considered a pioneer of American science. Josiah C. Nott was an eminent physician who published *The Types of Mankind* (1855). Jean Louis Rudolphe Agassiz (1807–73) is considered to be one of the key figures in geology and organic biology. He was in contact with important intellectuals such as Ralph Waldo Emerson and Henry Wadsworth Longfellow, founded the Museum of Comparative Zoology, and formulated a highly influential theory of the ice ages. In addition to these groundbreaking studies, Agassiz was also known for his theory that God had created a number of different human species and that "Negroes," in particular, were not just biologically different from but also inherently inferior to the white race. According to the *Journal of Blacks in Higher Education*, Agassiz should be remembered as "the father of scientific racism" (*Zapata* 1995: 38).

7. Section 4 upheld the provision that excluded criminals: "All foreign convicts except those convicted of political offenses, upon arrival, shall be sent back to the nations to which they belong and from whence they came."

8. For the most part, the Immigration Act of 1917 reiterated the criteria used in previous laws. In particular, section 3 held that "the following classes of aliens shall be excluded from admission into the United States: All idiots, imbeciles, feebleminded persons, epileptics, insane persons, . . . persons with chronic alcoholism; paupers; professional beggars; vagrants; persons afflicted with tuberculosis in any form or a loathsome or dangerous contagious disease; persons not comprehended within any of the foregoing excluded classes who are found to be and are certified by the examining surgeon as being mentally or physically defective, such physical defect being of a nature which may affect the ability of such alien to earn a living; persons who have been convicted . . . of a felony or other crime or misdemeanor involving moral turpitude; polygamists or persons who practice polygamy or

believe in and advocate the practice of polygamy; anarchists or persons who advocate the overthrow by force or violence of the Government of the United States, or of all forms of law . . . or who advocate the assassination of public officials, or who advocate and teach the unlawful destruction of property; . . . prostitutes, or persons coming to the United States for the purpose of prostitution or unmoral purposes; . . . persons hereinafter called contract laborers; . . . persons likely to become public charges; . . . persons whose ticket or passage is paid for with the money of another."

9. Interestingly, the Immigration Act of 1917 does not exempt the unmarried or widowed sons of U.S. citizens and legal permanent residents from the literacy requirement.

10. In 1929, President Hoover changed the quota system yet again. While he retained the 150,000 cap on immigration, he allocated quotas based on the 1920 census. This system remained in place until 1965.

11. Under this act, the spouses and unmarried children of U.S. citizens were not subject to any numerical limitations.

12. The spouses and unmarried sons and daughters of U.S. citizens were given special priority. As "immediate relatives," they were not subject to direct numerical limitations.

13. *Boutilier v. INS* (387 U.S. 118), a 1967 Supreme Court decision that affirmed the common practice that homosexuals were held excludable under 212(a)(4) of the 1952 INA, cited the following evidence: "Beginning in 1950, a subcommittee of the Senate Committee on the Judiciary conducted a comprehensive study of the immigration laws and in its report found 'that the purpose of the provision against persons with constitutional psychopathic inferiority will be more adequately served by changing that term to persons afflicted with psychopathic personality, and that the classes of mentally defectives should be enlarged to include homosexuals and other sex perverts.' S. Rep. No. 1515, 81st Cong., 2d Sess., p. 345."

14. See Davis (2006), Edwards (2006), Green (1987), and Luibhéid (2002) for additional information about the treatment of gay and lesbian immigrants and the legal changes that affected their ability to immigrate to the United States.

15. This provision remained in place until 1990, when the 1990 INA withdrew the phrase "sexual deviation."

16. Twenty percent of all immigrant visas were reserved for the unmarried sons or daughters of U.S. citizens, the next 20 percent went to the spouses and unmarried sons and daughters of legal permanent residents, 10 percent were reserved for the married children of U.S. citizens, and an astonishing 24 percent of immigration visas were allotted to the brothers or sisters of U.S. citizens. The remaining 24 percent of green cards went to skilled (10 percent) and unskilled (10 percent) workers and refugees (6 percent).

17. Notably, this was the first time that the United States deemed it necessary to restrict immigration from Canada and Mexico, as well as from Middle and South America. Initially, the INA did not apply the preference system to the Western Hemisphere. On October 20, 1976, though, Congress amended the 1965 INA. As a result of the 1965 law, potential immigrants from the Western Hemisphere received visas on a first-come, first-served basis. This led to situations where immediate family members had to wait in excess of two years, while distant relatives received their paper work in a much more timely fashion. To rectify this situation, Congress extended the preference system to the Western Hemisphere.

18. Reimers (1985), cited in Luibhéid (2002, 22).

19. The original provision would have granted amnesty to all undocumented immigrants who had resided in the United States since before January 1, 1977. Those who had arrived between January 1, 1977, and January 1, 1980, would be given temporary legal status that could be turned into permanent status upon further review. Senator Edward Kennedy (D-MA) introduced an amendment that would have moved the cutoff date to December 31, 1981. However, that amendment was defeated by a wide margin (3–12). See Gimpel and Edwards (1999) for additional information.

20. E. Clay Shaw (R-FL), for example, offered an amendment that would have moved the eligibility date from January 1, 1982, to January 1, 1980, thus cutting off a significant number of newly arrived immigrants. "The Shaw effort failed on a 177–246 vote" (Gimpel and Edwards 1999, 163).

21. In the end, the IRCA granted legal resident status to all undocumented immigrants who had entered the United States before January 1, 1982, and had worked at least 90 days per calendar year. The aforementioned language and American history requirements were stricken from the final version of the bill.

22. Their bill eliminated the preferential treatment of immediate relatives of U.S. citizens, who had been exempt from the numerical limits in the past, and capped the total number of immigrant visas at 600,000 per year—480,000 for family members and 120,000 for immigrants who possessed special skills (Gimpel and Edwards 1999, 187).

23. The following number of visas were allocated for each preference category:
- *First preference.* Unmarried adult sons and daughters of U.S. citizens (23,400 plus visas not required for fourth preference)
- *Second preference.* Spouses and unmarried minor children of permanent residents; unmarried adult sons and daughters of permanent residents (114,200 plus visas not required for first preference)
- *Third preference.* Married sons and daughters of U.S. citizens (23,400 plus visas not required for first or second preference)
- *Fourth preference.* Brothers and sisters of adult U.S. citizens (65,000 plus visas not required for first, second, or third preferences)

In addition, 55,000 visas were reserved for the new diversity category.

24. Originally, the commission was chartered to focus on illegal immigration only, but its mandate was soon extended to provide an analysis of the legal immigration system as well. The commission consisted of Vice Chair Lawrence H. Fuchs (Jaffe professor of American civilization and politics, Brandeis University), Michael S. Teitelbaum (program officer, Alfred P. Sloan Foundation), Richard Estrada (associate editor, *Dallas Morning News*), Harold Ezell (president and founder, Ezell Group), Robert Charles Hill (partner, Jenkens & Gilchrist, PC), Warren R. Leiden (executive director, American Immigration Lawyers Association), Nelson Merced (chief executive officer, Inquilinos Boricuas en Acción / Emergency Tenant Council), and Bruce A. Morrison (chairman, Federal Housing Finance Board).

25. According to Gimpel and Edwards, "the pro-immigration ethnic groups, such as the National Council of La Raza and various Asian-Pacific American organizations, wondered if Simpson and Smith had influenced the Commission's findings and recommendations. There were rumors that the staff of the Commission had not arrived at their decisions independently, but had been subject to political pressures from Capitol Hill" (Gimpel and Edwards 1999, 220).

26. This task force went on several fact-finding missions, one of which became mired in scandal. On June 10, 1995, the task force toured various immigration facilities in Miami (including Krome Service Processing Center and Miami International Airport). Soon after the visit, forty-seven INS employees sent a letter to the attorney general. In this letter, the INS officers claimed that INS management deliberately deceived the task force to create the impression that these facilities were well managed and efficiently run. A few days before the task force's visit, INS management increased staff and moved almost 40 percent of the detainees at Krome to other detention facilities and local jails. Apparently, some criminal aliens were also released to the community. Assistant Attorney General Stephen Colgate and Assistant Deputy Attorney General David Margolis reviewed the record and decided that serious misconduct had occurred.

27. Proposition 187 was passed in California in November 1994. Among other things, Proposition 187 established that undocumented immigrants should be excluded from all public social services (§ 5), publicly funded health care (§ 6), and public elementary and secondary schools (§ 7).

28. There were two earlier reform proposals: On January 4, 1995, Representative Bob Stump (R-AZ) introduced H.R. 373, the Immigration Moratorium Act of 1995. The next day, Senator Richard Shelby (R-AL) presented a similar act in the Senate (S. 160). However, both bills died quickly.

29. Senators Kennedy (D-MA) and Simon (D-IL) were the only two committee members who opposed the bill.

30. This bipartisan amendment, which had been proposed by Representatives Dick Chrysler (R-MI), Howard Berman (D-CA), and Sam Brownback (R-KS),

was agreed to by a comfortable margin (238–183). Not only did the majority of Democrats support the amendment; Chrysler, Berman, and Brownback also garnered the support of seventy-five Republicans.

31. However, the conference committee was not yet ready to give up on the Gallegly Amendment. After the amendment was deleted from the general immigration bill, it was reintroduced as a stand-alone legislation (H.R. 4134). The House passed H.R. 4134 (254–175), but the bill stood no chance of Senate passage. See Gimpel and Edwards (1999, 280ff) for additional information.

32. Due to the focus of this particular project, I will not discuss the PRWORA in its entirety. See Gilens (1999), Mink (1998), Seefeldt (2002), Sidel (1998), and Smith (2002) for a detailed analysis of the Welfare Reform Act.

33. The other titles were (1) "Reducing Illegitimacy," (2) "Requiring Work," (3) "Capping the Aggregate Growth of Welfare Spending," (4) "Restricting Welfare for Aliens," (5) "Consolidating Food Assistance Programs," (6) "Expanding Statutory Flexibility of States," and (7) "Drug Testing for Welfare Recipients" (H.R. 4, January 6, 1995—version 1).

34. For instance, on September 14, 1995, the Senate rejected the Feinstein Amendment (no. 2513), which would have limited the deeming of income to cash and cash-like programs and retained SSI eligibility by a recorded vote of twenty yeas and seventy-eight nays. The next day, the Senate also rejected the Simon Amendment (no. 2509), which attempted to eliminate the retroactive deeming requirements for those legal immigrants who were already present in the United States, by a recorded vote of thirty-five yeas and sixty-four nays.

35. The entire bill had been reorganized multiple times. The seventh and final version of H.R. 4 contained the following ten sections: (1) "Block Grant for TANF," (2) "SSI," (3) "Child Support," (4) "Restricting Welfare and Public Benefits for Aliens," (5) "Reductions in Federal Government Positions," (6) "Reform of Public Housing," (7) "Child Protection Block Grant Program and Foster Care and Adoption Assistance," (8) "Child Care," (9) "Child Nutrition Programs," and (10) "Food Stamps and Commodity Distribution."

36. Refugees were not subject to these limitations. They had full access to all federal services as soon as they arrived in the United States.

37. This section is only concerned with legal immigrants. With regard to this group of immigrants, Congress never even questioned the idea that their children should have access to a free public school education. They were only concerned with the availability of additional programs.

38. The list of programs included assistance or benefits under the National School Lunch Act and the Child Nutrition Act of 1966; programs of student assistance under titles IV, V, IX, and X of the Higher Education Act of 1965 and titles III, VII, and VIII of the Public Health Service Act; means-tested programs under the Elementary and Secondary Education Act of 1965; as well as benefits

under the Head Start Act. In addition, Congress agreed to exempt benefits under the Job Training Partnership Act.

39. According to Capps, Ku, and Fix, "Large proportions of immigrant families experiencing food insecurity do not receive food stamps, indicating that there is substantial unmet need for food stamps in both cities. About four-fifths of food insecure families (82 percent in Los Angeles and 78 percent in New York) did not receive benefits during the year before the survey" (Capps, Ku, and Fix 2002, iv).

40. In addition, there were also a few minor reform proposals that focused on specific aspects. For instance, on January 9, 1995, Senator William V. Roth (R-DE) introduced S. 179, the Criminal Alien Control Act of 1995, which streamlined the deportation procedures for all criminal aliens and eliminated opportunities for judicial review for aliens who were not legal permanent residents. A few weeks later, on February 2, 1995, Senator Olympia Snowe (R-ME) proposed S. 347 (Terrorist Exclusion Act), which made membership in a terrorist organization a basis for exclusion from the United States.

41. Some politicians also claimed that Timothy McVeigh did not count as a "real American." Orrin G. Hatch (R-UT), for example, went on record with the following proclamation: "What is shocking to so many of us is the apparent fact that those responsible for the Oklahoma atrocity are U.S. citizens. To think that Americans could do this to one another. Yet, these killers are not true Americans—not in my book" (United States Congress, Senate, May 25, 1995).

42. In addition to its two main sponsors, S. 735 had the following seven co-sponsors: Hank Brown (R-CO), Dianne Feinstein (D-CA), Phil Gramm (R-TX), Jon Kyl (R-AZ), Don Nickles (R-OK), Alan K. Simpson (R-WY), and Strom Thurmond (R-SC).

43. On a similar note, Representative Patrick J. Kennedy (D-RI) reminded Congress that "sacrificing our Constitution and the integrity of our judicial system is too high a price to pay for an antiterrorism bill" (United States Congress, House, April 18, 1996).

44. This section bars repetitious habeas corpus petitions by all federal and state prisoners and establishes a one-year deadline within which a prisoner must file his/her habeas corpus claim.

45. Title II increases the funding for victim compensation programs and narrows the immunity of foreign governments who support terrorist organizations.

46. Subtitle A designates certain organizations as "terrorist organizations" and establishes a system of penalties for financial institutions that refuse to freeze the assets of these organizations. Subtitle B offers an expanded definition of "assistance to terrorist organizations."

47. This section places additional restrictions on the possession of materials that could be used to assemble a bomb.

48. In addition to increasing the penalties for certain terrorism-related offenses, title VII also expands the reach of federal law beyond the boundaries of the United States.

49. Title VIII provides an additional $1 billion to fund antiterrorism efforts.

50. More specifically, section IV establishes that "an alien subject to removal under this title shall not be entitled to suppress evidence that the alien alleges was unlawfully obtained." In addition, the defendant and his or her attorney have no right to access classified evidence "if the attorney general determines that public disclosure would pose a risk to the national security of the United States." Instead, the defendant is presented with an unclassified summary of the evidence (Pub. L. No. 104-132, § 401).

51. According to Bruce Robert Marley, "before the enactment of AEDPA and IIRIRA, aggravated felony offenses included: (A) murder; (B) illicit trafficking in a controlled substance; (C) illicit trafficking in firearms or destructive devices or in explosive materials; (D) 'money laundering' of amounts over $100,000; (E) certain firearms and explosive material offenses; (F) a crime of violence for which the term of imprisonment imposed was at least five years; (G) a theft offense (including receipt of stolen property) for which the term of imprisonment imposed was at least five years; (H) ransom (kidnapping) offenses; (I) child pornography offenses; (J) RICO offenses for which a sentence of at least five years' imprisonment may be imposed; (K) involuntary servitude and management of prostitution offenses; (L) national security and treason offenses; (M) fraud or tax evasion where the loss exceeds $200,000; (N) alien smuggling for commercial advantage; (O) a trafficking in fraudulent documents offense; (P) failure to appear for service of sentence if the underlying sentence is punishable by a term of imprisonment of 15 years or more; (Q) an attempt or conspiracy to commit an aggravated felony" (Marley 1998, note 40).

52. This was only one among a number of different scenarios that Senator Kennedy discussed on this particular day. He also pointed out that "an immigrant with an American citizen wife and children sentenced to 1-year probation for minor tax evasion and fraud would be subject to this procedure. And under this provision, he would be treated the same as ax murderers and drug lords" (United States Congress, Senate, June 7, 1995). Later, he added that "under this provision, an older immigrant who came to the United States as a child but was never naturalized gets tired of a rash of robberies on her store and buys a firearm which she doesn't realize is illegal. She is convicted of a felony. Even though she is married to an American and has four U.S.-citizen children, she must be placed in expedited deportation proceedings with no recourse to the courts" (United States Congress, Senate, June 7, 1995).

53. Legal scholar Sara A. Martin begins her article with a very similar case. She provides a lengthy account of the deportation hearings of Martin Muñoz, a

thirty-seven-year-old Mexican immigrant. Despite the fact that he was married to a U.S. citizen and supported his three U.S. citizen children and four stepchildren, he was deported for a crime that he had committed almost ten years prior. See Martin (1999) for additional information.

54. For more information on the Uniting American Families Act, see Farber (2010) and Titshaw (2010).

55. In addition to these three principles, there is a concern about admitting refugees for humanitarian reasons. However, the debate surrounding humanitarian admission is outside of the scope of the current project. See Barbee and Parcells (2010) for more information.

56. The seventeen states are Arizona, Idaho, Indiana, Maryland, Michigan, Minnesota, Missouri, New England, Nevada, New Jersey, Ohio, Oklahoma, Pennsylvania, Rhode Island, South Carolina, Texas, and Utah.

2. Family Values and Moral Obligations

1. As mentioned in the previous chapter, the commission was mandated by the Immigration Act of 1990 (Pub. L. No. 101-649) to make recommendations regarding the implementation and impact of U.S. immigration policy.

2. In particular, the U.S. Commission on Immigration Reform proposed to reduce immigrant admissions from over 675,000 immigrants and refugees to about 550,000 per year. These numbers were to be divided as follows: (1) nuclear family immigration would be reduced to 400,000 (currently 480,000), (2) skill-based immigration would be reduced to 100,000 (currently 140,000), (3) refugee resettlement would remain the same (currently 50,000), and (4) the diversity lottery would be eliminated (currently 55,000).

3. Similar to Senator Kennedy, Steve Chabot (R-OH) made the following comment: "I deeply value the fundamental character of this nation as a land of hope and opportunity and because I cherish our unique American heritage as a country of immigrants, united by shared values, a strong work ethic, and a commitment to freedom. Let us not tarnish that heritage or ignore our greatest strength, which is our people" (United States Congress, House, March 21, 1996).

4. The Immigration Act of 1990 (Pub. L. No. 101-649) determined that the United States should try to increase the immigrant population's national diversity by giving immigrants from underrepresented nations an opportunity to immigrate, even if they did not have a family or a job in the United States. Consequently, the INA established a lottery system that randomly selected fifty-five thousand nationals from countries that had sent fewer than fifty thousand immigrants to the United States over the previous five years and provided them with an immigrant visa. In their 1995 report, the U.S. Commission on Immigration Reform recommended that the diversity lottery should be abolished. The Legal Immigration

Act of 1996 (S. 1665) wanted to reduce the number of diversity visas from fifty-five thousand to twenty-seven thousand. In the end, though, Congress decided to leave the diversity lottery unchanged. The U.S. Commission on Immigration Reform also recommended the elimination of the visa category for unskilled laborers and the reduction of skill-based visas to 100,000 (from 140,000); S. 1665 left the number of skilled immigrants at 140,000, while eliminating the 10,000 special visas for unskilled workers. Eventually, Congress did not make any changes to the employment preference category in 1996.

5. Interestingly, Senator Phil Gramm (R-TX) does not mention a specific country. Throughout his account, he refers to his Korean in-laws as "Asian immigrants" or "Asian Americans."

6. On April 25, 1996, Senator Mike DeWine (R-OH) proclaimed, "Immigration policy in its best days, most enlightened, has been based on two principles. One is that the United States should be a magnet, a magnet for the best and the brightest, yes, but also a magnet for the gutsiest, the people who have enough guts to get up, leave their country, get on a boat or get on a plane or somehow get here, come into this country because they want a better future for their children and their grandchildren and their great grandchildren" (United States Congress, Senate, April 25, 1996).

7. Many supporters of a generous family reunification system portrayed families as an important support structure. Sheila Jackson-Lee (D-TX) argued that "at a time when strong family bonds are more important than ever, restriction in family based immigration will hurt legal immigrant families in America" (United States Congress, House, March 20, 1996). The next day, Rick A. Lazio stressed that "keeping families—including extended families—intact, is culturally and empirically a way to keep people off the public dole" (United States Congress, House, March 21, 1996).

8. One such mechanism to shift responsibility is the "affidavit of support," which will be discussed in more detail in the following section.

9. It is important to acknowledge that it was not just politicians who described immigrants as strong believers in traditional family values. Karen K. Narasaki, executive director of the National Asian Pacific American Legal Consortium, also confirmed the idea that immigrants from all over the world could help to initiate a return to traditional family values. She testified that "the Consortium believes that our nation is enriched by cultures which honor the family, not just the nuclear family but also among generations and brothers and sisters. This notion of the family is important not only to Asian Pacific Americans, but to Latinos, Eastern Europeans, Irish, Italians, and countless other Americans" (United States Congress, House, June 29, 1995).

10. Please note that there are important differences between the rhetoric used to discuss elderly immigrants and refugees' SSI usage. Generally speaking,

politicians were much more generous toward refugees, who were described as innocent victims of war, terror, and persecution. Due to their traumatic experiences,
they could hardly be expected to become productive members of U.S. society
overnight. For reasons of space, though, I will limit my discussion to elderly
immigrants.

11. Undocumented immigrants and temporary residents/visitors have always
been ineligible for SSI.

12. Jane L. Ross claimed that 5.5 percent of all SSI recipients are noncitizens,
while Carolyn Colvin argued that this proportion might be as high as 6.2 percent
(United States Congress, Senate, February 6, 1996).

13. In *Department of Mental Hygiene for the State of California v. Renel* (173
N.Y.S.2d 678 [1959]), the defendant had signed an affidavit of support for their
nephew, who had come under the care of the California Department of Mental
Hygiene. The State of California sued the sponsors to recover their costs. However, the court ruled against them. In later cases, the Supreme Court of Michigan
(Michigan ex. rel. Attorney General v. Binder, 96 N.W.2d 140, 143 [1959]) and the
California Court of Appeals (County of San Diego v. Viloria, 80 Cal. Rpt. 869, 873
[1969]) reached similar verdicts. See Sheridan (1998) for more information on the
legal history of the affidavit of support.

14. In the original provision, this deeming period was limited to three years.
However, when politicians realized that a significant number of elderly immigrants applied for SSI as soon as this deeming period was over, they lengthened
the deeming period to five years. However, this was only meant as a short-term
solution, and the deeming period reverted to three years in October 1996.

15. This deeming provision did not apply to refugees, who had unlimited access to public support as soon as they arrived in the United States.

16. In a similar vein, Norman Matloff, professor of computer science at the
University of California, Davis, cautioned that large numbers of Chinese seniors
eagerly immigrate to take advantage of the American welfare system. According to
his statistics, 55 percent of elderly Chinese were on welfare in 1995 (United States
Congress, Senate, February 6, 1996).

17. To my astonishment, no one questioned the validity of Matloff's "research"
and asked whether his methods, which he did not explain in much detail, were
ethical. He simply claimed that "as someone who has been immersed in the Chinese immigrant community for 20 years," he had a unique opportunity to talk
to people, gather information, and get a much more honest response than other
researchers (Senate Judiciary Committee, February 6, 1996).

18. Even though a few politicians indicated that they were reluctant to make
any radical changes and depart from America's commitment to family reunification, not a single person spoke in favor of the current system. Dick Chrysler
(R-MI), for instance, proposed an amendment that would have restored the current

definition of the nuclear family, which allowed parents as well as siblings and adult children to immigrate (United States Congress, House, March 21, 1996). In addition, Ileana Ros-Lehtinen (R-FL) argued that parents were undeniably part of the nuclear family—which she described as "a basic building block in the cultural development of our United States"—and thus deserved special protections (United States Congress, House, March 21, 1996).

19. At different points in the debate, Congress discussed income requirements that varied between 125 percent of the federal poverty line (with exception for sponsors who were on active military duty) and 200 percent of the federal poverty line. In the end, the IIRIRA established that potential sponsors had to "demonstrate . . . the means to maintain an annual income equal to at least 125 percent of the Federal poverty line." A person on active duty in the armed forces of the United States was only required to "maintain an annual income equal to at least 100 percent of the Federal poverty line" (Pub. L. No. 104-208, § 551).

20. As a reaction to the discussion about "deadbeat dads" in the context of welfare reform proposals, Lamar S. Smith (R-TX) introduced the term "deadbeat sponsor." He argued that "just as we require deadbeat dads to provide for the children they bring into the world, we should require deadbeat sponsors to provide for the immigrants they bring into the country. By requiring sponsors to demonstrate the means to fulfill their financial obligations, we make sure that taxpayers are not stuck with the bill" (United States Congress, House, September 25, 1996).

21. According to 8 U.S.C.A. § 1227(a)(5), any alien who, within five years after the date of entry, has become a public charge from causes not affirmatively shown to have arisen since entry, is deportable. However, even though this provision has been in the books for a long time, very few immigrants have actually been deported because they became public charges. The Office of Immigration Statistics' 2003 *Yearbook of Immigration Statistics* shows that between 1971 and 1980—the last dates for which this data is available—only thirty-one immigrants were deported because they had become public charges. (A total of 231,762 aliens were deported during that decade.) Between 1961 and 1970, a mere eight public charges were deported. In contrast, however, public charge deportations were still fairly common in the first half of the twentieth century (9,086 between 1911 and 1920 and 10,703 between 1921 and 1930).

22. H.R. 373 also contained a provision that would have lengthened the moratorium indefinitely until "the President submits a report to Congress, which is approved by a joint resolution of Congress, that the flow of illegal immigration has been reduced to less than 10,000 aliens per year and that any increase in legal immigration resulting from termination of the immigration moratorium would have no adverse impact on the wages and working conditions of United States citizens, the achievement or maintenance of Federal environmental quality standards, or the capacity of public schools, public hospitals, and other public facilities to serve

the resident population in those localities where immigrants are likely to settle" (H.R. 373, § 2).

23. See section 7, which redefined "immediate relatives" as follows: "During the immigration moratorium, the term 'immediate relatives' for purposes of section 201(b) of the Immigration and Nationality Act means the children and spouse of a citizen of the United States" (H.R. 373).

24. Like S. 1664, S. 1665 adopted a priority system that would have allowed a very limited number of nonnuclear family members, including elderly parents, to immigrate over the next ten years. In ten years, this system would have phased out, and parents would only be allowed to immigrate if visas were not taken by other, more immediate family members.

25. S. 1664 was actually intended to reduce illegal immigration. After Senator Spencer Abraham (R-MI) had proposed to split the original comprehensive bill (S. 1394) into a legal immigration part (S. 1665) and an illegal immigration part (S. 1664), Congress tried to examine these two issues separately. The aforementioned amendment, however, clearly violated this rule.

26. A few days later, Senator Simpson (R-WY) proposed an amendment to amendment 3725. Under this amendment, legal immigration would be reduced by 10 percent. Immediate family members would receive 480,000 of the 607,000 yearly visas. Yet, in accordance with the Kennedy Amendment, the Simpson Amendment would have made these visas available first to the spouses and minor children of U.S. citizens, then to immediate family members of legal permanent residents, and eventually to parents (United States Congress, Senate, April 25, 1996).

27. This discussion was limited to the main reform proposals that actually warranted a longer discussion. Yet in addition to the aforementioned proposals, there were also several other, more obscure provisions that were quickly removed from the respective act. For instance, the first version of the Immigration in the National Interest Act (H.R. 2202) contained a provision that would have denied family-based immigration opportunities to parents unless at least half of their children resided permanently in the United States. This provision was struck out after Henry J. Hyde (R-IL), who found this provision to be overly restrictive, offered a more generous amendment.

28. See 8 U.S.C. § 1151 (b)(2)(A)(i). For all other family-sponsored immigrants, the preference system is organized as follows: (1) unmarried sons and daughters of U.S. citizens, (2) spouses and unmarried sons and daughters of lawful permanent residents, (3) married sons and daughters of citizens, and (4) brothers and sisters of citizens (see 8 U.S.C. § 1153[a]).

29. See 8 U.S.C. § 1183a(a)(1)(B).

30. See 8 U.S.C. § 1183a(a)(1)(A) and 8 U.S.C. § 1183a(a)(2) and (3).

31. See Luibhéid (2005a) for a much more detailed discussion of the affidavit-of-support system.

32. Early on in the debate, Senator Alan K. Simpson (R-WY) proclaimed, "Neither the Government of these United States, nor the American people are responsible in any way for 'breaking up' extended families abroad. Please hear that. No, immigrants who have come here consciously chose to do so and, by doing so, they personally chose to leave most of their family behind—to 'break up' their family. No one else is responsible" (United States Congress, Senate, November 3, 1995). Similarly, Lamar S. Smith (R-TX) argued, "We need to remember that immigration is not an entitlement; it is a privilege. An adult immigrant who decides to leave his or her homeland to migrate to the United States is the one who has made a decision to separate from their family. It is not the obligation of U.S. immigration policy to lessen the consequences of that decision by giving the immigrant's adult family members an entitlement to immigrate to the United States" (United States Congress, House, March 21, 1996).

33. Dan Stein, executive director of the Federation of American Immigration Reform (FAIR), strongly supported the elimination of several family preference categories. (In particular, he wanted to keep siblings of citizens and adult offspring of citizens and legal permanent residents from immigrating). He justified these changes in the following terms: "This is key and essential to stopping the pyramiding chain migration system put in place in 1965. It was wrongly conceived then, and it should be changed now" (United States Congress, House, June 29, 1995).

34. This viewpoint was also endorsed by Senator Mike DeWine (R-OH).

35. In addition, politicians argued, "We have gotten away from the brand of immigration represented by [our] grandparents and others of that proud generation" (Bill Martini [R-NJ], United States Congress, House, March 21, 1996).

36. Jan Meyers (R-KS) took an even more extreme position. In response to a lengthy debate about America's reliance on qualified scientists and technicians, Meyers asked the following question: "How much of this supposed shortfall could be fixed by tracking more American students into technical fields and fixing our educational system so that our students are actually taught science and math rather than self-esteem and multiculturalism?" (United States Congress, House, March 19, 1996). According to Meyers, the growing significance of multicultural awareness not only keeps immigrants from assimilating; it also keeps native-born students from focusing on more important issues.

37. Norman Matloff was particularly concerned about the negative impact that bilingual education had on "many urban black parents." He argued that these parents "believe that their children's education is being diluted by the forced bilingual environment their children are subjected to" (United States Congress, House, April 5, 1995). To solve this problem, Matloff suggested "we should 'end bilingual education as we know it.'" In addition, he wanted to develop an immigration policy that required "as a condition for being granted immigrant status, that persons

over age 12 have a conversational knowledge of English" (United States Congress, House, April 5, 1995).

38. Interestingly, Charles T. Canady chose to limit the scope of his amendment to the diversity visa lottery and the employment preference category, instead of requiring family-sponsored immigrants to pass the same test. At no point in the debate did he offer an explanation for this decision. However, he added that it would be a possibility to give preferential treatment to those family members who already possessed superior English-language skills.

39. John Bryant (D-TX) asked repeatedly for evidence to show that immigrants refused to learn English. Representative Canady was unable to provide this evidence.

40. Notably, this kind of argument, which accuses the U.S. government of practicing reverse discrimination, is not unique to the immigration discourse; it can be found in many debates about affirmative action as well.

41. In addition, Senator Alan K. Simpson (R-WY) was convinced that U.S. reform proposals were fairly moderate in comparison to the changes that were taking place in Western Europe. He hypothesized that if "we had a man running for the Presidency of the United States, perhaps [he] would pick up 17 to 20 percent of the vote based on a lashing out about immigration or a move toward xenophobia, just as has happened in Germany, with a person receiving 17 to 20 percent of the vote, or in France, with another man with such views garnering 17 percent to 20 percent of the vote. Those things are out there" (United States Congress, Senate, April 15, 1996).

42. In a similar fashion, Elton Gallegly (R-CA) voiced his concern that "immigration reform is an issue on the minds of nearly all Americans, and nearly all express deep dissatisfaction with our current system and the strong desire for change" (United States Congress, House, March 19, 1996). Tellingly, these concerns have influenced the debate from the very beginning. On January 4, 1995, Representative Bob Stump (R-AL) reported, "Americans are deeply concerned about immigration and its impact on their lives. They are anxious about the changing face of this country and the problems associated with our system of immigration" (United States Congress, House, January 4, 1995).

43. On March 19, 1996, Tillie Fowler (R-FL) cited evidence to prove that "support for immigration reform cuts across all economic strata, as well as ethnic and social lines" (United States Congress, House, March 19, 1996). On April 25, 1996, Senator Jon Kyl argued, "A recent Roper poll showed that only 2 percent of the respondents supported the current levels of immigration; only 4 percent of blacks and Hispanics supported the current level. There is overwhelming view [sic] in our country that immigration numbers should be somewhat reduced" (United States Congress, Senate, April 25, 1996).

44. In particular, Frank L. Morris, past president of the Council of Historically Black Graduate Schools, was adamant in his claim that "the economic plight of African Americans in the US is made more precarious by the record levels of immigration into the US" (United States Congress, House, June 29, 1995). Vernon Briggs of Cornell University added that low-skilled workers of all races are bearing the brunt of this negative impact (United States Congress, House, April 5, 1995). Demographer Lindsay Lowell cautioned "there were small impacts overall." However, she confirmed, "the black population seemed to be somewhat moderately negatively affected by undocumented Mexicans. And we found interestingly enough a positive effect of illegal Mexicans on the white population" (United States Congress, House, April 5, 1995).

45. See his testimony on April 5, 1995, and June 29, 1995, before the House Judiciary Committee.

46. Representative Xavier Beccera (D-CA) recounted this story on several occasions. See United States Congress, House, March 20, 1996, and United States Congress, House, April 5, 1995.

47. Diana Aviv, director of the Council of Jewish Federations, voiced similar concerns about the negative repercussion of exclusionary laws. She testified, "The Jewish community also knows, however, the consequences of policies that scapegoat immigrants as the source of many of society's problems. Government anti-immigrant policies give rise to irrational fears of the foreign born and even of native born ethnic populations" (United States Congress, House, January 27, 1995).

48. Lamar S. Smith agreed that it was necessary for politicians not to be too compassionate. After he went to great lengths to prove that immigrants are "wonderful people," he went on to say that it was important not to lose sight of the fact that "America cannot absorb everyone who wants to journey here as much as our humanitarian instincts might argue otherwise" (United States Congress, House, March 19, 1996). On a similar note, Representative George W. Gekas (R-PA) argued that, since he was the son of immigrants, he was particular susceptible to immigrants' needs and desires. However, he was convinced that "that prejudice I must set aside in the greater good of our country." And, "as a responsible public official," he had to ignore the human aspect and "do something about the total number of individuals who live in our country or who will be coming into our country" (United States Congress, House, March 19, 1996). In addition, John Bryant (D-TX) acknowledged that immigrants were great people. However, he continued, "the bottom line question, though, is how many people can we have come in here and still manage the country in a way that our economy will continue to promise in the future that people who are willing to work hard can get their foot on the bottom rung of the economic ladder and climb up into the middle class" (United States Congress, House, March 19, 1996).

Moreover, Frank L. Morris argued that immigrants tended to be more racist and sexist than most U.S. citizens. He supported the idea that "we should require that all immigrants show an understanding of American history and language by having to pass a test that they understand and are willing to accept some hard won parts of our American tradition on such issues as racial and gender equality. Many immigrants come from cultures where these concepts are foreign to their experience and they are less likely to have the opportunity to understand and address them if they also have no command of the English language" (United States Congress, House, June 29, 1995).

3. Dehumanizing the Undocumented

1. Legomsky specifically mentioned the case of undocumented immigrants who had an asylum case pending and who might eventually be granted legal status (1995, 1469f).

2. On a similar note, David Dreier (R-CA) claimed, "Illegal immigration has reached crisis proportions in my State of California. We deal daily with a flood of illegal immigrants who are coming across the border seeking government services, job opportunities, and family members" (United States Congress, House, March 19, 1996). Two days later, Christopher H. Smith (R-NJ) argued, "Illegal immigration has reached epidemic proportions in the United States. Each year our borders are flooded with many thousands of people who enter the U.S. undocumented, usually unskilled, often without the resources to provide for their own needs" (United States Congress, House, March 21, 1996).

3. Other politicians preferred military analogies. For example, Elton Gallegly (R-CA), one of the most outspoken critics of undocumented immigrants, claimed that "our country is, in effect, under a full-scale invasion by those that have no legal right to be here" (United States Congress, House, September 25, 1996).

4. Several expert witnesses made similar points. Gus De La Vina, regional Immigration and Naturalization Service (INS) director (western region), for example, explained, "Four years ago, the evening hours were the shadowy domain of bandits, drug traffickers and alien smugglers, but the lighting initiative is helping to level the playing field and, as a result, our agents in San Diego are taking back the night" (United States Congress, House, March 10, 1995). On the same day, INS Commissioner Doris Meissner testified that "smugglers and illegal aliens had the advantage of darkness on an unlit border; fences hung in tatters; allowing easy access for drive throughs; and agents patrolled the border from dirt roads, where they existed. It simply could not do the job" (United States Congress, House, March 10, 1995).

5. For more information on the legal background and an overview of the legal process during the 104th Congress, see chapter 2.

6. On the same day, Senator John McCain (R-AZ) stated, "Each year many highly skilled and exceptionally talented individuals legally migrate to the United States. In addition, many hard-working individuals who have come to this Nation and contributed their skills, ideas, and cultural perspectives. . . . Illegal immigration is an entirely different matter and presents a whole host of problems that need to be addressed" (United States Congress, Senate, April 25, 1996). In addition, Mike DeWine (R-OH) asserted, "Illegal immigrants are lawbreakers. . . . Legal immigrants, on the other hand, are by and large great citizens. They are people who care about their families. They are people who work hard. They are people who played by the rules to get here, got here legally, and add a great deal to our society" (United States Congress, Senate, April 25, 1996). A few days earlier, DeWine expressed a similar perspective when he argued, "Illegal immigrants are lawbreakers. . . . On the other hand, legal immigrants are people who follow the law. They are an ambitious and gutsy group. They are people who have defined themselves by the fact they have been willing to come here, play by the rules, build a future, and take chances" (United States Congress, Senate, April 15, 1996).

7. On the previous day, Jay Kim (R-CA) declared, "As a legal immigrant myself, I believe it is important to recognize the difference between legal and illegal immigration. My compliance with the law and subsequent naturalization has instilled in me a sense of pride and responsibility. I am sure that these same feelings are shared by all legal immigrants who come to the United States in search of American dreams and a better life for their families" (United States Congress, House, March 20, 1996). Robert Menendez (D-NJ) added, "As an American-born son of legal immigrants, I can tell you this bill sends the wrong message. Instead of saying to potential immigrants that if you play by the rules, wait your turn, and follow the law, you will benefit by becoming a permanent resident, we say, we're going to treat you just about the same as an illegal immigrant" (United States Congress, House, March 21, 1996).

8. Gallegly made it clear that he would have liked to stop these payments completely. However, such an amendment would have violated the constitutional rights of U.S. citizens who happened to be born to undocumented parents.

9. Marge Roukema (R-NJ), for example, argued that "pregnant women cross the border into the United States as illegals, give birth to a child and then claim the right to immigrate legally based on the citizenship of that child" (United States Congress, House, May 24, 1995).

10. Contrary to these alarmist descriptions, however, research has shown that a significant number of undocumented women were afraid to deliver their baby in a public hospital in the United States (Chavez 1998). For fear of deportation, these women either returned to their home country to deliver their baby or decided to give birth in their private home, sometimes with the help of a midwife. As a result,

these children do not get an official birth certificate and are thus ineligible for U.S. citizenship.

11. A few months later, Alan K. Simpson (R-WY) provided his colleagues with the following statistical information: "When we have 60 percent of the live births in a certain hospital in California attributed to illegal undocumented mothers who then give birth to a U.S. citizen . . . that stirs people up. They don't like it" (United States Congress, Senate, September 16, 1996). By the end of the debate, the statistics had become even more extreme. On September 25, 1996, Randy (Duke) Cunningham (R-CA) proclaimed that "in California over two-thirds of the children born in our hospitals are to illegal aliens" (United States Congress, House, September 25, 1996). In contrast to Ezell and Simpson, who had at least indicated that these numbers were only based on a small selection of public hospitals in certain parts of the state, Cunningham implied that undocumented immigrants' birth rates were extremely high all over the state. In the course of debate, the alarmist rhetoric thus continued to escalate.

12. Bryant explicitly noted that his amendment should only be applied to undocumented immigrants who were at least eighteen years of age. See amendment 8 printed in part 2 of H.R. 104-483 for additional information.

13. In a different context, Edward M. Kennedy (D-MA) pointed out that a similar provision "upsets the basic values of our social service system after years of community assistance. Outreach clinics, day care centers, schools, and other institutions will now become the menacing presence because they will be seen as a branch of the INS to determine who is here illegally. This is going to have a chilling effect on those immigrants again that are legally here" (United States Congress, Senate, April 29, 1996).

14. A total of 161 Republicans supported the amendment, and 71 voted against it. Most Democrats were opposed to the amendment. However, 9 Democratic representatives voted for the amendment: Blanche Lambert Lincoln (D-AR), Gene Taylor (D-MS), Robert Andrews (D-NJ), Robert Torricelli (D-NJ), Sherrod Brown (D-OH), James Traficant (D-OH), Bob Clement (D-TN), Bart Gordon (D-TN), and Charles Wilson (D-TX).

15. Elton Gallegly added that "New York spends $634 million; Florida, $424 million; Texas, $419 million" (United States Congress, House, March 20, 1996).

16. In addition, William Clay (D-MO) rose "to oppose [the Gallegly] amendment because it is unconstitutional, runs counter to our Nation's commitment to the value of education, and is morally repugnant." Anthony C. Beilenson (D-CA) maintained that Gallegly's reform plans were "ineffective and overly punitive," and Lincoln Diaz-Balart (R-FL) added, "We do not blame the children for the conduct of their parents. That, among other reasons, is why we are the moral leader of the world" (United States Congress, House, March 20, 1996).

17. On a similar note, Sheila Jackson-Lee (D-TX) argued, "The Gallegly amendment unfairly punishes undocumented children for the actions of their parents. Denying children access to education will create an underclass of illiterate, uneducated individuals. . . . The goal of American public education is to impart the values of democracy such as equal opportunity and justice for all people and a respect for your neighbor, no matter what his or her ethnicity, race, or religion. Public education prepares our young people to become productive citizens and mature adults" (United States Congress, House, March 20, 1996).

18. In addition, Elton Gallegly described his amendment as "pro-education." He argued that "this is not anti-education, it is pro-education. It is pro-education for the students that have a legal right to be in this country, that are either legal residents or citizens" (United States Congress, House, September 25, 1996).

19. Later in the debate, Dana Rohrabacher (R-CA) argued, "It is absolutely wrong to spend $2 billion on the children of foreigners who have come here illegally. That $2 billion should be going to benefit the children of the people of the United States of America. That is what this vote is all about; it is to determine what our priorities are. Our priorities should be what is in the interest of the people of the United States. We can care for the children of foreigners, we can care about their well-being, but we must first care about our own children, our own families" (United States Congress, House, September 25, 1996).

20. This rhetoric about magnets was of particular importance throughout the debate about undocumented immigrants. On the same day, David Dreier (R-CA) told his colleagues that they needed "to recognize that this is not a mean-spirited amendment. . . . If we look at where we are headed, we are trying to decrease the magnet which draws people illegally into this country. There are [sic] a wide range of reasons they come in. Seeking family members . . . was the number one reason; job opportunities, obviously, another very important reason. But the tremendous flow of government services is obviously another magnet which draws people illegally into this country" (United States Congress, House, March 20, 1996). A few months later, Frank Riggs (R-CA) argued that "one of the more compelling of the border magnets is the free public education California and the other border States are mandated to provide the children of illegal immigrants, who are themselves illegal immigrants" (United States Congress, House, September 25, 1996).

21. For example, Ron Packard (R-CA) reminded Congress that "illegals cannot legally work in this country. If we educate them, they still cannot work legally here in this country" (United States Congress, House, March 20, 1996).

22. On September 25, 1996, Brian Bilbray (R-CA) reiterated this concern: "I would ask my colleagues on the other side of the aisle, if you don't care about the cost to the working class people, because this illegal immigration does not affect the rich white people, illegal immigration hurts those who need our services

and our jobs in this country more than anything else, those who are legally here" (United States Congress, House, September 25, 1996).

23. Soon after the introduction of the Hyde Bill, Bob Barr (R-GA) introduced an amendment that eliminated the controversial idea that "guilt by association" was a good enough reason to deport a legal permanent resident without a proper hearing. After a lengthy debate, the Barr Amendment passed by a relatively wide margin—246 yeas, 171 nays, 14 not voting. On the following day, Congress discussed the Conyers-Berman-Nadler substitute, which restored the provision that made it illegal to raise funds for terrorist organizations. However, the substitute also contained several provisions to protect the civil liberties of suspected terrorists. (It restored opportunities for meaningful judicial review, gave defendants the right to bring in their own evidence and their own witnesses, and gave them access to due process.)

24. On a similar note, Jerrold Nadler (D-NY) argued that the Barr Amendment "does not do the job. It is no longer an antiterrorism bill. It no longer even pretends to stop groups like Hamas or Hezbollah from raising funds in the United States. It no longer gives us the ability to get alien terrorists out of the country expeditiously" (United States Congress, House, March 14, 1996).

25. Solomon added, "According to the Immigration and Naturalization Service, in 1980, the total foreign-born population in Federal prisons was 1,000 which was less than 4 percent of all inmates. In 1995, the foreign-born population in Federal prisons was 27,938, which constitutes 29 percent of all inmates. The result is an enormous extra expense to be picked up by the Federal taxpayers" (United States Congress, House, March 19, 1996).

26. Shortly after Representative Solomon's comment, Porter J. Goss (R-FL) insisted, "Today more than one quarter of all Federal prisoners are illegal immigrants; fraudulent employment and benefit documentation is rampant; and criminal aliens linger in our country at significant taxpayer expense." Greg Ganske (R-IA) added, "Our current immigration laws are broken and they must be fixed. One-quarter of all Federal prisoners are illegal aliens" (United States Congress, House, March 19, 1996).

27. In the meantime, Bill Martini (R-NJ) claimed, "Nearly 20 percent of the legal immigrants in this country are on welfare. Furthermore, one-quarter of all federal prisoners are illegal aliens" (United States Congress, House, March 21, 1996).

28. Interestingly, a few months earlier, Lamar Smith (R-TX) argued, "An increasing number of crimes are being committed by noncitizens: both legal and illegal aliens. Over one-quarter of all federal prisoners are noncitizens—an astounding 42 percent of all federal prisoners in my home state of Texas" (United States Congress, House, April 18, 1996).

29. This misuse of statistical information is not the only instance where politicians misquoted—or maybe even fabricated—statistics to make a certain point.

On March 14, 1995, for example, Dianne Feinstein (D-CA) claimed that "ninety percent of the methamphetamine labs in this country are located in southern California and 90 percent of them are run by illegal immigrants" (United States Congress, Senate, March 14, 1995).

30. Benjamin A. Gilman (R-NY) was not the only politician to make such a claim. On June 7, 1995, for example, Spencer Abraham (R-MI) testified, "The Immigration and Naturalization Service does not have adequate facilities to house this many criminal aliens. As a result, the great majority of these convicted felons are released back to our streets after serving their sentences, with instructions to report several months later for a hearing before the INS. Needless to say, the majority of criminal aliens released from custody do not return for their hearings. Having been returned to the streets to continue their criminal predation on the American citizenry, many are rearrested soon after their release" (United States Congress, Senate, June 7, 1995).

31. However, Toby Roth (R-WI) made one noteworthy distinction between documented and undocumented immigrants: Whereas legal permanent residents still had the opportunity to appeal a deportation order while remaining in the United States, "aliens who are not permanent residents and who wish to appeal deportation orders [were required] to do so from their home countries, after they have been deported" (United States Congress, Senate, January 9, 1995).

32. Interestingly, Toby Roth's bill also contained a provision that tried to make sure that suspects had their work permits taken away while their appeals process was pending. Roth testified that "one INS deportation officer told my staff that he spends only about 5 percent of his time looking for criminal aliens because he must spend most of his time processing their work permits" (United States Congress, Senate, January 9, 1995). According to this provision, "criminal aliens" would be left without any means of support—especially since they were no longer eligible for welfare benefits either.

33. Edward M. Kennedy (D-MA), for example, appealed to Congress's sense of fairness and compassion: "An immigrant with an American citizen wife and children sentenced to one-year probation for minor tax evasion and fraud would be subject to this procedure. And under this provision, he would be treated the same as ax murderers and drug lords" (United States Congress, Senate, June 7, 1995). In addition, Nydia Velazquez (D-NY) reminded her colleagues of the differential impact this provision would have on poor people in particular: "The Constitution says we are all entitled to equal protection under the law, but in today's society some of us are more equal than others. The reality is, if you have the money to hire a good lawyer, you can make it through our legal system. But, if you are a poor minority, lacking those resources, you will lose and not have the opportunity to prove you are innocent. By severely limiting this ultimate right to appeal more

innocent Americans will unfairly die. Their blood will be on your hands" (United States Congress, House, April 18, 1996).

34. In a similar fashion, Henry J. Hyde (R-IL) argued that Congress needs to "protect a free people from those evil forces who seek our destruction through violence and terrorism. The bill, the conference report that we have before us today, does that in exemplary fashion. It maintains the delicate balance between liberty and order, between our precious freedoms and defending this country" (United States Congress, House, April 18, 1996).

35. Anthony C. Beilenson (D-CA), for example, reminded Congress that "in fact, to crack down on the more than 50 percent of illegal immigrants who come here legally and overstay their visas and remain often permanently, improving employer sanctions is essential, because we cannot obviously stop those immigrants from settling here permanently simply by improving border control" (United States Congress, House, March 19, 1996). On the same day, Bill McCollum (R-FL) argued, "The only way that we are going to stop people from coming here is by cutting off the magnet of jobs. No matter how many Border Patrol we put up on the border, and I am all for doing that, we will never completely stop it. Plus, about 50 percent or so of those who come here or were here illegally are visa overstays. They never crossed the border illegally in that sense, anyway, but they are here illegally" (United States Congress, House, March 19, 1996).

36. For example, Anthony C. Beilenson (D-CA) maintained that in order "to succeed in reducing illegal immigration, we must do two things; tighten control of our borders and remove to the greatest extent possible the incentives that encourage illegal immigration. The most powerful incentive of all, Mr. Speaker, is the opportunity to work in this country." Edward M. Kennedy (D-MA) agreed, "We must shut off the job magnet by denying jobs to illegal immigrants" (United States Congress, House, March 19, 1996).

37. According to the Immigration Reform and Control Act of 1986, employers are required to verify that their employees are eligible to work in the United States. If they fail to do so, they are not just "accomplices" but lawbreakers who can be charged a fine for hiring an unauthorized worker.

38. Specifically, Fix said, "A large share of the illegal immigrant working population is working in the informal and not the formal sector of the economy. A lot of the employment of those illegal workers is consensual between the employer and employee, and in those cases, fraudulent documents wouldn't be necessary. I consider, for example, domestic workers" (United States Congress, House, April 5, 1995). Robert L. Bach spoke in his position as the executive associate commissioner of the INS. In response to Sonny Bono's (R-CA) assertion that employers were the real victims, he said, "You'd be very surprised, if we could show you some of our investigations, at how bad the cards are when we find employers who knowingly and systematically hire illegal workers for certain types of businesses.

So even though it is very possible to get through the system well, there are many employers out there who continue to hire illegal workers in a knowingly [*sic*] way" (United States Congress, House, March 30, 1995).

39. In addition, Collins believed that "the U.S. Government's welfare system has lowered the work ethic in many areas of the labor market and has almost ruined the farm labor. As a result of this shortage, farmers are forced to import laborers from other countries" (United States Congress, House, March 21, 1996).

40. Bob Goodlatte (R-VA), for instance, argued, "There is now a great surplus of domestic farm workers." In addition, John Bryant (D-TX) claimed, "We have an American work force that can do this work." At the same time, he admitted that "maybe they do not want to do it at dirt-level wages. Maybe they need to have their wages raised. But we have the people to do this work" (United States Congress, House, March 21, 1996).

41. Along similar lines, Doc Hastings (R-WA) argued that his "constituents realize that our biggest industry—agriculture—must be protected," and Ron Lewis (R-KY) added, "again and again farmers tell me that one of the biggest problems they face is a willing and qualified work force. These jobs are mostly seasonal, temporary, and there simply are not enough domestic workers to do the hard work for short periods" (United States Congress, House, March 21, 1996).

42. Representative Richard W. Pombo (R-CA) described his own amendment in the following words: "My amendment supports and enhances immigration control. The increased employer sanctions already in H.R. 2202 for hiring illegals—coupled with strong incentives to leave this country when the growing season ends—creates a vast improvement over current law. Added to that is the mandatory withholding of 25 percent of the worker's salary to be returned to his country of origin and collected when he returns" (United States Congress, House, March 21, 1996).

43. Politicians who represented rural areas with many fruit and vegetable growers gladly embraced the Pombo Amendment. David Funderburk (R-NC), for example, believed that the new guest-worker program was an essential step toward ensuring the economic survival of countless farmers: "Without this Pombo Amendment, our cucumber, sweet potato, tobacco, and other farmers could be out of business, meaning a tremendous loss of food and jobs" (United States Congress, House, March 21, 1996). Other politicians painted an even more frightening picture. Helen Chenoweth (R-ID) reminded Congress that "without this amendment immigration reform could have the unintended consequence of causing a widespread labor shortage for American agriculture. That in turn could cause the industry to lose valuable markets to foreign competition and could cause hardships to millions of American consumers by raising the cost of the food they buy" (United States Congress, House, March 21, 1996).

44. In addition, Kika de la Garza (D-TX) argued, "One cannot say to people, you cannot bring your mother, you cannot bring your father, you have to speak English, you cannot come, we do not want you, get the dickens out of this country, but if you come to work temporarily then we can withhold 25 percent of your wages" (United States Congress, House, March 21, 1996).

45. For example, Bob Goodlatte (R-VA) pointed out, "This program will let in 250,000 unskilled foreign workers a year. That is four times the number of skilled workers we are going to admit. We are limiting the number of visas for family reunification. What is the point if we create this new program? This flies in the face of evidence that there is now a great surplus of domestic farm workers" (United States Congress, House, March 21, 1996).

46. Xavier Becerra (D-CA) summarized this contradiction in the following terms: "We just finished a day and a half worth of debate, where we were talking about eliminating about 300,000 visas for U.S. citizens to be able to bring in their family members. . . . Now we are dealing with an amendment that says, 'Let us bring in 250,000 imported foreign workers to do work in our fields'" (United States Congress, House, March 21, 1996).

47. Along similar lines, Thomas M. Barrett (D-WI) argued, "I find it ironic that we are hearing for the last 2 days how terrible it is that we have all these people coming into our country, we do not want these people in our country, we do not want these people who cannot pass an English test to come to our country. But we do want them if they will be cheap labor, we do want them if it is going to be easy for us to send them home like they are widgets at the end of a period of time" (United States Congress, House, March 21, 1996).

48. The Pombo Amendment was rejected (180 representatives voted for and 242 against the amendment; 9 representatives did not vote). In response, Bob Goodlatte (R-VA) offered an alternative amendment that would have reformed the H-2A Program. This amendment was even less popular and was rejected by a wide margin (yeas 59, nays 357, not voting 15).

4. Manufacturing the Crisis

1. In "Truth and Power," for instance, Foucault explains that it is his understanding that "truth" is a broader and more fundamental concept than "ideology." He writes, "This regime [of truth] is not merely ideological or superstructural; it was a condition of the formation and development of capitalism" (Foucault 1984, 74). See also Foucault, *The Archeology of Knowledge* (1972), and "Two Lectures" (1976).

2. According to *Editor & Publisher International Yearbook 1996*, the *New York Times* ranked third on the list of most widely circulated newspapers in 1995. On September 30, 1995, the date *Editor & Publisher* used to create their rankings, the

New York Times sold 1,081,541 copies. Only the *Wall Street Journal* (1,763,140 copies) and *USA Today* (1,523,610) had higher circulation numbers.

3. *Editor & Publisher International Yearbook 1996* ranked the *Houston Chronicle* ninth on its list of most widely circulated newspapers. On September 30, 1995, the *Houston Chronicle* sold 541,478 copies—more than any other newspaper in Texas. The *Dallas Morning News* ranked eleventh (500,358), and the *Fort Worth Telegram* (225,080) and the *San Antonio Express News* (221,556) came in forty-ninth and fiftieth, respectively.

4. According to the 2000 Census, San Diego was home to 606,254 immigrants, with 48.3 percent from Mexico. Los Angeles had almost 3.5 million immigrants; 44.2 percent had migrated to Los Angeles from Mexico, 13.9 percent came from other Central American countries, and 29.6 percent came from Asia.

5. The *SFC* was also one of the most widely circulated newspapers in California. On September 30, 1995, the *SFC* sold 489,238 copies and was thus ranked thirteenth by *Editor & Publisher International Yearbook 1996*. The *Los Angeles Times* was the only newspaper in California with higher circulation numbers (1,012,189).

6. A few days later, the *New York Times* added a special report about the impact that work requirements would have on certain welfare recipients. This report came back to the controversial comments about wolves and alligators. Journalist Sara Rimer wrote, "Recently, even as some Republicans in Washington were comparing welfare recipients to alligators and wolves in captivity who become dependent on food handouts, 21 welfare mothers were attending their first GAIN-sponsored Job Club meeting in Chula Vista, just south of San Diego" (*NYT*, April 10, 1995). Several participants critically interrogated the notion that they were "dependent" on benefits.

7. Consider the following examples:

- "A surge of immigration has led to the worst school overcrowding in four decades." (*NYT*, September 14, 1996)
- "School officials said enrollment has surged partly because of immigration of young families from the Dominican Republic, Mexico, and Asia." (*NYT*, September 6, 1996)
- "The overcrowding is a result of a combination of factors: immigrants flooding into the system, the effects of a miniature baby boom, fewer students dropping out and the failure to build new classrooms in time to accommodate the overflow." (*NYT*, September 5, 1995)
- "'They are coming to register in droves,' said Phyllis Gonon, the Superintendent of District 18, citing a stream of immigrants from Russia, Poland, and the Caribbean." (*NYT*, September 6, 1996)

8. The *New York Times* reported about the case on May 12, 1996. In addition, there were numerous special reports on individual families. For example,

the *Houston Chronicle* gave an account of the Vietnamese-born Truong family, whose children had all attended the University of Texas and were now established in technical, white-collar jobs (*HC*, Claudia Feldman, October 1, 1995). The next chapter will provide an in-depth analysis of these types of stories and their references to specific races and nationalities.

9. In some cases, the authors actually commented on their use of personal stories and rationalized this approach. In October 1996, for instance, the *Houston Chronicle* published a ten-part series that followed the lives of four Hispanic families. The authors, Thaddeus Herrick and James Pinkerton, claimed that this was an effective way "to illustrate the challenges facing today's inner-city Hispanic immigrants and also to put a human face on the larger immigration debate" (*HC*, "Out of the Shadows—About This Report," October 20, 1996).

10. In response to the question "How likely is it that the growing number of Hispanic immigrant children will cause the quality of education in public schools to decline?," 25.2 percent of all people responded that this was extremely or very likely, 33.4 percent found this somewhat likely, whereas 41.5 percent thought that this was not at all likely. White readers had the most negative attitudes (27.5 percent answered "extremely or very likely" and 35.3 percent picked the "somewhat likely" category). Not surprisingly, Hispanics had a much more positive attitude: only 18.9 percent thought that this outcome was extremely or very likely, 28 percent deemed it somewhat likely, and 53 percent thought that this was not at all likely (*HC*, "Out of the Shadows—Poll: Language and Education," October 20, 1996).

11. Not surprisingly, Hispanic respondents had the most positive attitude towards this cultural transformation: 89.3 percent said that these positives changes were likely to occur. Interestingly, however, the majority of black and white respondents agreed: 71.5 percent of blacks and 74.9 percent of whites thought that Hispanic immigrants were at least somewhat likely to exert a positive influence over American culture.

12. Please note that not all English-only policies demanded to put an end to bilingual education. However, since these two issues were inextricably linked within the larger discourse, the following section will examine them simultaneously.

13. Several letters to the editor made even more problematic connections and blamed multiculturalism for a host of different societal problems. For example, Mike Donnelly wrote, "Now we encourage and reward laziness, anti-Americanism. Most despicably we have made our country one that magnifies differences (Hispanic, African American, Asian American, etc.) instead of a country that strives to be a melting pot where the best and brightest, and those who work the hardest, reap the rewards" (*HC*, September 8, 1995). In addition, Tom Lovell argued, "'multiculturalism' is not a reality but a construct of minority activists" (*HC*, September 27, 1996).

14. These claims were factually incorrect. Previous immigrant groups have been known to set up school systems in foreign languages. German immigrant Joseph A. Herman, for instance, was among the first to develop a German-language school in Cincinnati, Ohio, in the 1840s. By 1860, there were dozens of German-language schools all over the country.

15. William Celis, for example, argued, "Even if bilingual programs are better, why should the 1 in 20 public school students in the nation who can't speak English be taught in their own language today when the immigrant children who entered school speaking only Italian or Russian or Yiddish or German or Greek or Finnish a century ago managed to get along just fine?" (*NYT*, October 15, 1995). Along similar lines, Constance L. Hays reported, "Some parents of children in the regular curriculum are opposed to bilingual education, considering it an unnecessary expense since previous immigrant generations survived without it" (*NYT*, February 19, 1995).

16. In a different context, the discourse compared bilingual education to affirmative action. William Celis wrote, "Like affirmative action, bilingual education has been derided by the descendants of immigrants as an entitlement, a form of preferential treatment that, because it costs more in the short term, is bought at the expense of other school services" (*NYT*, October 15, 1995).

17. Using a similar rhetoric, Lourdes Burrows, the project director of the Newcomers Academy for New Americans claimed that it is "our responsibility to maximize and expand the rich resources of our new immigrant population" (*NYT*, March 30, 1995).

18. These two remarks are representative of a large body of similar comments by politicians as well as journalists. For example, the *New York Times* reported, "Speaker Newt Gingrich criticized the requirement as a magnet for illegal aliens and an unfair financial burden on states. California alone spends $1.7 billion a year to educate more than 300,000 illegal immigrant pupils, Mr. Gingrich said. 'This is totally unfair,' he said" (*NYT*, Eric Schmitt, March 21, 1996). Three months later, the *New York Times* wrote, "Casting the issue as one of fairness, Bob Dole said today that taxpayers should not be forced to pay for the education of illegal immigrants. . . . 'It's not that we don't care,' Mr. Dole said. 'It's not that we're not compassionate. Where do you draw the line?'" (*NYT*, Katharine Q. Seelye, June 20, 1996). And, in a letter to the *Houston Chronicle*, Susan Garfield cast the issue as one of "fairness": "I wish it were possible for everybody on the planet to receive a decent education. It would do more to eradicate hunger, disease, poverty, crime, and just plain meanness than almost anything else. But this is not a perfect world; we have the responsibility of educating U.S. citizens above all others in this country" (*HC*, February 17, 1996).

19. On the same day, Purdy Cole demanded to know why the state did "not take action to deport the family, solving the immigration problem and eliminating

the controversy about whether their children should be allowed to attend public schools?" (*HC*, July 13, 1996).

20. This letter sparked another controversy among readers. On December 6, 1996, Claudia Macia asked whether Toney's suggestions were based on "anti-Hispanic and/or an anti-immigrant sentiment . . . Surely not every student's parents are going to be asked for proof of legal status." In addition, she reminded readers that "no human is 'illegal'—especially not any child" (*HC*, December 6, 1996). Kevin Ledkins, in turn, responded with the following letter: "How could she detect anything about Hispanics? They were not mentioned in Toney's letter. There are many non-Hispanic illegal aliens in this country. And his letter was not anti-immigrant, but anti–illegal immigrant" (*HC*, December 13, 1996).

21. Ira Mehlman continued: "We need to cut up the magnet of public services, but the real magnet is jobs and we've got to deal with that. The only way to do that is to have a mandatory verification process. Without that nothing else is going to work" (*SFC*, March 25, 1996).

22. George Borjas agreed. In a *New York Times* editorial, he maintained, "We need deterrence, but barring illegal aliens from our public schools is not an effective way of stopping illegal immigration" (*NYT*, July 11, 1996).

23. On other occasions, Arthur Hoppe criticized Congress's stance on welfare, at one point suggesting they deport "middle-class, native-born welfare bums [who] have developed that most debilitating of all inflictions—a welfare mentality" and allow immigrants to stay since "these are the people who swam shark-infested waters, climbed fences and crossed deserts to start their lives again in a strange land with strange customs, strange money and a strange language" (*SFC*, February 17, 1995).

24. In the introductory paragraph, Gunnison argued that Governor Pete Wilson "has repeatedly painted menacing villains—gang members are 'thugs,' teenagers are 'promiscuous,' affirmative action is a 'virus'—to appeal to voters who might otherwise give him low marks in public opinion polls" (*SFC*, February 19, 1996). Later on, however, Gunnison focused on President Bill Clinton's rhetoric and his attempts to turn his political adversaries—such as Newt Gingrich—into villains.

25. The editorial started with the following sentence: "Fear, blame, and resentment were introduced into presidential politics long before Pat Buchanan started stumping against 'Jose' and Bob Dole responded by scaring his Republican brethren by recalling the electoral math lesson of 1964." A few paragraphs later, the editorialist states that "the point is well established: Fear works as a campaign device" (*SFC*, March 3, 1996).

26. In particular, Carroll cited the results from a *New York Times* opinion poll, where white readers came up with the following estimates: "Percentage of the United States population that white Americans think is Hispanic: 14.9. Percentage that is Hispanic: 9.5. Percentage that white Americans think is Asian: 10.8. Percentage that

is Asian: 3.1. Percentage that white Americans think is black: 23.8. Percentage that is black: 11.8. Percentage that white Americans think is white: 49.9. Percentage that is white: 74" (*SFC*, March 27, 1996).

27. Fleeing an abusive husband, Maria T. enlisted the services of a "coyote," who held her captive for three months and beat and raped her repeatedly. After she managed to escape, Maria T. was homeless, penniless, eight-months pregnant and had two small children with her. In the beginning, she had to beg for food and money. Yet "slowly, she clawed her way up" (*NYT*, January 7, 1996).

28. In addition, Rayner argues, "When people complain about immigration, about the alien 'flood,' it's Latin Americans they mean" (*NYT*, January 7, 1996).

29. There was one positive response to Rayner's article. Ilze A. Choi, an immigrant from Sweden, wrote that she "welcome[s] Rayner, who, judging by his article, is not only intelligent but has a good heart. We badly need people like him in these darkening times" (*NYT*, January 28, 1996).

30. In a similar fashion, William E. Murray Jr. dismissed Rayner's approach as irrelevant. Murray insisted that "ultimately . . . his largely anecdotal analysis contains the seeds of its own counterargument. America is a nation of laws. The flagrant abuse of our borders, even by sympathetic figures like Maria T. and Maria V., is unacceptable—as it should be" (*NYT*, January 28, 1996).

31. Pointing to Richard Rayner's own immigrant roots, another writer angrily suggests that "debating immigration policy is such dirty work, it seems best left to immigrants" (*NYT*, William E. Murray Jr., January 28, 1996).

32. Throughout the article, Dugger added more definite comments to make her stance crystal clear. For instance, Dugger states matter-of-factly that "the growth of the Asian community in Flushing . . . is proving painful, even traumatic, for many elderly white voters, who reared their children in Flushing and once regarded it as theirs" (*NYT*, March 31, 1996).

5. Entrepreneurial Spirits and Individual Failures

1. On October 9, 1996, the *New York Times* reported, "Isolated from schools, playmates and playgrounds, Jessica, 5-year-old Danny and 3-year-old Jorge seem to fall ever further behind; even Jessica cannot read or write basic words in English or Spanish, and she stammers over the simplest phrases. . . . Danny, 5, who has two dimpled cheeks and wraps his arms around his mother's legs as she walks around the room, rarely utters a complete sentence. More often, he pokes and shrieks his way to being understood. When he speaks, it is with a slur, a lisp and an enormous smile. He often wets the family bed, so Miss Castillo makes him wear diapers. . . . And pudgy-faced Jorge, 3, is the most stoic, at ease about being the youngest, cautious about getting too close to people. He, too, relies on grunts and gestures" (*NYT*, October 9, 1996).

2. According to "Out of the Shadows," the five leading thinkers on immigration are Roy Beck, George Borjas, Michael Fix, Julian Simon, and Peter Brimelow.

3. The opening page featured a picture of a young Mexican couple with their little daughter, standing in front of a model of the Statue of Liberty at the immigration service's office in Houston. The opening paragraph read, "It was a grand experiment. Invite millions of illegal immigrants out of their hidden world, then slam the door shut on those who would follow. But 10 years later, the Mexican border remains porous. And while some who accepted the government's amnesty offer flourish, hundreds of thousands came out of the shadows only to vanish again in America's dead-end culture of urban poverty. These are the stories of three immigrant families that accepted amnesty and one that didn't."

4. The original newspaper coverage did not contain any Spanish accent marks on names. The following chapters adhere to the spelling in the original source.

5. "Maria's parents live two blocks away. Her sister Silvia lives on the next street over with sister Blanca and yet another sister, Marlene, is only a few blocks away. 'We help each other out,' said Maria" (*HC*, "Out of the Shadows—Part III," October 20, 1996).

6. Earlier in the same installment, the authors had already explained, "Life afterward [after they were legalized in 1986] was not much different for Marcelina and Victor. They were raising five U.S.-born children—Brenda, Victor, Reynaldo, Gloria, Marisa—and would have two more—Alicia and Patricia—over the next four years. Neither Marcelina nor Victor learned to speak English. And the most they could afford on Victor's salary of less than $200 a week were rickety rentals deep in the barrio" (*HC*, "Out of the Shadows—Part III," October 20, 1996).

7. See Briggs (2002) for a critique of the "culture of poverty" thesis.

8. In the first few articles, Pedro Sotelo is referred to as Adela Quintana's boyfriend. Yet after the Children Protective Services filed sexual assault charges against Sotelo, his attorney Nancy Revelette made a case that they were actually married. She argued that "in some areas of rural Mexico, when a man proposes, he offers to let her move in, leave all of her family belongings, and begin a life that he will make for her. The ritual begins when they set a date for her to leave. The bride leaves her home and goes with her groom to consummate their union. After a few days, the groom's friends visit the 'grieving' father, and try to console him with alcohol and the benefits of a son-in-law. The father is consoled, and welcomes the union. Revelette said she found that Sotelo and Quintana followed much the same ritual in February 1995" (*HC*, June 17, 1996).

9. What is even more interesting about this particular article is the fact that it advanced the same "cultural difference" rhetoric that dominated the media discourse about Pedro Sotelo and Adela Quintana. The *Houston Chronicle* reported, "Supporters of Lazo say they are amazed that a young man who rose so fast now risks an equally precipitous fall because of a mistake they believe originated out

of a difference in cultures. 'It shocks our American notion of how kids should behave' when children have children, said Jacob Monty, Lazo's attorney. 'But it's normal in Central America and Mexico'" (*HC*, July 7, 2006).

10. Deputy District Attorney Susan Breall was acutely aware of this dilemma. In support of her decision to drop charges, she asked the following (rhetorical) question: "Do we want to spend a lot of time and money prosecuting a person and putting on trial this particular culture when the victim is uncooperative and when I and many other San Franciscans pride ourselves on being sensitive to someone's culture?" (*SFC*, August 7, 1996).

11. On November 19, 1996, the *Houston Chronicle* reported that "Quintana has returned to school to finish her education," and two days later, Quintana told the judge, "I want to get my GED (general equivalency diploma)" (*HC*, November 19, 1996, and November 21, 1996, respectively).

12. It was not until a few days later that the *Houston Chronicle* revealed that Adela Quintana's mother had purchased a fake birth certificate with the wrong name ("Garcia") when she wanted to enroll her daughter into elementary school. On the same day, Kurt Kilpatrick wrote that he found "it appalling that so much taxpayer money has been and will be fruitlessly spent in trying to rectify a problem that should have been stopped at the border" (*HC*, February 1, 1996). In a slightly more sympathetic response, Juanita Garza argued that Quintana and Sotelo were "going through a very difficult situation because the state became involved. . . . Send them back to Mexico, but please, no prison" (*HC*, February 1, 1996).

13. In February 1996, presidential candidate Patrick J. Buchanan spoke at a rally against the local meat-packing plant, which actively recruited immigrant workers. According to the *New York Times*, it "is no coincidence that Mr. Buchanan chose this small farming and university town set amid rolling prairie in northwestern Iowa to make his nativist appeal. In the past 25 years, Storm Lake has undergone a startling metamorphosis as immigrants have flocked here to work in two packing plants. In 1970, the town of 8,591 people had 22 minority residents—mainly faculty members and students at Buena Vista University, including two young blacks who had been adopted by a white family. Today, town officials estimate that Storm Lake's population, now 8,769, is 10 percent minority, mainly recent immigrants from Mexico and Southeast Asia" (*NYT*, February 17, 1996).

14. The *New York Times* reporter seemed to endorse the idea that the influx of immigrants had created these conflicts. Journalist Celia W. Dugger wrote that "in Mount Kisco, the friction between longtime residents, many of Italian and Irish descent, and the Spanish-speaking newcomers has created feelings of loss and anger . . . roiling the idyllic surface of this picturesque town" (*NYT*, December 1, 1996).

15. Linda Skiba and Beth Vetare Civitello wrote, "The overwhelming amount of incidents that involve intoxicated persons should be alerting us to a major problem. . . . Check the police records concerning arrests made involving Hispanics

(for lack of a better term); undocumented or legal, either driving while intoxicated or throwing beer bottles or tearing street signs out of the ground or knifing one another" (*NYT*, December 1, 1996).

16. On May 4, 1995, the *San Francisco Chronicle* reported, "Under pressure from local communities, the Immigration and Naturalization Service began rounding up day laborers around the Bay Area this week in a new crackdown on illegal immigrants and their employers. Thirty-four suspects were taken into custody. . . . Although no employers were arrested, some of the suspects provided key information that will help agents target businesses for prosecution" (*SFC*, May 4, 1995).

17. The *New York Times* reported, "The lawsuit claims that the town was selectively enforcing the housing code and violating Hispanic residents' constitutional right to free speech, free assembly and due process. . . . Lawyers for the town say that its laws are equitably enforced and that the housing code is applied without regard to ethnicity" (*NYT*, December 1, 1996).

18. A similar case happened in Elgin, Illinois, where two-thirds of the 268 occupancy code violations were issued to families with Hispanic surnames between 1995 and 1998, despite the fact that less than one in four of Elgin's 87,000 inhabitants was Latino. The case was reported widely by news outlets around the country.

19. A few weeks later, the *Houston Chronicle* repeated the same point in another story about the Gulfton work stop. They wrote that "civic organizers say crime in the Gulfton area has since dropped about 17 percent, and the neighborhood's overall appearance and atmosphere have improved" (*HC*, July 1, 1995).

20. The article also narrated a "more subtle success story [that] involves a Costa Rican family in East Hampton" who were "saving to buy the three-bedroom rental home where they live" (*NYT*, February 25, 1996). In addition, the story repeatedly emphasized that thirty-five-year-old Juan and his family were likely to succeed.

Conclusion

1. For example, Raul Yzaguirre, the president of the National Council of La Raza, wrote a letter to Congress to express his dissatisfaction with politicians' attempts to combine justifiable concerns over undocumented immigrants with exaggerated anxieties about documented immigrants. On March 15, 1996, he wrote that H.R. 2202 "unfairly exploits public concern over illegal immigration to impose unwarranted restrictions on legal immigration." While NCLR was opposed to "unnecessary, extremist, and ineffective proposals embodied in—and being proposed as amendments to—the pending legislation," Yzaguirre also "acknowledges the right and duty of any sovereign nation to control its borders" (United States Congress, House, March 28, 1996).

Bibliography

Agrawal, Shantanu. 2008. "Immigrant Exclusion from Welfare: An Analysis of the 1996 Welfare Reform Legislative Process." *Politics and Policy* 36 (4): 636–75.

Akram, Susan, and Kevin R. Johnson. 2002. "Race, Civil Rights, and Immigration Law after September 11, 2001: The Targeting of Muslims and Arabs." *NYU Annual Survey of American Law* 58: 295–355.

Alba, Richard D., and Victor Nee. 2003. *Remaking the American Mainstream: Assimilation and Contemporary Immigration.* Cambridge, Mass.: Harvard University Press.

Albiston, Catherine, and Laura Beth Nielsen. 1995. "Welfare Queens and Other Fairy Tales: Welfare Reform and Unconstitutional Reproductive Controls." *Howard Law Journal* 38: 473–520.

Aldana, Raquel, and Sylvia R. Lazos Vargas. 2005. "'Aliens' in Our Midst Post 9/11: Legislating Outsiderness within the Borders." *U.C. Davis Law Review* 38: 1683–723.

Aleinikoff, Thomas Alexander, David A. Martin, and Hiroshi Motomura. 2007. *Immigration and Citizenship: Process and Policy.* 6th ed. St. Paul, Minn.: West Group.

Andreas, Peter. 1999. "Borderless Economy, Barricaded Border." *NACLA Report on the Americas* 33 (3): 14–21.

Arguelles, Lourdes. 1990. "Undocumented Female Labor in the United States Southwest: An Essay on Migration, Consciousness, Oppression, and Struggle." In *Between Borders: Essays on Mexicana/Chicana History*, edited by Adelaida R. Del Castillo, 299–314. Encino, Calif.: Floricanto Press.

Bailey, Silvia Pedraza. 1991. "Women and Migration." *Annual Review of Sociology* 17: 303–25.

Bâli, Asli Ü. 2005. "Changes in Immigration Law and Practice after September 11: A Practitioner's Perspective." *Canada–United States Law Journal* 30: 161–77.

Barbee, Alexandra, and Ashley Parcells, eds. 2010. *Protection and Resettlement Policy: Reforming United States Policy towards Refugees, Asylum Seekers and Forced Migrants.* Task Force 2010. Seattle, Wash.: The Henry M. Jackson School of International Studies, University of Washington.

Barkan, Elliott, Hasia R. Diner, and Alan M. Kraut, eds. 2007. *From Arrival to Incorporation: Migrants to the U.S. in a Global Era*. New York: New York University Press.

Barry, Andrew, Thomas Osborne, and Nikolas Rose, eds. 1996. *Foucault and Political Reason: Liberalism, Neo-Liberalism and Rationalities of Government*. Chicago: University of Chicago Press.

Basch, Linda, Nina Glick Schiller, and Cristina Szanton Blanc. 1994. *Nations Unbound: Transnational Projects, Postcolonial Predicaments, and Deterritorialized Nation-States*. Amsterdam: Gordon and Breach.

Beall, Jennifer A. 1998. "Are We Only Burning Witches? The Antiterrorism and Effective Death Penalty Act of 1996's Answer to Terrorism." *Indiana Law Journal* 73: 693–710.

Bean, Frank D., Robert G. Gushing, Charles W. Haynes, and Jennifer V. W. Van Hook. 1997. "Immigration and the Social Contract." *Social Science Quarterly* 78 (2): 249–68.

Bean, Frank D., Georges Vernez, and Charles B. Keely. 1989. *Opening and Closing the Doors: Evaluating Immigration Reform and Control*. Washington, D.C.: Urban Institute.

Beasley, Vanessa B. 2006. *Who Belongs in America? Presidents, Rhetoric, and Immigration*. 1st ed. College Station, Tex.: Texas A&M University Press.

Beck, Roy Howard. 1996. *The Case against Immigration: The Moral, Economic, Social, and Environmental Reasons for Reducing U.S. Immigration Back to Traditional Levels*. New York: W. W. Norton.

Berger, Susan. 2009. "Production and Reproduction of Gender and Sexuality in Legal Discourses of Asylum in the United States." *Signs: Journal of Women in Culture and Society* 34 (3): 659–85.

Blank, Rebecca M. 2002. "Evaluating Welfare Reform in the United States." Working Paper 8983. Cambridge, Mass.: National Bureau of Economic Research.

Bommes, Michael, and Andrew Geddes. 2000. *Immigration and Welfare: Challenging the Borders of the Welfare State*. New York: Routledge.

Boris, Eileen. 1995. "The Racialized Gendered State: Constructions of Citizenship in the United States." *Social Politics* 2 (3): 160–80.

Borjas, George J. 1990. *Friends or Strangers: The Impact of Immigrants on the U.S. Economy*. New York: Basic Books.

———. 1994. "The Economics of Immigration." *Journal of Economic Literature* 32 (4): 1667–717.

———. 1995. "Assimilation and Changes in Cohort Quality: What Happened to Immigrant Earnings in the 1980s." *Journal of Labor Economics* 2 (3): 201–45.

———. 1999. *Heaven's Door: Immigration Policy and the American Economy*. Princeton, N.J.: Princeton University Press.

———. 2001. "Welfare Reform and Immigration." In *The New World of Welfare*, edited by Rebecca M. Blank and Ron Haskins. Washington, D.C.: Brookings Institution.

Borjas, George J., Richard B. Freeman, and Lawrence F. Katz. 1992. "On the Labor Market Effects of Immigration and Trade." In *Immigration and the Work Force*, edited by George J. Borjas and Richard B. Freeman, 213–44. Chicago: University of Chicago Press.

Borjas, George J., Jeff Grogger, and Gordon H. Hanson. 2006. *Immigration and African-American Employment Opportunities: The Response of Wages, Employment, and Incarceration to Labor Supply Shocks.* Cambridge, Mass.: National Bureau of Economic Research.

Borjas, George J., and Lynette Hilton. 1995. *Immigration and the Welfare State: Immigrant Participation in Means-Tested Entitlement Programs.* Cambridge, Mass.: National Bureau of Economic Research.

Bosniak, Linda. 1994. "Membership, Equality, and the Difference That Alienage Makes." *New York University Law Review* 69: 1047–149.

———. 1996. "Opposing Prop. 187: Undocumented Immigrants and the National Imagination." *Connecticut Law Review* 28 (3): 555–619.

———. 2006. *The Citizen and the Alien. Dilemmas of Contemporary Membership.* Princeton, N.J.: Princeton University Press.

Briggs, Laura. 2002. "La Vida, Moynihan, and Other Libels: Migration, Social Science, and the Making of the Puerto Rican Welfare Queen." *Centro Journal* 14 (1): 74–102.

Briggs, Vernon M. 1996a. *Mass Immigration and the National Interest.* 2nd ed. Armonk, N.Y.: M. E. Sharpe.

———. 1996b. "The Administration of U.S. Immigration Policy: Time for Another Change." In *Immigration and the Social Contract: The Implosion of Western Societies*, edited by John Tanton, Denis McCormack, and Joseph Wayne Smith, 44–51. Aldershot, U.K.: Avebury.

Briggs, Vernon M., and Stephen Moore. 1994. *Still an Open Door? U.S. Immigration Policy and the American Economy.* Washington, D.C.: American University Press.

Brimelow, Peter. 1995. *Alien Nation: Common Sense about America's Immigration Disaster.* New York: Random House.

Brown, Michael K. 1999. *Race, Money, and the American Welfare State.* Ithaca, N.Y.: Cornell University Press.

Brown, Wendy. 2006. "American Nightmare: Neoliberalism, Neoconservatism, and De-Democratization." *Political Theory* 34 (6): 690–714.

Bryson, Valerie, and Ruth Lister. 1994. *Women, Citizenship and Social Policy.* Bradford, Conn.: University of Bradford/Joseph Rowntree Foundation.

Buchanan, Patrick J. 2006. *State of Emergency: The Third World Invasion and Conquest of America*. New York: Thomas Dunne Books.

Buff, Rachel Ida. 2008. "The Deportation Terror." *American Quarterly* 60 (3): 523–51.

Buijs, Gina, ed. 1993. *Migrant Women: Crossing Boundaries and Changing Identities*. Oxford, U.K.: Berg.

Burchell, Graham, Colin Gordon, and Peter Miller, eds. 1991. *The Foucault Effect: Studies in Governmentality*. Chicago: University of Chicago Press.

Burns, Peter, and James G. Gimpel. 2000. "Economic Insecurity, Prejudicial Stereotypes, and Public Opinion on Immigration Policy." *Political Science Quarterly* 115 (2): 201–25.

Calavita, Kitty. 1992. *Inside the State: The Bracero Program, Immigration, and the I.N.S.* New York: Routledge.

Cammisa, Anne Marie. 1998. *From Rhetoric to Reform? Welfare Policy in American Politics*. Boulder, Colo.: Westview.

Cantú, Lionel. 2000. "Entre Hombres/Between Men: Latino Masculinities and Homosexualities." In *Gay Masculinities*, edited by Peter Nardi, 224–46. Thousand Oaks, Calif.: Sage.

———. 2001. "A Place Called Home: A Queer Political Economy of Mexican Immigrant Men's Family Experiences." In *Queer Families, Queer Politics: Challenging Culture and the State*, edited by Mary Bernstein and Renate Reimann, 112–36. New York: Columbia University Press.

Capps, Randy, Leighton Ku, and Michael Fix. 2002. "How Are Immigrants Faring after Welfare Reform? Preliminary Evidence from Los Angeles and New York City." The Urban Institute. March 4, 2002. Accessed August 11, 2011. http://www.urban.org/UploadedPDF/410426_final_report.pdf.

Carter, Thomas J. 2005. "Undocumented Immigration and Host-Country Welfare: Competition across Segmented Labor Markets." *Journal of Regional Science* 45 (4): 777–95.

Castles, Stephen, and Alastair Davidson. 2000. *Citizenship and Migration: Globalization and the Politics of Belonging*. New York: Routledge.

Chacón, Justin Akers, and Mike Davis. 2006. *No One Is Illegal: Fighting Violence and State Repression on the U.S.-Mexico Border*. Chicago: Haymarket Books.

Chang, Grace. 2000. *Disposable Domestics: Immigrant Women Workers in the Global Economy*. Cambridge, Mass.: South End Press.

Chang, Howard F. 1997. "Liberalized Immigration as Free Trade: Economic Welfare and the Optimal Immigration Policy." *University of Pennsylvania Law Review* 145 (5): 1147–245.

Chang, Robert S. 1999. *Disoriented: Asian Americans, Law, and the Nation-State*. New York: New York University Press.

Chavez, Leo R. 1998. *Shadowed Lives: Undocumented Immigrants in American Society.* 2nd ed. New York: Wadsworth.

———. 1999. "Immigration Reform and Nativism: The Nationalist Response to the Transnationalist Challenge." In *Immigrants Out!*, edited by Juan Perea, 61–77. New York: New York University Press.

———. 2001. *Covering Immigration: Popular Images and the Politics of the Nation.* Berkeley, Calif.: University of California Press.

———. 2007. "A Glass Half Empty: Latina Reproduction and Public Discourse." *Women and Migration in the U.S.-Mexico Borderlands*, edited by Denise A. Segura and Patricia Zavella, 67–91. Durham, N.C.: Duke University Press, 2007.

Chavez, Manuel, Scott Whiteford, and Jennifer Howe. 2010. "Reporting on Immigration: A Content Analysis of Major U.S. Newspapers' Coverage of Mexican Immigration." *Norteamérica* 5 (2): 111–25.

Chin, Gabriel J., ed. 2000. *The United States Commission on Immigration Reform: The Interim and Final Reports and Commentary.* Buffalo, N.Y.: William S. Hein & Co.

Citrin, Jack, et al. 1997. "Public Opinion toward Immigration Reform: The Role of Economic Motivations." *The Journal of Politics* 59 (3): 858–81.

Clark, Rebecca, and Jeffrey Passel. 1993. *How Much Do Immigrants Pay in Taxes? Evidence from Los Angeles County.* Washington, D.C.: Urban Institute.

Clinton, Bill. 1994a. *Accepting the Immigration Challenge: The President's Report on Immigration.* Washington, D.C.: U.S. Office of the President.

———. 1994b. "Statement on Signing the Antiterrorism and Effective Death Penalty Act of 1996." *Public Papers of the President.* April 24, 1996. Accessed April 12, 2013. http://www.gpo.gov/fdsys/pkg/PPP-1996-book1/pdf/PPP-1996-book1-doc -pg630.pdf.

———. 1996. "Remarks on Welfare Reform Legislation and an Exchange with Reporters." *Public Papers of the President.* July 31, 1996. Accessed April 12, 2013. http://www.presidency.ucsb.edu/ws/index.php?pid=53140.

Cohen, Robin. 1996a. *Theories of Migration.* Cheltenham, U.K.: Edward Elgar.

———. 1996b. *The Sociology of Migration.* Cheltenham, U.K.: Edward Elgar.

Cole, David. 2003. *Enemy Aliens: Double Standards and Constitutional Freedoms in the War on Terrorism.* New York: New Press.

Cooper, Emilie. 2004. "Embedded Immigrant Exceptionalism: An Examination of California's Proposition 187, the 1996 Welfare Reforms, and the Anti-Immigrant Sentiment Expressed Therein." *Georgetown Immigrant Law Journal* 18: 345–72.

Cornelius, Wayne A. 2004. *Controlling Immigration: A Global Perspective.* 2nd ed. Stanford, Calif.: Stanford University Press.

Cornwall, Andrea, Jasmine Gideon, and Kalpana Wilson. 2008. "Reclaiming Feminism: Gender and Neoliberalism." *IDS Bulletin* 39 (6): 1–9.

Dallmayr, Fred R., and José; María Rosales. 2001. *Beyond Nationalism? Sovereignty and Citizenship.* Lanham, Md.: Lexington Books.

Daniels, Roger. 1990. *Coming to America: A History of Immigration and Ethnicity in American Life.* New York: Harper Collins.

———. 2004. *Guarding the Golden Door: American Immigration Policy and Immigrants since 1882.* New York: Hill and Wang.

Daniels, Roger, and Otis L. Graham. 2001. *Debating American Immigration, 1882–Present.* Lanham, Md.: Rowman & Littlefield.

Das Gupta, Monisha. 2006. *Unruly Immigrants: Rights, Activism and Transnational South Asian Politics in the United States.* Durham, N.C.: Duke University Press.

Davis, Tracy. 2006. "Opening the Doors of Immigration: Sexual Orientation and Asylum in the United States." March 26. http://www.wcl.american.edu/hrbrief /v6i3/immigration.htm.

Dean, Mitchell. 1999. *Governmentality: Power and Rule in Modern Society.* London: Sage.

De Genova, Nicholas, and Ana Y. Ramos-Zayas. 2003. *Latino Crossings: Mexicans, Puerto Ricans, and the Politics of Race and Citizenship.* New York: Routledge.

Demleitner, Nora V. 2003. "How Much Do Western Democracies Value Family and Marriage: Immigration Law's Conflicted Answers." *Hofstra Law Review* 32: 273–311.

DeSipio, Louis, and Rodolfo O. De la Garza. 1998. *Making Americans, Remaking America: Immigration and Immigrant Policy.* Boulder, Colo.: Westview Press.

Dietz, Mary G. 1985. "Citizenship with a Feminist Face: The Problem with Maternal Thinking." *Political Theory* 13 (1): 19–37.

———. 1987. "Context Is All: Feminism and Theories of Citizenship." *Daedalus* 116 (4): 1–24.

Dobkin, Donald S. 2009. "Race and the Shaping of US Immigration Policy." *Chicana/o-Latina/o Law Review* 28 (19): 19–41.

Duggan, Lisa. 2003. *The Twilight of Equality: Neoliberalism, Cultural Politics and the Attack on Democracy.* Boston: Beacon.

Eager, Paige Whaley. 2004. *Global Population Policy: From Population Control to Reproductive Rights.* Burlington, Vt.: Ashgate.

Edwards, James R. 2006. "Homosexuals and Immigration: Developments in the United States and Abroad." Center for Immigration Studies. March 26. http://www .cis.org/articles/1999/back599.html.

Entman, Robert M., and Andrew Rojecki. 2000. *The Black Image in the White Mind: Media and Race in America.* Chicago: University of Chicago Press.

Epps, Bradley S., Keja Valens, and Bill Johnson González. 2005. *Passing Lines: Sexuality and Immigration.* Cambridge, Mass.: Harvard University Press.

Espenshade, Thomas J., Jessica L. Baraka, and Gregory A. Huber. 1997. "Implications of the 1996 Welfare and Immigration Reform Acts for US Immigration." *Population and Development Review* 23 (4): 769–801.

Espenshade, Thomas J., and Katherine Hempstead. 1996. "Contemporary American Attitudes toward U.S. Immigration." *International Migration Review* 30 (2): 535–70.

Espin, Olivia, ed. 1997. *Latina Realities: Essays on Healing, Migration and Sexuality*. Boulder, Colo.: Westview Press.

———. 1999. *Women Crossing Boundaries: A Psychology of Immigration and Transformations of Sexuality*. New York: Routledge.

Fairclough, Norman. 1995. *Critical Discourse Analysis*. London: Longman.

———. 2003. *Analysing Discourse: Textual Analysis for Social Research*. London: Routledge.

———. 2005. "Critical Discourse Analysis." *Marges Linguistiques* 9: 76–94.

Fairclough, Norman, Simon Pardoe, and Bronislaw Szerszynski. 2006. "Critical Discourse Analysis and Citizenship." In *Analyzing Citizenship Talk*, edited by Heiko Hausendorf and Alfons Bora, 98–123. Amsterdam: John Benjamins.

Family, Jill E. 2010. "Conflicting Signals: Understanding US Immigration Reform through the Evolution of US Immigration Law." Widener Law School Legal Studies Research Paper Series, no. 10–18.

Farber, Sara E. 2010. "Presidential Promises and the Uniting American Families Act: Bringing Same-Sex Immigration Rights to the United States." *Boston College Third World Law Journal* 30 (2): 329–57.

Fix, Michael, and Jeffrey S. Passel. 1994. *Immigration and Immigrants: Setting the Record Straight*. Washington, D.C.: Urban Institute.

———. 2002. "The Scope and Impact of Welfare Reform's Immigrant Provisions." Assessing the New Federalism Discussion Paper No. 02-03. Washington, D.C.: Urban Institute.

Flores, Lisa. 2003. "Constructing Rhetorical Borders: Peons, Illegal Aliens, and Competing Narratives of Immigration." *Critical Studies in Media Communication* 20 (4): 362–87.

Flores, William C. 1997. "Citizens vs. Citizenry: Undocumented Immigrants and Latino Cultural Citizenship." In *Latino Cultural Citizenship: Claiming Identity, Space, and Rights*, edited by William C. Flores and Rina Benmayor, 255–77. Boston: Beacon.

Flores, William C., and Rina Benmayor, eds. 1997a. "Constructing Cultural Citizenship." In *Latino Cultural Citizenship: Claiming Identity, Space, and Rights*, edited by William C. Flores and Rina Benmayor, 1–26. Boston: Beacon.

———. 1997b. *Latino Cultural Citizenship: Claiming Identity, Space, and Rights*. Boston: Beacon.

Foucault, Michel. 1972. *The Archaeology of Knowledge and the Discourse on Language*. Translated by A. M. Sheridan Smith. New York: Pantheon.

———. 1980. *Power/Knowledge*. Edited by Colin Gordon. New York: Pantheon.

———. (1976) 1984. "Truth and Power." In *The Foucault Reader*, edited by Paul Rabinow, 51–75. New York: Pantheon.

———. 1991. "Governmentality." In *The Foucault Effect*, edited by Graham Burchell, Colin Gordon, and Peter Miller, 87–104. London: Harvester Wheatsheaf.

Fox Piven, Frances, and Richard A. Cloward. 1993. *Regulating the Poor: The Functions of Public Welfare*. 2nd ed. New York: Vintage.

Fraser, Nancy. 1999. "Rethinking the Public Sphere: A Contribution to the Critique of Actually Existing Democracy." In *The Cultural Studies Reader*, edited by Simon During, 518–36. New York: Routledge.

Fraser, Nancy, and Linda Gordon. 1992. "Contract versus Charity: Why Is There No Social Citizenship in the United States?" *Socialist Review* 22 (3): 45–67.

Fujiwara, Lynn. 2005. "Immigrant Rights Are Human Rights: The Reframing of Immigrant Entitlement and Welfare." *Social Problems* 52 (1): 79–101.

Gales, Tammy. 2009. "Diversity as Enacted in US Immigration Politics." *Discourse and Society* 20: 223–40.

Giddens, Anthony. 1998. *The Third Way*. Cambridge, U.K.: Polity Press.

Gilchrist, Jim, and Jerome R. Corsi. 2006. *Minutemen: The Battle to Secure America's Borders*. Los Angeles: World Ahead.

Gilens, Martin. 1999. *Why Americans Hate Welfare: Race, Media, and the Politics of Antipoverty Policy*. Chicago: University of Chicago Press.

Gimpel, James G., and James R. Edwards Jr. 1999. *The Congressional Politics of Immigration Reform*. Boston: Allyn and Bacon.

Glenn, Evelyn Nakano. 2002. *Unequal Freedom. How Race and Gender Shaped American Citizenship and Labor*. Cambridge, Mass.: Harvard University Press.

Goffman, E. 1974. *Frame Analysis*. New York: Harper and Row.

Gomberg-Muñoz, Ruth. 2009. "Not Just Mexico's Problem: Labor Migration from Mexico to the United States (1900–2009)." *The Journal of Latino-Latin American Studies* 3 (3): 2–18.

Gonzalez, Roberto. 2011. "Learning to Be Illegal: Undocumented Youth and Shifting Legal Contexts in the Transition to Adulthood." *American Sociological Review* 76 (4): 602–19.

Green, Allison, and Jack Martin. 2004. "Uncontrolled Immigration and the U.S. Health Care System." *The Journal of Social, Political, and Economic Studies* 29 (2): 225–41.

Green, Linda. 2011. "The Nobodies: Neoliberalism, Violence and Migration." *Medical Anthropology* 30 (4): 366–85.

Green, Richard. 1987. "'Give Me Your Tired, Your Poor, Your Huddled Masses' (of Heterosexuals): An Analysis of American and Canadian Immigration Law Policy." *Anglo American Law Review* 16 (2): 139–59.

Grewal, Inderpal. 2005. *Transnational America: Feminisms, Diasporas, Neoliberalisms*. Durham, N.C.: Duke University Press.

Griffin, Penny. 2007. "Sexing the Economy in a Neo-Liberal World Order: Neo-Liberal Discourse and the (Re)Production of Heteronormative Heterosexuality." *The British Journal of Politics and International Relations* 9 (2): 220–38.

Habermas, Jürgen. 1989. *The Structural Transformation of the Public Sphere: An Inquiry into a Category of Bourgeois Society*. Translated by Thomas Burger. Cambridge, Mass.: MIT Press.

———. 1992. "Citizenship and National Identity: Some Reflections on the Future of Europe." *Praxis International* 12 (1): 1–19.

———. 1996. "The European Nation-State—Its Achievements and Its Limits. On the Past and Future of Sovereignty and Citizenship." In *Mapping the Nation*, edited by Gopal Balakrishnan, 281–94. London: Verso.

Hanson, Gordon H. 2005. *Why Does Immigration Divide America? Public Finance and Political Opposition to Open Borders*. Washington, D.C.: Institute for International Economics.

Hanson, Gordon H., and Antonio Spilimbergo. 1996. *Illegal Immigration, Border Enforcement, and Relative Wages: Evidence from Apprehensions at the U.S.-Mexico Border*. Cambridge, Mass.: National Bureau of Economic Research.

Harper, Philip Brian, et al., eds. 1997. "Queer Transexions of Race, Nation, and Gender." *Social Text* 52–53 (Special issue).

Hartry, Allison. 2012. "Gendering Crimmigration: The Intersection of Gender, Immigration, and the Criminal Justice System." *Berkeley Journal of Gender, Law and Justice* 27: 1–27.

Hernandez, Donald J. 1999. *Children of Immigrants: Health, Adjustment, and Public Assistance*. Washington, D.C.: National Academy Press.

Hernandez-Truyol, Berta Esperanza. 2008. "The Gender Bend: Culture, Sex, and Sexuality—A LatCritical Human Rights Map of Latina/o Border Crossings." *Indiana Law Journal* 83 (4): 1283–331.

Hernandez-Truyol, Berta Esperanza, and Kimberly A. Johns. 1998. "Global Rights, Local Wrongs, and Legal Fixes: An International Human Rights Critique of Immigration and Welfare 'Reform.'" *Southern California Law Review* 71 (3): 547–616.

Hiemstra, Nancy. 2010. "Immigrant 'Illegality' as Neoliberal Governmentality in Leadville, Colorado." *Antipode* 42 (1): 74–102.

Hing, Bill Ong. 1993. *Making and Remaking Asian America through Immigration Policy, 1850–1990*. Stanford, Calif.: Stanford University Press.

——. 1998. "Don't Give Me Your Tired, Your Poor: Conflicted Immigrant Stories and Welfare Reform." *Harvard Civil Rights-Civil Liberties Law Review* 33: 159–82.

——. 2003. *Defining America through Immigration Policy*. Philadelphia, Penn.: Temple University Press.

Hoefer, Michael, Nancy Rytina, and Bryan C. Baker. 2011. "Estimates of the Unauthorized Immigrant Population Residing in the United States: January 2010." Department of Homeland Security, Office of Immigration Statistics.

Hondagneu-Sotelo, Pierrette. 1994. *Gendered Transitions: Mexican Experiences of Immigration*. Berkeley, Calif.: University of California Press.

——. 1999. "Women and Children First: New Directions in Anti-Immigrant Politics." In *American Families: A Multicultural Reader*, edited by Stephanie Coontz, Maya Parson, and Gabrielle Raley, 288–304. New York: Routledge.

——. 2003. *Gender and U.S. Immigration: Contemporary Trends*. Berkeley, Calif.: University of California Press.

Huang, Priscilla. 2008. "Anchor Babies, Over-Breeders, and the Population Bomb: The Reemergence of Nativism and Population Control in Anti-Immigration Policies." *Harvard Law and Policy Review* 2: 385–406.

Huddle, Donald. 1993. *The Costs of Immigration*. Washington, D.C.: Carrying Capacity Network.

Hursh, David. 2005. "Neo-Liberalism, Markets and Accountability: Transforming Education and Undermining Democracy in the United States and England." *Policy Future in Education* 3 (1): 3–15.

Hutchinson, E. P. 1091. *A Legislative History of American Immigration Policy, 1798–1965*. Philadelphia, Penn.: University of Pennsylvania Press.

Inda, Jonathan Xavier. 2005. *Targeting Immigrants: Government, Technology, and Ethics*. Malden, Mo.: Blackwell.

Inniss, Lolita Buckner. 1996. *California's Proposition 187: Does It Mean What It Says? Does It Say What It Means? A Textual and Constitutional Analysis*. Washington, D.C.: Georgetown University Law Center.

Jackson, Richard. 2007. "Constructing Enemies: 'Islamic Terrorism' in Political and Academic Discourse." *Government and Opposition* 42 (3): 394–426.

Jacobson, Robin Dale. 2008. *The New Nativism: Proposition 187 and the Debate over Immigration*. Minneapolis: University of Minnesota Press.

Jäger, Siegfried, and Jürgen Link. 1993. *Die Vierte Gewalt: Rassismus und die Medien*. Duisburg, Germany: Diss.

Jäger, Siegfried, and Florentine Maier. 2009. "Theoretical and Methodological Aspects of Foucauldian Critical Discourse Analysis and Dispositive Analysis." In *Methods of Critical Discourse Analysis*, edited by Ruth Wodak and Michael Meyer, 34–61. London: Sage.

Jefferies, Julian. 2008. "Do Undocumented Students 'Play by the Rules'?" *Journal of Adolescent and Adult Literacy* 52 (3): 249–51.

Johnson, Kevin R. 1993–94. "Free Trade and Closed Borders: NAFTA and Mexican Immigration to the United States." *U.C. Davis Law Review* 27: 937–78.

———. 1995. "Public Benefits and Immigration: The Intersection of Immigration Status, Ethnicity, Gender, and Class." *UCLA Law Review* 42: 1509–75.

———. 1996. "Fear of an 'Alien Nation': Race, Immigration, and Immigrants." *Stanford Law and Policy Review* 7: 111–19.

———. 1997. "The Antiterrorism Act, the Immigration Reform Act, and Ideological Regulation in the Immigration Laws: Important Lessons for Citizens and Noncitizens." *St. Mary's Law Journal* 28 (4): 833–82.

———. 2002. "The End of 'Civil Rights' as We Know It? Immigration and Civil Rights in the New Millennium." *UCLA Law Review* 49: 1481–511.

———. 2003. "September 11 and Mexican Immigrants: Collateral Damage Comes Home." *DePaul Law Review* 52: 849–70.

———. 2004. *The "Huddled Masses" Myth: Immigration and Civil Rights*. Philadelphia, Penn.: Temple University Press.

———. 2007. *Opening the Floodgates: Why America Needs to Rethink Its Borders and Immigration Laws*. New York: New York University Press.

Johnson, Kevin R., and Bill Ong Hing. 2007. "The Immigrant Rights Marches of 2006 and the Prospects for a New Civil Rights Movement." *Harvard Civil Rights-Civil Liberties Law Review* 42: 99–138.

Jonas, Susanne. 2006. "Reflections on the Great Immigration Battle of 2006 and the Future of the Americas." *Social Justice* 33 (1): 6–20.

Kelson, Gregory A., and Debra L. DeLaet. 1999. *Gender and Immigration*. New York: New York University Press.

Kil, Sang Hea, and Cecilia Menjivar. 2006. "The 'War on the Border': Criminalizing Immigrants and Militarizing the U.S.-Mexico Border." In *Immigration and Crime: Race, Ethnicity, and Violence*, edited by Ramiro Jr. Martinez and Abel Valenzuela Jr., 164–88. New York: New York University Press.

King, Desmond S. 1999. *In the Name of Liberalism: Illiberal Social Policy in the USA and Britain*. New York: Oxford University Press.

King, Shani. 2010. "U.S. Immigration Law and the Traditional Nuclear Conception of Family: Toward a Functional Definition of Family That Protects Children's Fundamental Human Rights." *Columbia Human Rights Law Review* 41: 509–67.

Klusmeyer, Douglas B., and Thomas Alexander Aleinikoff. 2000. *From Migrants to Citizens: Membership in a Changing World*. Washington, D.C.: Carnegie Endowment for International Peace.

Knijn, Trudie, and Monique Kremer. 1997. "Gender and the Caring Dimension of Welfare States: Toward Inclusive Citizenship." *Social Politics* 4 (3): 328–61.

Kretsedemas, Philip. 2008. "Immigration Enforcement and the Complication of National Sovereignty: Understanding Local Enforcement as an Exercise in Neoliberal Governance." *American Quarterly* 60 (3): 553–73.

Kyungwon Hong, Grace. 2011. "Existentially Surplus: Women of Color Feminism and the New Crises of Capitalism." *GLQ* 18 (1): 87–106.

Laqueur, Walter. 1999. *The New Terrorism: Fanaticism and the Arms of Mass Destruction*. New York: Oxford University Press.

Larner, Wendy. 2000. "Neo-Liberalism: Policy, Ideology, Governmentality." *Studies in Political Economy* 63: 5–25.

Lazar, Michelle M., ed. 2005. *Feminist Critical Discourse Analysis: Gender, Power and Ideology in Discourse*. London: Palgrave.

Legomsky, Stephen H. 1995. "Immigration, Federalism, and the Welfare State." *UCLA Law Review* 42: 1453–74.

LeMay, Michael C. 2006. *Guarding the Gates: Immigration and National Security*. Westport, Conn.: Praeger Security International.

LeMay, Michael C., and Elliott Robert Barkan. 1999. *U.S. Immigration and Naturalization Laws and Issues*. Westport, Conn.: Greenwood Press.

Light, Ivan. 2010. "Federal/State Cost Sharing of Immigrant Welfare." *California Journal of Politics and Policy* 2 (1): 1–19.

Lister, Ruth. 1997. *Citizenship: Feminist Perspectives*. New York: New York University Press.

———. 1999. "What Welfare Provisions Do Women Need to Become Full Citizens?" In *New Agendas for Women*, edited by Sylvia Walby, 17–31. Basingstoke, U.K.: Palgrave Macmillan.

Lodhia, Sharmila. 2010. "Constructing an Imperfect Citizen-Subject: Globalization, National 'Security,' and Violence Against South Asian Women." *WSQ: Women's Studies Quarterly* 38 (1/2): 161–77.

Logan, Robert A. 2006. "Analyzing News Content by Using the *New York Times*." August 18. http://www.nytimes.com/ref/college/faculty/coll_mono_loga.html.

Lowe, Lisa. 1996. *Immigrant Acts: On Asian American Cultural Politics*. Durham, N.C.: Duke University Press.

Luibhéid, Eithne. 2002. *Entry Denied: Controlling Sexuality at the Border*. Minneapolis: University of Minnesota Press.

———. 2005a. "Heteronormativity, Responsibility, and Neo-Liberal Governance in U.S. Immigration Control." In *Passing Lines: Immigration and (Homo)Sexuality*, edited by Brad Epps, Bill Johnson Gonzalez, and Keja Valens, 69–104. Cambridge, Mass.: Harvard University Press.

———. 2005b. "Introduction: Queering Migration and Citizenship." In *Queer Migrations: Sexuality, U.S. Citizenship, and Border Crossings*, edited by Eithne Luibhéid and Lionel Cantú, ix–xlvi. Minneapolis: University of Minnesota Press.

———. 2011. "Nationalist Heterosexuality, Migrant (Il)legality, and Irish Citizenship Law: Queering the Connections." *The South Atlantic Quarterly* 110 (1): 179–204.

Luibhéid, Eithne, and Lionel Jr. Cantú, eds. 2005. *Queer Migrations: Sexuality, U.S. Citizenship, and Border Crossings.* Minneapolis: University of Minnesota Press.

Mann, Michael. 1997. "Has Globalization Ended the Rise of the Nation-State?" *International Review of Political Economy* 4 (3): 472–96.

Marchevsky, Alejandra, and Jeanne Theoha. 2006. *Not Working: Latina Immigrants, Low-Wage Jobs, and the Failure of Welfare Reform.* New York: New York University Press.

Marley, Bruce Robert. 1998. "Exiling the New Felons: The Consequences of the Retroactive Application of Aggravated Felony Convictions to Lawful Permanent Residents." *San Diego Law Review* 35 (3): 855–96.

Marshall, Thomas H. 1965. "Citizenship and Social Class." In *Class, Citizenship, and Social Development: Essays by T. H. Marshall,* edited by Seymour Martin Lipset. Garden City, N.J.: Doubleday.

Martin, Sara A. 1999. "Postcards from the Border: A Result-Oriented Analysis of Immigration Reform under the AEDPA and IIRIRA." *Boston College Third World Law Journal* 19 (2): 683–708.

Martinot, Steve. 2007. "Immigration and the Boundary of Whiteness." *Race/Ethnicity* 1 (1): 17–36.

Massey, Douglas S. 1988. "Economic Development and International Migration in Comparative Perspective." *Population and Development Review* 14: 383–413.

———. 1996. "The Social and Economic Origins of Immigration." In *Immigration and the Social Contract: The Implosion of Western Societies,* edited by John Tanton, Denis McCormack, and Joseph Wayne Smith, 22–26. Aldershot, U.K.: Avebury.

Massey, Douglas, Jorge Durand, and Nolan J. Malone. 2002. *Beyond Smoke and Mirrors: Mexican Immigration in an Era of Economic Integration.* New York: Russell Sage Foundation.

McCluskey, Martha T. 2003. "Efficiency and Social Citizenship: Challenging the Neoliberal Attack on the Welfare State." *Indiana Law Journal* 78: 783–878.

McCormack, Karen. 2005. "Stratified Reproduction and Poor Women's Resistance." *Gender and Society* 19 (5): 660–79.

McDonald, William F. 2010. "US Immigration Reform: From G. W. Bush to B. H. Obama." *People and Place* 18 (3): 1–13.

McHoul, Alec, and Wendy Grace. 1993. *A Foucault Primer: Discourse, Power and the Subject.* New York: New York University Press.

McKinnon, Sara. 2009. "Citizenship and the Performance of Credibility: Audiencing Gender-Based Asylum Seekers in U.S. Immigration Courts." *Text and Performance Quarterly* 29 (3): 205–21.

Melamed, Jodi. 2006. "The Spirit of Neoliberalism: From Racial Liberalism to Neoliberal Multiculturalism." *Social Text* 24 (4): 1–24.

———. 2011. *Represent and Destroy: Rationalizing Violence in the New Racial Capitalism.* Minneapolis: University of Minnesota Press.

Merrill, Heather. 2006. *An Alliance of Women: Immigration and the Politics of Race.* Minneapolis: University of Minnesota Press.

Miller, Alice. 2005. "Gay Enough: Some Tensions in Seeking the Grant of Asylum and Protecting Global Sexual Diversity." In *Passing Lines: Sexuality and Immigration,* edited by Brad Epps, Keja Valens, and Bill Johnson Gonzalez, 137–87. Cambridge, Mass.: David Rockefeller Center for Latin American Studies, Harvard University.

Mink, Gwendolyn. 1998. *Welfare's End.* Ithaca, N.Y.: Cornell University Press.

Mink, Gwendolyn, and Rickie Solinger, eds. 2003. *Welfare: A Documentary History of U.S. Policy and Politics.* New York: New York University Press.

Moore, Kathleen M. 2000. "U.S. Immigration Reform and the Meaning of Responsibility." *Studies in Law, Politics, and Society* 20: 125–55.

Morgan, Deborah A. 2006. "Not Gay Enough for the Government: Racial and Sexual Stereotypes in Sexual Orientation Asylum Cases." *Law and Sexuality: A Review of Lesbian, Gay, Bisexual, and Transgender Legal Issues* 15: 135–62.

Muller, Thomas. 1997. "Nativism in the Mid-1990s: Why Now?" In *Immigrants Out!,* edited by Juan Perea, 105–18. New York: New York University Press.

Myrdal, Gunnar. (1944) 2009. *An American Dilemma: The Negro Problem and Modern Democracy.* New Brunswick, N.J.: Transaction.

Naples, Nancy. 2003. *Feminism and Method: Ethnography, Discourse Analysis, and Activist Research.* New York: Routledge.

Neubeck, Kenneth, and Noel Cazenave. 2001. *Welfare Racism: Playing the Race Card against America's Poor.* New York: Routledge.

Ng, Doris. 2002. "From War on Poverty to War on Welfare: The Impact of Welfare Reform on the Lives of Immigrant Women." In *Work, Welfare, and Politics. Confronting Poverty in the Wake of Welfare Reform,* edited by Frances Fox Piven, et al, 277–88. Eugene, Ore.: University of Oregon Press.

Ngai, Mae M. 1999. "The Architecture of Race in American Immigration Law: A Reexamination of the Immigration Act of 1924." *The Journal of American History* 86 (1): 67–92.

———. 2003. "The Strange Career of the Illegal Alien: Immigration Restriction and Deportation Policy in the United States, 1921–1965." *Law and History Review* 21 (1): 69–107.

Omi, Michael, and Howard Winant. 1994. *Racial Formation in the United States: From the 1960s to the 1990s.* New York: Routledge.

Ong, Aihwa. 1999. *Flexible Citizenship: The Cultural Logics of Transnationality.* Durham, N.C.: Duke University Press.

Orloff, Ann Shola. 1993. "Gender and the Social Rights of Citizenship: The Comparative Analysis of Gender Relations and Welfare States." *American Sociological Review* 58: 303–28.

Park, Edward J. W., and John S. W. Park. 2005. *Probationary Americans: Contemporary Immigration Policies and the Shaping of Asian American Communities.* New York: Routledge.

Pascall, Gillian. 2003. "Citizenship—a Feminist Analysis." In *New Approaches to Welfare Theory,* edited by Glenn Drove and Patrick Kerans, 113–26. Aldershot, U.K.: Edward Elgar.

Passel, Jeffrey S. 1994. *Immigrants and Taxes: A Reappraisal of Huddle's "The Cost of Immigrants."* Washington, D.C.: Urban Institute.

Peck, Jamie, and Adam Tickell. 2007. "Conceptualizing Neoliberalism, Thinking Thatcherism." In *Contesting Neoliberalism: Urban Frontiers,* edited by Helga Leitner, Jamie Peck, and Eric S. Sheppard, 26–50. New York: Guilford.

Pedraza, Silvia. 1996. "Origins and Destinies: Immigration, Race, and Ethnicity in American History." In *Origins and Destinies: Immigration, Race, and Ethnicity in America,* edited by Silvia Pedraza and Rubén G. Rumbaut, 1–20. Belmont, Calif.: Wadsworth.

Peffer, George Anthony. 1999. *If They Don't Bring Their Women Here: Chinese Female Immigration before Exclusion.* Urbana: University of Illinois Press.

Perea, Juan F. 1997. *Immigrants Out! The New Nativism and the Anti-Immigrant Impulse in the United States.* New York: New York University Press.

Phelan, Shane. 2001. *Sexual Strangers: Gays, Lesbians, and the Dilemmas of Citizenship.* Philadelphia, Penn.: Temple University Press.

Pickus, Noah M. J. 1998. *Immigration and Citizenship in the Twenty-First Century.* Lanham, Md.: Rowman & Littlefield.

Podnanski, Robert. 1983. "The Propriety of Denying Entry to Homosexual Aliens: Examining the Public Health Service's Authority over Medical Exclusions." *University of Michigan Journal of Law Reform* 17 (2): 331–60.

Portes, Alejandro, and Rubén G. Rumbaut. 1996. *Immigrant America: A Portrait.* 2nd ed. Berkeley, Calif.: University of California Press.

Quadagno, Jill. 1994. *The Color of Welfare: How Racism Undermined the War on Poverty.* New York: Oxford University Press.

Rapoport, David. 1984. "Fear and Trembling: Terrorism in Three Religious Traditions." *American Political Science Review* 78 (3): 658–77.

Rector, Robert, and William Lauber. 1995. "America Is Becoming a Deluxe Retirement Home." *The Social Contract* 6 (1): 58–59.

Reddy, Chandan. 2005. "Asian Diasporas, Neoliberalism, and Family: Reviewing the Case for Homosexual Asylum in the Context of Family Rights." *Social Text* 23 (3–4): 101–19.

Reimers, David. 1985. *Still the Golden Door: The Third World Comes to America.* New York: Columbia University Press.

Reimers, David M. 1998. *Unwelcome Strangers: American Identity and the Turn against Immigration.* New York: Columbia University Press.

Robertson, Susan. 2000. *A Class Act: Changing Teachers' Work, the State, and Globalization.* New York: Falmer.

Romero, Victor C. 2004a. *Alienated: Immigrant Rights, the Constitution, and Equality in America.* New York: New York University Press.

———. 2004b. "Decoupling 'Terrorist' from 'Immigrant': An Enhanced Role for the Federal Courts Post-9/11." *Journal of Gender, Race and Justice* 7: 201–11.

Rose, Nikolas. 1990. *Governing the Soul: The Shaping of the Private Self.* New York: Routledge.

———. 1996. "Governing 'Advanced' Liberal Democracies." In *Foucault and Political Reason: Liberalism, Neo-Liberalism, and Rationalities of Government,* edited by Andrew Barry, Thomas Osborne, Nikolas Rose, 37–64. Chicago: University of Chicago Press.

———. 1999. *Powers of Freedom: Reframing Political Thought.* Cambridge, Mass.: Cambridge University Press.

Rytina, Nancy. 2002. "IRCA Legalization Effects: Lawful Permanent Residence and Naturalization through 2001." U.S. Immigration and Naturalization Service. Accessed April 13, 2013. http://www.dhs.gov/xlibrary/assets/statistics /publications/irca0114int.pdf.

Santa Ana, Otto. 1999. "'Like an Animal I Was Treated': Anti-Immigrant Metaphor in U.S. Public Discourse." *Discourse and Society* 10 (2): 191–224.

———. 2002. *Brown Tide Rising: Metaphors of Latinos in Contemporary American Public Discourse.* Austin: University of Texas Press.

Sassen, Saskia. 1996. *Losing Control? Sovereignty in an Age of Globalization.* New York: Columbia University Press.

———. 1998. *Globalization and Its Discontents: Essays on the Mobility of People and Money.* New York: New Press.

Schneider, Anne, and Helen Ingram. 1993. "Social Construction of Target Populations: Implications for Politics and Policy." *American Political Science Review* 87 (2): 334–47.

Schuck, Peter. 2003. *Diversity in America: Keeping Government at a Safe Distance.* Cambridge, Mass.: Belknap Press.

Seefeldt, Kristin S. 2002. *Welfare Reform.* Edited by Ann Chih Lin. Washington, D.C.: CQ Press.

Segura, Denise A., and Patricia Zavella, eds. 2007. *Women and Migration in the U.S.-Mexico Borderlands.* Durham, N.C.: Duke University Press.

Semati, Mehdi. 2010. "Islamophobia, Culture and Race in the Age of Empire." *Cultural Studies* 24 (2): 256–75.

Shapiro, Stephanie. 2005. *Reinventing the Feature Story: Mythic Cycles in American Literary Journalism*. Baltimore: Apprentice House.

———. 2006. "Return of the Sob Sisters." American Journalism Review. August 16. http://www.ajr.org/Article.asp?id=4117.

Sheridan, Michael J. 1998. "The New Affidavit of Support and Other 1996 Amendments to Immigration and Welfare Provisions Designed to Prevent Aliens from Becoming Public Charges." *Creighton Law Review* 31: 741–66.

Shulman, Robert J. 1995. "Children of a Lesser God." *Pepperdine Law Review* 22: 669–725.

Sidel, Ruth. 1998. *Keeping Women and Children Last: America's War on the Poor*. New York: Penguin.

Simcox, David. 1994. The Costs of Immigration: Assessing a Conflicted Issue. Center for Immigration Studies. November 14. http://www.cis.org/articles/1994/back294.htm.

———. 1996. "Population Growth and the American Future." In *Immigration and the Social Contract: The Implosion of Western Societies*, edited by John Tanton, Denis McCormack and Joseph Wayne Smith, 35–43. Aldershot, U.K.: Avebury.

Simon, Rita James, and Susan H. Alexander. 1993. *The Ambivalent Welcome: Print Media, Public Opinion, and Immigration*. Westport, Conn.: Praeger.

Smith, Anna Marie. 2002. "The Sexual Regulation Dimensions of Contemporary Welfare Law: A Fifty State Overview." *Michigan Journal of Gender and Law* 8: 121–93.

Smith, James F. 1995. "A Nation That Welcomes Immigrants? An Historical Examination of United States Immigration Policy." *U.C. Davis Journal of International Law and Policy* 1 (2): 227–47.

Somerville, Siobhan S. 2005. "Notes toward a Queer History of Naturalization." *American Quarterly* 57 (3): 659–75.

Suro, Roberto. 1996. *Watching America's Door: The Immigration Backlash and the New Policy Debate*. New York: Twentieth Century Fund Press.

———. 1998. *Strangers among Us: How Latino Immigration Is Transforming America*. New York: Alfred A. Knopf.

Tancredo, Tom. 2006. *In Mortal Danger: The Battle for America's Border and Security*. Nashville: WND Books.

Tanton, John, Denis McCormack, and Joseph Wayne Smith. 1996. *Immigration and the Social Contract: The Implosion of Western Societies*. Aldershot, U.K.: Avebury.

Tichenor, Daniel J. 2002. *Dividing Lines: The Politics of Immigration Control in America*. Princeton, N.J.: Princeton University Press.

Titshaw, Scott. 2010. "The Meaning of Marriage: Immigration Rules and Their Implications for Same-Sex Spouses in a World Without DOMA." *William and Mary Journal of Women and the Law* 16: 537–611.

United States Census Bureau. 2003. "The Foreign-Born Population: 2000." *Census 2000 Brief.* Accessed April 15, 2003. http://www.census.gov/prod/2003pubs /c2kbr-34.pdf.

United States Commission on Immigration Reform. 1994. *U.S. Immigration Policy: Restoring Credibility: A Report to Congress.* Washington, D.C.: U.S. Commission on Immigration Reform.

———. 1995. *Legal Immigration: Setting Priorities. A Report to Congress.* Washington, D.C.: U.S. Commission on Immigration Reform.

———. 1997. *Becoming an American: Immigration and Immigrant Policy. 1997 Report to Congress.* Washington, D.C.: U.S. Commission on Immigration Reform.

United States Congress. 1988. *Grounds for Exclusion of Aliens under the Immigration and Nationality Act: Historical Background and Analysis.* Washington, D.C.: U.S. GPO.

———. 1996. *Illegal Immigration Reform and Immigrant Responsibility Act of 1996: Conference Report (to Accompany H.R. 2202).* Washington, D.C.: U.S. GPO.

United States Congress, House. 1993. "Employer Sanctions, June 16, 1993." *Committee on the Judiciary, Subcommittee on International Law Immigration and Refugees.* Washington, D.C.: U.S. GPO.

———. 1993. "Border Violence, on H.R. 2119, Immigration Enforcement Review Commission Act, September 29, 1993." *Committee on the Judiciary, Subcommittee on International Law Immigration and Refugees.* Washington, D.C.: U.S. GPO.

———. 1993. "Impact of Immigration on Welfare Programs, November 15, 1993." *Committee on Ways and Means, Subcommittee on Human Resources.* Washington, D.C.: U.S. GPO.

———. 1993. "Controlling the Flow of Illegal Immigration at U.S. Land Borders, December 10, 1993." *Committee on Government Operations, Information Justice Transportation and Agriculture Subcommittee.* Washington, D.C.: U.S. GPO.

———. 1994. "Criminal Aliens, February 23, 1994." *Committee on the Judiciary, Subcommittee on International Law Immigration and Refugees.* Washington, D.C.: U.S. GPO.

———. 1994. "Access to Public Assistance Benefits by Illegal Aliens, May 11, 1994." *Committee on the Judiciary, Subcommittee on International Law Immigration and Refugees.* Washington, D.C.: U.S. GPO.

———. 1994. "Employment Eligibility Verification System, October 3, 1994." *Committee on the Judiciary, Subcommittee on International Law Immigration and Refugees.* Washington, D.C.: U.S. GPO.

———. 1995. "Reform Immigration Laws, January 5, 1995." *Extension of Remarks.* Washington, D.C.: U.S. GPO.

———. 1995. "Contract with America: Welfare Reform, Part 1, January 27, 1995." *Ways and Means Committee, Subcommittee on Human Resources.* Washington, D.C.: U.S. GPO.

———. 1995. "Foreign Visitors Who Violate the Terms of Their Visas by Remaining in the United States Indefinitely, February 24, 1995." *Committee on the Judiciary, Subcommittee on Immigration and Claims.* Washington, D.C.: U.S. GPO.

———. 1995. "Worksite Enforcement of Employer Sanctions, March 3, 1995." *Committee on the Judiciary, Subcommittee on Immigration and Claims.* Washington, D.C.: U.S. GPO.

———. 1995. "Border Security, March 10, 1995." *Committee on the Judiciary, Subcommittee on Immigration and Claims.* Washington, D.C.: U.S. GPO.

———. 1995. "Removal of Criminal and Illegal Aliens, March 23, 1995." *Committee on the Judiciary, Subcommittee on Immigration and Claims.* Washington, D.C.: U.S. GPO.

———. 1995. "Verification of Eligibility for Employment and Benefits, March 30, 1995." *Committee on the Judiciary, Subcommittee on Immigration and Claims.* Washington, D.C.: U.S. GPO.

———. 1995. "Impact of Illegal Immigration on Public Benefit Programs and the American Labor Force, April 5, 1995." *Committee on the Judiciary, Subcommittee on Immigration and Claims.* Washington, D.C.: U.S. GPO.

———. 1995. "Legal Immigration Reform Proposals, May 17, 1995." *Committee on the Judiciary, Subcommittee on Immigration and Claims.* Washington, D.C.: U.S. GPO.

———. 1995. "Members' Forum on Immigration, May 24, 1995." *Committee on the Judiciary, Subcommittee on Immigration and Claims.* Washington, D.C.: U.S. GPO.

———. 1995. "Immigration in the National Interest Act of 1995, on H.R. 1915, June 29, 1995." *Committee on the Judiciary, Subcommittee on Immigration and Claims.* Washington, D.C.: U.S. GPO.

———. 1995. "Guest Worker Programs, December 7, 1995." *Committee on the Judiciary, Subcommittee on Immigration and Claims.* Washington, D.C.: U.S. GPO.

———. 1995. "Societal and Legal Issues Surrounding Children Born in the United States to Illegal Alien Parents, December 13, 1995." *Committee on the Judiciary, Subcommittee on Immigration and Claims.* Washington, D.C.: U.S. GPO.

———. 1995. "Agricultural Guest Worker Programs, December 14, 1995." *Committee on the Judiciary, Subcommittee on Immigration and Claims.* Washington, D.C.: U.S. GPO.

———. 1996. "Field Hearing on Public Benefits, Employment, and Immigration Reform, February 26, 1996." *Committee on Economic and Educational Opportunities.* Washington, D.C.: U.S. GPO.

——. 1996. "Comprehensive Antiterrorism Act of 1995 (H.R. 2703), March 13 and 14, 1996." *General Debate*. Washington, D.C.: U.S. GPO.

——. 1996. "Immigration in the National Interest Act (H.R. 2202), March 19, 20, 21, and 28, 1996." *General Debate*. Washington, D.C.: U.S. GPO.

——. 1996. "Antiterrorism and Effective Death Penalty Act (S. 735), April 18, 1996." *Conference Report*. Washington, D.C.: U.S. GPO.

——. 1996. "Illegal Immigration Reform and Immigrant Responsibility Act of 1996 (H.R. 2202), September 25, 1996." *Conference Report*. Washington, D.C.: U.S. GPO.

——. 2006. "Field Hearing: How Does Illegal Immigration Impact American Taxpayers? August 2, 2006." *Committee on the Judiciary*. Washington, D.C.: U.S. GPO.

United States Congress, Senate. 1993. "Terrorism and America: A Comprehensive Review of the Threat, Policy, and Law, April 21 and 22, 1993." *Committee on the Judiciary*. Washington, D.C.: U.S. GPO.

——. 1993. "Terrorism, Asylum Issues, and U.S. Immigration Policy, on S. 667, May 28, 1993." *Committee on the Judiciary. Subcommittee on Immigration and Refugee Affairs*. Washington, D.C.: U.S. GPO.

——. 1994. "Proposals for Immigration Reform, June 15, 1994." *Committee on the Judiciary*. Washington, D.C.: U.S. GPO.

——. 1994. "Increasing Costs of Illegal Immigration, June 22, 1994." *Senate Appropriations Committee*. Washington, D.C.: U.S. GPO.

——. 1994. "Proposals for Immigration Reform, August 3, 1994." *Committee on the Judiciary. Subcommittee on Immigration and Refugee Affairs*. Washington, D.C.: U.S. GPO.

——. 1995. "The Immigration Moratorium Act of 1995 (S.160), January 5, 1995." *Statements on Introduced Bills and Joint Resolutions*. Washington, D.C.: U.S. GPO.

——. 1995. "The Criminal Alien Control Act of 1995 (S.179), January 9, 1995." *Statements on Introduced Bills and Joint Resolutions*. Washington, D.C.: U.S. GPO.

——. 1995. "The Immigrant Control and Financial Responsibility Act (S.269), January 24, 1995." *Statements on Introduced Bills and Joint Resolutions*. Washington, D.C.: U.S. GPO.

——. 1995. "Proposals to Reduce Illegal Immigration and Control Costs to Taxpayers, on S. 269, March 14, 1995." *Committee on the Judiciary*. Washington, D.C.: U.S. GPO.

——. 1995. "Comprehensive Terrorism Prevention Act (S. 735), May 25 and June 7, 1995." *General Debate*. Washington, D.C.: U.S. GPO.

———. 1995. "The Immigration Reform Act of 1995 (S. 1394), November 3, 1995." *Statements on Introduced Bills and Joint Resolutions*. Washington, D.C.: U.S. GPO.

———. 1996. *Immigration Control and Financial Responsibility Act of 1996: Report Together with Additional and Minority Views (S. 1664)*. Washington, D.C.: U.S. GPO.

———. 1996. *Legal Immigration Act of 1996: Report Together with Additional and Minority Views (to Accompany S. 1665)*. Washington, D.C.: U.S. GPO.

———. 1996. "The Use of Supplemental Security Income and Other Welfare Programs by Immigrants, February 6, 1996." *Committee on the Judiciary, Subcommittee on Immigration*. Washington, D.C.: U.S. GPO.

———. 1996. "Legal Immigration Act of 1996 (S. 1665), April 10, 1996." *Committee on the Judiciary*. Washington, D.C.: U.S. GPO.

———. 1996. "The Immigration Control and Financial Responsibility Act of 1996" (S. 1664), April 15, 25, and 29, 1996. *General Debate*. Washington, D.C.: U.S. GPO.

———. 1996. "Illegal Immigration Reform and Immigrant Responsibility Act of 1996, September 16, 1996." *General Debate*. Washington, D.C.: U.S. GPO.

———. 2006. "Immigration: Economic Impacts, April 25, 2006." *Committee on the Judiciary*. Washington, D.C.: U.S. GPO.

United States General Accounting Office. 1995. *Illegal Immigration, INS Overstay Estimation Methods Need Improvement: Report to the Chairman, Subcommittee on Immigration, Committee on the Judiciary, U.S. Senate*. Washington, D.C.: U.S. GAO.

United States Immigration and Naturalization Service, Office of Policy and Planning. 2000. *Estimates of the Unauthorized Immigrant Population Residing in the United States: 1990 to 2000*. Washington, D.C.: U.S. GPO.

Valkenburg, Patti M., Holli A. Semetko, and Claes H. De Vreese. 1999. "The Effects of News Frames on Readers' Thoughts and Recall." *Communication Research* 26: 550–69.

van Dijk, Teun A. 1999. "Discourse and Racism." *Discourse and Society* 10 (2): 147–48.

———. 2000. "New(s) Racism: A Discourse Analytical Approach." In *Ethnic Minorities and the Media*, edited by Simon Cottle, 33–49. Philadelphia, Penn.: Open University Press.

van Dijk, Teun A., et al. 1997. "Discourse, Ethnicity, Culture and Racism." In *Discourse as Social Interaction*, edited by Teun A. van Dijk, 144–80. Thousand Oaks, Calif.: Sage.

Wacquant, Loïc. 2008. "Extirpate and Expel: On the Penal Management of Postcolonial Migrants in the European Union." *Race/Ethnicity* 2 (1): 45–52.

Widener, Daniel. 2008. "Another City Is Possible: Interethnic Organizing in Contemporary Los Angeles." *Race/Ethnicity* 1 (2): 189–219.

Williams, Lucy A. 1995. "Race, Rat Bites, and Unfit Mothers: How Media Discourse Informs Welfare Legislation Debate." *Fordham Urban Law Journal* 22 (4): 1159–96.

Wodak, Ruth, and Martin Reisigl. 1999. "Discourse and Racism: European Perspectives." *Annual Review of Anthropology* 29: 175–99.

Wong, Carolyn. 2006. *Lobbying for Inclusion: Rights Politics and the Making of Immigration Policy.* Stanford, Calif.: Stanford University Press.

Wygonik, Blythe. 2005. "Refocus on the Family: Exploring the Complications in Granting the Family Immigration Benefit to Gay and Lesbian United States Citizens." *Santa Clara Law Review* 45 (2): 493–530.

Yoo, Grace J. 2001. "Shaping Public Perceptions of Immigrants on Welfare: The Role of Editorial Pages of Major US Newspapers." *International Journal of Sociology and Social Policy* 21 (7): 47–62.

———. 2008. "Immigrants and Welfare: Policy Constructions of Deservingness." *Journal of Immigrant and Refugee Studies* 6 (4): 490–507.

Zapata, Martin. 1995. "New and Views: The Father of Scientific Racism." *Journal of Blacks in Higher Education* 8: 38.

Zimmerman, Wendy, and Karen C. Tulmin. 1999. "Patchwork Policies: State Assistance for Immigrants under Welfare Reform." Urban Institute Occasional Paper 24.

Index

abortion, 3, 11
Abraham, Spencer, 42, 44, 91, 118, 135, 266n25, 275n30; chain migration and, 95
Abu Sayaf, 55
abuse, 50, 217, 224, 249, 283n27; welfare, 20, 88, 143, 207
adoption-assistance programs, 50
AEDPA. *See* Antiterrorism and Effective Death Penalty Act
affidavit of support, 86, 92–93, 263n8, 264n13, 266n31
affirmative action, 11, 37, 101, 189, 268n40, 281n16
AFL-CIO, 60
Agassiz, Jean Louis Rudolphe, 26, 255n6
Agricultural Job Opportunity, Benefits, and Security Act (2003), 63
agriculture, 32, 104, 143, 149; cheap labor and, 145; labor shortage in, 146, 277n41, 277n43
Albert, Larry, 224
Aleinikoff, T. Alexander, 135
Alfred P. Murrah Federal Building: bombing of, 54, 131
Alien and Sedition Acts (1798), 255n4
Alien Nation (Brimelow), 96
Alqazzaz, Iyad, 218
Alsreafi, Mohammed, 195, 217, 218, 219, 220

Alverson, Susie, 224
American Civil Liberties Union, 229
American Competitiveness in the Twenty-First Century Act (2000), 61
American Dilemma, An (Myrdal), 20, 212
American Immigration Control Foundation (ACIF), 65
American Immigration Lawyers Association (AILA), 41–42
Americanization, 97, 100
American Legion: Dole at, 169, 170
American Psychiatric Association, 22
Americans for Legal Immigration (ALIPAC), 68
amnesty, 10, 36, 60, 62, 167, 247, 284n3; undocumented immigrants and, 64, 161, 201, 204, 207, 257n19
Andrews, Robert, 272n14
anticitizens, 15, 56, 68, 111, 115, 136, 176, 202, 229, 245, 248–49, 270n4; illegal aliens as, 17, 203, 243; undocumented immigrants as, 178, 241
Anti–Drug Abuse Act (1988), 58
anti-immigrant climate, 151, 185, 186–87, 282n20
anti-immigrant discourse, 18, 60, 115, 152, 154, 155, 175, 183, 188, 208, 226–27, 242; illegal aliens and, 15
antiterrorism, 8, 16, 18, 132, 134, 135, 139, 236, 237, 261n49; legislation, 37, 54–60, 245

Antiterrorism and Effective Death Penalty Act (AEDPA) (1996), 38, 57, 69, 70, 253n1, 261n51; discretionary relief and, 60; immigration/immigrants and, 55; passage of, 58, 59–60, 245; sponsors of, 260n42
anxieties, 26, 152, 208, 225; anti-immigrant, 241, 242; cultural, 225, 233; gender, 16, 20; racial, 3, 16, 27, 96, 97, 187, 189, 192, 199, 220, 250; sexual, 16, 20, 123; terrorism, 139, 236
Archaeology of Knowledge and the Discourse on Language, The (Foucault), 8, 74, 108, 134
Arizona SB 1070. *See* Support Our Law Enforcement and Safe Neighborhoods Act
Ashcroft, John, 61, 62
Asian American Alliance, 192
Asian American rights groups, 42, 192
Asian Americans, 263n5; hostile remarks toward, 189–90; stereotypes of, 190–91
Asian immigrants, 159, 193, 263n5; assault on, 26; attitudes on, 32; attracting, 101; desirability of, 167; portrayal of, 30, 190, 198; preference categories and, 103
Asian-Pacific American organizations, 258n25
assimilation, 2, 97–98, 100, 118, 168, 171, 206; cultural, 212; immigrants and, 1; refusing, 3
asylum, 23, 57, 157, 161
asylum seekers, 41, 91, 160; descriptions of, 157–58; gay/lesbian, 22, 23
Avendo, Carolina, 231
Aviv, Diana, 269n47

Bach, Robert L., 144, 276n38
Barr, Bob, 133, 274n23

Barr Amendment, 133, 274n23, 274n24
Barrett, Thomas M., 147, 148, 278n47
Bates, Jeffrey, 187
Becerra, Xavier, 95, 124–25, 269n46, 278n46
Beck, Roy, 254n6, 284n2
behavior: codes, 230; day laborer, 231; immigrant, 101, 230; policing, 230; sexual/reproductive, 225; social, 11–12
Beilenson, Anthony C., 127, 272n16, 276n35, 276n36
Benmayor, Rina, 101
Berman, Howard L., 36, 105, 147, 258n30, 259n30
Biden, Joseph R., 131, 138
Bilbray, Brian, 104, 116, 130–31, 273n22
bilingual education, 154, 165, 171, 182, 246, 281n15, 281n16; ending, 168, 169, 172, 267n37, 280n12; opposition to, 170, 172; support for, 173–74; welfare and, 172, 173
biology, 20, 76, 171
birth rates, 123, 163, 272n11
births out-of-wedlock, 213, 214, 216
Boggs, Clara Alicia, 223
Bonilla, Henry, 61
Bono, Sonny, 144, 276n38
booty-strapping, 122–23
border control, 39, 62, 66, 150, 161
Border Patriots, 193
border patrol, 64, 236, 276n35
Border Protection, Antiterrorism, and Illegal Immigration Control Act (2005), 64, 65, 243
Borjas, George, 179, 282n22, 284n2
Boutilier v. INS (1967), 256n13
Boxer Amendment, 50
Bracero Program, 32
Bradley, Bill, 133
Brandon, Joseph, 227

Breall, Susan, 218, 219, 285n9
Briggs, Vernon, 269n44
Brimelow, Peter, 96, 97, 284n2
Brown, Hank, 260n42
Brown, Sherrod, 272n14
Brown, Wendy, 15
Brownback, Sam, 258n30, 259n30
Brown Tide Rising (Santa Ana), 152
Bryant, Ed, 124–25, 144
Bryant, John, 36, 94, 268n39, 269n48, 272n12, 277n40
Buchanan, Patrick J., 282n25, 285n12
Buff, Rachel Ida, 240
Bureau of Immigration and Customs Enforcement (ICE), 240
Burrows, Lourdes, 173, 281n17
Bush, George H. W., 11
Bush, George W., 61, 62, 64, 160; immigration reform and, 64, 66, 237; on terrorism, 238

California Court of Appeals, 264n13
California Department of Mental Hygiene, 264n13
Canady, Charles T., 102–3, 268n38, 268n39
capitalism, 33, 278n1; racial, 109
Carroll, John, 185, 282n26
Carvajal, Doreen, 165
Castaneda, Jorge, 61
Castillo, Juana, 197, 198, 283n1
Celis, William, 281n15, 281n16
Chabot, Steve, 262n3
chain migration, 44, 94–95, 96, 267n33
Chavez, Leo, 221, 254n7
Chen, Ethel, 189
Chenoweth, Helen, 277n43
Chertoff, Michael, 63
childbirth, 123, 271n9, 271n10
child care, 3, 83, 87
Child Nutrition Act (1966), 51, 259n38

Children's Protective Services Agency (CPS), 216, 284n7
Chiles, Lawton, 99
Chinese Exclusion Act (1882), 27, 96
Chinese immigrants, 29, 96, 264n17
Choi, Ilze A., 283n29
Christensen, Annette, 188
Chrysler, Dick, 259n30, 264–65n18, 284n30
Chrysler-Berman-Brownback Amendment, 42
Chung, Josephine, 191
citizen interest, 103–4, 117
citizenship, 21, 49, 64, 113, 123, 143, 190, 237, 272n10; birthright, 122; children and, 122, 271n9; elderly immigrants and, 90; global, 153, 154; liberal notions of, 16, 24; nation-based, 249; neoliberal, 6, 199, 216, 241, 246, 247; obtaining, 122, 174, 244; potential, 207; preclusion of, 30; rethinking, 249; self-sufficient, 17
civil rights, 6, 34, 243
Civitello, Beth Vetare, 227, 285n14
class, 2, 5, 16, 27, 130, 165
Class A medical exclusion certificates, 34
Clay, William, 272n16
Clement, Bob, 272n14
Clinton, Bill, 46, 51, 53, 57, 282n24; AEDPA and, 56; antiterrorism legislation and, 54; appointments by, 39; discriminatory employment practices and, 47; Gallegly amendment and, 177; illegal immigrants and, 175, 184; immigration reform and, 37, 182; PRWORA and, 47; welfare state and, 11
Cold War: immigration reform and, 33
Cole, Purdy, 281n19

Colgate, Stephen, 258n26
Collins, Mac, 144, 277n39
color-blind rhetoric, 120, 189, 199, 241, 250
Colvin, Carolyn, 85, 264n12
Comprehensive Immigration Reform Act (2006), 65
Comprehensive Immigration Reform Act (2011), 69
Conference on Asian Pacific American Leadership, 191
Congressional Task Force on Immigration Reform, 40
Conyers, John, 133
Cornelius, Wayne, 253n3
cost-benefit assessment, 5, 16, 127, 148, 180, 199, 236, 248
Council of Historically Black Graduate Schools, 106
Craig, Larry, 133
Cramer, Gary C., 220
cram schools, 165
Creel, Santiago, 61
crime, 28, 31, 43, 112, 115, 120, 127, 143, 212, 233, 237, 243, 244, 274n28; concerns about, 140; culture of, 208; hate, 238; immigrants and, 26, 113; increase in, 139, 167; undocumented immigrant, 68, 137; violent, 136–37, 138; youth, 179
Criminal Alien Control Act (1995), 138, 260n40
criminal aliens, 38, 58, 69, 70, 131–39, 140, 157, 193, 275n32; deportation of, 59; detaining, 160; discourse about, 135, 141; terrorists and, 56, 57, 236
criminal justice, 12, 207, 250
criminals, 139, 149, 181, 184, 237, 247; exclusion of, 150; noncitizen, 135; portrayal of, 150; terrorists and, 138, 239

Cubin, Barbara, 160
cultural clashes, 198, 217, 222, 225–27, 233
cultural contributions, 40, 77, 84, 96, 112
cultural difference, 20, 96, 99, 171, 212, 215, 221, 222, 223, 225–26
culture, 97, 212, 239; attacking, 169; black, 20; economic success and, 213; escaping, 233; focus on, 213; immersion in, 206; improving, 101, 167; mainstream, 101, 241; patriarchal, 217; race as, 213; shared, 169; urban, 210, 233
Cunningham, Randy (Duke), 117, 118, 171, 272n11

Dallas Morning News: circulation of, 279n3
Daniels, Roger, 27, 37
Das Gupta, Monisha, 6, 249
day laborers, 234; neighborhood conflicts and, 225–32; portrayal of, 198, 199, 225–26
Deal, Nathan, 122–23
Dean, Mitchell, 13, 253n5
deeming requirements, 46, 259n34
Defense of Marriage Act (DOMA) (1996), 3, 83, 101, 109, 253n1
De la Garza, Kika, 146, 278n44
De La Vina, Gus, 270n4
Demleitner, Nora, 82
Department of Mental Hygiene for the State of California v. Renel (1959), 264n13
deportation, 29, 32, 55, 58, 59, 96, 131, 133, 134, 175, 176, 177, 184, 201, 216–17, 225; childbirth and, 271n10; criminal alien, 138; drive for, 31; hearings, 261–62n53; proceedings for, 63; public charge, 89, 265n21;

streamlining, 260n40; suspension of, 60; terror of, 240
detention centers, 160
Development, Relief, Education for Alien Minors Act (DREAM Act) (2003), 63, 65, 69, 246, 247; support for, 244–45
DeWine, Mike, 42, 44, 78, 267n34; on family reunification, 81; on illegal immigrants, 271n6; on immigration policy, 263n6; risk management and, 80
Diaz, Alex, 224
Diaz-Balart, Lincoln, 272n16
discrimination, 42, 101, 104, 107, 126, 130, 162, 167, 201, 212, 248; employment, 46, 47, 213; ending, 34; language and, 182–92; lawsuit, 240; reverse, 104, 268n40; structural, 3
discursive formation, 74, 75, 77, 134
discursive strands, 7, 75, 76, 84, 87–88, 108, 156
diversity, 21, 37, 98, 170
Diversity Category, 37, 258n23
diversity lottery, 262n2, 262–63n4, 268n38
Dobbs, Lou, 14, 254n7
documented immigrants, 113; immigration reform and, 120; portrayal of, 149; undocumented immigrants and, 242
Dole, Bob, 55, 181, 281n18, 282n25; immigration reform and, 182; on multilingual education, 169; opposition to, 170
DOMA. *See* Defense of Marriage Act
dominant discourse, 15, 168, 171, 188, 211
Donnelly, Mike, 280n13
Dornan, Robert K., 52
DREAM Act. *See* Development, Relief, Education for Alien Minors Act

Dreier, David, 270n2, 273n20
drug dealers, 31, 131–39, 270n4
Dugger, Cecilia W., 189, 190, 191, 283n32, 285n13
Duncan, John J., 74
Dunlavey, J. L., 177
Durbin, Richard, 63, 244

economic impact: immigrants and, 4–5, 17, 77–78, 94, 112, 241
economic issues, 13, 42, 60, 96, 107, 140–48, 151, 182, 196, 197, 225, 230, 232; immigration policy and, 19; solving, 184
economic objectives, 15, 20, 233
economic reforms: focus on, 76
economic success, 76, 78–79, 82, 213
Editor & Publisher International Yearbook 1996, 278–79n2, 279n3, 279n5
education, 5, 8, 12, 50, 52, 79, 87, 96, 119, 160, 202, 205, 241, 273n18; access to, 175, 179, 248, 259n37; ban on, 177–80, 182, 193; deeming requirements and, 46; denying, 125, 126–27; deterioration of, 129, 131; expenses for, 130; media coverage on, 162–82; multicultural, 169; privatization of, 162, 163; providing, 131, 246; quality, 167, 214; social inequalities in, 165; undocumented immigrants and, 1, 44, 114, 116–17, 125, 127–31, 157, 159, 163, 175, 176–77, 178, 180, 193, 244, 280n10, 281n18, 282n22
education magnet, 113, 115
Edwards, James R., 48, 75
Effective Death Penalty and Public Safety Act (1996), 132–33
elderly immigrants, 73, 83–93, 94
Elementary and Secondary Education Act (1965), 259n38

Emerson, Ralph Waldo, 255n6
employers: discrimination charges against, 46; as victims, 276n38
employment magnet, 115, 276n36
employment verification, 66, 141, 144, 149, 161
English language, 101, 151, 188, 203, 268n38, 278n44; learning, 168, 169, 171, 202, 206, 268n39, 270n48; melting pot and, 102, 168; proficiency in, 36, 102, 173; Spanish-speaking immigrants and, 169
English-only laws, 168, 171, 173, 182, 280n12
Enhanced Border Security and Visa Entry Reform Act (2002), 62
Estrada, Richard, 258n24
ethnic groups, 98, 105, 118, 123, 184, 258n25; immigration reform and, 106, 107; neoliberal policy and, 109
ethnicity, 2, 15, 77, 97, 101; anxieties about, 96; importance of, 103–8
Exclusion Act (1924), 103
exclusions, 16, 19, 20, 24–37, 47, 57, 150, 239, 242, 258n27
Ezell, Harold W., 123, 258n24, 272n11

FAIR. *See* Federation for American Immigration Reform
family: dominant model of, 83; extended, 94, 206; focus on, 200–13; mixed-status, 121; neoliberal policy and, 109; networks, 82, 93; productiveness of, 80; traditional notions of, 82, 108, 109, 208, 253n2
family reunification, 4, 17, 23, 28, 29, 34, 38, 44, 67, 78, 83, 263n7, 264n18; categories, 41; controversy about, 75, 85, 111; discourse about, 71, 84, 108; economic impact of, 97; homosexual immigrants and, 82;

provisions for, 103; self-sufficiency and, 84; support for, 79, 80–81, 84; visas for, 38, 278n45
Family Self-Sufficiency Act (1995), 50, 51, 52, 259n35
family structure, 2, 3, 76, 213, 253n2; changing, 109; heteronormative, 77, 82, 94, 109; narrow definition of, 30
family values, 4, 87, 94, 101, 149, 206, 208; commitment to, 76, 83, 92, 93; conservative ideology and, 3; heteronormative, 8, 18, 34, 43, 48, 70, 82, 84, 111, 199, 215, 223; importance of, 10, 11, 81; neoliberal, 205, 232, 248; rhetoric, 81, 111
Farhat, Laina, 220
Federation for American Immigration Reform (FAIR), 14, 65, 179, 253n3, 254n6, 267n33
Feingold, Russell D., 42, 45, 64, 139
Feinstein, Dianne, 40, 260n42; amendment by, 259n34; on children/citizenship, 122; on meth labs, 275n29
felonies, 28, 38, 261n51, 275n30; aggravated, 47, 60, 137
feminists, 11, 22
First Quota Act (1921), 29
Fix, Michael D., 4, 5, 144, 276n38, 284n2
Flatten, John, 177
flood imagery, 114–20, 164–65, 185, 186, 270n2
Flores, Lisa, 31, 43
Flores, William, 101
Flushing: racial makeup of, 189, 190–91
food grants, emergency, 50
Food stamps, 51, 84, 121, 185, 211, 242, 260n39
Ford, Harold E., 49
foreign languages, 169, 172, 281n14
Fort Worth Telegram: circulation of, 279n3

Foucault, Michel, 8, 74, 108, 134; discourse and, 7, 77; social order and, 155; truth and, 155, 278n1
Fourteenth Amendment, 25–26, 122
Fowler, Tillie, 268n43
Fox, Vicente, 61, 62, 237
fraud, 138, 261n52, 275n33
free market, 5, 7, 10, 148, 153
free trade, 6, 7, 141, 142
Friedman, Thomas L., 170
Frost, Martin, 125
Fuchs, Lawrence H., 258n24
Funderburk, David, 277n43

Gallegly, Elton, 40, 179, 182, 268n42, 271n8, 272n15; amendment by, 44, 125, 126–27, 273n18; criticism of, 178; editorial by, 160; on illegal immigration, 120; support for, 176, 178; testimony of, 128–29; undocumented immigrants/education and, 175, 270n3; welfare distribution system and, 121
Gallegly amendment, 46, 131, 176, 177, 193, 259n31, 272n16, 273n17, 273n18; academic achievements and, 130; criticism of, 44, 121, 125, 126–27, 127–28; political purpose of, 179, 180; support for, 128, 130
gangs, 179, 203, 210, 211
Ganske, Greg, 274n26
Garcia, Adela, 224
Garfield, Susan, 281n18
Garza, Juanita, 285n11
gay immigrants, 33, 34, 67, 82, 256n14
Gekas, George W., 269n48
gender, 2, 7, 21, 23, 27, 32, 248; claims based on, 22; immigration reform and, 13
gender identity, 23, 76, 77
gender relations, 3, 24, 33, 109

genital mutilation, 22, 157
Gilman, Benjamin A., 137, 275n30
Gimpel, James G., 48, 75
Gingrich, Newt, 40, 46, 102, 281n18, 282n24
Giuliani, Rudolph W., 163, 192
Glen Cove, 227, 228
global economy, 6, 76–77
globalization, 141, 248
Goffman, Erving, 75
Goldsmith, Jan, 117, 118
Gonon, Phyllis, 279n7
Goodlatte, Bob, 277n40, 278n45, 278n48
Gordon, Bart, 272n14
Goss, Porter J., 274n26
Graham, Bob, 45
Gramm, Phil, 78, 79, 80, 160, 177, 260n42, 263n5
Grassley, Chuck, 104–5
Great Depression, 31, 43, 96
green cards, 23, 37, 63, 67, 218, 244, 256n16
Greene, Enid, 125
Griffin, Peggy, 76–77
guest-worker program, 62, 65, 146, 147, 148, 149, 237, 249, 277n43
Gunnison, Robert B., 184, 282n24
Gutierrez, Luis, 80–81

Ha, Annette, 151–52
Hamas, 133, 274n24
Hanson, Gordon H., 15, 254n8
harassment, 184, 228, 229, 238
Harris, David, 187
Harrison, Julia: hostile remarks by, 189–90, 191–92
Hastings, Doc, 277n41
Hatch, Orrin G., 44, 55, 131, 260n40; DREAM Act and, 63, 244
Hays, Constance L., 281n15

Head Start, 52
health care, 116, 127, 175, 209
Hedgecock, Michael, 14
Heritage Foundation, 14, 87, 88, 254n6
Herman, Joseph A., 281n14
Hernandez, Erasmo, 203, 204, 207
Hernandez, Mari, 203, 204, 205, 207, 208–9, 233
Herrick, Thaddeus, 167, 200, 201, 202, 203, 205, 209, 211, 280n9
heteropatriarchal structure, 29, 32, 33
Hiemsta, Nancy, 239
Higher Education Act (1965), 51, 259n38
Hill, Robert Charles, 258n24
Hing, Bill Ong, 196
hiring practices, 144, 229, 234
HIV/AIDS, 52
Hoekstra, Pete, 66
homeland security, 18, 62, 236, 239
Homeland Security Act (2002), 62
Homeland Security Committee, 254n6
homosexuals, 11, 33, 34, 162, 256n13
Hoover, Herbert, 256n10
Hoppe, Arthur, 180–81, 282n23
House Judiciary Committee, 103, 106, 269n45
House Republican Conference, 66
House Subcommittee on Human Resources, 49
House Subcommittee on Immigration and Claims, 135
housing code, 197, 229, 286n16
Houston Chronicle, 165, 177, 185, 199, 201, 202, 213, 216, 217, 221, 222–23, 232; analysis of, 17, 154; circulation of, 279n3; on day laborers, 230; human-interest stories and, 161, 188, 195; on illegal immigrants/ education, 281n18; immigrant labor and, 161; immigration issue

and, 160; interviews in, 167; on Lazo, 284n8; personal stories and, 280n8, 280n9; positions of, 156; Quintana and, 195, 285n10, 285n11; stylistic differences with, 158; on Wheelan, 222
Houston Livestock Show and Rodeo, 160, 165
Houston Police Department, 228
H.R. 2202: 44, 45, 46, 136, 137, 146, 150, 277n42, 286n1
human-interest stories, 154, 157, 158, 195, 196, 197, 198, 217–18, 220, 225–26, 229–31, 233; individual, 161; media and, 18; race and, 199–200; reading, 201; selecting, 158; types of, 198–99
human rights, 6, 16, 21, 65, 242, 245, 249
Hutchinson, Kay Bailey, 160, 177
Hyde, Henry J., 132–33, 274n23, 276n34; amendment by, 266n27; antiterrorism bill and, 56; on undocumented aliens, 117

identity categories, 12, 22, 108
IIRIRA. *See* Illegal Immigration Reform and Immigrant Responsibility Act
illegal immigrants, 2, 15, 107, 116, 129, 271n6, 271n7, 273n21, 276n35, 284n3; benefits for, 121; children of, 123, 273n20; criminal, 184; as federal prisoners, 136; hiring, 276–77n38; legal immigrants and, 43, 112, 118, 203, 244; population of, 114, 185; portrayal of, 118, 139, 144, 186, 189, 236, 239, 243
illegal immigration, 53, 105–6, 111, 237, 243, 254n7, 270n2, 271n6, 271n7, 276n36; concerns about, 140; coverage of, 186–87; curbing, 142; impact

of, 127, 207, 273–74n22; legal immigration and, 119; reform of, 41, 45; stopping, 41, 201–2, 265n22; wave of, 115

Illegal Immigration Act (1996), 44, 45, 46, 69, 92, 266n24, 266n25

Illegal Immigration Control and Enforcement Act (1995), 40

Illegal Immigration Reform and Immigrant Responsibility Act (IIRIRA) (1996), 3, 37, 69, 215, 242, 261n51; affidavit of support and, 92–93; final version of, 47; legacy of, 235–36; passage of, 245; poverty line and, 265n19

immigrant rights, 188; restricting, 54–60

immigrant rights organizations, 42, 45, 65, 228, 242, 243, 244, 250

immigrants: contemporary, 4, 94–103; cultural/ethnic heritage of, 1; desirable/undesirable, 16, 24, 99, 165, 205; diversity of, 158, 159; family-sponsored, 77, 92, 93, 266n28, 268n38; fear of, 170; hostility toward, 105, 188, 248; ideal, 8, 94; influx of, 225–26; opportunities for, 202; portrayal of, 81–82, 160, 211, 250; qualified, 34; racial composition of, 26, 99; rights/responsibilities of, 37; role of, 38; successful, 5, 105, 203; targeting, 240

Immigrants' Rights Project, 229

immigrant students, 174; school overcrowding and, 164; successful, 167, 246, 247; well-educated, 166

immigration, 8, 18, 155; attitudes toward, 118, 201, 250; decisions on, 104; flow of, 25, 279n7; impact of, 2, 19, 38; injustices of, 237; limiting, 14; periods of, 19

Immigration Act (1917), 29, 33, 86, 298, 255n8, 256n9

Immigration Act (1924), 30–31

Immigration Act (1990), 58, 262n1, 262n4

Immigration and Control Act (1983), 35–36

Immigration and Nationality Act (INA) (1952), 32, 33, 256n13

Immigration and Nationality Act (INA) (1965), 19, 34, 257n17, 266n23; racist provisions of, 35

Immigration and Nationality Act (INA) (1990), 39, 256n15, 262n4; immigration level and, 37

Immigration and Naturalization Service (INS), 39, 59, 62, 63, 86, 135, 144, 188, 227, 258n26, 270n4, 272n13, 274n25; border enforcement and, 148, 286n15; criticism of, 275n30; homosexuals and, 33; immigration laws and, 149; mayor of Pomona and, 107; study by, 185; unauthorized resident population and, 235

Immigration Control Act (1891), 28

Immigration Control and Financial Responsibility Act (1996), 1, 40, 91

immigration crisis, 5, 8, 186, 206

immigration debate, 4, 42, 100, 280n9

immigration discourse, 5, 15, 16, 21, 83–84, 99, 151–52, 182, 189, 192, 205, 207, 220, 250, 268n40; complexity of, 164; formation of, 75; local contexts of, 155–62; media and, 154, 167–68; Mexican immigrants and, 159; neoliberalism and, 8; racism and, 18

Immigration in the National Interest Act (1995), 41, 266n27

immigration laws, 1, 7, 16, 39, 66, 200, 274n26; changes in, 105; colonial,

immigration laws *(continued)*
25; debate surrounding, 20; disregarding, 249; economic purposes of, 29; effective, 103; enforcing, 64–65, 68, 140; family structure and, 32; invasive, 237; norms/values/social hierarchies and, 24; racist effects of, 250; restrictive, 28, 70, 74, 98; violation of, 139, 140
immigration levels, 19, 104, 106, 205; changes in, 37, 91, 94
Immigration Moratorium Act (1995), 91, 92, 258n28, 265n22
immigration policy, 15, 28, 51, 76, 86, 103, 105, 107, 143, 263n6; economic considerations and, 19; logic behind, 93; national security and, 19; overhaul of, 60; preferential treatment and, 21; racist/sexist effects of, 16; shifts in, 29; trade agreements and, 6
immigration reform, 6, 15, 9, 24, 103, 122, 142, 182, 202, 215; bipartisan, 35; complexity of, 200; comprehensive, 64, 65, 67, 69, 75, 91, 92, 120, 150, 243; criticism of, 181; debate over, 7, 8, 20, 36, 157, 250; early, 242; examining, 76; heteronormative logic of, 82; justifying, 120; neoliberal, 9, 13, 14, 214; in 1990s, 39–47; support for, 107
Immigration Reform Act (1995), 41, 83, 91, 92, 118, 266n25
Immigration Reform and Control Act (IRCA) (1986), 10, 36, 149, 161, 200–201, 257n21, 276n37
immigration reform discourse, 2, 4, 7–8, 16, 21, 70–71, 84, 96, 114–15, 139, 141, 142, 153, 163, 210, 237, 243, 245, 248; debates about, 108–9; logic behind, 24; neoliberal, 13–14, 24

immigration system, 1, 17, 76, 95, 156; developing, 26; economic profitability of, 76, 232; employment-based, 79–80; generous, 104; loopholes in, 147; merits/effects of, 16; objectives of, 73; reorganization of, 149
immunization programs, 50, 51, 124
INA. *See* Immigration and Nationality Act
Inda, Jonathan Xavier, 15, 174, 175
inequality, 109, 154, 213, 250
INS. *See* Immigration and Naturalization Service
Intel: coalition with, 42
IRCA. *See* Immigration Reform and Control Act
Islamic Jihad, 132–33
Issa, Darrell, 67

Jackson-Lee, Sheila, 127, 263n7, 273n17
James, Bill, 177
Japanese immigration, 27, 165
Jefferies, Julian, 246
jobs, 5, 37, 78, 201, 248, 276n36
job skills, 5, 36, 87
job training, 50, 248
Johnson, Kevin R., 38, 55, 96, 142
Johnson, Lyndon B., 10
Johnson-Reed Act (1924), 29, 30
Jordan, Barbara, 39, 73
Jordan Commission. *See* U.S. Commission on Immigration Reform
Journal of Blacks in Higher Education, 255n6
judicial review, 133, 260n40, 274n23
jus sanguinis/jus soli, 122

Kasich, John R., 51–52
Kemp, Jack, 160, 182
Kennedy, Edward M., 59, 61, 65, 66,

119, 262n3, 272n13; amendment by, 257n19, 266n26; compromise solution and, 74; humanistic argument of, 124; on immigrants/ fraud, 261n52, 275n33; immigration reform and, 35, 36, 40, 73; on job magnet, 276n36; opposition by, 258n29; Special Registration and, 63
Kennedy, Patrick J., 126, 260n43
Kil, San Hea, 15
Kilpatrick, Kurt, 285n11
Kim, Jay, 119, 120, 271n7
King, Peter T., 160, 172–73
King, Shani, 82
Kingston, Jack, 144
Klepfer, F., 225
Kraut, David, 191
Kretsedemas, Philip, 240
Kumar, Rohit, 79
Kyl, Jon, 98, 260n42, 268n43

labor: agriculture and, 145; cheap, 141, 145, 278n47; free flow of, 142; immigrant, 161, 231; shortages, 34, 146, 148; temporary, 143
labor market, 33, 54, 198, 239, 248; demands of, 73, 76; immigrants and, 140–48
labor migration, 32, 141, 142
language: discrimination and, 182–92
Laqueur, Walter, 132
Latinas: children and, 196; portrayal of, 208
Latino and Immigration Fairness Act, 61
Latinos, 164, 203; desirability of, 167; education and, 193, 202; focus on, 200; representations of, 153, 198, 202, 226–27; targeting, 99, 101
LaTourette, Steven C., 50, 118

Lattie, George L., 223
Lauber, William, 88
Lazarus, Emma, 27
Lazio, Rick A., 263n7
Lazo, Jose, 216–17, 284n8
League of United Latin American Citizens (LULAC), 14, 254n6
Leahy, Patrick, 67
Ledkins, Kevin, 282n20
legal immigrants, 2, 10, 45, 53, 120, 135, 149, 176, 243, 244, 259n37, 271n7; citizens and, 117; illegal immigrants and, 42, 43, 112, 118, 203, 245; portrayal of, 111, 113, 118, 186; poverty line and, 47; targeting, 120
legal immigration, 41, 71, 105–6, 111, 116, 139, 254n3, 271n7, 286n1; illegal immigration and, 119; reducing, 266n26; reform of, 36, 41, 42, 45
Legal Immigration Act (1996), 44, 262–63n4, 266n24, 266n25
Legal Immigration Family Equity Act (LIFE Act), 61
"Legal Immigration: Setting Priorities" (U.S. Commission on Immigration Reform), 40, 73
legal status, 10, 68, 176, 179, 253n4; lack of, 239, 245, 247; temporary, 257n19
Leggio, Richard, 227
Legomsky, Stephen, 114, 270n1
Leiden, Warren R., 258n24
lesbian immigrants, 33, 34, 67, 82, 256n14
Lewis, Oscar, 213, 214
Lewis, Ron, 277n41
LGBTQ, 23; immigration reform and, 22
Lieberman, Joseph E., 160
Limbaugh, Rush, 14
Lincoln, Blanche Lambert, 272n14
literacy requirements, 29, 256n9

Logan, Robert A., 195
Longfellow, Henry Wadsworth, 255n6
Los Angeles Times, 152, 164, 279n5
Lovell, Tom, 280n13
Lowell, Lindsay, 269n44
Luibhéid, Eithne, 12, 26, 33

Macia, Claudia, 282n20
magnets, 122, 130; education, 113, 115;
    employment, 115, 276n36; rhetoric
    about, 190, 273n20; welfare, 84, 113,
    114–20
Mann, Donald, 176, 177
Manton, Thomas J., 192
Margolis, David, 258n26
Maria T.: story of, 185–86, 187
market forces, 20, 171
Marley, Bruce Robert, 56, 59, 261n51
marriage, 2; arranged, 196, 221;
    interests of children and, 253n2;
    patriarchal, 23; successful society
    and, 83
Martin, Sara A., 261–62n53
Martin, Susan, 85, 86, 89, 90
Martini, Bill, 56–57, 99, 267n35,
    274n27
Massachusetts Bay Colony: immigra-
    tion and, 25
Massachusetts Province: immigration
    and, 25
Massachusetts Province Laws (1756),
    255n5
Matloff, Norman, 87, 88, 254n16,
    264n17, 267n37
McCain, John, 65, 271n6
McCarran-Walter Act. *See* Immigra-
    tion and Nationality Act (1952)
McCaul, Michael, 254n6
McCluskey, Martha, 15
McCollum, Bill, 133, 276n35
McCormack, Karen, 215

McGrath, Martin, 227
McVeigh, Timothy, 54–55, 260n41
media, 187, 193, 196, 199, 217, 250;
    competition for, 195; education
    controversy and, 162–82; illegal im-
    migrants and, 174, 185; immigrant
    students and, 164, 165; immigration
    discourse and, 151, 154, 167–68;
    immigration reform and, 3, 157,
    183; mainstream, 154, 156, 157, 193;
    racial inequalities and, 166; repre-
    sentations by, 3, 120, 132, 151–52,
    236; undocumented immigrants
    and, 174–75, 178; unskilled laborers
    and, 203
media discourse, 43, 153, 160, 162, 192
Medicaid, 51, 53, 84, 121, 122, 242
medical care, 1, 122, 124–25; emer-
    gency, 50, 123, 124
medical certificates, 22, 30
Mehlman, Ira, 179, 282n21
Meissner, Doris, 270n4
Melamed, Jodi, 76, 213
melting pot, 1, 3, 97; English language
    and, 102, 168
Menendez, Robert, 68–69, 119, 120,
    271n7
Menjivar, Cecilia, 15
Merced, Nelsen, 258n24
metaphors, 152–53, 164–65, 210
Mexican American Legal Defense and
    Education Fund (MALDEF), 14,
    254n6
Mexican Americans, 43, 164, 209
Mexican immigrants, 158, 279n4;
    deportation of, 96; as flexible labor
    force, 31–32; immigration discourse
    and, 159; perception of, 97; self-
    control and, 209; threat from, 43;
    undocumented, 118
Mexican nanny: story of, 186

Mexico–U.S. Migration Working
 Group, 61
Meyers, Jan, 267n36
Mica, John L., 159–60
Microsoft: coalition with, 42
Miller, George, 148
Milstead, Milton E., 224
Mink, Patsy, 103
Minuteman Civil Defense Corps, 193
Minuteman Project, 15
Monty, Jacob, 285n8
Morris, Frank L., 106, 269n44,
 269–70n48
Morrison, Bruce A., 36, 258n24
Morton, Samuel G., 26, 255n6
Mount Kisco, 226–27, 285n13; class
 action suit against, 228–29
Mount Kisco Planning Board, 227
Mount Kisco Worker's Project v. The
 Village/Town of Mount Kisco
 (1996), 229
multiculturalism, 3, 20, 98, 267n36;
 controversy over, 100, 101–2; dam-
 aging effects of, 2, 280n13; ethnic
 community and, 97; melting pot
 and, 1; neoliberal, 21, 213
Muñoz, Celia, 107
Muñoz, Martin, 261–62n53
Murray, William E., Jr., 283n30
Muslim culture: beliefs about, 220
Muslim immigrants, 132; arranged
 marriages and, 196
Muslim terrorists, 238, 240
Myrdal, Gunnar, 20, 21, 212, 213

Nachemin, Sol, 191
Nadler, Jerrold, 58, 67, 140, 274n24
NAFTA, 6, 7, 141, 142, 143, 253n3
Narasaki, Karen K., 80, 103, 263n9
National Asian Pacific American
 Council, 80

National Asian Pacific American Legal
 Consortium (NAPALC), 103, 263n9
National Council of La Raza (NCLR),
 107, 258n25, 286n1
nationality, 15, 27, 32, 165
National School Lunch Act (1966), 51,
 259n38
national security, 57, 60, 70, 112, 238,
 261n50; immigration policy and, 19;
 threats to, 182
National Security Entry and Exit
 Registration System (NSEERS), 62,
 63, 64
nativism, 28, 31, 96
Naturalization, 6, 25, 254n2
Negative Population Growth, 14, 176
Nenney, Susan, 223
neoliberal agenda, 18, 82, 141, 234, 246
neoliberal approach, 11, 12, 23, 240
neoliberal consensus: emergence of,
 8–13
neoliberal discourse, 76, 101, 105, 148,
 153, 189, 199, 212, 248; compassionate, 13; racist discourses and, 18
neoliberal framework, 156, 158, 165, 247
neoliberal ideals, 18, 158, 215, 239, 241;
 living up to, 199, 203
neoliberalism, 254n5; advanced, 9, 155,
 253n5; as gender- and race-blind
 project, 15; immigration reform
 and, 9; integration discourse and,
 8; as political/social philosophy, 11;
 racial capitalism and, 109; racial/
 sexual politics of, 13–16
neoliberal reform, 8, 45, 51, 52, 121, 145,
 149–50; analysis of, 11–12; antiracism and, 21; beneficiaries of, 154;
 discourse, 37–39; education and, 163
neoliberal subjects, 111; ideal, 156, 204,
 248; responsible, 225, 236, 241, 242;
 self-sufficient, 130, 165, 166, 199, 233

Newcomers Academy for New Americans, 173, 281n17
newcomer schools, 174
New Deal: social welfare programs of, 10
New York State Supreme Court, 86
New York Times, 180, 185, 187, 227, 230, 231, 279–80n8, 281n18, 282n22, 283n1, 285n13; analysis of, 17, 154; on Buchanan, 285n12; on Castillo, 197; circulation of, 278–79n2; coverage by, 159, 191; on cram schools, 165; on Harrison, 189–90; on housing code enforcement, 286n16; human-interest stories in, 161, 195; on immigrants/assimilation, 1; on immigrant students, 174; immigration and, 2, 160; Latino immigrants and, 164; on national language law, 169; poll by, 282n26; positions of, 156; on school overcrowding, 163; stylistic differences with, 158; on undocumented immigrants/education, 177; Velázquez in, 173; work requirements and, 279n6
Ngai, Mae, 30–31
Nickles, Don, 260n42
Ninety-Eighth Congress: immigration reform and, 35
Ninety-Ninth Congress, 36
norms: cultural, 196, 213, 226; neoliberal, 3; social, 24, 26, 27, 38, 113, 211, 224, 230; stereotypical, 22
Nott, Josiah C., 26, 255n6
NSEERS. *See* National Security Entry and Exit Registration System
nuclear family, 5, 22, 75, 82; immigrants and, 29–30; redefining, 83–93; successful, 94–103; support of, 33, 77–83

Obama, Barack, 67, 68
Office of Immigration Statistics, 265n21
Oklahoma City bombing, 54–55, 131
Omi, Michael, 218
Omnibus Consolidated Appropriations Act (1996), 47
Omnibus Counterterrorism Act (1993), 54
104th Congress, 37, 40, 45, 69, 70, 91, 120, 134, 135, 138, 270n5; terrorism and, 56; undocumented immigrants and, 140, 150; welfare reform and, 48, 49, 50
108th Congress, 64
109th Congress, 65
110th Congress, 65
111th Congress: immigration and, 67
Operation Wetback, 32
organized crime, 160; terrorism and, 134
Ortiz, Maria, 203, 205, 206, 207, 208–9, 233
Ortiz, Marisol, 205
Ortiz, Nathalie, 205
Other, 217, 218
"Out of the Shadows" (*Houston Chronicle*), 199, 200, 201, 202, 208, 213, 225
Ozawa v. United States (1922), 30

Packard, Ron, 273n21
Page Law (1875), 25–26, 27
Park, Robert E., 212
Passel, Jeffrey S., 4, 5
Pastor, Ed, 147
Pataki, George E., 192
Patent Trader, The, 226–27
Peffer, George Anthony, 26
Pell Grants, 66

Pelosi, Nancy, 128
Personal Responsibility and Work Opportunity Reconciliation Act (PRWORA) (1996), 3, 11, 38, 47, 53, 69, 83, 214, 253n1; analysis of, 48; introduction of, 51–52; passage of, 245; poverty/welfare/family structure and, 253n2
Pinkerton, James, 167, 200, 201, 205, 209, 211, 280n9; immigration reform and, 202; successful immigrants and, 203
Planned Parenthood of Houston, 223
polygamy, 255–56n8
Pombo, Richard W., 146, 147, 148, 277n42
Pombo Amendment, 146, 149–50; criticism of, 148, 278n48; support for, 277n43
Pomeroy, Earl, 126, 148
poverty, 2, 11, 31, 41, 93, 120, 128, 193, 202, 203, 204, 205, 210, 212, 215, 241; African American, 106; culture of, 208, 213, 233, 284n3, 284n6; cycle of, 211, 214; depictions of, 198; escaping, 18, 199, 211, 213; federal, 46, 47, 265n19; fighting, 11, 80; immigrant, 54, 152, 195
Powell, Colin, 61
power, 7, 155
Powers of Freedom (Rose), 9
preference categories, 17, 21, 103, 257n23, 267n33, 268n38
prejudice, 3, 20, 162, 184, 187, 223
prisons: foreign born in, 274n25, 274n26; illegal aliens in, 274n26, 274n27
privatization, 12, 154, 162, 163
profamily rhetoric, 17, 80, 94
Proposition 187 (California) (1994), 40, 44, 105, 106, 122, 159, 175; debate

on, 183; undocumented immigrants and, 258n27
prostitutes, 26, 27, 256n8
Province Law (1700), 255n5
PRWORA. See Personal Responsibility and Work Opportunity Reconciliation Act
public discourse, 75, 153, 176, 192
public expenditures, 3, 52–53, 119; decrease in, 152, 248; demands on, 15
public health, 32, 149; assistance, 52; immigrants and, 26, 30; protecting, 39; risks to, 43, 150; threats to, 182
Public Health Service: homosexual immigrants and, 34
Public Health Service Act (1965), 259n38
Public Law 104–93 (1996), 53
Public Law 104–208 (1996), 92
public opinion, 75, 157, 160, 282n24
public safety, 39, 198, 203, 227
Pyun, Chun Soo, 189

Quintana, Adela, 216, 217, 221–25, 233, 284n7, 284n8, 285n11; articles about, 195
quotas, 2, 34, 44, 97, 250, 256n10; census and, 29

race, 2, 15, 24, 27, 30, 77, 97, 101, 200, 239, 248; biology and, 20; as culture, 20, 171, 213; human-interest stories and, 199–200; immigration and, 13, 186; importance of, 20, 21, 100, 103–8, 130, 250
race-neutral language, 3, 7, 99, 104–5, 120
racial backgrounds, 118, 123, 200
racial bias, 102–3
racial difference, 97, 215

racial inequalities, 153, 166, 213
racial minorities, 100, 105; immigration reform and, 106, 107; neoliberal policy and, 109
racial politics, 13–16
racial profiling, 67, 238
racism, 1, 3, 15, 18, 26, 42, 101, 104, 152, 153, 154, 162, 164, 175, 182, 187, 190, 193, 219, 232; anti-Asian, 192; centrality of, 20; color-blind rhetoric and, 250; disguised, 7, 8; elimination of, 21; expression of, 106; scientific, 255n6
racist discourse, 2, 18, 153, 192, 193, 225
Rankin, Clarease Mitchell, 225
Rayner, Richard, 283n28, 283n29, 283n31; story by, 185–86, 187–88
Reagan, Ronald, 10–11, 76
REAL ID Act (2005), 64, 253n1
Rector, Robert, 87, 88, 90–91, 254n6
refugees, 41, 91, 259n36, 262n2; economic, 239; female, 22; suicide by, 92
Reid, Harry, 66
Reimers, David, 35
relatives: immediate, 92, 256n12, 266n23; sponsoring, 4
removal procedures, 61, 64, 137
residency: applying for, 10; requirements, 36, 255n4
responsibility, 25, 37, 89, 230, 233; financial, 90, 93, 157, 232; personal, 20, 45, 158, 209, 211, 215, 247
Revelette, Nancy, 284n7
Reyes, Brenda, 209
Reyes, Guillermo, 210
Reyes, Jesus, 210
Reyes, Kimberly, 207, 209
Reyes, Marcelina, 207, 208, 209, 210, 211
Reyes, Rey, 207, 209, 210
Reyes, Roberto, 207, 211, 212
Reyes, Teresa, 207, 210, 211

Reyes, Victor, 207
Rhee, Michael I., 191
Richardson, Bill, 127
Riggs, Frank, 129, 273n20
rights, 237; civil, 6, 34, 243; human, 6, 16, 21, 65, 242, 245, 249; immigrant, 54–60, 188; national borders and, 6; transnational complex of, 7
Rimer, Sara, 279n6
risk management, 20, 80; strategies for, 48, 70, 85, 90, 92, 158
Robertson, Susan, 163
Rodriguez, Nestor, 188
Rogin, Michael, 184
Rohrabacher, Dana, 115, 130, 273n19; on Gallegly amendment, 129; HIV/AIDS and, 52; on illegal immigrants, 114
Rosales, Rosa, 14, 254n6
Rose, Nikolas, 13, 155, 229, 254n5; advanced liberalism and, 9, 253n5; on discursive fields, 156; on neoliberal governments, 225; on social behavior, 11–12
Rosenthal, A. M., 180, 181–82
Ros-Lehtinen, Ileana, 126, 265n18
Ross, Jane L., 85, 264n12
Roth, Toby, 102, 138, 168, 275n31
Roth, William V., 260n40
Roukema, Marge, 122, 129–30, 143, 271n9
Roybal-Allard, Lucille, 121
Rubio, Refugio, 59–60

Said, Edward, 218
San Antonio Express News: circulation of, 279n3
Sanchez, Edward J., 224
San Francisco Chronicle, 177, 180, 185, 195, 221, 227, 231, 286n15; analysis of, 17, 154; anti-immigrant rhetoric and, 183; circulation of, 279n5; on day laborers, 230; on FAIR, 179;

human-interest stories in, 161, 217–
18; immigration issue and, 151, 160,
161–62, 164, 188; positions of, 156,
162; on Save-Our-State II initiative,
184; stylistic differences with, 158
Santa Ana, Otto, 152–53, 155, 164
Saunders, Debra, 179
Savage, Michael, 14
Save-Our-State II initiative, 183, 184
savings-and-loan industry: collapse
of, 10–11
scapegoating, 104, 129, 151, 184, 186,
245, 269n47
school overcrowding, 163, 164, 166,
279n7
Schumer, Charles E., 37, 133, 137
Sciales, Nancy, 191
Sciales, William J., 191
Secure Borders, Economic Opportunity, and Immigration Reform Act
(2007), 65, 66
security: financial, 205; homeland, 18,
62, 236, 239; national, 19, 57, 60,
70, 112, 182, 238, 261n50; spending
on, 128
security risks, 32, 58; immigrants as,
131–39
segregation, 13, 165, 168; legal, 213;
racial, 212
self-sufficiency, 45, 54, 92, 94, 214
Semati, Mehdi, 218
Senate Immigration Subcommittee, 41
Senate Judiciary Committee, 33–34,
42, 85, 86, 87, 256n13
Sensenbrenner, F. James, 64, 65, 243
September 11th, 18, 62, 218, 237, 238, 243
sexism, 7, 21
sex perverts, 34, 256n13
sexuality, 2, 21, 23, 76, 98, 113, 248;
Latino/a, 123; nonnormative, 196;
normalized, 109; uncontrolled, 87,
96, 98, 112, 123, 208

sexual politics, 13–16
Shapiro, Stephanie, 197
Shaw, E. Clay, 257n20
Shelby, Richard C., 74, 98, 258n28;
assimilation and, 2, 100; citizen
interest and, 103–4; on immigrants/
education, 1; immigration reform
and, 91, 94, 103; on multiculturalism, 100
shelter grants, emergency, 50
Shije Ribao: on SSI, 88
Simon, Julian, 284n2
Simon, Paul, 40, 42, 45, 258n29,
259n34
Simpson, Alan K., 86, 107, 260n42,
267n32, 268n41, 272n11; amendment by, 44, 266n26; on Americanization, 100; assimilation and,
97–98; chain migration and, 95, 96;
Commission and, 258n25; comprehensive approach of, 41; family
reunification and, 84; immigration
reform and, 35, 36, 40, 91, 105; on
petitions, 95; on public benefits, 89
single motherhood, 208, 214, 215, 241
Sixth Amendment, 56
Skiba, Linda, 227, 285n14
skilled workers, 5, 73, 96
slavery, 180–81, 254n1
Smith, Christopher H., 270n2
Smith, Lamar S., 36, 61, 106, 267n32,
269n48; chain migration and, 94–
95, 96; Commission and, 258n25;
deadbeat sponsors and, 265n20; on
illegal aliens, 136; immigration reform and, 111; Jordan Commission
and, 41; national interest and, 104;
on noncitizens/crimes, 274n28
Snowe, Olympia, 133, 139, 260n40
social climate, 24, 199
social constructions, 83, 157
social contract, 38, 47, 55, 71

social contributions, 77, 112
social costs, 178, 181
social equality, 15, 162
social government, 9, 156
social inequalities, 7, 154, 165, 166
social problems, 10, 75, 109, 151, 175, 193, 215, 245; framing, 157, 161; solving, 184
social safety net, 10, 23, 71
Social Security, 23, 85
Social Security Act: elderly immigrants and, 93
Social Security Administration (SSA), 85, 86
social services, 3, 12, 15, 37, 39, 94, 101, 121, 163, 174, 225; availability of, 158; elderly immigrants and, 89; limiting access to, 14, 258n27; undocumented immigrants and, 44, 159, 175, 177
social welfare, 8, 10, 11, 35, 80, 214
Solomon, Gerald, 136, 274n25, 274n26
Sotelo, Bryant, 222–23, 225
Sotelo, Pedro, 216, 217, 223, 224, 284n7, 284n8, 285n11; charges against, 221–22; deportation of, 225
Sourcebook of Federal Sentencing Statistics, 136
Special Agricultural Workers, 253n4
special-needs children: services for, 225
Specter, Arlen, 42, 65, 66
sponsors, 4, 37, 86, 93, 260n42; deadbeat, 89, 265n20; responsibility for, 89
SSA. See Social Security Administration
SSI. See Supplemental Security Income
statistics, 123, 274–75n29
status, 67, 123; economic, 88, 94, 170; legal, 10, 68, 176, 179, 239, 245, 247, 253n4, 257n19; social, 170; violation of, 61

Stein, Daniel, 253n3, 254n6, 267n33
stereotypes, 22, 83, 95, 142, 151, 152, 185; Asian American, 190–91; confirming, 193, 196, 198; cultural, 132; illegal alien, 114, 247; racial, 165, 186, 187, 210
Stoke, Louis, 74
Stop Out of Control Problems of Immigration Today (STOP IT), 193
Storm Lake, 226, 285n12
Storrow, Amy, 172–73
structural inequalities, 21, 54, 154, 199, 201, 213, 246, 248
Stump, Bob, 91, 258n28, 268n42
Supplemental Security Income (SSI), 51, 84, 92, 222, 264n11; elderly immigrants and, 87, 90, 264n14; eligibility for, 86–87, 259n34, 264n11; immigrants and, 88, 263–64n10
Support Our Law Enforcement and Safe Neighborhoods Act (Arizona SB 1070), 67–69
Swenson, John, 81

TANF. See Temporary Assistance for Needy Families
Targeting Immigrants (Inda), 15
Tate, Randy, 117
taxes, 5, 9, 10, 129, 138, 275n33
Taylor, Gene, 272n14
technology, anticitizenship, 174
teen pregnancy, 81, 213–25, 241
Teitelbaum, Michael S., 258n24
Temporary Agricultural Worker Amendments (1996), 146
Temporary Assistance for Needy Families (TANF), 51, 53, 84, 112, 242
temporary worker program, 62, 64, 146
terrorism, 54, 60, 64, 135, 160, 243, 276n34; debate about, 132, 140; fear of, 131, 239; fighting, 55, 133, 139; illegal immigration and, 20,

113, 237, 239; immigration reform and, 24, 56; Islamic, 55, 132; organized crime and, 134; social ills from, 245
Terrorist Exclusion Act (1995), 260n40
Terrorists, 131–39, 149, 237, 240, 260n45, 260n46; criminals and, 56, 57, 138, 236, 239; exclusion of, 28, 150; personal information of, 62; threat from, 135
Thurmond, Strom, 35, 260n42
Tolson, Mike, 188
Toney, Bill, 177, 178, 282n20
Torres, Esteban Edward, 128, 147, 148
Torricelli, Robert G., 160, 272n14
trade agreements, 6, 141, 142, 248
tradition, 98, 196, 217, 220, 231, 233
Traficant, James, 272n14
transgender immigrants, 82
Trasvina, John, 14, 254n6
Types of Mankind, The (Nott), 255n6

Unaccompanied Alien Child Protection Act (2007), 66
Underwood, Robert A., 102–3
undocumented children, 113, 120–31, 182; education and, 114, 116–17, 127, 128, 129, 175, 177, 244; innocence of, 126
undocumented immigrants, 32, 37, 39, 41, 43, 44, 53, 58, 60, 69, 136, 137, 148, 149, 152, 232; benefits for, 119; concerns about, 189, 241, 286n1; conscious decisions and, 116; criticism of, 71, 243; deterring, 120, 150, 157, 159, 182, 235; discourse about, 112, 113, 116, 120, 143–44, 150; economic impact of, 17, 112, 118, 244; hiring, 10, 36; as lawbreakers, 17, 140; as legal problem, 36, 244; portrayal of, 8, 113–19, 127, 141, 149, 184, 188, 189, 241, 245; support for,

43, 242; threat from, 174, 182, 236; treatment of, 139
undocumented students, 63, 126, 129, 130–31; deserving, 246; education and, 157, 178; legalization for, 246
unemployment, 11, 31, 69, 106, 120, 214
United States v. Thind (1923), 30
Uniting American Families Act (2009), 67, 262n54
unskilled labor, 5, 29, 73, 119, 209, 230, 263n4; African American, 106; hiring, 147, 148; visas for, 114
Urban Institute, 4
USA Patriot Act (2001), 62
USA Today: circulation of, 279n2
U.S. Commission on Immigration Reform, 85, 86, 89, 112, 121, 123, 262n2, 262n4; elderly immigrants and, 90; recommendations by, 39; report by, 40, 41, 44, 73; visa categories and, 263n4
U.S. Department of Homeland Security, 62, 63, 253n4
U.S. Department of Justice, 62, 63, 68, 188
U.S. Immigration Policy: Restoring Credibility (U.S. Commission on Immigration Reform), 39
U.S. Sentencing Commission, 136
U.S. State Department, 62
U.S. Supreme Court: decisions by, 30

Valkenburg, Patti, 195, 196
values, 24, 26, 97, 200, 214, 217; Confucian, 87; cultural, 217, 220, 233; heteropatriarchal, 81; Judeo-Christian, 3, 101, 122; moral, 38; neoliberal, 94; social, 122; violation of, 220
Velázquez, Nydia M., 121, 160, 173, 275n33
Velázquez/Roybal-Allard Amendment, 122

violence, 203, 208, 212, 275n34; domestic, 198, 199, 211, 233; female survivors of, 22, 23; gender-specific forms of, 22

visas, 30, 36, 38, 239, 263n4, 278n46; applications for, 91–92; eliminating categories of, 242; employment-based, 91; expired, 140, 150, 236; family reunification, 38, 93, 242, 278n45; guest workers and, 65; H-1B, 23, 65; H-2A, 61, 63, 278n48; H-2B, 146; H-4, 23; immigrant, 34, 248, 256n16, 257n22; K, 61; overstaying, 129, 141, 236; reallocation of, 40, 67; temporary, 5; unskilled labor and, 114; V, 61

Von Hayek, Friedrich, 9

Wallis, Robert A., 188

Wall Street Journal: circulation of, 279n2

War on Poverty, 214

War on Terror, 237, 238, 239

Waters, Maxine, 56

Watson, Robert P., 171

Watt, Melvin L., 56

welfare, 2, 16, 75, 87, 151, 193, 202, 242, 253n2; access to, 88; bilingual education and, 172, 173; dependency, 80, 172, 208, 211, 213; eligibility for, 48, 53, 112, 275n32; exclusion from, 175, 180, 215; immigrants and, 1, 14, 49, 51, 69; injustices of, 237; noncitizens and, 49; policies, 161, 162; public perceptions of, 88; receiving, 8, 121, 211, 216; undocumented immigrants and, 70, 145; work requirements for, 279n6

welfare magnet, 84, 113, 114–20

welfare mothers, 208, 215

welfare programs, 173, 222; responsibility for, 89; wolf, 160

welfare reform, 2, 8, 18, 45, 101, 144, 189, 213, 214; comprehensive, 37; debates about, 12, 109; discourse, 87, 205, 208, 211; immigrants and, 24, 47–54

Welfare Reform Act (1996), 83, 259n32

welfare state, 4, 9, 11, 48, 90–91, 116, 236; dismantling of, 121, 214; neoliberal attack on, 15; reorganizing, 8

welfare system, 9, 11, 73, 85, 224, 277n39; economic objectives and, 48; information about, 87; staying away from, 205; taking advantage of, 123, 249; threats to, 182

Wheelan, Dick, 222

Wigal, Delores, 223

Wilson, Charles, 272n14

Wilson, Pete, 160, 175, 176, 184, 186, 282n24

Winant, Howard, 218

Wong, Carolyn, 42

work ethic, 199, 206, 209, 231, 262n3, 277n39

Workforce Improvement and Protection Act (WIPA) (1998), 253n1

work permits, 130, 230

work stops/work centers, 229, 230

World Trade Center: bombing of, 54, 55, 131, 218

Wyden, Ron, 145

xenophobia, 103, 105, 140–41, 151, 152, 183, 220, 268n41

Yearbook of Immigration Statistics (Office of Immigration Statistics), 265n21

Yoo, Grace, 88

Young, Bill, 115

Yousef, Ramzi, 55

Yzaguirre, Raul, 107, 286n1

CHRISTINA GERKEN is assistant professor of women's studies at Indiana University South Bend, where she teaches classes on immigration, global women's issues, and race and reproductive rights. Her research examines how anxieties about immigrants' race, class, gender, and sexuality affect public discourse and the legislative process.